The Unwanted

Great War Letters from the Field

JOHN McKENDRICK HUGHES

The Unwanted

Great War Letters from the Field

Edited by JOHN R. HUGHES

The University of Alberta Press

Published by
The University of Alberta Press
Ring House 2
Edmonton, Alberta, Canada   T6G 2E1

Copyright Original Manuscript © 1956
    John McKendrick Hughes
Copyright Edited Manuscript © 2005
    John R. Hughes
Copyright Introduction © 2005
    Craig Gibson

Printed and bound in Canada by
    Houghton Boston Printers, Saskatoon,
    Saskatchewan.
First edition, first printing, 2005

ISBN 0-88864-436-1

LIBRARY AND ARCHIVES CANADA
CATALOGUING IN PUBLICATION DATA

Hughes, John McKendrick, 1882–1967.
    The unwanted : Great War letters from
the field / John McKendrick Hughes ;
edited by John R. Hughes.

Includes bibliographical references
and index.
ISBN 0-88864-436-1

    1. Hughes, John McKendrick,
1882–1967. 2. Hughes, John McKendrick,
1882–1967—Correspondence. 3. World War,
1914–1918—Food supply. 4. World War,
1914–1918—Personal narratives, Canadian.
5. Great Britain. Army—Biography.
I. Hughes, John R. (John Richard), 1949–
II. Title.

D640.H87 2005   940.4'8171
C2005-902338-4

The University of Alberta Press is committed
to protecting our natural environment. As
part of our efforts, this book is printed on
stock produced by New Leaf Paper: it
contains 100% post-consumer recycled
fibres and is acid- and chlorine-free.

The University of Alberta Press gratefully
acknowledges the support received for its
publishing program from The Canada
Council for the Arts. The University of
Alberta Press also gratefully acknowledges
the financial support of the Government
of Canada through the Book Publishing
Industry Development Program (BPDIP)
and from the Alberta Foundation for the
Arts for our publishing activities.

Scratchboard Illustrations of wheat, a
potato, a cow and an onion used
throughout the book are by Michael
Halbert and are used by permission of
the artist.

Canada Council   Conseil des Arts
for the Arts   du Canada

Canadä

To my grandfather John McKendrick Hughes,
for writing the letters and then the manuscript.

To my grandmother, Sara Maria Purdy Hughes,
for keeping the letters safe for many, many years.

To my father, John Paul Hughes, for supporting
and encouraging me through the long, complex
process of publication.

Contents

Author's Notes

THIS IS A STORY. It is not to be read as exact history. There is no doubt that in many cases we have placed the wrong units in the wrong place. Any soldier who was in France knows how hard it was to locate a unit other than his own. Just so, no doubt, we have made many mistakes as to units and places. Place names may be spelt wrongly, but European maps give many different spellings.

We want you to notice that where letters are quoted and place names, unit numbers, and so on are in square brackets—[ ]—these items have been added to the original script. Naturally they were left blank when written, for military reasons. In many cases we have only these old letters to give battalion numbers of many of our comrades. These may not be correct, and if so we apologize. We make no apologies for mentioning their names. They were a grand bunch of fellows doing a fine service for the country under the most difficult of circumstances.

Some of our friends have criticized us for writing this story in first person plural. No doubt in doing so we have made many mistakes in grammar. Our reason is that in the first person singular it sounds like patting ourself on the back if we said, "I did this" or "I did that." Actually this was not correct. I seldom did anything alone. I seldom went anywhere alone. I had my driver and an interpreter with me a great deal of the time, or other officers. In the army one seldom acts as an individual; he acts as a unit. There is plenty of first person in the quotations from my letters to my wife.

I was given a marvelous opportunity to do, to see, to talk, to observe. These opportunities were not given to Major John Hughes. They were given to a Canadian major who happened to be on the spot. As "we," we represented Canadians away from home.

J. McK. HUGHES
Lieut. Colonel (retired)
Circa 1956

Editor's Notes

An army marches on its stomach.

—Attributed to both Napoleon Bonaparte and Frederick the Great

MOST "WAR STORIES" FOCUS on trench life, combat, and death. They usually pay little or no attention to how the troops who fought and died in those trenches were fed, or where the food came from—meals are mentioned only in passing, or food appears as if by magic. Anyone who has planned a meal for 40 or 50 people, however, will appreciate how much food such a group can go through. Now expand that group to a million men and feed them not for one evening, but for four years. That is the task in which my grandfather played a small part, and about which he wrote this book, some 38 years after the end of WWI. Although he went overseas as an infantry officer, his contribution to the war effort involved agriculture. But as he said in his Author's Notes, he was in a unique position to see, hear, and do much more than most combat troops.

Although Granddad was a farmer all his life, he was also a passionate writer and over the years he wrote hundreds of short stories and several full-length novels, as well as these memoirs of his time in England and Europe during WWI. When he died in 1967, two cardboard boxes of his stories and writings were willed to my father. Some years later, Dad gave me all these documents—including the original (hand-written) manuscript and a typed copy of *The Unwanted*. I did virtually nothing with any these papers until the late 1990s. By then, I had the time and energy to revive an earlier interest in family history, and in 2000, Dad and I collaborated on his autobiography. After allowing the dust to settle somewhat, I suggested we do a biography of his parents, which we began in late 2002. Part of my research for this project involved reading *The Unwanted* for details that could be used in the biography. In doing so, I realized that this was a story that needed to be told. Dad agreed with me, then decreed that I was just the person to do it.

Converting Granddad's manuscript into a publishable version was a labour of love, but there was no doubt that it was a labour. First, the text was keyed in by Isabel Milne, who then did a light copyedit for spelling, punctuation, and grammar. All the quotations from Granddad's letters were left as they had been written in 1916–19 and copied in 1956, except for the occasional, absolutely necessary change in punctuation or spelling. These letters (and a few other items that Granddad quoted) are presented in indented, sans-serif text to distinguish them from the 1956 narrative.

Next I checked the spelling of all the place names, using Granddad's WWI-era maps as references, so spellings are circa 1918, not necessarily as they are today. Many facts and personal names were also checked, and corrected as required. Finally, I did a light edit of the overall document for clarity and flow. The occasional sentence was rephrased, several "chapter" titles were revised, the occasional block of text was moved, and in several instances, two "chapters" were merged into one. The vast majority of the book, however, is exactly as it was written in 1956. (It should be noted that the hand-written manuscript appears to have been a first draft; as near as I can tell, Granddad rarely, if ever, went back and reviewed or revised a story once he finished writing it. He simply got on with the next one.) All of these changes were reviewed and, with a few minor quibbles, approved by my father. Our intent was to ensure it was still my grandfather's story, not my version of his story.

JOHN R. HUGHES

Acknowledgements

THIS BOOK IS DEDICATED to the three people who made it possible: my grandfather, John McKendrick Hughes, 1882–1967, for writing the letters and then the manuscript; my grandmother, Sara Maria Purdy Hughes, 1890–1966, for keeping the letters safe for many, many years; and my father, John Paul Hughes, 1912–2005, for supporting and encouraging me through the long, complex process of actually getting it into print.

Books usually do not get published without the support of and help from many people, and this one is no exception. I wish to thank my family, especially Paul Hughes, Ross Hughes, Allan Hughes, Henk Mostert, Barbara Anderson, and Ann Campbell; my friends who volunteered time and effort far above and beyond the call of simple friendship, especially Isabel Milne and Jean Armstrong; the people whom I have never met but who nonetheless responded to my requests for technical help, especially Dr. Craig Gibson who has written the Introduction, the folks at the Centre for First World War Studies (University of Birmingham, UK), and Robert E. Monk; and finally, Michael Luski, who convinced me that this was a book that really deserved to be published.

The Great War and John McKendrick Hughes's Western Front Experience

Craig Gibson

From Vegreville to the Western Front

DURING THE GREAT WAR, 1914–1918, the notion of doing one's bit for the war effort—of performing an essential wartime service on active duty—transcended traditional stereotypes. The vast majority of military personnel rarely had the opportunity to display the sorts of bravery warranting official recognition. Of the 2,044,627 British and Dominion officers and other ranks in France and Flanders in the British Expeditionary Force (BEF) during the first week of August 1917, only 700,000–800,000 belonged to combatant arms such as the infantry, artillery, engineers and the like.[1] The rest belonged to the army's support services—medical personnel, camp staff, clerks, typists, headquarters staff, servants, mechanics, labour companies, railway companies, ammunition and transportation columns—not directly involved in military operations but by that date essential to them nonetheless.[2] Most had joined up in the expectation of fighting in combatant arms. Either through injury, age, special skill, or simply fate, however, they found themselves performing other sundry tasks.

John McKendrick Hughes was one of these men. Of lengthy Canadian pedigree, Hughes's parents moved west from the Maritimes across late 19th century North America before settling in Alberta when John was sixteen. There, besides developing a work ethic typical of settler communities, he also cemented close ties with the local militia, rising quickly through the ranks of the Canadian Mounted Rifles. Married with two children at the war's outbreak, he did not immediately enlist. That had to wait until June 1915, when he enlisted in the 66th Battalion. At the end of that year, he transfered to the 151st Battalion, and devoted the next five months to recruiting and training men for it in the Vegreville/ Vermilion area. This was a common practice across much of Canada. In this, he was eminently successful. Although Hughes did eventually travel overseas with *his boys* in the fall of 1916, all did not end well. Rumours surfaced that as the four Canadian divisions presently serving in France and Flanders could not sustain current casualty levels without reinforcement from home, the breaking up of battalions now in transit was being considered. The rumours proved accurate. As soon as 151st made St. Martin's Plain, near Folkestone, Kent, officers and men were separated, the latter being sent on to reinforce units at the front. The 151st ceased to exist.

The experience of the 151st's officer cadre was not unique. They joined an already burgeoning surplus of battalion commanders, company commanders and other junior officers—often prominent men in their home communities—who were, at least for the moment, *unwanted* by the Canadian Expeditionary Force (CEF). Having risen to a lieutenancy on the basis of his militia service and a majority on the basis of his recent home service, Hughes soon discovered that there were precious few openings for untried battalion-level officers. Not surprisingly, veteran battalions preferred the promotion of those who had already proven themselves in the peculiar nastiness pervading operations on the western front to officers such as Hughes who had attained their ranks while on home service. Would the Royal Flying Corps, which lost newly-trained pilots at a prodigious rate, take him? Unwilling to accept married men, the RFC rejected Hughes's application.

Despite savouring the freedom to explore country lanes and pubs, to meet the locals and to take in London shows (passes were easily obtained—anything to help the unwanted pass the time), Hughes yearned for the chance to proceed to France on active service, a not uncommon sentiment. A brief training spell with the 29th Battalion, CEF, in late December 1916/early January 1917 near Souchez merely whetted his appetite. In July 1917, an opportunity, not without conditions, finally presented itself in the form of a request for officers who were willing to work on the lines of communication and willing to revert to the rank of Staff Lieutenant, Second Class, with a commensurate pay cut.[3] After many months of languishing in England, Hughes eagerly volunteered.

The latter half of 1917, when, in effect, Hughes's active service was just beginning, was arguably the darkest time of the war for the allies. They were not immune to the feelings of fatigue and deprivation and futility that had led to revolution in Russia. In France, defeatism was gathering strength; labour unrest was rife. People openly questioned the purpose and costs of the war, especially the casualties. General Robert Nivelle, who had earned celebrity at Verdun, succeeded a Joffre whose squandering of French lives during the previous two and half years had already rendered the prospect of any imminent French victory very pyrrhic indeed. Nevertheless, Nivelle managed to convince the French government and even the new British prime minister, David Lloyd George, that the German lines could be broken within twenty-four hours, with a victorious pursuit to follow. Without consulting his own field commander, General Douglas Haig, Lloyd George agreed to place British forces temporarily under French command in spring 1917. An infuriated Haig reluctantly agreed to attack north of Arras, while the French attacked further south in Champagne. The Germans pre-empted allied strategy, however, by withdrawing to the so-called Hindenburg Line—prepared field fortifications— behind a swathe of French territory now razed to the ground. With the salient he wanted to pinch off with simultaneous attacks from north and south now gone, Nivelle was given the opportunity to reconsider his offensive. Most wanted him to. He did not. While the British attack known as the battle of Arras began well with the Canadian Corps' capture of Vimy Ridge, little further headway could be made. When the French attacked in Champagne a week later, Nivelle proved himself a far better self-promoter than prognosticator: the French were cut to shreds. Such was the state of the French Army that by the beginning of May 1917 several divisions refused orders to return to the front.

Relieved of his obligation to cooperate with the French, Haig turned his attention to Flanders, where ever since assuming command of the BEF in December 1915 he had wanted to mount an offensive.[4] Now was his chance. Besides French problems, which were justification enough in his mind to launch an offensive and to distract German attention away from the French front, Haig hoped to clear the Passchendaele ridge, and push on to the important rail junction of Roulers, the capture of which would render the German Flanders position untenable. Whether or not Haig's ambitious plan stood any realistic chance of success—based on the previous three years of operations on the western front, it did not—it is worth mentioning that there were also other, indeed more pressing, factors to consider. The war at sea was one of these. From Ostende and Zeebrugge, it was (wrongly) believed, the Germans were launching the submarines so devastating to allied shipping. While it was true that these same submarines had served the purpose of bringing the United States into the war on the side of the allies, Germany's policy of unrestricted submarine warfare threatened to starve the Entente into submission before United States power could be brought to bear where it was needed most—on the western front. Like Canada, the United States retained a small professional force of peacetime soldiers. It would take many months to field a force capable of playing a decisive role on the western front. One thing was sure: the strains on allied shipping were enormous and increasing daily. The tonnage of shipping lost to submarines jeopardized Anglo-French lifelines to colonies, overseas markets and other theatres. Furthermore the ongoing process of ferrying tens of thousands of American soldiers across the Atlantic, not to mention the supply of some 2 million soldiers of the BEF already in France and Flanders, became increasingly problematic. In short, economizing on overseas shipping became a military issue of the first magnitude.

Rarely in the first two years of the Great War on the western front had the BEF as an institution considered the agricultural environment

Agricultural Officers attending a potato-spraying demonstration at Le Touquet, France, 18 June 1918, arranged by the Director of Agriculture to show how to decrease disease in Army grown potatoes in France. Used with permission from the Imperial War Museum, Q.9027.

of northern France and Flanders in anything other than military, or occasionally, aesthetic, terms. Attitudes and the events that shape them, however, were slowly changing. The summer of 1916 was crucial. With no effective riposte to German submarines in sight and the Somme offensive having liberated a tract of French territory, however small in area, British troops harvested the ripening crops, and remarkably, planted some abandoned land, using German POWs as labourers. It was becoming increasingly clear that no longer could anything be wasted, a feeling that the events of 1917 intensified. Being proactive, not reactive, would eventually guide British efforts. The logical culmination of this new-found interest in things agricultural came in January 1917. GHQ appointed agricultural experts, known as Agricultural Officers, or AOs, to each army and corps headquarters staff, to coordinate help for local farmers who otherwise found it difficult if not impossible to pursue their normal vocation under conditions that deprived them of labour and beasts.

With the fate of nations and empires hanging in the balance, for sheer drama nothing matches the war of grand manoeuvre in northern France and Flanders from August to November 1914. It is arguable, though, that the ensuing period of trench warfare has captivated the popular imagination in Canada, as elsewhere to a far greater extent. Especially for Canadians, this is not too surprising. En route for England in October 1914, Canada's initial 30,000-man contingent missed the Marne and the first battle of Ypres. It did not, however, escape the subsequent carnage on the western front. Indeed, the very words *western front* conjure up a variety of images for most people, and these are often associated with trenches, mud, barbed wire, and the seemingly futile killing that went on there for over four years. It was here that the British Empire lost, in rough figures, 600,000 lives, including almost 60,000 Canadians, France, 1 million lives, and the Germans, 1.5 million lives. Battles such as Verdun, Somme and Passchendaele became bywords for the horrors and waste of that type of warfare known as attrition. Such battles and such staggering casualty figures can neither be ignored nor easily explained away.[5]

Indeed, making sense of the western front, then or since, has not been easy. Its history has invariably become confused and intertwined with things that had little or nothing to do with actual events. With censorship all pervasive, little was written at the time that was not outright fiction, or at least one or another of the government's officially-sanctioned version of events. When they began to write about their experiences, the soldiers presented alternative and often conflicting versions. An accurate portrayal of life at the front, Henri Barbusse, *Under Fire*, is remarkable more for when it was published (1916) than what it said—that the western front was not a very pleasant place.[6] Trenches were not always of the immaculately clean and orderly sort written about in the press and constructed in various town and city squares across the empire. Focusing his study on the sorts of public-schools educated poets and writers who found the western front impossible to fathom, live through and conventionalize, Paul Fussell, in his highly-influential *The Great War and Modern Memory* (1975), argued the war represented a fundamental departure from literary conventions.[7] As a corpus of literature, however, most postwar authors were either highly ambivalent or in fact rather positive about their wartime experiences: the war was not purpose-less, officers were not all unfeeling cads, and the trenches, though lethal on occasion, could be, during quiet spells, a good place to catch up on one's sleep.[8] As Frederic Manning, *The Middle Parts of Fortune*, makes plain, there was always comradeship, time in billets, and rousing nights in *estaminets* behind the lines.[9] Even Erich Maria Remarque, *All Quiet on the Western Front* (1929), though now firmly ensconced as the greatest icon of anti-war literature, embraces the redeeming qualities of male bonding.[10] There were those at the time, however, who criticized Remarque and authors of a similar ilk for their frank depictions of soldiers imbibing, fornicating, and defecating. Controversy was fuelled because, it was believed, the memory of the fighting man—the embodiment of the nation-state—was under assault.[11] Which explains why, even now, even in Canada, it remains bad form in some circles to suggest that Canada's participation in the Great War was anything but entered for the noblest of reasons, that the capture of Vimy Ridge was anything but the western front's finest feat of arms, that the Canadian soldier was anything but the finest product of a youthful and emergent society. No conscripts, shirkers, adulterers, drunks or bad shots here.[12]

Even for professional historians, making sense of western front is not an easy task. Outside of specific unit histories, military and diplomatic historians have examined the circumstances that brought the soldiers to that front, the strategic considerations that determined how they were used, and the weapons and tactics that created and eventually overcame the strategic deadlock. To this day, nearly a hundred years after the war's outbreak, the conduct of the war, the numbers of dead, and the seeming futility of a war that needed to be refought in less than a generation weigh heavily on the combatant nations. Fierce debates still rage, about political direction, about the military conduct, about the memory and meaning of the events that transpired in France and Flanders. There is a profound desire, or more precisely, need, to understand the military events, to make sense of the nonsensical. This pursuit often leaves a bad taste in one's mouth. The military events are neither readily explicable nor neatly resolved. The battles of 1914 were not decisive, that much is clear. And neither were those that followed. Even in 1918, there were no decisive victories, no beaten and demoralized enemy fleeing the battlefield, just battering and more battering, with more and more artillery, more and more troops, more and more sophisticated weaponry against increasingly clever defenders, and a German Army only grudgingly leaving the field. No, the Great War did not end with a knock-out punch: this was a heavy-weight prize fight, both sides bloodied and staggering at the final bell but still on their feet. Perhaps for this very reason, those who did the fighting, at once deified and pitied, remain objects of enduring fascination.[13]

So what was Canada's role in all this?[14] After a brief introduction to trench warfare in late February-March 1915 in the Armentières sector, the 1st Division took up a position on the north-east shoulder of the Ypres salient, that infamous bit of Belgian Flanders that jutted around the medieval town whose name has become synonymous with the sacrifice and tenacity of the BEF. Having been introduced to the appalling conditions of an overwhelmed British military facility, Salisbury Plain, the previous autumn, the Canadians now faced a cruel introduction to trench warfare. Seeking to continue the rolling up of the allied flank begun the previous autumn, the Germans resorted to a method of attack both unconventional and illegal, poison gas.

After the second battle of Ypres, where it was commonly believed that Canada's finest sons had proven their mettle, the Canadians' reputation grew, as did their numbers. The 2nd Canadian Division arrived on the western front in September 1915, where in conjunction with the 1st Division it formed the nascent Canadian Corps. Obliged to take over British trenches near St. Éloi in early April 1916, the 2nd receiving a mauling from German forces intent on capturing blown mine craters, a speciality. Under the command of Lieutenant-General Sir Julian Byng, the Corps suffered another reverse only two months later. Surprised by a massive artillery barrage and the blowing of several German mines, the 3rd Division was struck in the early hours of 2 June 1916, at Mount Sorrel. After the 1st and 2nd Divisions had also been drawn into the maelstrom, most of the ground lost to the Germans was eventually recaptured. Typical of the many local actions that raged along the western front, both the Germans and Canadians suffered thousands of casualties for very little in ground gained—in this case, none. Until this point, much praise had been heaped on the Canadians, some of it deserved, much of it not. The efforts of the Max Aitkens, the future Lord Beaverbrook, cannot be trivialized. An unabashed publicist and the self-proclaimed official historian of the CEF, he invariably glossed over deficiencies and setbacks while downplaying the crucial work of British staff officers. His *Canada in Flanders* (1916)—"patriotic, sanitized, and uncritical"—became an instant best-seller, going through twelve printings in four months. Canadians were the pick of the empire, pronounced Aitkens. Products of the frontier, they were a hardy people, natural soldiers, quick learners, the fiercely proud products of a vibrant new democracy.[15]

While trench warfare, with its random death and maiming and occasional quiet spells, was a common experience, there were also major offensives, or *pushes*. For the Canadian Corps, the first of these was the Somme. Journeying from Flanders where they had spent most of 1915 and 1916, the first three Canadian divisions arrived in the Somme in late August 1916. In mid-September 1916 they spearheaded the Flers-Courcelette offensive, which featured the first use of tanks. As the Somme offensive petered out in November 1916, 4th Canadian Division, the last and final Canadian division to arrive on the western front (in August 1916), took part in the capture of Regina trench. Overall, the Canadians' first experience of attacking an experienced, well dug-in German foe was also their first exposure to a new type of warfare, attrition, whose main goal was not a breakthrough, or otherwise strategic, but simply the gaining of limited objectives that had as a corollary the wearing down of enemy forces, and the acceptance of a large number of casualties to the attacker. This first entailed concentrating heavy artillery at the point of attack, to destroy fortifications, wire, and to keep the enemy below ground for as long as possible, and then following up with infantry attacks to kill or capture any survivors. Having pushed the enemy from one line of defence, the procedure was repeated.[16]

The capture of Vimy Ridge, one of the centrepieces of German defences on the western front and which many observers believed impregnable, in April 1917 bolstered the reputation of the Canadian Corps still further. It proved itself capable of conducting successful offensive operations in difficult circumstances. Other operations ensued. A lesser action at Hill 70 in August made the German position at Lens increasingly untenable while at the same time distracting the Germans from the overture taking place further north, at Ypres, where the third battle bearing the forlorn town's name was commencing. Later that year, the Canadians were asked to capture the red dust that was once the pretty Flemish village of Passchendaele, which once crowned the gentle ridge east of Ypres. None of these successes were dramatic ruptures of the German lines, through which thousands of allied troops and tanks could have funnelled and fanned out, pursuing the enemy in open terrain: whatever initial tactical successes an attacker may have enjoyed, the long-term advantages still lie with the defender, whose communications generally extended over unbroken ground to the rear. Moreover, both Byng, who commanded the Canadians at Vimy, and Sir Arthur Currie, a real estate salesman from Victoria who commanded the Corps from June 1917 onwards, were sticklers for staff work and refused to squander Canadian lives. Currie, in particular, used political connections to ensure his troops attacked only under the most favourable conditions possible, bearing in mind that on the western front most attacks—even under the best conditions and even if extremely successful—incurred significant losses.

The events of 1918 did nothing to dim the lustre of the Canadian Corps' earlier accomplishments. Having escaped the worst of the German spring and summer offensives, the four Canadian divisions were extremely well rested and prepared (they were withdrawn from the line in mid-May for training) for their participation in the highly-successful 8 August Amiens offensive, dubbed the German Army's Black Day by its *de facto* commander-in-chief, Erich von Ludendorff. Later successful attacks on the Hindenburg Line, the Canal du Nord, and Cambrai were meticulously-planned operations on which all the ingenuity and innovation bred by three-and-a-half years of strategic stalemate were brought to bear. Backed by plenty of artillery, especially heavy tanks where available, secrecy if possible, and with limited objectives in mind, *set piece* or *bite and hold* attacks became the order of the day. By the time it entered Mons on the morning of 11 November 1918, just hours before the armistice came into effect, it was widely believed that the Canadian Corps was among the finest if not the finest formation to have emerged on the western front. By its efforts, paid in blood and recognized on the world stage, Canada came of age, securing a seat at the Paris peace conference.

Canada's experience during the Great War is told here in a conventional fashion. This historical account begins with the heady days of August 1914 when the young colony, still less than 50 years old, embarks on a great European adventure. Eager to help the mother country but short on experience, Canadian troops soon find themselves on the western front, where the adventure turns sour. German gas at the second battle of Ypres reveals a new, nasty side to modern warfare, and Mount Sorrel and St. Éloi, just how much the Canadians need to learn, as do the spike in casualties during major offensives such as the Somme. But learn they do. By spring 1917 a great victory won on the slopes of Vimy, under a British commander but with all four Canadian divisions fighting side-by-side for the first time, shows just how far the amateurs have progressed. With a Canadian commander directing operations for the first time, the Corps proves itself again and again, first at Hill 70, then at Passchendaele, Amiens, the Hindenburg Line, and throughout the so-called Hundred Days. Arriving on the western front as novices, the Canadians depart in full knowledge that they, perhaps more than any other troops, have mastered the art of modern warfare.[17] In the process the young dominion has taken the first step towards attaining political autonomy.

Behind the Lines

Whatever its use and pedigree in the construction of a post-colonial Canadian identity, such a narrative is not without its weaknesses. Focusing narrowly on the military exploits of the Canadian Corps in France and Flanders, and in particular on the efforts of the fighting troops, does a disservice to those who did not belong to combatant arms, of whom there were thousands, and even to the combatant troops themselves, who were not in the front lines all the time. Even before the Canadians arrived on the western front, a BEF-wide system of rotation was in the process of evolving into a sophisticated means of ensuring that troops could be rested at regular intervals behind the lines. Though the system could be flexible, it did ensure that Canadian troops, like their British and Australian counterparts, did not spend all of their time manning the parapet in front line trenches—one of the enduring misconceptions of the western front. Thus, of the 10,000 men comprising a typical British division at near full strength, only 1,000 men could be expected to be actually manning the forward-most trenches and saps at any one time.[18] More to the point, raids were infrequent and large-scale offensives even rarer. *Going over the top*, despite its currency in everyday English, was very much the exception, not the rule. Occasionally, too, divisions were withdrawn from the line altogether, for rest, training and refitting. In reality, an infantryman could expect to spend a majority of his time on the western front behind the lines, in relative safety.

Besides the system of rotation, the BEF as a whole was continually evolving, a process that had begun nearly as soon as siege-like conditions gripped the western front in November-December 1914. Though the love of horses generally and cavalry specifically was ingrained among the largely aristocratic senior British officer corps—no defensive position, it was commonly believed, could withstand a determined cavalry charge—there was no disputing the fact that, dream though they might, there were few opportunities for the use of horses in trench warfare, other than lugging of artillery and General Service (GS) wagons. Thus cavalry was the first to go, with some units like the Canadian Mounted Rifles (CMR) converting to infantry. Admittedly the British retained a reserve of cavalry that at least partially repaid the faith shown in it at Cambrai in November 1917 and during the final allied offensives of October-November 1918. In numbers if not nostalgia, however, cavalry gradually gave way to the Machine Gun Corps, Royal Flying Corps and the Tank Corps. In a war dominated by gunners, artillery—both field and especially heavy—showed the largest increases of any branch.[19]

Specialization continued apace.[20] Many were directed to engineering, tunnelling, railway and forestry companies.[21] Labour shortages, however, were endemic. While tens of thousands of black South African ("Kaffirs") and Chinese ("chinks" or "coolies") were recruited to work at the docks and depots and dumps and on the roads behind the lines, there were ongoing manpower shortages, especially closer to the front where foreign labourers were not brought. Leaving aside for the moment large-scale offensives that posed their own logistical difficulties, just supplying the needs of the troops at the front during trench warfare was an enormous undertaking. Trains could bring supplies to railheads 10 to 15 miles behind the front, but it was generally ill-advised if not impossible to proceed farther. From railhead, lorries, animals or small-gauge railways brought supplies to divisional dumps, within some 5–10 miles of the front. The final stage of the journey, getting supplies to units at the front, required manpower—and plenty of it. Though there were (by 1917 at least) labour companies for such tasks, in reality battalions at rest or in reserve were often used. Undertaken at night, such fatigues were universally abhorred. Adding to their disaffection, soldiers *at rest* were often detailed to engineering companies where their tasks could range from digging communication trenches, burying signalling cable, humping all manner of trench stores, often coils of wire and stakes and duck-boards and boxes of ammunition, to disposing of the spoil from tunnelling operations. Justifiably the *Poor Bloody Infantry* complained.

With the BEF's lines of communication extending from northern France and Flanders to the channel ports and thence to Britain, logistics were a far from insignificant consideration. Never before had a nation tried to keep an army the size of large city supplied for a lengthy, apparently indefinite, period. Every shell, every reinforcement, every gallon of petrol, every tin of Bully Beef, every letter and parcel—the list was endless—had to be brought from Britain. It required an organizational effort of unprecedented proportions. Though mechanization was increasingly important to its operations, the BEF maintained an army of animals. This, in turn, presented its own problems. Fodder consumed huge amounts of cross-channel shipping.[22]

Rarely do discussions of the Great War on the western front touch on such matters. They rarely move beyond traditional military narratives, focusing as they often do on military leadership, strategy, campaigns, alliance relations, and tactics. As for the soldiers themselves, those through whom the nation-state wielded its monopoly over violence, little is said beyond their role in trying to kill the enemy—that is, either in the trenches or during combat. It is possible, though perhaps difficult to prove, that many military historians simply feel uncomfortable looking beyond the trenches and the major offensives, or that the history of the BEF beyond these venues holds little interest, either for themselves personally or their publishers.[23] Whatever the case, they simply do not document other aspects of the British war effort in northern France and Flanders.

Even products of the New Military History school—which, given its origins are often dated to the publication of John Keegan, *The Face of Battle* (1976),[24] is now no longer very *new* at all—that examine the day-to-day life of the British and Dominion soldier, spill precious little ink on his life behind the lines, in billets or rest camps, at leisure and play, his relations with local inhabitants, or on the hundreds of thousands of noncombatant troops who worked in repair shops, schools, dumps, in hospitals, on the railways, in the woods, in salvage companies.[25] The heroic narratives traditionally deployed to describe military operations dispense with them, if at all, in perfunctory fashion. A number of recent works catering to a popular market, including the recent History Television series, Norm Christie, *For King and Empire*, Christie's CEF Books, and J.L. Granatstein, *Hell's Corner: An Illustrated History of Canada's Great War, 1914–1918*, fall into this category.[26] The Canadian media exhibits similar tendencies. Come the anniversaries of Remembrance Day and Vimy Ridge, they focus on operations, combat, and the personal valour of individuals at the front—the memory of the dead and those who risked their lives—not on the myriad of tasks undertaken in the rear by forgotten thousands. Fitting uneasily beside far more commonplace heroic and sacrificial images of a nation at war, the lives of noncombatant troops behind the lines have been relegated to insignificance, and their contribution to the largely anonymous infastructure that supported the BEF and CEF's operations forgotten.[27] Essential though such tasks were, they were—indeed, *are*—hardly heroic according to the traditional definition of wartime heroism—of exceptional bravery in the face of the enemy.

Joining the 9th Corps: Soldier to Farmer

Unwanted as an officer with the CEF, John McKendrick Hughes arrived in France in mid-July 1917, having agreed to a posting on the lines of communication. Initially, he became an Area Commandant in French Flanders under the auspices of 9th Corps, a British formation. His duties, mainly ensuring that billets in the rural area under his jurisdiction were left in

Soldiers tending the potato crop in Béthune, France, 15 August 1918. Used with permission from the Imperial War Museum, Q.9781.

a sanitary state, were far from arduous. The following month, however, 9th Corps' Agricultural Officer returned to his unit, and General Cooke, the Quartermaster General of 9th Corps offered the post to Hughes, a farmer in civilian life. He readily accepted. From August 1917 until his eventual demobilization in 1919, Hughes became immersed in this largely unexplored dimension of the British war effort in France and Flanders.[28]

The BEF's agricultural efforts went through three distinct phases. The first began in early 1917 as a means of placing aid to local farmers on a firmer institutional basis, which is where it stood at the time Hughes joined 9th Corps in summer 1917. In late 1917 and early 1918, under increasing pressure from Whitehall to conserve cross-channel shipping space by increasing the production of bulky food items such as potatoes in France, and with the appointment of Earl Radnor as Director of Agricultural Production at GHQ, the establishment of British-run army farms on abandoned French land was added to AO's chores. Though both of these activities were curtailed by the German offensives of March-June 1918, the summer and autumn of the same year brought new tasks.

Now 4th Army's AO, Hughes spent most the war's final weeks coordinating efforts to harvest ground recently captured from the Germans—ironically, some that had been planted by the British the previous winter. In other locations they contained the crops of inhabitants recently made refugees or at least in dire need of outside help. Often undertaken just behind the fighting front, among the shell-holes and detritus of recent combat, this was a harvest few who participated in it would soon forget. No stranger to stray shells and bullets, Hughes took a certain amount of pride in finally working in conditions that regularly brought him close to the front, amidst British and Canadian combat troops, and near enough to the German lines that casualties to the troops undertaking agricultural work were not uncommon.

John McKendrick Hughes's Great War and post-armistice experiences are vividly told in his memoir, *The Unwanted*. Crammed with details about life behind the lines difficult to find elsewhere, amusing anecdotes on a host of subjects, a rich cast of characters, many drawn from the British aristocracy, an intense pride in his westerner's roots and *being* Canadian, as well as strong opinions on everything and everyone from Sam Hughes, the election of December 1917, French brothels, Winston Churchill, and Lord Radnor—to name just a few—Hughes's contemporaneous letters and post-war narrative tell the story with immediacy and verve. Even though he was not, he readily admits, an historian (he occasionally offers explanations for events that were, at best, simply educated guesses on his part) or even pedantically accurate (he also assures us that he has, on more than one occasion, confused dates and misspelt local place-names) he is an effective story-teller, training for which was honed both before and after the war, writing hundreds of tales on a variety of subjects.

As its very strength lies in its history it is easy to overlook a few quirks. There were thousands of officers and men behind the lines, like Hughes, discharging their military obligations in perfectly honourable and necessary ways. Unlike Hughes, few have told their stories. Not at the sharp end, they were usually not deemed worthy of recording either by the participants themselves, who perhaps believed, not entirely without foundation, that when compared to the momentous events transpiring at the front, no one would credit such mundane efforts. Or was it the guilt at having secured a *bomb-proof* posting that ensured their survival but also their post-war reticence? Or does some of the blame reside with publishers eager to cash in on the powerful allure of mud and blood and the comradeship of the trenches but not much else?[29] While such musings must remain conjecture, what is clear is that in having spent much of the war behind the lines Hughes was not alone. There were thousands like him. Yet in terms of his posting, the freedom he enjoyed, the people he met, and the type of work he supervised, his experience was unique. This historical uniqueness makes it historically important.

Critics will undoubtedly point to the fact that Hughes never took part in those events on which historians have since constructed the edifice of Canada's western front experience—of Canada's birth as a nation. On all counts they would be right. Hughes did not rush to the colours in 1914. He did not spend a miserable winter at Salisbury Plain. He was not gassed at 2nd Ypres. He did not attack Regina trench. He did not storm Vimy Ridge. And he never spent more than a few days in a trench, that archetype *par excellence* of the western front experience, or wander from billet to billet and camp to camp, as did the typical battalion-level junior officer and soldier. Yes, it is all true. Even defining the archetypal Canadian experience in the very broadest of terms, Hughes does not fit the mould. On the contrary, he did not reach the western front until late 1916, after the battles of 2nd Ypres, St. Éloi, Mt. Sorrel, and the Somme had been fought, and then, only for a few days. With a car at his disposal, and a freedom to roam, he surmises likely unmatched by virtually any other posting on the western front, he spent the Great War touring the towns and villages of Picardy and Flanders and, in the post-armistice era, Belgium and the Rhineland. He did not *muck in* with a platoon of infantry, or know the cramped familiarity of a battalion or company headquarters, or lead a raid across no man's land. Nor did he ever go *over the top*. But he did belong to a mess of senior officers, did have a driver and French interpreter at his disposal, did develop relationships with senior army officers as well as local farmers, and, in the end, did come to supervise an enterprise that comprised dozens of officers and thousands of troops. And while his agricultural work took him far and wide, across the length and breadth of the British-held sector of the western front, and occasionally beyond—attending meetings, visiting farms, surveying plots of land, acquiring tools and supplies—he moved billets on only a handful of occasions, spending most nights in a cosy bed, sometimes a hotel—no trench or barbed wire in sight. He did not, it seems, hate, or even dislike, the Germans. If anything, his experience as part of the post-war occupation force engendered a certain admiration. He always sought out old Canadian friends and offered them good jobs if possible, believing them intrinsically the best men available, but he never served in a Canadian formation while in France. He respected his superiors, nearly all of whom were British, believed the war needed to be fought, especially after witnessing some of the wanton destruction caused by the Germans, and never doubted the importance of his own efforts, despite their essentially non-military character. He returned home to a loving wife and family, to whom he had devotedly written at least once a day during the conflict, and lived out a lengthy and fulfilling life.

The Unwanted is very much a personal glimpse of the Great War on the western front. But it is a glimpse fundamentally at odds with the generally accepted version of Canada's passage to nationhood, relying, as the latter does, on the accomplishments of those who fought and, even more significantly, on the sacrifices of those who rest in the troublingly beautiful Commonwealth War Graves cemeteries dotting the now eerily quiet countryside of northern France and Belgium. History, however, ignores John McKendrick Hughes's war at its peril. Unassuming though it may be, his war is as much a part of Canada's heritage as those who performed more frequently-heralded deeds. As the purpose of scholarship is the pursuit of the truth, whatever that entails, including the questioning of robust national discourses, myths and memories, the publication of this memoir should be lauded. Though Hughes never believed his own contribution to the canon of Great War memoirs would ever be anything other than modest, it is far from that. As a means of undermining popular perceptions of Canada's role on the western front, it is a welcome addition to the literature. Even more significantly, as a vehicle for highlighting a side of the British war effort on the western front not generally well known, much less understood, Hughes's literary effort stands apart. His is a work that introduces us to another side of that most terrible of conflicts—a side that is little studied and barely remembered. We are in John McKendrick Hughes's debt for recording his war experience for a new generation of readers and military historians and for his grandson, John R. Hughes, for sharing them with us.

ABOUT THE CONTRIBUTOR

A graduate of the University of Toronto (B.A., M.A.) and the University of Leeds (Ph.D.), historian Craig Gibson has been studying the Great War for the past fifteen years. His first book, *Behind the Western Front, 1914–1918: British Troops and French Civilians*, is forthcoming with Cambridge University Press.

NOTES

1. War Office, *Statistics of the Military Effort of the British Empire in the Great War, 1914–1920* (London, 1922; repr., London, 1992), table facing p. 64.
2. Haig's GHQ at Montreuil-sur-Mer housed over 3,000 officers and support staff. For an excellent exposition of its multi-faceted functions, see G.S.O., *G.H.Q. (Montreuil-sur-Mer)* (London: Philip Allan & Co., 1920).
3. Records indicate that Hughes was cut back only to Captain's pay a few days after getting to France, from $6 to $4.75 per diem. National Archives of Canada, RG 150, Box 4594–38.
4. Haig's diaries and letters have recently been re-edited. See Douglas Haig, *The War Diaries: The Diaries of Field Marshal Sir Douglas Haig: War Diaries & Letters, 1914–1918*, eds. Gary Sheffield, John Bourne (London: Weidenfeld & Nicolson, 2005).
5. On the variation in casualty estimates, as well as other developments in recent Great War historiography, see the review essay, Terry Castle, "Our First View of the End of the World," *The Chronicle of Higher Education* 51, no. 11 (5 November 2004), pp. B6.
6. Henri Barbusse, *Under Fire: the Story of a Squad*, translated by W. Fitzwater Wray, Introduction by Brian Rhys (1916; 1st Eng. trans., London and Melbourne: J.M. Dent, Everyman's Library, 1917; New York: E.P. Dutton, 1926; reprint, 1988).
7. Paul Fussell, *The Great War and Modern Memory* (New York and London: Oxford University Press, 1975). For the latest critique of Fussell, see Richard Holmes, *Tommy: The British Soldier on the Western Front, 1914–1918* (London, UK: Harper Collins, 2004), pp. xvii–xviii. For an outstanding critique of the war writers by a military historian, see Correlli Barnett, "A Military Historian's View of the Great War," in *Essays by Divers Hands Being the Transactions of the Royal Society of Literature*, ed. Mary Stock, New Series, 36 (London: Oxford University Press, 1970), pp. 1–18.
8. On the extent to which informal truces pervaded sectors of the western front see Tony Ashworth, *Trench Warfare, 1914–1918: The Live and Let Live System* (London and Basingstoke: The MacMillan Press Ltd., 1980).
9. Frederic Manning, *The Middle Parts of Fortune: Somme and Ancre, 1916*, Introduction by Niall Ferguson (orig. pub., 1930, as *Her Privates We*) (London: Penguin Classics, 2000).
10. Erich Maria Remarque, *All Quiet on the Western Front*, trans. A.W. Wheen (Boston: Little, Brown, 1929).
11. On the controversies immediately following the publication of *All Quiet*, see Modris Eksteins, *Rites of Spring: The Great War and the Birth of the Modern Age* (Toronto: Lester & Orpen Dennys, 1989), pp. 285–99.

12. Jeffrey Keshen in "The Great War Soldier as Nation Builder in Canada and Australia," in *Canada and the Great War: Western Front Association Papers*, ed. Briton C. Busch (Montreal and Kingston: McGill-Queen's University Press, 2003), writes (p. 15) well that: "Over the last generation, as those directly connected to, and particularly interested in, protecting the image of Canada's Great War soldiers have died off, the historical portrayal of these men has shown signs of losing its lustre." See also Jonathan F. Vance, *Death So Noble: Memory, Meaning and the First World War* (Vancouver: UBC Press, 1997).

13. For more on the history of the western front versus its popular understanding, see Brian Bond, *The Unquiet Western Front: Britain's Role in Literature and History* (Cambridge, UK: Cambridge University Press, 2002).

14. See Col. G.W.L. Nicholson, *The Canadian Expeditionary Force, 1914–1919: The Official History of the Canadian Army in the First World War* (Ottawa: Queen's Printer, 1964), available (May 2005) online at http://www.dnd.ca/hr/dhh/downloads/Official_Histories/CEF_e.PDF

15. Tim Cook, "Immortalizing the Canadian Soldier: Lord Beaverbrook and the Canadian War Records Office in the First World War," in *Canada and the Great War: Western Front Association Papers*, ed. Briton C. Busch, (Montreal and Kingston: McGill-Queen's University Press, 2003), pp. 52–53.

16. Though they are extremely rough, casualty estimates for the Somme generally put German losses at about 400,000–450,000, and those for the Allies at about 600,000.

17. Norm Christie's recent *For King and Empire* series, a popular account of Canadians on the western front, entitles the 1918 episode, "Masters of War."

18. Cited in Holmes, *Tommy*, p. 277.

19. See *Statistics of the Military Effort of the British Empire*, pp. 65–66.

20. On the evolution of some of the logistical considerations discussed in this introduction, see Martin van Creveld, *Supplying War: Logistics from Wallenstein to Patton* (Cambridge, UK: Cambridge University Press, 1977; reprint, 1980).

21. See *Statistics of the Military Effort of the British Empire*, pp. 65–66.

22. While largely ignoring the BEF's agricultural efforts, Ian Malcolm Brown, *British Logistics on the Western Front, 1914–1919* (Westport, Conn.: Praeger Publishers, 1998), is excellent in other respects.

23. While many talk about *sacrifice* and *dying for a cause*, few have tackled *killing*, the soldier's *raison d'être*. For a welcome addition to the literature, see Joanna Bourke, *An Intimate History of Killing: Face-to-Face Killing in Twentieth-Century Warfare* (London: Granta Books, 1999; New York: Basic Books, 1999).

24. John Keegan, *The Face of Battle* (London: Jonathan Cape, 1976).

25. We number among these, John Ellis, *Eye-Deep in Hell: Trench Warfare in World War I* (Baltimore: John Hopkins University Press, 1977); William L. Gammage, *The Broken Years: Australian Soldiers in the Great War* (Victoria, Australia: Ringwood, 1975; New York: Penguin Books, 1975); Holmes, *Tommy*; Desmond Morton, *When Your Number's Up: The Canadian Soldier in the First World War* (Toronto: Random House of Canada Ltd., 1993), and Denis Winter, *Death's Men: Soldiers of the Great War* (London: Allen Lane, 1979). J.G. Fuller, *Troop Morale and Popular Culture in the British*

and Dominion Armies, 1914–18 (Oxford: Clarendon Press, 1991) predicates the BEF's morale on the importation of homespun forms of popular amusement, including variety shows, sports, and musical performances.

26. CEF Books, Ottawa, have republished numerous classic Canadian memoirs, while at the same time published new ones. J.L. Granatstein, *Hell's Corner: An Illustrated History of Canada's Great War, 1914–1918* (Vancouver: Douglas & McIntyre, 2004), is an extremely recent publication, using the Canadian War Museum's collection of photographs.

27. See also Craig Gibson, "'My Chief Source of Worry': An Assistant Provost Marshal's View of Relations between 2nd Canadian Division and Local Inhabitants on the Western Front, 1915–1917," *War in History* 2000, 7 (4), pp. 413–41.

28. Two articles that explore this subject further are: Craig Gibson, "The British Army, French Farmers and the War on the Western Front 1914–1918," *Past & Present* 180 (August 2003), pp. 173–237; and S.F. Wise, "The Gardeners of Vimy: Canadian Corps' Farming Operations during the German Offensives of 1918," *Canadian Military History* VIII, 3 (1999), pp. 39–47.

29. On a related note, the hundreds of memoirs, edited collections of letters, and novels from experience authored by fighting troops generally display similar tendencies. Despite the fact most combatants spent a majority of time behind the lines, their unpublished and published writings are weighted towards life in the trenches and during combat.

Prologue

ODE TO THE RAT

Here's to the Rat, the curse of all
Who listen to their country's call.
In good old France's mud you'll find
The Rat was never left behind.

You'll find their holes on every beat
But chiefly underneath your seat.
In every dugout big or small
There'll be a Rat if he can crawl.

If you'll be still I'll tell to you
A little bit of harm they do.
They eat great holes in our haversacks
They raise their young ones in our packs.

If we leave our bread out on our bunk
The Rat will eat it, every chunk.
And many a Rat has caused us fright
While standing-to on darksome nights.

Even while we sleep we have no grace
They fight and crawl about our face.
And hold conventions round our head
The noise they make would wake the dead.

They get into our ration bags
And break and dirty all our fags.

"Runner," called the Company Commander.

"Here, Sir."

"Take this note to Battalion Headquarters."

"Yes, Sir," and the company runner laid aside his own small notebook, turned, and climbed up the narrow stairway out of the dugout in the chalk before Vimy Ridge.

Was the ode ever finished? We do not know. Neither do we know the poet's name. All we know is that he was runner for D Company, 29th Battalion, Canadian Expeditionary Force (CEF) on New Year's Day, 1917.

We apologize for using his verse as a prologue to our own story. We were attached to the 29th for instructional duty at that time. Sitting on our bunk—a sheet of corrugated iron—we had noticed the preoccupation of the runner-poet as he crouched under his ground sheet, on the steps of the dugout, while water dripped from the ceiling overhead. Another runner, whose name we also do not know, seeing our interest in the writing, picked up the scribbled sheets and passed them over with a smile.

To our mind they typified the spirit of these brave (although they would have laughed at the word) lads, who, when carrying messages, defied death a dozen times a day.

Amidst death and destruction, filth and corruption, the snap of rifle bullets that missed by inches, and the crump of exploding mortar shells, one of them excluded all these things from his mind and composed verse about our greatest curse of trench life—the rat.[1]

Gardens

"**HUGHES,** I want you to start a kitchen garden for me."

"Yes, Sir. Where will you have it?"

"Oh, wherever you find room."

"How large do you want it, Sir?"

"Oh, make it large enough to supply potatoes and vegetables for a million men."

Major General Holman,[2] Quartermaster General of the 4th Army, which held the salient in Belgium and Northern France, sat behind his army table that served as a desk. The General, with his greying hair and deep-set eyes that seemed at times to slumber, but never did, was intently watching the officer before him.

Watching and weighing, the officer thought, but—being a Canadian—tried to show no undue concern at the tremendous order laid on his shoulders. In a flash he had the answer to the General's next question even before it was finished being asked.

"Where can you make such a garden?"

"Up in the forward areas, south from Poperinghe and Ypres,[3] along Messines Ridge.[4] There are forty thousand acres of idle land along our front, and all good farm land."

"How do you know all that?"

"As you know, Sir, I am a farmer."

"Do you think you can do what I suggest?"

"Yes, Sir, provided you give me a free hand."

"Where would you find the farm implements, plows, and so forth?"

"Large quantities of farm implements have been gathered up from the devastated farms and are being repaired near Péronne and near Bapaume. Also there are large stocks of new implements available in Paris."

"What about horses? We have none to spare here in the Army."

"There are five thousand idle horses in horse lines just outside of Calais. Many of them are blind, while many more have sore feet. They are useless up the line on the hard roads, but would be quite serviceable on farms."

"How do you know this?"

"Again, Sir, I am a farmer and I have passed these lines."

"What about manpower?"

"We have hundreds, yes, thousands, of convalescent men around our hospitals. We have hundreds of partially shell-shocked men in our battalions who would be brought back to health if given a few weeks of farm life. Then, troops out in rest could each give a limited amount of help. In addition to these there are the labour battalions."[5]

"What about seeds, and potatoes for seed?"

"France had always been a great vegetable country, so seed will be available at any of the big centres. Send to Scotland and Ireland for seed potatoes."

"Hughes, what I like about you Canadians is that nothing stumps you. You have a job, and a damn big one. Cotton," he said, turning to his assistant, "tell the Director of Labour I want to see him."

"Yes, Sir," replied Major Cotton,[6] Assistant Adjutant to the Quartermaster General.

When the Director of Labour came into the room, the Quartermaster General's orders were short and to the point: "Colonel, Major Hughes here has been assigned to the job of producing vegetables and potatoes for our Army, here in our Army area. This is a project of immense importance and will take every effort we can put forth. Will you see that Army Orders are promulgated to the effect that every Corps will assist in every way possible. They will issue orders to this effect to every Division in their command.

Also, all Army units that have available farmers are to allow Major Hughes to have these men for this project."

"I will see to this at once, Sir. More than that, Sir, personally I think this a fine thing to do, and I will assist the Major in every way possible."

"Thank you, Colonel. Now, Major Cotton, will you arrange for Major Hughes to have the use of any necessary transport vehicles he needs from time to time. Also make arrangements so that he can draw on our supply of horses now in sick lines near Calais.

"Now, Major, one other thing. What about money, cash with which to buy the innumerable things this project will need?"

"That, Sir, is a question I cannot answer, but as your question indicates, you know that if we always have to wait until requisitions go through GHQ or the War Office, we won't make very good time."

"Sir," broke in Major Cotton, "could we not use the Fat Fund for this purpose? This whole project is to supply extra rations for the good of our men, and that is what the Fat Fund was established for."

"That's the idea. You understand about our Fat Fund, Hughes?"

"Only partially, Sir. I know we are ordered to save all surplus fats and we have had the experience of inhaling the aroma of the extraction plant down near Étaples."

"Well, as you say, we save all surplus fats and these are valuable. Their value in money is credited back to units so that extra rations, not usually on the provided list, may be bought for the men. Now this vegetable project fits right into our plans.

"Cotton, arrange that Major Hughes, as our Agricultural Officer,[7] has discretionary powers to draw on this fund as he deems advisable. Understand, Hughes, this is a very special privilege. Our Army Commander himself does not have this privilege.

"Now, let's sum it up. You are appointed 4th Army Agricultural Officer. We will endeavour to make this a permanent unit in the Army, but until this is accomplished, and you know the War Office sometimes moves slowly, you must use your Canadian ingenuity and initiative to get this project under way. You will have the wholehearted backing of Q Branch. Come in and see me personally whenever you see fit. Major Cotton will be your line of communication at all times. Is that all clear?"

"Yes, Sir. Thank you very much."

A young Canadian farmer, temporary gentleman and junior field officer and, for the time being, a Staff Lieutenant Second Class, shook hands with a hard-working, keen-eyed, temporary Major General of the British Army, who had the biggest non-fighting job in the Army in France, for at that moment (late 1917), he was charged with feeding a million men.

The *California*

Steadily the steamship *California*[8] of the Anchor Line plowed her way eastward. On board was the 151st Battalion, CEF, and four batteries of artillery. Down in the holds were stored great quantities of ammunition that had been loaded in New York.

The troops had come aboard at Halifax and were now settled down for the long run across the Atlantic. Well ahead steamed the cruiser *Gloucester*, followed by the steamship *Saxonia*, next came the *California*, and last the *Missanabia*.

The Captain of the *California* did not like this convoy idea one little bit. He would have much preferred to go it alone, even though he knew that the ocean-going German submarine U53[9] was lurking somewhere off the Atlantic coast and had already sent several ships to their watery graves.

Fortunately for the troops on board, the sea was moderately calm and the 7000-ton ship rode steady. The *California* was a nice ship in which to travel. She had good high ceilings on all decks and the air conditioning was excellent. All ranks were reasonably happy and most were enjoying this first experience on the water.

The officers gathered in the main cabin did not seem to have a care in the world. The day was fine, the sea was calm, and lunch had been

A studio portrait of John taken in about 1917 in England, wearing his wool battledress with one crown on the shoulder, indicating his rank of Major. The photo was made into a postcard, as was commonly done in those days, but this copy was never used as a postcard.

excellent. Lieutenant Chipman was pounding the piano and others were singing. Only a small group seated around the table seemed to have something to worry about. These were the senior officers, captains and majors. They were not worrying about German submarines. In fact, the colonel coming into the cabin rebuked them for not wearing their life belts as had been ordered.

Their trouble was something quite different from this. Rumour had seeped through that there was not a hope that the battalion would go to the front as a unit, despite the assurance of the Minister for War back in Ottawa.

Worse than this, a senior officer who had been met in Halifax, on his way home from England, had been very bitter on the subject. He had stated, "I am going home in disgust. Officers above the rank of lieutenant are just not wanted in England. There are hundreds of captains, majors, and lieutenant colonels kicking their heels in idleness all over the country, nothing for them to do, and our government is too damn cowardly to send them home."[10]

If this was true, it was a gloomy outlook for those around the table, and it took much of the enthusiasm out of every one of them.

After long months of training, they were on their way to the Western Front. They knew they had as fine a bunch of men as ever came from Canada. Now, if all this was true, they were not going to have the chance to lead the lads they had worked so hard to train.

Of course there was nothing they could do but hope. Finally the small party broke up and drifted away to their cabins. One of the party, Major Hughes, Officer in Command (OC) of C Company, went in search of his Quartermaster Sergeant. Finding him, he said, "Pilkie,[11] how about distributing those boxes of apples our friends from Vermilion gave us."

"Good idea, Major. I'll attend to it at once."

On leaving Edmonton, Alberta, friends from Vermilion[12] had loaded ten boxes of BC apples into C Company baggage car. The major went among his men, his "boys" as he called them, as the apples were distributed. He knew every one of them by name. He had personally enlisted every one of them and they were his friends. Now, knowing he might be parted from them within a few days, it was like preparing himself to part with members of his own family.

The privates of C Company were absolutely at their ease with their OC, and why should they be anything else? They were his neighbours at home, and hoped to be his neighbours when this little unpleasantness was over.

Sadly, the major made his way back to his own cabin and, sitting there alone, he knew there was only one thing under the circumstances he could do. He could tell his wife about his troubles.

Then and there, aboard the steamship *California*, he started a line of letters in which he poured out all his troubles to the one person he knew would understand—Sara Hughes,[13] who was then staying with his mother and father at Saddle Lake, Alberta.

Most people, when they have read a letter, think it best to give it to the flames, but not so this wife. Those letters were carefully preserved, and although in later years the mice did get into the packages and nibble many corners, in the main they were as on the day they were written.

Thirty-five years passed away. Then, one day, the writer of the letters unearthed those boxes from the attic and sat down to relive those days of the years 1916–19. The urge came to put in readable form a record of those days, taken from those letters that so largely dealt with a phase of the Great War that, so far as we know, has never appeared in print.

Those letters dealt largely with the problem that the senior officers had been discussing that day aboard the *California*—what of the unwanted officers of the CEF?

If, in the chapters that follow, readers are inclined to think that the words are but the vain imaginings of a feeble old mind, they are very much mistaken. Feeble the mind might have been, but not old, for all the most important wordings are taken almost verbatim from that file of letters written near on forty years ago.

While the names used are mostly those of Western units, the problem affected every part of our wide Dominion. The names and units are authentic as far as the writer knew at the time.

The whole story was one of heartbreak, disillusionment, and uncertainty as to what was the best course one could follow. These men had sacrificed all they held dearest—homes, successful businesses, professions—at their country's call. Now they were unwanted. Unwanted, when they had been placed in a position where, if they went home, few at home would give them credit for acting as gentlemen, even temporary gentlemen, as they were listed in Army records.

What could they do? Our story tells how many of them solved their problem and gave service to their country, in spite of difficulties, in spite of snubs, in spite of indifference by Army authorities, and proved the worth of Canadians amidst the most conservative group of men on earth, the officers of the British Army.

To a large extent, this is one man's story. It is not a history of the unwanted senior officers of the CEF, yet it typifies what others did as well. Let each man tell his own story, and added together they will be history. They were a splendid group of men. The writer is proud to have been one of those who did not go home until the game was finished.

England's Grass

MORNING BROKE, and the *California* was almost alone in the rough sea off the north coast of Ireland. Far ahead was a smudge of smoke fading into the distance. This, we were told, was the *Saxonia*,[14] which was the faster ship of the convoy, while, far behind, another smudge told that the *Missanabie*[15] was being outdistanced. Where the cruiser *Gloucester* was, no one knew. Those aboard the *California* felt very much alone, for this was known as good cruising ground for the Hun U-boats.

Then, far ahead, were seen specks on the waves, coming ever nearer. Among the hundreds that lined the decks there was almost complete silence. What were these specks? The troops did not have long to wait for the answer.

"Destroyers," rippled through the crowd. "Our own destroyers."

Then, as those little boats came abreast, every cap was waving and every throat was shouting wild greetings. Aboard the slim swift vessels a few men were seen, and these waved back to the happy group up on the transport.

How those destroyers could speed! There were four of them, and hour after hour they sailed circles around the much slower-moving transport ship. No U-boat could come through that tight circle and live, so the men on board could give their attention to the panorama to their right.

John at Saddle Lake Indian
Reserve, circa 1915–16, where his
father was the Indian Agent.
An undated note in Sara's
handwriting on the back says,
"Taken a year ago at the Agency
here. John has got a lot stouter
since this was taken. He tips the
scales between 150 and 160 lbs.
now. A slight difference to what
he did when you last saw him at
133 lbs." It is not known who the
note was intended for, as
the photo was still in John's
possession when he died.

Ireland. Ireland in all its checkerboard tints of green. Who has not seen picture post cards of the fields of the Emerald Isle? Those cards do but scant justice to the beauty of that land, especially when seen by weary travellers far away from land so long.

Later, away to the left was a dim cloudy mound that the sailors told us was the Mull of Kintyre, Scotland. Scotland, the homeland of some on board, and that of many of the sires of very many more.

We had crossed the Atlantic. Nine long days, a quiet uneventful trip, and safe, in spite of enemy U-boats. We did not know then that this splendid ship that had carried us in comfort and safety was so soon to meet one of those hated Hun boats and go down to her watery grave off the coast of Ireland.

Darkness came down during the long run down the Irish Sea, and when dawn came again the *California* rode at ease in the quiet waters of the Mersey.

Liverpool, one of the greatest harbours in the world.

Slowly, we were edged in by the tugboats to the vast floating dock. With what emotions we stepped down the gangplank and felt solid earth once more. Much was strange to those young men from the wilds of far Western Canada. Much to admire, much to praise, yet much to laugh and joke about.

For instance, those men carrying bags of wheat from that ship which we were told came from Australia. Carrying wheat in bags! Why, that had gone out of fashion years ago back home on the prairies. Why make beasts of burden out of men when machinery could do the work both quicker and easier?

"Come on boys, let's help these chaps carry the wheat," laughingly suggested someone.

"Of course. Why not?" Then the laughter ceased. Why not? Because the husky lads from the West could not lift and shoulder those bags that were being carried with apparent ease by older and smaller men. Men who were going at a half-trot up those narrow ways to storerooms. For the first time, we had laughed at Englishmen, then changed our mind and praised.

The second laugh came when the train of little railway cars was shunted into position for us to enter.

"See the dinky little cabooses? Come on boys, let's pick this one up and turn it around." Yes, jokes and jibes and laughter. That is, until we were out of the city and onto the straight runway. Then there was no laughter. A ride so swift and so smooth, a glass of water or a cup of tea could sit for miles and not spill a drop. Not much like some of our Western railroads that had been laid across the prairies.

It is said that when Mackenzie and Mann built the Canadian Northern Railway west from Winnipeg they did not even smooth out the knolls made by the gophers. Yet they built a road that developed an Empire.

England's cities are far from beautiful. In fact, they are drab and dirty and uninteresting, at least at first glance. England's countryside is always beautiful, go where you will—east, west, north, or south.

What a change from the limitless prairies to these small, well-kept farms. The hedges of green that marked the boundaries of the fields, in comparison to ugly barb wire fences. The homesteads, many with red-tiled

A studio portrait of John, Sara, and their first three children—William, John Paul, and Charles Edward—in the summer of 1915, shortly after John enlisted in the 66th Bn. The two pips in the embroidered portion of his left sleeve indicate he was a Lieutenant at the time.

roofs, in place of unpainted buildings that spoke of anything but beauty on the bald prairies.

Perhaps what caught the eye of those western lads most was the grass. How deeply green, how thick and velvety. Our grass is grey and uninteresting in comparison. True, uninteresting though it looks, it puts pounds onto steers in an amazing manner. But this English grass has beauty, and more than that.

Listening, the major could hear two of his boys talking.

Said one, "Jim, do you notice how many cows there are on each of those little pastures?"

"Sure did, Bob, and those cows are fat."

"Look at that one there. One, two, four, six, ten cows. How big is that field?"

"Not more than three or four acres."

"Lordy. Dad has a whole quarter section at Viking, and he thinks it does fine to carry twenty cows."

"Dinky little farms, Jim, but I guess we had better not laugh at them. We laughed at this dinky little train, but boy, she sure rides smooth."

"Do you know how they build these roadbeds?"

"No."

"Well, Dad told me. They move away all the topsoil till they come to the hard clay. Then they lay a heavy bed of rock, and on that make a fill of gravel and cinders, then lay their ties."

"Some different to the road I was working on last summer. We just piled up a ridge of topsoil for the bed. Several horses died on the job, so we just piled the bodies in the grade and covered them over."

"Not much wonder our cars jump and bound around. This road is sure smooth."

These contrasts we were to observe everywhere in this old land that had taken thousands of years to develop, in contrast to the hundreds for Canada and tens for the prairies.

The Unwanted

THE DAY HAD BEEN BEAUTIFUL as the swift train carried a thousand Canadian soldiers clear across England, from Liverpool to London, and then south to Folkestone.

London was disappointing. How could it be anything else from a railway-carriage point of view? That point of view consists mainly of chimney pots. Chimney pots by the tens and hundreds of thousands.

"Golly," said one lad after gazing for a long time at the unending line of pots, "these English folks must have a lot of stoves in their houses. I thought this was a warm country. I would sure hate to cut wood for a house with a dozen stoves."

Later, they were to think of England as anything but a warm country. They were to know the dampness that penetrates and chills as zero never does on the prairies. In fact, the dampness was coming in fast. When the train came to rest at Shorncliffe station, the air was full of moisture.

"This," said Regimental Quartermaster Sergeant Matt Brimacombe,[16] "is one of those Scotch mists they tell about. It wets an Englishman to the skin."

The march from Shorncliffe[17] to St. Martin's Plain, through the growing mist and growing dark, was anything but pleasant, yet at the same time a relief from the long day in the coaches.

Unit 151ᵗʰ Batt Rank Lieut Name Hughes John Mc

OFFICERS' DECLARATION PAPER.

CANADIAN OVER-SEAS EXPEDITIONARY FORCE.

151ST BN

QUESTIONS TO BE ANSWERED BY OFFICER.

(ANSWERS.)

1. (a) What is your Surname? *Hughes.*

   (b) What are your Christian Names? *John McK Hughes.*

2. (a) Where were you born? (State place and country). *Rexton Kent Co New Brunswick*

   (b) What is your present address? *Lavoy Alberta*

3. What is the date of your birth? *Aug 15 1883*

4. What is (a) the name of your next-of-kin? *Sara Marie Hughes.*

   (b) the address of your next-of-kin? *Saddle Lake Alberta*

   (c) the relationship of your next-of-kin? *Wife*

5. What is your profession or occupation? *Farmer*

6. What is your religion? *Anglican*

7. Are you willing to be vaccinated or re-vaccinated and inoculated? *Yes.*

8. To what Unit of the Active Militia do you belong? *19th Alberta Dragoons.*

9. State particulars of any former Military Service.

10. Are you willing to serve in the
    CANADIAN OVER-SEAS EXPEDITIONARY FORCE? *Yes.*

The undersigned hereby declares that the above answers made by him to the above questions are true.

J McK Hughes Lieut (Signature of Officer.)

CERTIFICATE OF MEDICAL EXAMINATION.

I have examined the above-named Officer in accordance with the Regulations for Army Medical Services.

I consider him* *fit* for the CANADIAN OVER-SEAS EXPEDITIONARY FORCE.

Date *June 29* 1915

Place *Edmonton*

Bernard R Mooney
Medical Officer.

*Insert here "fit" or "unfit."

M. F. W. 51.
20m—70-15.
H. Q. 1772-99 817.

This is the standard one-page Officers' Declaration Paper filled out by John McKendrick Hughes when he enlisted in the army in June 1915. He was taken on strength as an officer because he had experience as an officer in the militia, specifically the 19th Alberta Dragoons. Source: Library and Archives Canada, RG150, Box 4594–38.

It was dark, with not a mist but a steady rain, as the battalion formed up on the parade ground on St. Martin's Plain. Cold and wet and dark. Then a wait. Did anyone know we had arrived or, knowing, care?

A man, who proved to be the Adjutant of the 9th Reserve Battalion, came through the darkness along with a bunch of NCOs. His orders were short and to the point: "Officers, fall out."

There it was. Not even a courteous, "Colonel, ask your officers to fall out."

Did it strike any of us at that moment how little a lieutenant colonel amounted to in those days? That is, one who commanded, or who *had* commanded, a CEF battalion. Maybe not at that precise moment, but we were to know it more and more as time went on.

"A Company," said the Adjutant, "you are allotted to the 21st Reserve Battalion. Sergeant Major, march your company off. Follow this guide.

"B Company, you are allotted to the 11th Reserve Battalion. Sergeant Major, march your company off. Follow this guide.

"C Company." Our own. Our friends. Our neighbours. Our boys. "You are allotted to the 9th Reserve Battalion. Sergeant Major, march your company off. Follow this guide."

Company Sergeant Major Morris, an English gentleman who was to win his commission and lead of a company of his own Shire Regiment, the Buffs, and who was the best CSM in our outfit, swung our company so as to pass the spot where his company commander—his *late* company commander—was standing.

"Eyes...right!"

Our eyes were straight ahead. Our hand was at the salute. Our eyes were full of tears. We were proud of those boys. Maybe they even liked us. We like to think they did. We still have a gold-banded Malacca cane they gave us. Dimly, through our tears and the steady rain, our company disappeared into the darkness.

The Adjutant turned and left the parade ground.

There we stood:

One Lieutenant Colonel.
One Senior Major.
One Junior Major.
Four Company Majors.

Sixteen Lieutenants.

One Adjutant Captain.

Four Company Captains.

One Quartermaster Captain.

One Medical Officer Captain.

One Paymaster Captain.

Alone in the rain on St. Martin's Plain.

We had brought a thousand badly wanted men.

But we were *unwanted*.[18]

How Canada's Army Was Made

THROUGH THE GLOOM and steady drizzle of rain a junior lieutenant appeared.

"Gentlemen, if you will come to the messroom I think we can scare you up a bit to eat and some coffee."

A bit to eat and a mug of coffee.

What a welcome to a group of men (temporary gentlemen) who had left home and fireside at their country's call. Men who had left busy business offices, professional offices and clinics, fine farmsteads. Men who for years had given their spare time, sacrificed their earned holidays to train a scoffed-at militia. Men who had given long hours to train themselves so as to be able to train others in the ways of war.

The messroom was more crowded than any we had been used to in the past. Especially, there seemed to be a surplus of senior officers. A full half-dozen who wore both crown and pip. A dozen like ourself who wore the crown, and a score or more with three pips. Few with two pips.

"Hello chaps, where from?" was the usual greeting as we were welcomed into a crowded, smoke-filled mess. "From Edmonton, from Northern Alberta." Questions were poured at us. "Do you know so and so?", "How are things back home?", and on and on.

When it came our turn to ask questions there was silence in the room as our junior major led off. "Is this the way Canadian troops are welcomed in England? Our battalion smashed to bits without as much as by-your-leave. Officers left standing in the rain to wander God-knows-where. If it is, it's time we let the folks back home know what's up over here."

Major Jim Lowry was mad. Mad clear through and did not try to hide his anger. Also, Jim was a bit of a politician and used to speaking his mind.

For a moment there was silence. Then came the flood. If Jim Lowry was mad, there were a score or more who were madder still.

"We had Sam Hughes's[19] personal word we would go to the front as a unit. Damn his soul to hell."

"We were broken up the minute we landed on St. Martin's Plain."

"Our men are scattered God-knows-where."

"Half our men are already in France. We simps of officers are still here sitting on our backsides."

"If the people back home knew how we are treated there would be hell to pay."

"Let's go home and kick Sam Hughes out of Ottawa."

On and on, not only that evening but for days and months to come, this steady refrain that should have blistered the hide of the Minister of Militia and Defense back in Ottawa.

Now why all this? Was it justified? Was it righteous wrath? In other words, what had caused all this wild talk?

The writer is not a historian, neither has he all the information available on this point. All he has are the facts as appeared on those days in 1916.

At the outbreak of war in June 1914, Canada had a military system of sorts. It worked quite well, that is for peacetime, but now we were at war. Militia units were located in all the cities and large towns from coast to coast. They were grouped under District Commands that roughly corresponded to provincial boundaries, except in Ontario and Quebec, where more than one was located. These units were not grouped as brigades and divisions outside of the provincial boundaries. Nevertheless, there was a fair semblance of a Dominion Army. Yet when war came, even this semblance of an Army was not used.

The Garrison church at Shorncliffe Camp. A hand-written note on the back of this postcard says, "This is the place where Bob Pinkney is buried. It is a much better building than appears in this picture, particularly inside." Robert Charles Pinkney (1885–1916) was a resident of Vermilion whom John recruited for the 151st Bn. in January 1916. He died on 16 October 1916, just days after the unit arrived in England.

Sam Hughes was Minister of Militia.

Now Sam Hughes was a forceable man, a domineering type of man. A *very* domineering man. Apparently as far as the army went he was Dictator. It is a black mark against the government of the day that this state of affairs was allowed to exist. The fact that the party that was then in power has even to this day never again been the dominating power in Canada for any length of time is, to this writer's mind, attributable to the fact that Sam Hughes was master at Ottawa in those crucial days. The writer bears the same name, and Sam once tapped him on the shoulder and said, "See that you keep up our family name, my lad." Sam's family is Irish, ours is Welsh. We came to Canada a generation or more before his.

Canada overnight decided to raise an army, and she did just that. She raised the biggest and finest volunteer army in modern times. And Sam Hughes was the genius that did it. Was it all done with aforethought or did it just run wild without control? If it was the first, it was the cruelest, most cold-blooded plan ever developed in Canada. If the latter, then Sam Hughes never deserved his rank or his knighthood. (Judge not that you be not judged.) We do not know.

For our population, Canada raised an immense army; six hundred thousand or more in uniform. This for a country that never before had even fifty thousand men under arms.

How was it done?

By ruthless disregard of existing militia organization.

By favouritism unashamed.

Suddenly, from coast to coast, men were given authority to raise regiments, battalions, batteries, and brigades of artillery.

Canada, without inquiring as to the why and wherefore, flocked to the banners. Protests from established regiments, battalions, and batteries were cast in the discard.

True, many of the Officers Commanding of the established units were the OCs of these newly approved units, but most of the established units, as units, stayed at home.

This was a new army. Or was it any army?

Yes it was an army, a volunteer army. With *all its men in the first-line troops. There was no second line, no reserve.* Read that over again: *No reserves.*

Battalions started from number one and went on and on, to over three hundred or more, *and still no reserves.*

In all-out war, casualties are considered normal at seventy per cent every six months. Canada had three hundred battalions of a thousand men, each fully equipped from lieutenant colonel to bugle boy.

We all knew the table of casualties, that is all who had officer militia training. Sam Hughes knew it, for he was head of our militia, yet he disregarded this inescapable fact.

Some of our best and most respected citizens suddenly had command of battalions. Some were trained officers, that is militia-trained. A few—a very few—had seen actual war as officers in South Africa, though more as privates and troopers. Some men, whom we the people knew little or nothing about, suddenly appeared with command of battalions yet to be raised.

The established 19th Alberta Dragoons[20] had been allowed to recruit one squadron for overseas service. Major Fred Jamieson[21] received the command. With him went Major Billy Griesbach,[22] afterwards to be Major-

General, as second-in-command. Ten officers of the 19th were allowed to go. Our application to be one of those chosen came just a little too late for acceptance, but it did leave us in command of C Squadron (still waiting). Months went by. Slowly the stern fact came to light; this was not a war for cavalry, it was a foot-slugger's war.

Suddenly a man appeared in Edmonton, a Lieutenant Colonel J.W.H. McKinery,[23] with a call to raise the 66th Infantry Battalion, CEF.

Fifteen officers of the still-waiting 19th Alberta Dragoons assembled, debated, then marched as a body to the office of the 66th Battalion. They offered their services and were accepted at once, sworn in, and told to go to their respective homes and raise a platoon each. We did as ordered, went back home and, in and around Vegreville and Lavoy, raised a platoon. Arrived back in Edmonton on a morning train, reported to Battalion and was instructed to fall in on parade as OC Fourteen Platoon, and stood there in fear and trembling, without the faintest idea of how to give an infantry command. We lived through that day, thanks to a sergeant who wore a South African ribbon. We were no better or no worse than thousands of others (temporary gentlemen) who officered the new army.

The 31st Battalion had been raised in Edmonton. Billy Griesbach had come home to raise the 49th Battalion. Dr. Harwood had command of a new battalion named the 51st. George MacLeod received authority to raise the 63rd. MacLeod may not have had the military training such as that of the new Commanding Officer (CO) of the 66th, but at least he was a gentleman.

The CO of the 66th knew infantry drill even if his Lieutenant of Fourteen Platoon did not. He knew it well. He was a martinet at drill. He had an absolute disregard for the feelings of the officers under his command, and still less regard for the authority of the District Officer Commanding (DOC). Canada, that is in so far as the army was concerned, was on the Indian list. That is, no alcoholic drinks were allowed. The CO of the 66th disregarded this openly, both in the Sergeants' Mess and the Officers'.

Complaints were made and the DOC came up from Calgary to investigate. Apparently (or so it seemed to us at the time) he decided that there was no evidence to support the complaints.

Came mess dinner time. After the meal came time for toasts. Two decanters were placed in front of the OC, the one port, the other sherry,

H.J. (Jack) Frost, D Company, 10th Canadian Railway Troops worked with John on one of his farms in France. He may also have served as John's batman. This photograph is believed to be of Jack Frost, somewhere in England.

and were passed right and left around the long table. It was good port and also good sherry. We junior officers knew, we had paid for it. Came the time for the toast, "Our King," and from officers of field rank, "God bless him."

The DOC smacked his lips. "God damn fine grape juice, Colonel."

"Yes," replied the Colonel, "nothing but the best for the 66th."

Had the DOC never tasted port? We wonder.

Later the writer was to transfer to the 151st Battalion, [to] enlist, command, and train C Company.

Edmonton raised the 9th, part of the 31st, the 49th, the 51st, the 63rd, the 66th, the 151st, the 202nd, the 218th and others, *with no reserves.*

The Canadian Army had its baptism of fire at the Battle of Ypres, a bloody, gas-filled battle and the casualties were heavy. Reserves were needed and at once. Did those hard-stricken battalions have reserves to fill their depleted rank? No.

Why, oh why, did not the Army Command at home in Canada wake up then and there to the fact that it was not battalions that were needed but men, men, and more men?

Was it that the Prime Minister, the Minister of Militia, and the rest of the Cabinet got together and said one to the other:

"If we just ask for men to fill the ranks we won't get them."

"The only way we can get the men is to play on the vanity of our leading men, the vanity of our cities and towns."

"Let's give any man who has standing in his town the command of a battalion, make him a Lieutenant Colonel, pat him on the back, tell him that the unit he raised will go overseas as a battalion, go to France as a battalion."

"Let's play one town, one city, against another, so that they will be viewing each other to see which can raise the most men."

Was there one among that group that had the right of the prefix Honourable to their names, who said "shame"?

Anyway, apparently this is just what was done.

What actually was the situation? Sam Hughes was master at home and hated overseas. British officers, that is ranking British officers, absolutely refused to recognize the authority of the Minister of Militia of Canada over Canadian troops once they had arrived in England, and, considering the facts already stated, rightly so.

These men knew war. By comparison, Sam Hughes was a newly recruited trooper. Yet the same Sam Hughes was their master when it came to raising a volunteer army of free Canadians.

Officers of the 66th, 63rd, 82nd, and other Alberta battalions were sent east in the fall of 1915 to take a musketry course at Rockcliffe Range, Ottawa. As was quite usual apparently, the Minister of Militia came to the ranges one day on a tour of inspection. A demonstration was arranged by the OC Musketry School. We were to strip a rifle, explain its working parts, and re-assemble it.

An officer from an Ontario battalion was selected to go through the detail. This officer held a rifle in his hands. We stood six feet from him on one side. Sir Sam Hughes, Minister of Militia, the same approximate distance on the other side.

Let us follow this officer's discourse:

"This is a Ross rifle.[24] It weighs nine-and-one-quarter pounds.

"This rifle is divided into three main parts, namely the barrel, lock, and stock.

"The barrel is so-many inches long, calibre 303.

"The lock is made up of so-many parts and operates so-and-so.

"The stock is owned by Sir Sam Hughes."

We gasped and held our breath for moments. Not a word was said by anybody. The Minister of Militia did not bat an eye or change colour.

We were aghast. Furtively we looked around at others who were taking the course. Everyone was staring straight ahead.

We forget now how the tension was broken, but we do remember that afterwards we gathered in small groups and freely discussed this, which, if true, was a damning indictment and, if false, was slander and open to a charge of criminal libel.

We had occasion later in the day to ask this officer if he wanted to be charged with conduct unbecoming to an officer and a gentleman.

His answer was, "I hope I am. But I won't be. He doesn't dare."

This was a shock to ourself. Had our idol feet of clay? We were young and rather proud that one of our name was the most important man in Canada and, moreover, remember he had called us "Sonny."

Now in England, we were to remember that day at Rockcliffe Range. We were to listen to the ribald jests as all our leather equipment was thrown aside as junk. At least twenty thousand dollars' worth from each and every Canadian battalion. Who were the profiteers? We heard stories, but did not believe them until we were in the trenches in France, but there was proof—Ross rifles were used as stakes to hold up the parapet. Every man carried a Lee Enfield.

From a letter we wrote to our wife back home in Alberta:

9th Reserve Battalion
St. Martin's Plain
22–11–16

Dearest:
The feeling here among soldiers [officers in particular] is bitter against the Government, although a great majority are Conservatives. The feeling against Sam Hughes is more than bitter. He has nearly pulled the present government out of power. Of course, now Borden may be able to save the situation. Sam's downfall was hailed with delight among Canadian troops in England

and France. His stubborn stupidity in trying to force the Ross rifle on the Canadian troops at the front has been only one of his many mistakes. He jarred the War Office here until Chief of Staff Robertson said he would rather do without the assistance of the Canadians than have Sam around the War Office. A polite invitation was issued to our Minister of Militia to go home.

Canada put four divisions in the field. Four divisions make one corps. Four divisions of about twenty thousand men each. She tried hard to make it five divisions, but there was just not enough men to go around. (Of officers there were more than enough.)

Four divisions of sixteen battalions each (when at full strength), even this had to be cut in the end. Sixty-four battalions and we had three hundred. There was one lieutenant colonel, six majors, and eight captains to a battalion. Count them yourself. Leave out the captains and still you have a battalion of senior officers, and unwanted in England.

Officer casualties were heavy, extremely heavy in France. Then why not send these men to the front? This raises another problem. If it was a tragedy to send completely officered battalions to England, it was not only a tragedy but a disgrace to send untrained men to war.

Was the Canadian Army untrained? you ask with a lift of the eyebrows.

Yes, just that.

By the end of 1915 it was known that this World War was something new.

Julius Caesar dug trenches in England. They are still there. Climb Caesar's Hill just outside Folkestone and there on that high rounded hill overlooking the English Channel you can still, after two thousand years, trace those trenches. Yet World War One was the first and maybe the last war fought nine-tenths in the trench. Then why, oh why, were we trained for the old-fashioned war of movement? Was the Government of Canada, the War Department asleep?

When we arrived in England we had ten years of service behind us, one complete year of training for a war actually going on. Yet until we had a turn of duty in the trenches down in the Suchey Valley looking up the rise to Vimy Ridge, we knew practically nothing about trench warfare.

We hope that Colonel Wilfred Bovey will forgive us for quoting from his article on training in the Legion Magazine.

John at Sarcee Camp, Calgary, in 1915 or 1916. The three pips on his left sleeve indicate he was still a Captain at the time, and, as indicated by the tents in the background, living under canvas.

We first learned about the complicated system of German trenches (far better constructed than ours) with deep dugouts and comfortable housing from a long report of a raid carried out by Lieut. Colonel Embury's 5th Battalion. The report reached us quite unauthorized, but had excellent maps and was a blessing. Needless to say, the officer who brought it over should have been courtmartialed, but there never was any evidence.

Then he goes on to tell how he and others, quite unofficially, started the real training for trench warfare (that unfortunately did not reach us in Canada).

Our next step was the result of a letter from Division officer Major Victor Buchanan, killed soon afterwards, which said, "At last we have got rid of those damned Ross rifles. We now have Enfields taken off British corpses." Not long afterwards our redoubtable Minister of Militia, who I think by this time had become both a Knight and a Major General, came to look over our training and his eagle eye spotted the Enfields.

"Why are these men being trained on Enfields?" he asked.

"Because they are for the First Division, and the First has Enfields."

"Then turn them in at once and get Rosses," he said.

"Can't do it Sir," was the natural answer, "these men have to use the Enfield in the field."

That was the first time he had even heard that his new rifle had gone into the discard. But I must say that never, by word or deed, did Sam Hughes take any note of my unauthorized activities.

The Mills hand grenade[25] had been in use for a year at least, but the only grenades the troops training at Sarcee had seen were the few, very few, hand-made ones that they themselves had constructed with blasting powder and old tomato cans.

Now keep all this in mind, then let's consider the position of the battalions already in France. These units had learned war the hard way, that is usual. But they had learned, and at a terrific cost of life. Gradually they had become accustomed to, and knew how to maintain their end and live in, those ditches that had been dug in a continuous line from Ostend to Switzerland.

They had learned the hard way; now they could hold their own. Then they were asked to absorb a swarm of officers who knew absolutely nothing about the type of war raging in France and Belgium. Can you wonder that they said *no*, emphatically *no*. They went on to say, "We have NCOs better, far better, qualified to lead our men than officers with years of training for an open war of movement." And they were right. No army in the world since time began contained more officer material than the CEF of 1914–18. In our own company, we could count fifty men who could fill with distinction officers' uniforms. Many eventually did.

France

UNDER PRESSURE from Canada House, the units in France did accept us in batches for training purposes in the line.

The Colonel OC of 9th Reserve said, "we are sending you chaps to a Brigade school to teach you how to use hand grenades. You will report to Colonel Murray, 61st Battalion."

To school to learn something the Colonel knows full well we will never use. But it keeps us busy and out of his sight, at least 'til mess time. There are so many officers in the mess that there has to be two sittings. But there is a rumour in the air. There is something doing.

The rumour said we were going to France after all. Then the full import came home to us—a spell in the trenches for training purposes only. Well, even that was to the good, we might even see some of our boys. Or they see us and give us credit for being over there.

So we went to France and were attached to the 29th BC Battalion. We had gone to France on a training course that we could have had to a large extent back in Canada. We could have learned to dig trenches, zigzag them so as to lend a degree of safety. We could have dug deeper for company and battalion headquarters. We could have learned how to string barbed wire and at night. We could have learned how to crawl out onto no-man's-land in the dark of the night and try to be inconspicuous under Very light flares.

No, we must see that no one got hurt, that no one was annoyed by not being back in camp and all tidied up by 5 P.M. at the latest. Sure, ordinary basic training is needed. But that is *all* we got, at least up to mid-1916. What happened after that in Canada we do not know.

Then, in France, we went into the trenches. It was December and raining. In fact, it rained all the time we were there. Mud and filth and corruption and rats. Especially rats. Our chance of hitting a German was small, maybe we did, we never knew. We did cause one casualty, a rat. Should one make a nick in the butt of one's Webley revolver for a rat?

1–1–17

Dearest

Last night I watched the New Year come in while out in no-man's land. We got within thirty yards of Fritzies line. I cannot say I was not afraid, because I was. I had a guide, a boy officer of twenty-one who was through the fight at Ypres, and it would not do to let him know that I was shaky. The second time we went out it was not so bad. We made an awful noise slushing through the mud and water. It was just a slow crawl, drawing one foot after another out of the mud. We were out an hour and a half. I know how it is to stand still when the flares light up everything. Stand and try to look like the stump of a tree. Stand perfectly still, face away from the enemy. The face shows up very plain in the glare. Pictures, stories and books can give you but a faint idea of the awful conditions of the ground out on no-man's-land. Just a mass of shellholes filled with water, and we creep from edge to edge, stumble over wire, stone and every conceivable manner of rubbish. There is enough wire tangled in every manner of shape out in front of our sector to fence all the farms between Vegreville and Saddle Lake. Posts, shovels, picks, boxes, bags of chalk, trunks of trees, and all churned into an awful mess. Our Boys, many of them still clean-faced, are clinging to this land and will never give it up.

I certainly admire the boys who have held this line all these months. This company is commanded by a lad who was a private a year ago. The three lieutenants who are with him were privates a year ago.

A page from John's Soldier's Own Diary with his brief notes indicating that for the first few days of 1917 he was in the front-line trenches for training purposes, and even experienced a "heavy bombardment" on Wednesday 3rd, before going back to a "Rest Hut" for several days, and then leaving for Bethune on Saturday evening.

Could you blame these veteran officers for not wanting untrained officers much senior to themselves and just arrived from Canada in their company? No.

> The rats are having a great time tonight behind the corrugated iron that forms the sides of our dugout. The officers practice revolver shooting on them during the day.

We did cause, as we said before, one casualty—a rat—then we went back to England.

England

WHEN THOSE TRAINING PERIODS were over and we were once more back in England there was little or no complaint in so far as the attitude of the front-line battalion commanders was concerned.

But this only added fire to that already raging among senior officers who were kicking their heels in England. More clearly than ever they realized how they had been hoodwinked into a position from which they seemingly could not escape *with honour*.

Letters, telegrams by the scores, to persons in authority in England or back in Canada. Pleading, demanding, threatening for something to be done. A few succeeded, but only a few of the large number.

The weeks and months went by, in which we had little or nothing to do. Go on leave. Yes, sure, the OC Reserve was happy to grant week-long or weekend passes. Go where you like, do what you like. Go to London. Go to the Royal Automobile Club (we were all honourary members). Go to shows, for London had the best in the world. Go to the pub, drink more whiskey than was good for you, see more women of a kind not good for you. Anywhere, anytime, anything just to kill time.

Then at last the authorities in Canada saw that they had to do something, something drastic. Reluctantly, we suspect with fear and trembling, the order went forth:

We were to report to Canada House.

Plainly and—we must admit—very courteously, the situation was explained to us.

"Owing to circumstances beyond the control of the Canadian Army in England, a very large surplus of officers has accumulated in England. Much as it is regretted, there is no alternative but to ask you to revert to the rank of lieutenant or return to Canada."

We listened to the lieutenant colonel just ahead of us. He was mad clear through and was letting the officer behind the desk have the length of his tongue.

"Revert to the rank of lieutenant? No, Sir. Be damned if I do. I'll go home to Canada and raise hell in Ottawa. I have served my country for twenty years. I was a trooper in South Africa. I have been a commissioned officer for ten years. No Sir. To hell with you," and he stamped out of the office.

There was a resigned look on the face of the officer behind the desk. We wondered how many such outbursts he had listened to in the past weeks.

Our turn was next. "Never mind going over the story again, Major," we said. "I heard what you said to the Colonel. But there is one question. What hope is there of actually getting to France in case one does revert?"

A tired smile came over his face, and his reply indicated that he too wanted to be anywhere but in London. "God knows, Major. I wish I did. Anyway it seems our only chance. What are you going to do?"

"Go to France. That's what we came for, is it not?"

"Sure," he said. "Well, sign here, then go back to your reserve, but best take a couple of days in London while you are here. Hope to see you in France. Bye."

We never met in France. We don't even know his name, but we are betting that he did not go home until the curtain came down.

Actually our rally cry was given to us by Major Billy Wilkin,[27] 194th Battalion of Edmonton. "To hell with going home," he said. "I served as a trooper in South Africa and I can serve as a private in France. I go home when the war is over." And he did.

The spring of 1917 was beautiful. England in spring is always beautiful. The fields are green with daffodils growing in their uncounted thousands among the trees of the parks, private and public, making a carpet of gold.

It is unfortunate that so many men, and no doubt women, imagine that the place to have a good time is in the city. How foolish, how very foolish! Cities are the same the world over, drab and unlovely, the only difference is that some are more drab, more unlovely than others. But the country, and especially the English country, is a joy unto itself anywhere and everywhere. Naturally there are some spots more beautiful than others. Take for instance the lanes and byways of Sussex, Essex, and Devon. Row after endless row of lilacs, hawthorns, rhododendrons, plums, apples, and cherries. The very air heavy with scents of bloom all intermixed with each other. How best to see all this beauty? Go for a ride in a charabanc,[28] or stroll slowly along secluded lane and bypath. Stop and talk to the carters on the road, the farmer in the fields. They take one look at your shoulder badge, CANADA, and time is nothing to them.

We still cherish a snapshot we took. One day on the road along which Captain Jim MacQueen[29] of Edmonton and myself were bicycling, from Liphook to Portsmouth, we met an old carter. Seventy and five years he said he was. An old soldier himself of many years ago. He was leading his horse hitched to a two-wheeled cart. We were soldiers, he had been a soldier, proudly he showed us a ribbon. That dark red of the Victoria Cross, his grandson had won it at Ypres, gave his life in exchange. Proudly he stood erect, right hand on the horse's bridle, left hand stiffly at his side as we snapped his picture. Later, when we had gone to France, a comrade (with whom we left our camera) took that film and entered and won a snapshot contest with the picture of our carter, age seventy-five, and his horse.

Yes, England is beautiful. Unfortunately many Canadians had little opportunity to see that beauty.

We, who for a time were unwanted, had that opportunity. Those who did not avail themselves of this wonderful opportunity perhaps do not know what they missed. Those of us who did, have a book crammed full of memories of the glory of a glorious land, of kindly people who would

Hindhead, In Nutcombe Valley

Two postcards of Hindhead, near Bramshott Camp, where John was station for a while in early 1917. He wrote notes on the backs of both, presumably to Sara. On the card to the left; "One of the Lanes I spoke about in one of my letters in the valley between the camp and Haselmere about fifteen minutes walk from the camp." ' On the card below; "A very beautiful spot about two miles from Camp. Am sending you a book that tells about these places." The required postage for postcards was a halfpenny stamp.

Hindhead View near the Devils Jumps

sit and talk, answer questions without end, just so long as they in turn could ask questions, seemingly without end, about one subject, Canada.

Here along these secluded roads one finds something that just is not in Canada. Wayside inn or, to the locals, pub. Quaint names. One afternoon stroll from Bramshott camp we came across the *Woodcock*, the *Cock and Bull*, the *Black Raven*, the *Red Lion*, the *Half Moon*, and—poetically speaking—the *Pride of the Valley*. Drop in and have a half-pint, maybe buy one for the oldster and have the history of the pub and neighbours.

Back to camp and be captured by Captain Forrester, Chaplain, who wants you to read his latest chapter of his story, *The Black Mark*. The captain is Irish, with the jolly chuckle we attribute to an Irishman. Maybe that Irish twinkle in his eye was what won him so many votes when he ran against Premier Scott of Saskatchewan and nearly beat him. We wonder where he is now. We last saw him at #2 Hospital at Boulogne.

Just to put in time, we arrange a party for London. Ostensibly to see the latest show. To some, the latest show is the ever-recurring spectacle of the streams of after-theatre people. Piccadilly Circus with every sidewalk crammed with people, and here is where some consider the evenings start. We are well instructed by a young lieutenant who apparently knows the ropes.

"You senior officers should get wise to yourself. Leave some rank badges at your hotel. The technique of those lassies on Piccadilly Circus is quite simple. They can't see your badges, but a hand on your shoulder soon gives them the cue. It runs like this, for the pleasure of their company for half an hour in some upstairs room; for a lieutenant, two bob; for a captain, ten shillings; a major, a pound. For a lieutenant colonel, well, they will roll him for what he has. Ours got something more than he expected, besides waking up next morning with only car fare left in his pocket. Get wise, boys."

Staff Lieutenant, Second Class

FINALLY, IN JULY, 1917, after more than six months of idleness, a notice appeared on the board:

> *The British War Office asks for Senior Officers who wish to go to France on duty on Lines of Communication to make application. All such officers will go as Staff Lieutenants, Second Class.*

"What is a Staff Lieutenant, Second Class? Is he a one-pip Louie?"

We don't know or seeming don't care as we hurry to the Orderly Room.

The writer beat most of his companions to the room that we had bombarded with requests so often, and managed to be third on the list. Get your name down and ask questions afterwards.

Ask questions, yes, but that is all the good it does you. Neither the Adjutant or the Colonel are any wiser than ourself.

The whole atmosphere of the reserve had changed, from looks of gloom and resignation to gay laughter. From Major Brown to Lieutenant Colonel Smith (who heretofore has been a bit stiffish), "The top of the day to you, Lieutenant Smith."

"The same to you, Lieutenant Brown. When do we leave for France?"

No one knows.

A studio portrait of John in his dress uniform, taken by Lambert Weston Ltd., Folkestone, England, probably shortly before he went over to France in the summer of 1917. The embroidery and crown on his sleeves identifies him as a Major; as he says in the text, he wore his major's crown through the entire war, although all the time he was in France he held the rank of Staff Lieutenant.

"What about pay? What does a Staff Lieutenant, Second Class draw anyway? Will it be Canadian pay or British pay?"

No one knows. What does it matter anyway?

"Do we take down our crowns and pips?"

No one knows, so let them stay until told.

Apparently the English Army wanted men, and wanted them in a hurry, for we had not long to wait. Each bus and train brings more officers back from leave. There is a rush to obtain clothing for the front, though we don't know what we will want.

Never perhaps in the history of the British Empire were there so many senior officers aboard the boat train for Folkestone, while a like train went to Southampton. Senior officers? Oh no, second-class lieutenants. Yet had someone slipped up on an order? We still wore our crowns, and crowns and pips.

Had we had the faintest idea that we would ever record this exodus, we no doubt would have caught the names of many. As it is, only the names of a few appear in a faded old mouse-eaten letter written on the train from Boulogne to the front. How many there were we do not know. We do know that the train was crowded, and the boat also.

Did ever a bunch of men head for war in a more happy mood? We did not know where we were going or what we would be doing. All we knew was that we were headed east, not west, not home to Canada.

The English Channel was as smooth as a mill pond. Very different than when we crossed last December. We sit on the covering of the old side-paddle-wheel. This is an old French boat that has crossed from Boulogne to Folkestone hundreds of times.

Majors Simmons, McMillan, Wilkin, Douglas, and myself speculate as to where and to what we are bound. No doubt when we arrive in France we will go many ways, scattered up and down the whole British Army front.

We learn that there are five British Armies in France and Belgium. In the North, the 2nd Army, then to the South, the 1st Army, of which our Canadian Corps is a part.[30] Also there is the Australian Army under General Birdwood,[31] and the Portuguese Army, of which we will hear more anon.

We land at Boulogne and immediately our group starts breaking up. From here our story will no longer be about Canada's unwanted senior officers. We are wanted, but we will be more or less alone. We will meet from time to time, greet, and pass on. This story becomes that of one Canadian among many Englishmen. Would that we could assemble the hundreds of stories that at that date still had to be lived. We would like to have the pleasure of combining them into one book, and then we could call it history. As it is, consider that there were hundreds like ourself, and you might say the unwanted made good.

On Active Service

France or Belgium
16–7–17

Dearest Girlie:
Am writing while sitting in my tent at Corps Headquarters. Simmons is asleep on his bed. McMillan is with us. Whyte and Rubbra are in another Corps. Wilkin, we left at Hazebrouck and Douglas at Boulonge. McMillan is going to be in charge of some railroad gang, but none of the rest of us are placed as yet. I believe we will see the Corps Commander tomorrow and will be told off to our various jobs. This is a beautiful place, right up on the hill, from which we can see many of the places whose names are household words to all Canadians, although the Canadians are not here now. You can hear the steady rumble of guns, and from the hill see their flash. This place has never been shelled. I don't know whether we are in France or Belgium. We know the messroom is in France. All the land around is highly cultivated and crops are splendid. Lots of wheat and oats and vegetables. The land is not so level as down where I was last winter. There seems to be no mining.

Lost track of Major Grant at Boulonge. Do you remember Captain Stevens, who was Adjutant of the 66th Battalion and was let out by Colonel McKinnery. Well, he is in this party somewhere. I met him at Folkestone. He

A small portion of one of the large-scale War Office maps that John used to find his way around France and Belgium. All main and many secondary roads are marked, as are wooded areas and rivers. Contour lines indicate changes in elevation. Cassel, where he was stationed with the 4th Army for about a year, is on the left-hand side, about half-way up. On the right side, slightly higher up, is Ypres; Armentieres is in the lower-right corner; St. Venant and Hazebrouck in the lower-left; and Wormhoudt in the upper-left. The shaded line running from top-centre to lower-right is the border between France and Belgium. From Cassel to Ypres was a 20-mile (32 km) drive.

A French postcard showing a three-cornered conversation between an Allied officer, a French peasant, and a French interpreter. John's note on the back says, "This is a common scene, the old lady trying to get three values for damage done by troops. That is one of the duties of an Interpreter to assist in settling all claims for small damages. The barn is a quite usual sight. Plastered in-between the joists with mud and lime, it quickly falls to pieces when not attended to every year. And now all the men are at war."

went to Winnipeg and joined the 90th [Little Black Devils] as a private, worked himself up to the rank of Major, and came over to England ten months ago. Will be glad when I get to my position, whatever it may be, and then I can send my address.

After tea. Back to the English habit of afternoon tea. You know we cut the tea out in England and had an earlier dinner to give the boys a longer evening. The band of the 5th Oxford and Bucks are playing just now on the lawn back of the Chateaux. They are playing "If You Were the Only Girl in the World." I always liked that piece. Last night we passed a battalion of Australians and they were singing "Smile, Smile, Smile." A fine hardy-looking bunch these Australians. Met one of their Captains who has come over to be A.P.M. [Assistant Provost Marshal]. That is a job some of our group are getting. Simmons has just been unpacking the picture of the girl he is engaged to in England. He is a widower and only met this girl a month ago.

He raves about her night and day. She is not a great beauty at that. My Girlie is much better looking. We are sheltered among a fine grove of oak, birch, pine, elm and larch. As you see, our party is gradually breaking up, by tomorrow it is likely we will all be separated. It will be a bit lonely until we make new friends. So far we have found all the Imperials very fine fellows.

*I am glad to be able to write **On Active Service** once more on all my letters. To a small extent at least I am sharing the danger of the other lads. I have written to no one but you since coming to France. I think I have told you all the news Dearest. So Good Night Sweetheart and pleasant dreams. John.*

Now what is wrong with that letter?

Lots. If this letter had come before us at a later date, when we had become an experienced censor, we certainly would not have let it pass. In fact, the writer would have been in for a severe reprimand.

Just for instance, we gave the location of the 9th Corps Headquarters (HQ). Actually it was at Mont Noir,[32] right on the boundary between France and Belgium. It is among trees, on high ground. How long do you think it would take a German officer with their excellent maps of all France and Belgium to spot that HQ? Then the Oxford-Bucks Battalion is there, and the Australians.

We were green, very green. Luckily the Base Censor did not open that letter as he did many others. Later we were to become a censor ourself. Our censor number was 6766. We still have the stamp as a war souvenir.

Area Commandant

WE KNOW NOW what the title Area Commandant means. Also Town Major. They are much the same, one rural, one urban. All this part of France and Belgium is divided into areas for billeting purposes. Troops not on duty in the line are billeted in camps, farm houses, towns and villages. These areas were about the size of a Western Canadian township, six miles square. In that area might be billeted from a brigade to a division. Our work was to keep the area clean and sanitary and ready for troops coming out of the line. We understand that many of our Canadian officers just arrived from England have been posted to this work. Some are in charge of Gun Parks, some are Agricultural Officers, some are in charge of Chinese labour companies.[33] Major Tom Douglas got one of these Chink outfits.

The British Army has been expanded to such a tremendous extent that they just have not enough older officers to go around. There are hundreds of officers who had retired that are now back on just this work we are doing. One was Captain Gaskell of the Wilts, a farmer from Wiltshire, who served as Agricultural Officer for this 9th Corps area. We will meet many others as we go on.

Sanitation. This is an English word. What the equivalent is in French we don't know. Neither do the French. It just is not. To illustrate, we will tell a little story, although it is a bit ahead of our main story. When the

47

Germans made their last desperate attempt to break through the Allied lines in April 1918, our northern front lines were cut to a corporals' guard and our lines pushed back and back. Two French divisions were sent north to help our hard-pressed army. They came in, helped steady the line, then went back south.

There was a certain farm house at the edge of the village of Caestre where we liked to stop for a cup of coffee. One of the three daughters of the home was a school teacher. (We have a liking for schoolmarms—we married one.) This school teacher taught English in the local school. This fact made it an agreeable place to spend an hour over the coffee.

We visited the farm home and quite casually asked our English-speaking schoolmarm, "Well, how did you enjoy having your own French troops for a while instead of English Tommies?"

We talk of the people of France as a volatile race, quick to anger, quick to laugh.

There was no laugh. "Frenchmen! Frenchmen!" she fairly spat the words at us. "Dirty scum."

We were surprised, and looked it no doubt.

"Frenchmen, I am ashamed of them. They walked into our house without knocking at the door as an Englishman does. Walked in, demanded coffee, wine, eats. Then they thought that Mama, my sisters and myself should be just delighted to strip off and get into bed and entertain them until morning. Just as if we were all whores. We have lived with Englishmen for two years now. They are gentlemen. They never ask for coffee or wine without offering to pay. They treat us as ladies. It is true that one of my sisters has a baby whose father is an Englishman. That just happened. He did not tell my sister to get into bed right in front of Mama and I. He sends her money every month. Maybe someday....

"We have English troops around the village and farm coming and going all the time. A company of English troops stop for an hour over there in the meadow you see from the window. What do they do? I have watched them often. The very first thing is that a small number are told off to dig a latrine. I know now how long the company is staying. If it is only for an hour, the men just turn the sod a few inches deep. If for overnight, a foot deep. Then, and not 'til then, do they go and relieve themselves. Then just before they move away, another group of soldiers go and turn the sod back again while others go around and pick up bits of paper, cigarette packs, etc. They have kept our meadow clean, although thousands of them have camped there. Now look out there."

We looked. The place was littered with bits of paper, bits of everything.

"Smell," and she sniffed.

One did not have to sniff. The effluvium was rank.

"Oh well," she said, "I suppose we cannot blame our men. Our village is not much better. Or it was not much better until the English troops came. We are learning about sanitation. *Après la guerre* it will be better in France."

By this story (absolutely true) you will understand what we mean when we say that the principal duty of an Area Commandant was to look carefully to sanitation. Water was a difficult question. When an English battalion or company moved into a French farmstead, the first thing that happened was that the Medical Officer went straight to the farm pump and on it hung a sign:

Not Fit For Use By British Troops.

Very definitely it was not. Nine times out of ten the well was only a few feet from the cesspool manure pile. Yet with all, those people were healthy. They, over the centuries no doubt, had built up an immunity to bacteria that would floor an Englishman.

As Area Commandant we first learned to know and admire the fortitude of the French people. Few of us here in Canada know the French people that live in northern France or southern Belgium. Remember, French Canada was populated mainly by people from seaboard France, not from the inland north. Also, these people have small resemblance to Parisian French whom we and the world know. These are farm people, a peasant people. If we were asked what is their dominating characteristic, we would say that they are *stayers*.

Their love of home, their love of their land, their love of their garden and livestock transcends all else.

Our area was close to the front line. Its eastern side was the limit of civilian habitation. To our way of thinking, there should have been no civilian habitation in the whole area. Hardly a farm house or barn but showed evidence of shell fire. A roof gone here, part of the tiles gone there, a building had been burnt. Yet they stayed. Would our Canadian women have stayed under those conditions? Stood at the door, dishcloth in hand, and looked and wondered if that last shell had hit their neighbour's home. Hurried out to gather the children around her when part of the barn had been blown sky high, and still stayed. Listened to the noise of an aeroplane going over at night, the dull thud as a bomb exploded, and still stayed.

Yet, look at the credit side of the ledger. Troops at your door, troops in your pasture, troops all around and hungry for eggs, for milk, for vegetables. Prices about what you asked. Of course they are money-wise, these peasants of Flanders. For that reason, they are not anxious for their own troops, who are paid about fifteen cents a day. Much better the English Tommies who had two shillings six pence. They really coined money when they are lucky enough to have as guests the boys from Canada with their dollar ten a day, but it's really gold-diggers' day when the Aussies are billeted there. Eggs double in price. However, they are a kindly folk. They like nothing better than having their big kitchen filled with Tommies of an evening when coffee and good cheer flow in spite of difficulty of language. They don't wait for Tommie to learn French—they learn English.

Agricultural Officer, 9th Corps

WE ONLY GAVE ONE CHAPTER to the Area Commandant. That is as long as we lasted at that pleasant job.

16–8–17

Dearest:

Today I found another of our Canadians, Lieut. Colonel Pritchard,[34] who is Area Commandant and Agriculture Officer. Also met a jovial old Scotchman at the same work, an Imperial, Lieut. Colonel Forbes by name. As per usual he produced a bottle of Scotch, and when I refused he told me I was a disgrace to my wife's people. [I married a Highland lassie.] He is a rare old character. A farmer in Scotland. Fritz started to shell the village, so we said farewell for the moment.

The Corps Quartermaster General, General Cooke,[35] sent for us. "Hughes, how would you like to be Corps Agricultural Officer?"

We knew that our friend Colonel Pritchard from the 153rd Ontario battalion had this post in the 10th Corps and seemed satisfied, so our answer was prompt, "Fine, Sir."

"All right. I thought maybe you would. Captain Gaskell has to rejoin his battalion, so we need someone to take his place. Gaskell will be here shortly. We will take his car and drive over the Corps area. You can become familiar with the work."

We had met General Cooke several times and liked him very much. A soldier he was, had been all his life, yet he longed for his time to expire so that he could get back to his farm in England. In the weeks to come we were to get to know this kindly English gentleman and consider him as a friend.

Now, before we go any further, let's take a look at the make-up of an army. We have G and O and Q:

- *G is the active fighting branch.*
- *O is ordnance.*
- *Q is what enables G to fight.*

G is the spectacular side, usually the dangerous side. The side that the public see and admire. The side that the press gives credit or blame for winning or losing battles.

Q is little heard about, although taken in all its branches it is as large as G. All that a soldier wears or eats or uses, except his gun and ammunition, which is ordnance, goes through the Quartermaster's Department. Without Q, the army is immobile within days, useless within weeks, and non-existent within the month. Practically all our unwanted Canadian officers (now Lieutenants, Second Class) went to Q.

Now we were being asked to be an Agricultural Officer (AO). Agriculture means food. Within a few months we were to find that twenty or more Canadian lieutenant colonels and majors were to be AOs. We had left the farm in Western Canada to be a soldier. Now, within reach of shells and bombs and the steady roar of artillery, we were asked to leave off being a soldier and be a farmer. Well, so be it. We were still in uniform and wearing a crown, although classed as Lieutenant, Second Class.

Again we must dip into facts not actually part of our story. France bore the brunt of World War I.[36] As we all know, she had not recovered when World War II again poured down on her fertile farm lands. Has not recovered yet. Pray God she may.

By 1917 France had stripped her lands of her manpower and nowhere more so than on the farms. The old men, over sixty-five, boys, women, and children were left to carry on. Nobly they were doing their work, but there was just too much for them to do. These peasant people asked their friendly new neighbours for manual help from time to time, and help was given where possible. The requests naturally increased, and the idea slowly spread through the whole army in France that there should be assistance given to the farmers wherever possible. The idea was sound, but it was new, and there was no such establishment on the Army List. The orderly-minded British generals decided that they must appoint an officer to supervise this work. Hence the name Agricultural Officer. The carrying out of the scheme was left to the Quartermaster Generals of the different corps of the line. The help was more or less haphazard as Battalion, Brigade, and Divisional OCs naturally were reluctant to have able-bodied men absent from duty for any length of time.

There were six armies holding the line in mid-1917. From north to south they were the 2nd, the 1st, the Aussies, the 4th, the 3rd, and the 5th. Each one was divided into three or more corps, which also remained steady in one sector. Each corps might have from three to five divisions, which were being continually shifted from corps to corps. Army and corps are only administrative organizations which maintain, equip, feed, give medical assistance, maintain ordnance supplies, and have general charge of operations.

There were three corps in the 2nd Army. Again from north to south, the 10th, where Lieutenant Colonel Pritchard was AO; the 9th, where we were AO; and the 4th, where Lieutenant Colonel Hind was AO. Some divisions had also appointed AOs, and these usually moved when the division moved.

The Quartermaster General of the 9th Corps was a farmer. We have named him before—General Cooke. He just could not help taking a strong and understanding interest in anything relating to the farm and the farmers' needs. He had established a system. There were lots of men available. First he talked to Battalion Commanders and Medical Officers.

He said, "Is it not true that you have many men in your units who actually are on the verge of a breakdown, men shellshocked but still able to carry on? Now, why not weed these men out? Send them out to the

French farms for a couple of weeks or a month. Let them live with the French people. Let them eat the soft foods, vegetables, eggs, milk, fruit instead of our hardy meat diet. See what a month's change will do. At the same time, they are near at hand in case we have a German push. We can get them back to their units within twenty-four hours."

"Good," said the COs. "Excellent," said the MOs.

The 9th Corps took up this work in earnest and was fast establishing it on a regular army plan by the time we took over from Captain Gaskell. An orderly system of agricultural leave (not counted against their regular fourteen-day leave every six months) was established. The results were a Godsend to the men. The French women—for they were running the farms—said, "Thanks to *mon Dieu* and the English Army."

The usual thing was to let two men go to a farm. The work of the Corps AO was largely an administrative job. We had to investigate the needs on the farms, place the men, visit them once a week to see that they were content yet not shirking their work, take them mail, collect their outgoing mail, and issue their tobacco ration.

Back of Corps was the 2nd Army and there was an Army AO who we were meeting more and more. At that time he was Major J. Aubrey-Smith,[37] on the staff of General Plumer,[38] OC, 2nd Army. The Army AO was allotted a motor car. A Corps AO was allotted two saddle horses and a groom. The attached French interpreters[39] had bicycles.

Now a groom should be of more importance than a horse, but as a rider from our youth we are afraid we paid more attention to our saddle horses, one in particular. He was a big, upstanding grey Irish steeplechaser as we afterwards found out. A magnificent horse, it was a joy to be up on him. We well remember the first day. We were coming along a country road at a fast clip. Ahead was a five-barred gate, shoulder high. Naturally when we saw the gate we eased up for a stop. Not so our Irish hunter, not by any means—he just gathered speed and within a moment we were sailing over the five-barred gate. We knew little or nothing about jumping, and if we had given the problem aforethought no doubt we would have landed on the roadway. But that magnificent horse sailed over the gate so smoothly we stayed in the saddle and were very proud of ourself. To our hunter it was just an ordinary event, which evidently he loved. We were to jump many gates in after days. We waited for our groom to catch

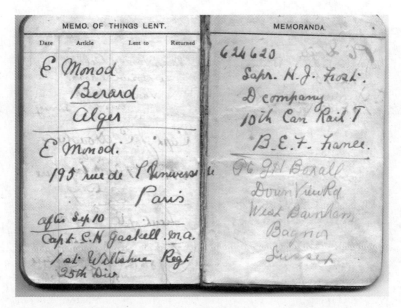

A page from John's Soldier's Own Diary showing several addresses for Émile Monod, the French interpreter for the 9th Corps, as well as addresses for Captain Gaskell, whom John replaced as AO of the 9th Corps when Gaskell when back to his unit, and for Sapper H.J. (Jack) Frost, 10th Canadian Railway Troops.

up. Wisely, he stopped and opened the gate and led his horse through. We think there was an added note of respect in our groom's eyes. He may have put it down to the fact that the major was a Canadian. We were to learn as time went on that it really meant something in the eyes of men, from grooms to generals, that word on our shoulders—CANADA.

With up to four hundred men scattered around the countryside, being a Corps AO was a busy, yet pleasant, job. Few of us could talk French, so to help in this work that was really appreciated by France, the French Army had allotted an interpreter to each AO, generally a junior French officer. Our first interpreter was Adjutant Lieutenant Émile Monod DCM, a farmer from Alger. When you see a French officer wearing an English medal you know it really means something. Monod was a Protestant. Much to our surprise we were to meet quite a number of French officers who were Protestants. The interpreter attached to the Aussies was also a farmer and a Protestant. His father was an English clergyman who married a

French girl and settled in France. We found these French officers very capable, always cheerful, and ready to take the heavy end of the work.

Each of us made the round of the farms once a week. The interpreter on a bike, we on horseback. Each starting from opposite ends of the district, we saw each soldier twice a week. Monod considered the farmer, we the soldier. If a farmer was not satisfied with his help, we took the help away and gave him another pair. If then not satisfied, we dropped him from our list. If the men were not satisfied, we took them to another farm. If then not satisfied, we sent them back to their units as unsatisfactory for this type of work. Usually there was little complaint on either side. The Tommies, glad to have a home instead of a trench, and eggs and milk and fruit and pudding instead of regular army food, grew fat.

The women loved them, and we witnessed many a weep when we went around to say that farm leave was over. Many a woman begged with tears in her eyes for Tommie to stay just one more week. Do you blame them? We don't. Their own men folks had been torn from home and bed and they were lonesome. Suddenly they had men again, men who needed feeding and loving.

We had the pleasure of taking forty men of the Hampshire Battalion back to their unit. When we had these late farmers lined up for inspection, the Battalion CO and MO came out for the inspection.

"Good Lord," said the MO, "are these the men we sent away a month ago? Colonel," he said, "let's let Hughes take the whole damned battalion on his farms for a month. When he brings them back, we will smash a hole in the Hun line, he won't know what happened."

The CO's reaction was summed up in his words; "Hughes, how many men can you handle for the next bunch?"

The Quiet Life of a Farmer

WE DECIDE TO SETTLE DOWN to the quiet life of a farmer. We find billets at the edge of the small town of Flêtre. In the meadow outside of our window is camped, in tents, a battalion of the Duke of Cornwall's Light Infantry. They are out of the lines on rest.

It is a peaceful moonlight night. How those tents show up in the moonlight. A peaceful night, and we slumber. Slumber, then waken to the intermittent hum of a German plane close overhead. The dull thud, thud, thud as bombs explode and windows are broken. What at that moment we do not know is that the ever-fertile German scientist had developed a new bomb. A bomb that exploded a foot from the ground and scattered, not upwards, but latterly, cutting a wide swath of destruction. The boys in those tents went down like ripe grain before a scythe. Forty and four are dead. Dead on a peaceful moonlight night. From then on we learned to build, at least a foot high, an earthen wall around every tent. The boys were strictly instructed to hug mother earth and live.

We will long remember that first mass burial there in that green meadow outside a French town. Forty in one long grave, four in another, with a single strand of barbed wire separating the forty from the four. The four were Roman Catholics.

Paddy, our little Irish batman looked on, and his face was grim. "Begorra and it will take more than a strand of barbed wire to keep those boys apart when they reach the first pub in heaven. Bless their souls."

We were to learn many things like this. The worst offence of all was to put a cross over the grave of a Bengal Lancer. He was to be buried in a sitting position with his face towards Mecca. A single straight staff as a marker to show where reposed a member of that famous regiment.

B.E.F.
[Meteren] France
19–8–17

Dearest:
Evening. Today has been clear and fine and the visibility good. One could see for miles. Days like this I like to ride to the high spots of the district where one can see for miles. You see the land as a rule is very level. Just gradual undulations that give a beautiful valley effect when seen from the heights. But here and there are small hills rising a few hundred feet above the plain, set out by themselves like great mounds and without an adjoining hill. These are great vantage points for observation. I wish you could have ridden with us today, to one of these hills over towards the line. And seen with me fifty or more miles of the firing line. You could pick it out by those captive balloons which watch from morn till dark for any movement in the enemy lines. North you can look away to the blue line which we know is the sea, and the other way to where our own boys [Canadians in the 1st Army] are doing such gallant work these days. Before you, you see a wilderness and utter destruction being still. churned up by bursting shells. Little is left to show that it was once a peaceful and happy country. Only here and there a bit of broken wall or splintered tree trunk. Part of a church tower still stands over to the left. What a wonderful aiming mark those church spires have made for the Hun gunners. As you know, there are churches everywhere, and around each church cluster a group of red tiled or thatched roofed houses, forming these innumerable little villages. When the German Uhlans rode through this land in those early days of the war, they entered these churches and climbed the spires and took away some part of the machinery of the clocks which adorned every spire. They said it was to stop them being used

as signals. So for miles around you see the village clock always pointing to the same hour. As we gazed on this wilderness we wonder if it will ever be restored to its old-time glory. No doubt it will take more than our life time to heal these awful scars on the land. The government may give money and have these houses and granaries and barns rebuilt. Towns and villages will spring up, roads will be repaired, but it will take generations to reclaim the land. All that clay and chalk and gravel will take a tremendous amount of work to make rich for vegetation. And those trees which were the pride of France will not be replaced short of two generations. You look for the remains of those villages which at one time dotted that plain and find nothing. Even the broken bricks and stones have been carted away to make roads which creep forward with our line. But let us not look too long on this scene. It is fascinating because it tells of the greatest chapter of this world's history of wars. And the chapter is not finished, for watch those great bursts making another hole in a land all holes.

The roar of the guns deafens one and sometimes the very earth rocks with the explosion of mine or dump. But let us not look that way any longer. Just about face and the contrast startles you, for before you lies one of the fairest scenes in all France, and for a picture of rural peace and plenty and beauty it can be surpassed by few spots on earth. One of the richest provinces of France stretches away to the sea in gentle undulations. No hills to obscure our vision of splendid trees, green and golden fields, countless red-roofed farm buildings, many little villages and several towns. Note how the roads cut the land in pieces like a giant jig-saw puzzle, not like a checker-board as ours is. See those splendid straight elms that line the roads. Is it not a pity that so many are falling every day, cut by experienced Canadian lumbermen? But necessity knows no laws. For an open plain, these trees grow wonder-fully tall and straight and make fine timber. Look at those fields of grain all in stooks. The stooks are in straight thick rows all across the fields. See over there, that man plowing between the rows of stooks. That is the reason for the extra labour of stooking that way. Yet we doubt if it pays to do all this, because some fields will be stacked shortly. But these farmers move in a very set groove. They hate to abandon the reaping hook that was used two thousand years ago. Only a small portion of the grain is cut by machinery. Saturday, while I was on my rounds, one of the widow ladies whom we are helping complained her new McCormack binder was not working right. So she took me out to the field to see it. It was like old times to get my coat off and use a wrench and pinchers, and to get my hands covered with oil and grease. Yet I liked it, and Madame thanked me in French and English and Flemish when the binder was at work again. Then I washed my hands in a ditch, dried them on Madame's apron and rode away to the next farm, feeling that I was helping to win the war. Now let us mount and ride down this winding road to the plain, then gallop along this earth road to the highway beyond. Along this high road you notice the trees still stand. This is one of France's main pike roads, and it brings my mind back to another such road further south that was a fine road also, but unsafe to travel day or night, because Fritz swept it with machine gun fire and played overhead with shrapnel. Yet our boys clattered up taking all sorts of chances. Gun fire would not kill as many horses as would die of exhaustion if they were forced through the mud of the lower safer road. Along that road no tree stood more than ten feet high. Just splintered stumps, weird things by night. Notice the paving of the road, wide pieces of cobble stone in the centre and on either side a hard road of pounded flint, making a hard fine road. Now there is one thing I want you to notice in the fields as we pass. Your mind will flash to the story in the Old Testament, Book of Ruth. For here are the Gleaners. Mostly young children and old women, picking up the heads of wheat one by one. The farmer has cut the grain either with hook or binder, stooked the grain and then gone over the fields with a hand rake and, after that, what is left is for the poor. No doubt, in fact I have noticed, that some farmers leave very little for the Gleaners and others leave quite a bit, even like in the Bible days. The right to glean the fields belongs to the public who are not tilling the land, to the poor of the villages and the towns. Like everywhere else, the real poor live in the towns, never in the country. These people, these peasants of France, are not rich as we understand riches, but as a whole class they are no doubt the wealthiest in the world. Remember, it is not because these people are poor that we are helping, but because it is of vital importance to the Allies in general that every bushel of grain be saved. Now we come to a quaint old village where you will find the people cheerful but nervous. Last night's experience would shake the nerves of many men, let alone women and children. Even men who have spent many months in the trenches confess to me today that they would sooner stand days of shelling than ten minutes of bombing. But the way our guns are roaring tonight, I think Fritz will find more important work nearer the line.

Now Dearie, I have been scribbling on and hardly know what I have said. I only try to make you see with my eyes and hear with my ears. But always after trying to get my ideas on paper I feel when I am done that what I have tried to impress most is but dry and stilted and uninteresting. But, my Dearie, it is a pleasure to tell you these things anyway and only wish I knew how better. Remember I told you I wrote a long letter to Wilma Hughes? Had an answer this week, and what do you think she did? Went and read my letter to their Young Folks Club. Hardly fair was it to subject my scrawls to such a critical audience. Then to cap the climax, Leila Battle [nursing sister from Edmonton] writes and says as they have no paper in which to publish my letters in Paris, she read them to her companions in the hospitals. Guess I will have to confine myself to "I'm well. Hope you are well. Good bye." if they continue to see such funny things in my writing.

Now this is the last page and my eyes are getting heavy.

Goodnight, Sweetheart.

We were also to learn that nothing on earth would keep these French people away from their church on a Sunday morning.

France. 20–8–17

Dearest.

Well Dearie, this has been a glorious day, a beautiful Sunday. The air is warm and yet not close. The sun is bright. I stood on the corner this morning watching the people stream to church. All in their Sunday best, and one is surprised when you see a person come along that yesterday you saw digging potatoes, looking very dirty and disheveled, and today is dressed in the height of fashion. These women and girls certainly know how to dress. As I said, I stood and watched them stream along to church. The stream was constantly interrupted as the people had to watch their chance and dodge between the horses and guns, as battery after battery went by in a string seeming without end, and between hurrying motor lorries and motor cars, not to mention motor cyclists who whizz past looking neither to right or left.

Horsemen going either way, and wagons and carts of all descriptions, and the church bells kept ringing, and a bit away the guns were roaring and cursing in a tone I have heard only once before. Yet, through the air came the sound of church bells from other nearby villages. And overhead the sharp crack of bursting anti-aircraft shells, and every once in a while the dull throbbing tearing crash of bursting bombs. The people hurrying along to church would pause and gaze up at the sky. One would clutch another and point skywards to a gleaming speck, around which you could see the smoke of bursting shells and you knew that the gleaming speck contained a daring Hun airman. Along with the chiming of the bells you heard the rat-tat-tat and the spit-spit-spit of machine guns, and the anties stopped firing, because some of our own airmen were tackling the Hun nearly overheud. The specks turned and twisted and dived and climbed, and worked their way out of sight towards the front. The bells chimed on, seeming to try and drown out the noise of guns and shells.

Women, girls, children and old men all dressed in their best poured in a steady stream towards the church. Flowers still bloom in the gardens, but not in all, because some gardens are but heaps of rubbish and holes full of water. The birds sing in the trees and the fruit is ripe on the branches. And a squadron of Indian Cavalry swing past, those great bronzed fellows with solemn faces and gleaming eyes that seem to see everything, yet look neither to the right or to the left. And so different from the battalion of Scots that are now going by. These men are near as bronzed as their Indian comrades and their eyes as bright, they laugh and sing and pass a word with the girls or comrades on the side of the street. They march with a swing of their own. Those pipes make one want to step in line. The kilt, a tartan, but covered with a khaki apron gives these men a distinction that none can rival. And their steady tramp-tramp shakes the earth, and the church bells chime on, seeming to keep time to the step of the bronzed and hardened soldiers. Oh how fit and fine they look. Such a contrast to the men in civilian clothes, but remember there are none here in civvies except the old men and the unfit. And a group of pretty little girls pass all dressed so nicely, with pretty hats on their heads and hair in ringlets. Then two boys about the age of Ted and Paul [about seven and five] who smiled at me as they passed and reminded me of home. Then a long string of ambulances coming down from last night's fight, not running very fast, so as to jar the poor broken bodies as little as possible. And several women, widows with the veils, pass up the church steps. And the great organ in the church peals forth as the service starts. Only it is drowned a moment later by a screeching shell that just passes overhead and buries itself in the nearby open field, then explodes. And throws a great column of dust and earth many feet into the air, and very little notice is taken. And the people still hurry into the church, and a battalion swings by followed by more batteries. And the kiddies playing in the back yard go on building mud pies, and motor lorries never cease. And it is rattle and bang and rumble and chime of bell and tramp and sound of organ on one side, and a gramophone is playing in an officers' mess nearby. The men of the passing battalion sing songs of love and homeland, and love and hate, peace and war, beauty and destruction, strength and weakness are all mixed up together. Why is it? Where is it going to end and when? Can any good come out of all this turmoil? I stand and watch all this go by and wonder. Oh what volumes a person of ability could write were they allowed and had the time. Although I have not the ability to make others feel what I see, yet I am glad to be here and watch this, the greatest convulsion of the world's history. Now Dearie I have no news to tell, so I must stop scribbling.

Good night Sweetheart.

Excerpts From Many Letters

6–7–17

Dearest:
Tuesday. Wet again this morning. Am just waiting for Paddy to come back from railhead with the mail and rations. He goes there every second day for rations, which are very good. We get fresh meat, bacon, potatoes, jam, marmalade, bread, butter, milk [canned], candles, oil for office lamp, a little coal, hay and oats for the horses. Oatmeal is not an issue, so last Sunday I wheeled over to _____ where there is a BEF canteen and bought a seven-pound tin. Cost me seven francs and fifty centimes. I don't like going without my porridge.

Belgium
20–7–17

Dearest:
Yesterday I saw something that shows how unconcerned the boys have grown in regards to danger or the war in general. In one of the battalions of the Brigade quartered in this area they held a boxing competition. Several thousand gathered to see. It was in the open and they never seemed to mind the fact that sometimes the roar of great guns drowned the voice of

the referee. No one ever glanced back to where shells were hurling great
columns of smoke and dust into the air. It was like a continual roar of thunder
and lightning.

We have been cut down to Captain's pay as we expected. As it is, even at
this reduced pay we are far better off than many Imperial Lieutenant Colonels.
They only get Lieutenant's pay, so we ought not to complain.

2–8–17

Dearest:
Billy Wilkin [Major Wilkin, 218th] rode over to see me and had dinner. The
218th officers, who are with the 10th Canadian Railway Troops, sent for him
to come up to their lines the night of the big push. They were to follow up
with the light railway line. He had a splendid view of the show. He saw the
first prisoners. Tells an amusing tale of seeing a little Irishman, not much
taller than his rifle, marching in four Hun officers. By gentle pressure of the
point of his bayonet making them hop along rather lively and at the same
time in broad Irish telling them how much he loved them.

Fritzie came over last night and dropped a bomb through the kitchen of
the house alongside ours. Rather a rude awakening at 2 A.M.

3–8–17

Had a letter from Lieutenant Tomlison, 9th Reserve, yesterday. Tells of several
changes. All Captains are to revert to Lieutenants at once or return to Canada.

So now even the captains are not being absorbed into line battalions
as lieutenants. Tomlison in later years was to command the Calgary
Highlanders and win renown as one of Canada's outstanding Red Cross
administrators.

23–8–17

Dearest:
I rode by way of [Poperinghe] and stopped with Major Simmons, 202nd, for
lunch. His work is not very heavy, complains he has not enough to do. You

see, his area is in one corner of my district, so I always stop to see him. Colonel Harrison DSO, who messes with him, is a very jovial chap.

Then, swinging back, I came to _____ where Major Lane [110th] and Major Whyte [194th] are both Area Commandants. Both complain, like Simmons, of not having enough work.

2nd Army Railhead
9–9–17

Dearest:
Just a few lines tonight before I start reading other fellows letters. Have a large stack to go through. Just occasionally one gets a letter that makes one smile. Found one the other day that was good. I took a note of a few things he said. This letter was in reply no doubt to one from his sister scolding him about finding fault, and here is part of his answer.

> I was never happier or more contented in my life. I don't want to come home. Since I have been in France I've never been hungry or thirsty. Never lost a wink of sleep or had a nightmare. Never had blisters on my feet or felt tired after a route march. Don't know there is a war on.

He has been wounded twice and shellshocked.

> I go to a music hall every night and twice on Sunday. Have a bath every day and a change every other. Have never been bitten by a louse or sworn at by an NCO. And never had more than my share of rum.
>
> Did you ever suffer from bladder trouble. I have discovered the finest remedy in the world: French beer. Had two glasses last night. Got up fourteen times to see what time it was during the night. It's splendid. I will send you some. No, on second thought, it might run through the bottle like it ran through me.

This chap was in for his mail this morning, and I asked him if he ever did any cooking. He said, a little. So I may bring him in from the farm to help in the office and to cook for Monod and I.

We did just what was suggested and it was a fine move. Marsden stayed with us for near a year. He was a fine clerk and a most excellent cook.

17—9—17

Dearest:

Was awakened by a Signaller with a message to return one hundred men today. Some task to get them gathered in from a dozen or more farms all over the country. These are hop-pickers and not my regular workers.

We had four hundred extra men out helping the farmers gather in their hop crop.

France
4—10—17

Dearest.

Today I am at my desk making my company roll. I am keeping a list of the battalions of the Imperial Army who have furnished men for this work. Few officers ever had a chance like this to observe the difference in training in battalions. As you know, in the Imperial Army there are no new regiments, but hundreds of new battalions. If only Sam Hughes had allowed us to carry on like this how much better it would have been.

Normally there are two battalions to each English regiment, one at home and one abroad. New battalions during war time could be either used as battalions for the line or as reserves.

I saw one of our own Regimental badges [the 19th Alberta Dragoons] today. A Belgian girl was showing me her collection of badges and this was among them. Of course you know that when they were the 1st Divisional Cavalry they were stationed here for some time. The girl also had some 3rd Canadian Mounted Rifle badges.

Colonel Fred Jamieson was in command of the 19th Dragoons at that time. Major Fane had C Company of 3rd CMRs.

Dearest:

I rode thirty-eight or forty miles today. Got out of my way down near
_____ and had to go way round. The land is level as the floor down here
and lots of wide ditches and small canals, and one has to keep to the roads.
Nearer around here I often go right across country, small ditches and fences
do not stop me. The farmers don't mind me riding over the fields and crops,
but raise a great howl when others do. Quite often they shout at me to
come back, that there is no road that way, and then when they see who it is
they say, "All right, go ahead." You see, they like to keep on good terms with
me. Nearly every farmer for ten miles around knows me now. There are
some farmers in that distance.

These are but a few of the items showing a busy life of an AO in France
in the summer and fall of 1917. We are informed that we have been promoted. We are now a Staff Lieutenant, First Class. Still wearing a major's
crown.

We Go to the 2nd Army

GENERAL COOKE'S KEEN INTEREST in agricultural affairs for the 9th Corps had allowed us to outdistance all the other Corps AOs. Our work was coming under the eyes of the Quartermaster General of 2nd Army. As it happened, Major J. Aubrey-Smith, AO for the Army, was being recalled to take over the job of Brigade Major, and he recommended that we take over his position at Army HQ. General Cooke was not keen on letting us go and only consented if another Canadian was available for his Corps. Finally Major Rowan of Vancouver took over at Corps and we went to Army in December.

We were not so sure that we liked the idea either. You see, at Corps our transportation was by saddle horse, while at Army we would rate a car. This may seem strange in this day and age, but remember this was near forty years ago and motor cars were not the everyday thing as of today. More than that, for years we had had a string of saddle horses on the farm. And if that was not enough, we were a cavalry man, although of necessity turned infantry man.

What at that moment we did not know was the entire new world this promotion would open up to a young man from the Western prairies.

Nevertheless we went up, in more ways than one. We went to the top of the sugar-loaf hill, where was the town of Cassel. Of Cassel it is said to have been the place where originated that nursery rhyme, "King William had ten thousand men. He marched them up the hill and he marched them down again." This may or may not be a fact, but many of the soldiers of World War I knew that hill and marched up and marched down it, for it straddled the main road to the Salient in Belgium that had Ypres as its goal, for which to hold untold thousands died. We held it, wisely or not, we held it for four long, hard, bloody years.

For most of those four years Cassel was Army Headquarters. At that moment, the 2nd Army under General Plumer held this hill top that looked away across the plains to Flanders to another sugar-loaf hill that so many knew as the Hill of the Cats (*Mont des Cats*[40]). From there you could see the perimeter of the front line ten miles away. Nearer again to the front line was Mont Noir, where first we came to the 9th Corps and became an AO. Now we were going back to the comparative safety of Army Headquarters. We were losing our grey Irish hunter. We acquired a motor car, a driver, and an assistant AO, one Major Charles Murray, member of the Parliament of Great Britain. A gentleman, a perfect gentleman, and a man old enough to be our father.

We also found that we were expected to administer a new department of the Army, for the Agriculture Department had been promulgated as a regular established army department. We found that coming under our direction we had eight lieutenant colonels, fourteen majors, five captains, and ten French officer interpreters. Our work would cover the whole 2nd Army area, all the way from Bergues in Belgium, where we joined the Belgian Army, to Merville, where we joined the 1st Army. What at first we did not realize was that we were going to live in a world new to us. We were to live among men of the old world, among men who knew all the rules and regulations, for they had lived with them from childhood.

Keep in mind that up until that time, very, very few men became officers in the British Army unless they came of a class called Gentlemen. We Canadians were only temporary gentlemen. In other words, they knew the rules, we only *thought* we knew the rules. Many of the men we were to live with were men of titles or sons of titled men. Lord this, or Lord that, but without exception gentlemen in the true sense of the word.

First thing was that we were allotted to a certain mess, K mess, which became quite well known as Spuds, Suds and Other Duds. We were Spuds, we were growing potatoes. Captain Robinson was Suds, he was Army

Laundry Officer. Then there was Captain Heyer, Professor of Language at Oxford University. He was Chief Requisition Officer. Captain Stone from Cornwall was Assistant Requisition Officer. Captain Truskett, eminent London lawyer, was Courts Martial Officer. Lieutenant Linton, Requisition Officer, was a nephew of the Duchess of Sutherland.

All university men, all brilliant talkers, men who had travelled the world over.

Captain Morgan of the Indian Army, Political Branch, who was afterwards knighted. Captain Hickey was Salvage Officer. A hard drinker, but a wonderful conversationalist. Captain Thomas was Transport Officer. An Irish gentleman who was to lose much of his estates in the Sinn Fein revolution in Ireland.

And myself, a farmer from the Prairies. The youngest of the group, who outwardly (we wore a crown) was senior of the mess.

Passchendaele—
We Must Have the Canadians

SO MUCH HAS BEEN WRITTEN about this famous battle,[41] where Canada's soldiers won undying glory, that perhaps we should not try to add our little bit. Nevertheless, a couple of incidents came home to us that may have escaped the historians. It was natural that, living in an Army HQ Mess, items of news reached us at times before they were known by Corps or Divisional generals. Let us tell the story as the old letters revive the memory. The terrible summer of blood and mud was drawing to a close; 1917 had cost the British armies more lives than any year in our long history. Yet France had suffered even more dreadful losses. France was staggering. Generalissimo Foch called a conference and told those in authority just how dangerous the situation had become.

Field Marshal Haig[42] in turn called a conference of his generals. He told the bald, naked truth; "France has fought her most bloody battle of all time. Verdun alone has cost her half a million men. France has been bled white. She cannot stand another such avalanche. We must take the weight off her shoulders for a time at least." Turning to General Plumer, who commanded our Army, the 2nd, he said, "General, you have got to take Passchendaele village and ridge."

"Impossible," replied General Plumer promptly. "Our Army is exhausted, we have fought through seas of mud and blood and can go no further. It cannot be done."

"Nevertheless, General, it has to be done," replied the Commander-in-Chief.

"Very well, Sir," replied General Plumer, "then we must have the Canadians."

"No. Absolutely not," shouted General Horne,[43] who commanded the 1st Army, of which the Canadian Corps was a part. "No. The Canadian Corps is going to take Lens. They have already fought a practice battle over similar ground. Every last move of every unit in the Corps is carefully planned. They will sweep the Huns from Vimy Ridge that they have held so long. No. The Canadians cannot go."

Slowly the Commander-in-Chief shook his head. "No, General Horne, I am sorry. You must send the Canadians north to General Plumer."

We have heard many high praises sung about our Canadian men, but was there ever higher praise than in those few simple sentences. The four divisions of the Canadian Corps picked as the shock troops of the British Empire.

The wording used may not have been exact so as to be actual history, but it was told to us around our mess room table by one who was there, on the day that these historic words were spoken. Did our Canadian Corps live up to that high praise? Ask the world, ask history.

The day of the great battle came. We at HQ had the opportunity to know early if for us it was victory or defeat. This incident was told to us within the hour.

General Plumer, who with his chiefs of staff planned the battle, waited the outcome. "What is the latest," he asked of the Chief of Staff, "what of our Imperials?"

"They have done well, but have not taken all their objectives," the Chief of Staff replied.

"What of the Australians?"

"They also have done splendidly but have not taken all their objectives," was the reply.

"What of the Canadians?"

"They have taken all their objectives."

"All their objectives," softly murmured the man to whom praise or otherwise would come for winning this great battle. Then smiling, he said, "All their objectives. All is well gentlemen. Good night. I am going to bed."

Again we are repeating hearsay, but hearsay that was repeated to us within the hour of it happening. As the lone Canadian in that group in K Mess, 2nd Army HQ, in that little town of Cassel that topped a sugar-loaf hill where one could look across the Flanders plain and watch the continuous glow from the sullen Hun guns that were still trying desperately to hold our Canadians at bay, was it to be wondered if we held our head high.

We had known that the Canadians were coming, so we went to meet them and had some enjoyable hours greeting friends of all ranks. They knew little of what was expected of them and it was not our duty to tell. Sadly we watched them go up.

We had the opportunity to be up near the line when they came back. (Back, back from the mouth of Hell, but not the six hundred.) We had lunch with the officers of the 49th Battalion, in which were many of our lieutenants of the 151st. We saw Ames, Lyall, Emsley, McQueen, Anderson, Meade, and Rollett. But were saddened when we heard that Bishopric, Knight, Percy Belcher, Bob Dow, Oakley, and Stone were killed. McMurdie, Bradburn, and Billy Tipton were wounded. Also three others whose names we did not record were killed and four wounded. There would be sad days in Northern Alberta. Next to the Pats, the 49th got it the worst.

France
8–11–17

Dearest:
But the whole Army rings with the news of what our Boys did. This is the highest compliment ever paid to our Canadian troops, to be picked to be the Storm Troops of the British Army. Monday's show was all ours. One Corps, brought from away down the line, to crack this, the hardest nut in the whole German line. But oh, the price was heavy.

AO for the 4th Army

D O Y O U R E C A L L the history of the war during the fall of 1917? In the South, our ally Italy was in trouble. Steadily the Austrian army had mounted the Alps and were pouring down towards the Po River and the ancient city of Venice. The whole of Italy seemed lost. The army was falling back in disorder and a total rout was imminent. Something must be done. The call was out—send a British Army to Italy and stop the Austrians.

Yes, but what army? The 2nd that had held the Salient in Belgium for so long was ordered to go south. Now, when we say an Army, it does not necessarily mean the fighting troops, the divisions, no, not even the corps. What actually happened was that General Plumer took his Army Staff and one Division—the 41st we believe—and sailed for Italy. General Plumer was not a dashing, spectacular sort of general. But he was as stubborn as a rock; the rock against which Prince Rupprecht of Bavaria had hurled uncounted divisions in vain.

General Plumer took over command in Italy. Within four months he had rebuilt the Italian Army and so filled it with the British spirit that they turned and hurled the Austrian Army back into and over the Alps and peace returned to Venice.

Now we had just been attached to the 2nd Army and as our work was not of the nature that was needed in Italy, we remained at Cassel. The 2nd Army was replaced by the 4th Army under General Lord Rawlinson.[44]

A small portion of a very large map showing the area that was to become the
Western Front. It was most likely published by a British newspaper in the autumn of
1914. It is not as detailed as the official War Office maps (see page 44), but it was probably easier to use for that very reason—less detail to confuse the reader. Many of the
places John mentions in the text—Armentieres, Bailleul, Neuve Eglise, Kemmel,
Messines, Meteren, and Wytschaete—are shown, although some of the spellings may
be slightly different.

Major General Holman was Quartermaster General (QMG). He was a farmer born, a driver, a man who demanded that things be done, and done in a hurry, and at that moment the 4th Army had half the British troops on the Western front. We were to know this general, and know him well, for he opened a new chapter in our life. Now turn back to page 3 and reread *Gardens*. This we consider was the starting point of the amazing months that were to follow.

Maybe we were stepping high as we wended our way back to our billet after that interview with Major General Holman, then sat down to evaluate the situation.

We took out pencil and paper, but where were we to start? The immensity of the job was for a moment overwhelming. Vegetables and potatoes for a million men. We did not need to refer to the army ration tables. One pound of vegetables and one pound of potatoes per man per day. The figures were staggering. Would we go to the general and say, "Sir, this undertaking is just too big for us."

We could still hear the General's words; "Hughes, what I like about you Canadians is that nothing stumps you."

Were we going to let Canada down? NO. Also there was the answer: Canadians. No figuring today, we would go and talk this over with fellow Canadians.

We called for our driver to bring around the car. The name of one man came to mind and he was not a senior officer, in fact he was not a commissioned officer, just an NCO, Regimental Quartermaster Sergeant Matt Brimacombe. Late Mayor of the town of Vermilion back in our own Province of Alberta. Matt had been our strong right hand when we were given the job of raising and training a company in the 151st Battalion. Now he was a Sergeant with the 4th Canadian Labour Battalion, up on the very spot where Canada had its baptism of blood and fire and gas—Ypres.

It is a drive of twenty miles from Cassel in France to Ypres in Belgium. We found the 4th just outside the walls of that ancient city and were greeted by many old friends.

I had known Matt as a contractor and builder of the town he started. My first question, after greetings, was something different. "Matt, do you know anything about gardening?"

"A little," he said. "Our family were market gardeners in Devon before we went to Canada. My Father took over a garden when we landed in Ontario and I worked on it before we went to Alberta. Why?"

"How would you like to have charge of one of the biggest gardens in France and raise enough vegetables to feed the Army?"

"Show me where it is and I am on my way. That is, if Colonel McKinery will let me go."

"McKinery isn't going to have much to say as it happens. Now, have you four men you know who you would like as helpers?"

"Yes, there are four of our old Company here—Corporals Compton, Gosnell, Doonely, and Robinson."

"Fine, Matt. You will get your marching orders soon."

We went to the Officers' Mess and met our old CO and other friends: Captains Grainger, Heeney, and Jones.

When we asked for Sergeant Brimacombe and the other men, McKinery's answer was definite and to the point. "Not by a damn sight. Take five of my best men? To hell with you, Hughes."

We did not argue. Once before we had heard almost the same outburst. We had applied for transfer from the 66th to the newly formed 151st, where we were to get a Company. A few days later the Colonel called us in and said, "Hughes, this bunch of greenbacks that call themselves the 151st Battalion are badly in need of trained officers. They have applied to me for help. I am sending you to them as I consider you one of my most efficient officers. Go and show them the lessons I have taught you."

We knew full well that this change of front was not because of any desire to help another battalion CO. It came about by the good will of our friend John MacKintosh of Edmonton, who had the ear of Ottawa, and Major Jim Lowery, who also was known at Ottawa.

We were to get an unexpected helper, and this time not a Canadian. An officer came with a letter from General Holman introducing Major Wheatley,[45] whom he was sure would be a valuable assistant in our big farm scheme. Valuable assistant was an understatement. Major Wheatley DSO, retired, had been in what perhaps is England's crack regiment, the Grenadier Guards. His fund of knowledge of the army and army ways was unlimited. He seemed to be on intimate terms with generals and men of distinction and rank in and out of the army. We were to learn that his

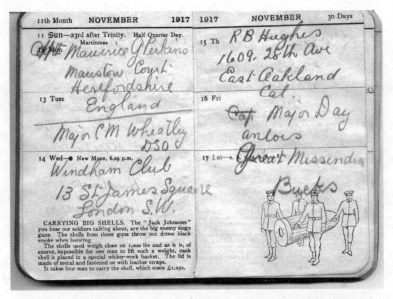

11th Month NOVEMBER 1917	1917 NOVEMBER 30 Days
11 Sun—23rd after Trinity. Half Quarter Day. Martinmas *Maurice G Perkins* *Maustow Court* *Herefordshire* 13 Tues *England* *Major CM Wheatley* *DSO* 14 Wed—● New Moon, 6.29 p.m. *Windham Club* *13 St James Square* *London S.W.*	15 Th *RB Hughes* *1609. 28th Ave* *East Oakland* *Cal.* 16 Fri *Major Day* *anlois* 17 Sat—*Great Missenden* *Bucks*

CARRYING BIG SHELLS. The "Jack Johnsons" you hear our soldiers talking about, are the big enemy siege guns. The shells from these guns throw out dense black smoke when bursting.

The shells used weigh close on 1,000 lbs and as it is, of course, impossible for one man to lift such a weight, each shell is placed in a special wicker-work basket. The lid is made of metal and fastened on with leather straps.

It takes four men to carry the shell, which costs £1,250.

A page from John's Soldier's Own Diary showing an address for Major C.M. Wheatley, John's chief assistant at his office—who just happened to outrank him, not that that seemed to bother anyone. The "R.B. Hughes" noted on the right-hand page is John's younger brother, who was unable to enlist because of an old leg injury.

father had been a general and Warden of the Royal Parks of England, and had his place in the household of Queen Victoria.

At one stroke we were given what we sadly lacked—inside knowledge of the working of the British Army. Yet this man never for one moment intimated that he, not we, should be in charge of this big new enterprise. We never asked General Holman, but perhaps he had sized up the situation clearly. He picked a Canadian to be his driver, a man who did not know very much about precedents and army regulations and who would waste no time on red tape, just because he did not know it was there. Then at the same time he picked a man who, knowing all these rules and regulations, could take advantage of the situation when the untaught Canadian waded in as if rules and regulations did not exist.

From time to time we stray from the time factor of our story, but memories of old flash into one's mind as old letters are read. So here let us tell of an incident that shows General Holman's character.

The general had called a conference of his staff and we were included. Included among an array of major generals, brigadier generals, colonels, lieutenant colonels, and a few majors, the youngest and greenest, ourself. The general saw to an introduction all the way around and we were not the only Canadian there, in fact there was quite a sprinkling of them.

All were seated. The general behind an Army table and this table loaded with books and pamphlets. Said the general, "Gentlemen, I have called this conference with a specific reason. We need, we must have, a decided speeding up of the work of our departments. We are too slow. Things are not moving as they should. Now, you see this table. On it are all the Orders pertaining to what we have to do in the Army; Standing Orders, Routine Orders, Orders of every kind. If you follow these orders you can not go wrong." Standing up and grasping the table by its side, he tilted the whole mass of orders onto the floor.

"Orderly," he called.

An orderly came in.

"Sweep all this junk out of the room."

The orderly obeyed.

"Gentlemen," he said, "you notice that we have quite a lot of Canadians at present on our staff. What I like about these men is that they are so damned ignorant." He paused. "Yes, ignorant about Army Orders. Do you know what these fools do? When anything needs doing, they do it. They don't consult Standing or Routine Orders, they just damn well go ahead and do it. Sure, they make lots of mistakes. Complaints come to me about how things are done by these chaps. Then I ask, well the thing is done is it not? The reply is, yes it's done, but not according to orders. The job is done. These fellows did not know how to do it, but they went ahead and did it. Now, do I make myself clear? Let's get things done, and in a hurry. If mistakes are made and it comes to my attention, you won't find me criticizing, that is, if the job is done.

"Now, Gentlemen, we have added a complete new department to our army. The Department of Agriculture. As you all know, the German U-boats have badly crippled our transports. France is short of food and we are feeling the pinch. There is much idle land here in France and Belgium. We are going to make use of it. We are going to grow a lot of our own food. Especially fresh vegetables that deteriorate so fast in transport. We have picked a young Canadian farmer to head this department. He is a farmer gardener. He does not know any orders about such work. In fact there are none. He will make them up as we go along. Now I want you to give Hughes every possible support, for we consider this a most important work. It means food and health for our troops."

We came away from the conference with a new concept of our work. We were fighting the U-boats. We were a factor in the health of the army.

Major Wheatley was organizing our own headquarters staff. He would take the office work, take care of reports, indents, records, and so on. We would look after operations. Within our department he would be Q, we would be G. This suited us fine. We would do the field work unhampered by the routine, army routine, of which we were woefully ignorant. We took a couple of days and drove about the country, sizing it up from an angle hitherto not considered by the Army. That is, its capability of producing food. Went right up to the front. Up beyond where any civilians were allowed. We studied the fields that were more or less clear from actual operations. None were fully clear. Here were some fine fields along the slopes of Messines Ridge. Between Messines Ridge and Kemmel Hill[46] was a fertile valley that stretched right up to Ypres, good land, but oh, what a mess man in his fury had made of those acres. Trenches zigzagged in every imaginable manner, taking advantage of each contour of the land. Gun emplacements by the hundreds with their embankments, shell holes by the thousands. Barbed wire by the hundreds of miles, twisted in every imaginable shape. An upturned broken gun, smashed General Service (GS) wagons, telephone lines, shells by the hundreds, abandoned when our men surged forward.

All this and more, much more, and call it a garden. But the soil was rich and had further been enriched by the blood of thousands. It would grow vegetables, grow potatoes. But the task of cleaning it up was greater than that given to Hercules when he was ordered to clean the Aegean stables.

Slowly Major Wheatley shook his head. "It will take a thousand men a year to clear this mess, and we are to plant potatoes in three months."

"We have been promised a thousand men. We will have a thousand acres ready by St. Patrick's Day," we replied. We had them ready, then the Hun came back.

Plows, Harrows, and Paris

HOW MANY CANADIANS ever went to Paris to buy a plow or a set of harrows? Thousands have gone there to buy dresses, of course, mainly female Canadians. We, being male and a war on, went for agriculture implements and we got them and, much to the surprise of some, we brought them home with us. Home being farm headquarters 4th Army, Cassel, France.

General Holman was never one to let the grass grow under his feet, he was a driver. Telegrams by the score had gone forth checking up on our leads about machinery, seeds, potatoes, horses, and a thousand and one other things needed.

With five three-ton lorries, our motor car with driver, and a French interpreter who knew Paris, we were on our way south. In our pocket were credit notes for five thousand pounds sterling, which we would deposit to our account in the Bank of France. Many Canadians went to Paris on leave, but not many with a motor car at their disposal and, as a guide, one who would show us a Paris others might miss. We picked a rendezvous where we would meet our lorry convoy and so arranged it that these drivers also had a couple of free days in the city many of us only dream about.

World War I did not dim the gaiety of Paris and it lived up to all our expectations. We picked a quiet hotel—quiet, that is, for that city—and lost no time looking up the agricultural sales offices. We wanted fifty plows and a like number of harrows. It did not take long to conclude our buying. The convoy of lorries having arrived, we loaded them at once and then returned to our hotel. There we ran up against trouble. A note was waiting for us with instructions to report to the Chief Purchasing Officer for the British Army. We did just that. While the Colonel was quite courteous, he nevertheless gave us a thorough dressing down for going ahead and ordering goods in France without going through the proper channels. That is, through his office. He informed us that all the British Armies had suddenly developed the agricultural spirit and were clamouring for him to purchase agricultural implements for them. He rather snorted at the idea of an army needing plows and harrows instead of guns and shells. Yet he would do it just as soon as the War Office in London gave him permission. Meantime we could wait.

Naturally we did not argue with him. It does not pay to enter into a dispute with a senior officer. Much better to be just Canadian. We asked if we should unload our lorries and send them back to the Army.

"Unload your lorries?" he almost shouted. "You don't mean to tell me that you have already taken possession of loads of implements?"

"Why yes. We have five lorry loads ready to pull out tomorrow morning."

"You mean to say a French implement firm let you load goods that are not paid for?"

"Oh no. They are all settled and paid in full."

"Paid in full! What do you mean? Did you have money? The Army does not use money! You have to get an order OK'd by the War Office."

"Yes, I had the money. I gave them a cheque on the Bank of France."

"Money! Cash! Bank of France! You Canadians will drive me crazy. You don't know a damn thing about army orders and still they let you run loose here in France. For heaven's sake, tell just what you mean."

We told him. Apologizing, of course, for not knowing the rules. (General Holman had told us not to know the rules.)

Slowly the Colonel shook his head and looked compassionately at one so dumb. "Well," he said, "seeing that you have completed your deal there is not much use me interfering at this stage. Best thing you can do is get the hell out of Paris before the other Army Agricultural Officers get word of this."

We took the hint. That is, we looked up our Sergeant Major in charge of lorries and told him to get moving, not in the morning, but within the hour. He did. We caught up with him before he reached Cassel.

Meantime, having completed our duties, we placed ourself in the hands of our interpreter, Lieutenant Falicon of the French Army. Now Falicon's home and business was in Nice, but he had been educated at the National School of Agriculture at Versailles. He proposed that we visit this school, for he said it was one of the show places of France. We spent a wonderful half day among the walled gardens of that famous institution and then were invited to have dinner with the Superintendent and his staff. We wanted to ask questions. Instead, we answered questions. What about? Canada and Canadian agriculture, of course. We spent several hours walking through the magnificent castle. No, a castle does not describe rightly the wonderful building a doting monarch poured untold millions into to please a willful woman who despised him, yet took the millions that, had they gone for food for the people, might have saved her neck from the kiss of the guillotine.

One of France's largest army encampments is just near Versailles. France had conceptions of the necessities of life to men in the Army that are foreign to our Anglo-Saxon ideas. Falicon said that we should see this side of Army life. We did. Those who wish may skip the next page. Some will call it sex in the raw. It is not so intended. It is just a simple statement of fact. French soldiers received the lowest pay of any of the great nations. During World War I it was half a franc a day, a full franc while in the front line trenches. At half a franc a day (ten cents Canadian) a man had little chance to buy female attentions. The French authorities looked on this subject in a clear, matter-of-fact light. To keep the men of the Army fit they must have the companionship of women who were free from venereal diseases. Therefore the women as well as the men must be under government medical supervision. Moreover, government assistance was necessary for the men drawing ten cents a day pay. Not far from the barracks were established homes for the women.

Falicon said, "Such as it is, it's a show place and absolutely clean." We went to see the show place on a Sunday morning. A clear cold morning, when one was glad of one's British Warm (overcoat). A girl was outside each house to welcome visitors. We said it was cold. What it would have been, had we been wearing the clothes of those out to give a welcome, we shudder to think. It could all have been stuffed into one pocket, a very small pocket. Big picture windows in those houses. Inside the window, the bathroom. We will let you imagine the rest.

Now we can hear the exclamations—bad, wicked, immoral! Yes, perhaps. Yet the French Army had a record of freedom from venereal diseases never even approached by the British Army. Army Commanders dreaded to see their men going home to England on fourteen days leave. The casualties there were much, much greater than from the fiercest battles of the war.

Naturally, as nearly everyone does, we went to the *Folies Bergères*. Not a particularly good show as far as a show went. We have seen better leg shows.

Stuck in a Snowdrift

WE NEEDED MORE PLOWS and more harrows. A Canadian, Major Hogg,[47] had charge of an army workshop near Péronne. Here he gathered plows, harrows, and every other kind of farm implement from the devastated farms in the area evacuated by the civilian population. Broken plows, broken implements from farms blown to pieces by shells and bombs and ravaged by fire. French blacksmiths, English blacksmiths, blacksmiths from all the armies were striving mightily to put together the plow and the sickle that the sword had broken.

Again, this time with three lorries, we went forth to find tools for our gardeners. Many Canadians know that long, wide, straight road that leads from Amiens to Arras past Bapaume. The weather was nice when we started, but that night it snowed. We think of sunny France. France can be just the opposite. There was two feet of snow—wet, heavy snow—and the roads were blocked for miles. A long column of our trucks, guns, and lorries were going up. A French division of like vehicles were coming out, in two feet of snow, and not a traffic policeman for miles. Can you imagine the confusion, the congestion? You cannot, that is unless you know something about the traffic control in the French army. There is none, at least not as we understand traffic control. As it happened, we were the senior officer on the spot. That is, we wore a major's crown,

86

although on paper we were a Staff Lieutenant First Class, therefore we had to take charge. There was only one hope: establish a one-way lane. So many vehicles one way, then stop, and so many the other way, then stop.

Fortunately we were just opposite a prisoner-of-war camp. The Commandant, another Canadian, whose name we have missed, seeing the jam immediately sent out a hundred German prisoners to help. Give us Germans anytime when a heavy job of work needs doing. They took it all as a lark, and laughed and sang as they dug, pushed, or pulled truck or gun out of snowdrifts. Along came a small French car in which were four French generals. They wanted the right of way, demanded the right of way. They snarled our otherwise now smooth-working plan. We tried to reason with them, but our French was bad, and their English was worse. They were holding up the whole line. We called to our Hun friends, "Pick up that car and put it in the ditch." They did just that. It was just play for twenty husky Germans, and how they enjoyed putting those French generals where in their opinion they should be. We did not have to know French to understand what was going to happen to us when these officers could get in touch with the Commander-in-Chief of the British Army. We had no time to worry about what was to happen, our job was to clear the block. When the turn of the Generals' car came, the same group of Germans again picked up the car and ironically waved the departing Frenchmen on their way.

Also, maybe ironically, when we were in Arras we were invited to a French officers' mess and treated right royally. Naturally we did not tell the story of the snowdrifts.

France

21–12–17

Dearest:

Starting from the city [Amiens], we swing out on one of the finest and straightest roads in France, only to be held up in the snowdrifts for two hours. The snow was two feet deep. A seeming hopeless block occurred, and no one to take charge. So I did it myself.

I would have given anything for a camera about that time. Just imagine, British officers and men, French officers and men, Hun prisoners, all pushing behind and alongside of those big lorries. All working together with the best good will as if there was no war on.

I think from the cheerful expression on those Boche faces that they would sooner be working on our roads than fighting in the trenches.

Well, at last we were clear and then we got into the cleared roads further forward and we sailed along a splendid road under a canopy of high wide-spreading trees all coated with white frost, like we see at home. The frost I mean. I doubt if such an avenue of regularly planted trees exists in Canada. Then we gradually got a change. Here a limb off, then a tree uprooted, then a great gash in the side made by a passing shell, then the trees became only tall naked pitted trunks, then only shattered stumps. The work and growth of generations destroyed by man's hate.

Along and along we whirled to a famous city [Bapaume], which is destroyed but not leveled like Ypres, past the remains of the ramparts of this ancient city. Here I had lunch at the Officers' Club. Think of it, an Officers' club in this advanced area, among these ruins, where good hot meals are served. I stayed here till nearly dusk arranging for some plows to be gathered by our lorries that were coming on behind me. Here was an Agricultural Officer, a Canadian, showing what an interest is taken in this work.

Then we swing more north and through another historic city [Arras], where I had dinner at a French Officers' Mess.

Then north again we went crawling slowly to avoid accidents, our lamps [carbide] seeming to only make the fog denser. A light would gleam ahead, coming gradually nearer but seeming to move slowly till right near, when with a whizz it swept past. Lorries, lorries everywhere, lorries through the gloom, they rumble up and past or, if going your way, you must sweep past, always looking out for others coming the other way. But on through the thickening gloom we went. A light would be swung in front. If white, the road is clear. If red, you must stop. "Who are you?" "Army Headquarters Staff." "Pass. All's well."

Then the question. "Can we still keep straight north?"

"Yes. But lights out for the next ten miles. We are close to the line."

So slower still we creep into the gloom. This piece of road gives me a certain cause for excitement, because presently along the side of the road I see a certain old disused trench. Just a year ago I crept along this trench on my first trip into the front line. There where a year ago the snipers' bullets *were always singing past and I first knew how to duck [after the bullets had passed], I swept past in my car. I can pick out our communication trench and an old unused dugout that was a YMCA hut where our boys had hot coffee.*

At last we reached our HQ and billets. We had travelled eighty miles, mostly over new roads and through the fog, and made it in just over four hours.

We must tell you about the Agricultural Officer of this area [Bapaume]. He is Major Hogg. Last September the British Government sent out from England several threshing machines to help with the harvest. This chap Hogg stole them all and had them working in his district for a month before the Army knew they were in France. There was a great row over it. But as our General Holman told me, "While the Government was thinking about the work, Hogg was working the machines and had threshed thousands of bushels of grain in a district where three years grain was unthreshed."

Goodnight Sweetheart.

The Earl of Folkestone

THE BRITISH PURCHASING AGENT in Paris had spoken rightly. The British Armies, including Australians and Canadians, were bitten with the agricultural bug. That, or orders came from higher up, from the War Office in London. We imagine the latter. On the scene appeared a Director of Agriculture, attached to the staff of the Commander-in-Chief, Field Marshal Haig.

We were instructed to proceed to GHQ. It is a pleasant drive down through some of France's finest farm lands, down to Montreuil-sur-Mer near the coast and on the Nocq River, to one of Europe's few remaining walled cities. There we were to meet the AOs of the four other British Armies, three of whom were Canadians who would not go home. The man who interested us most, however, was General Lord Radnor,[48] Earl of Folkestone, the Director of Agricultural Operations. Farmer and gentleman in the truest sense of the word. A man who called himself a socialist and voted as a conservative. During the next year we were to know this gentleman very well, not so much as a commanding officer but as a friend. We were to sit at his side while we drove many hundreds of miles up and down the roads of Flanders and tramp endless miles looking over farm operations carried on by British soldiers in a foreign land.

We were proud that day that such a man as General Holman was our direct OC at Army HQ, for we were far and away ahead of all others in our operations. We were operating, the others mostly planning. We were so far ahead that Lord Radnor made immediate arrangements to visit 4th Army farms.

True to his word, General Radnor arrived at 4th Army HQ within the week. We were called into a conference by General Holman who, with his senior assistants, was to tell the Director of Agricultural Operations what had been accomplished. This gave us an opportunity to tell of the great assistance we had received from our new second-in-command, Major Wheatley DSO. Wheatley was immediately sent for, and it turned out that he and General Radnor were old friends. Right away plans were made for a tour of our farms (proposed and operating) for the next day.

The Director, General Holman, Major Cotton, and ourself were in one car, while Major Wheatley, Major Murray MP, and the Director of Labour went in another. Cassel to Bailleul along that straight wide road that Napoleon built, past the villages of Caestre, Flêtre, and Meteren. Still east to where the hamlet of Wulverghem once stood, but now only rubble. There, at a crossroad close to the little River Douve and only a mile from where once stood the town of Messines, we had established our main camp. Major Bromley-Martin[49] was in charge and his chief assistant was Sergeant Harry Compton,[50] ex-blacksmith from the town of Vermilion in Alberta.

Messines, as many Canadians know, is a low ridge that stretches away to Wytschaete and St. Eloi. Between that road and the road from Neuve Eglise, Lindenhoek, Kemmel, and Voormezeele is a fine stretch of farm land, and on that land from Ploegsteert northward we were proposing to plant a thousand acres of potatoes. The front line was just a little more than a mile away. Were we a bit optimistic? Yes, very much so.

One of Canada's foremost authors, Will Bird,[51] went back along that line that he and fellow Canadians held for so long and then wrote a story, *Thirteen Years After*. In this story, he mentioned that a certain part of the battle field was further advanced in rehabilitation than any other he saw. Had he been with our party that day in December, 1917, he would have had the answer to his puzzle. On reading his story we were tempted to write to the author and give him the answer. We should have done as tempted and sent him our box of letters and let one so much more able write this story. Maybe, if the gods and some publisher are agreeable, Will Bird will yet have the answer.

It was a busy scene along this stretch of fertile farm land this day. Farming on a land that only Goethe could properly describe. Land that the Devil himself must have viewed and smiled. Yet man was undoing the havoc he so recently had created, and yet would do it again, although on a lesser scale.

Army horses driven by English farmers were actually hauling plows, followed by others with harrows. But, oh, the immense work that had to be done before even one furrow was turned. Men were rolling up great bundles of barbed wire. What was eventually done with the tangled mass we often wonder. Shell holes and old trenches were being filled by an army of men. Shells were being gathered up by crews and hauled away to dumps. Why shells, you may ask, were we not short of shells? We had been, but the versatile man who afterwards would tell Britain that only tears, sweat and blood would save the Isles had been made Minister of Munitions, and shells there were aplenty. So, when a battery moved forward they did not even pause to gather up the shells unfired. So now crews with GS wagons were gathering these and empty shell cases and carting them to the dump heap. We paused to watch the unloading of these shells, mostly eighteen-pounders. "Familiarity breeds contempt." The old saying never was more exemplified than by this crew of cleaners on Messines Ridge. They were tossing live shells on to the dump just like they tossed stones back on the farms at home. Had one exploded, well, there would be no need of a funeral. There would have been nothing to bury. We talked to those lads. Maybe talk is the wrong word, for our hair was carrying our steel helmet well off our skull. Yet there was nothing to do but leave them and hope.

A thousand men were working on the farm that day. True, an occasional shell came over and made a hole where a hole had just been filled in but an hour before. GS wagons were arriving from all directions loaded with horse manure. Had this been World War II, we would have been without this valuable fertilizer, as the motor has replaced the horse, but during World War I the British army had five hundred thousand horses and mules on the Western front. Every horse line far and near was being carefully cleaned to save the manure wherewith to rebuild Belgium's ravaged acres.

Major Cotton was a motor car dealer in civil life and therefore a forward-looking man in the motor field. He had persuaded General Holman to purchase a couple of farm tractors. These had arrived and nothing would do but Cotton should drive one of these a couple of times up and down the field. They were International Moguls. We could write a story that might be pleasing to the International Harvester Co. about their machines under shell fire.

This whole farm scheme was General Holman's baby. His idea, and he was proud to show it to one of England's foremost farmers, Lord Radnor, the Earl of Folkestone. And, incidentally, giving praise for the rapid development of his idea by a farmer from Western Canada. We took pains to point out and, at every opportunity, introduce Canadians working on this scheme.

North we went past Wytschaete, past St. Eloi, up to and through Ypres. There we made a blunder. We were supposed to be guide, but, what with looking at the ruins of the great Cloth Hall and other historic spots, we took the road east instead of north and found ourself out on the plank road. We had gone out the Menin Gate, or what was once that famous gate. An army traffic control sergeant wanted to know where in bloody hell we thought we were going. We managed to turn around and get back into the city, meantime we took quite a ribbing by our general. Anyway, they took it in good part. We had taken a motor car closer to the front line than any other car ever had been in broad daylight. As shells were falling in all directions anyway, we did not know if we were Fritzie's target or not.

We had farms started at Vlamertinghe and Elverdinghe, at Reninghelst and Poperinghe, and as one after the other we introduced Canadians in charge, it got so that Lord Radnor would ask, "Is there a Canadian in charge at the next farm?" Usually there was. It was good to introduce Lieutenant Colonel Pritchard, Colonel Harrison, Major Brown, Major Simmons, and Colonel Campbell and have them tell of the work they were doing. We hoped that the words of encouragement they received from two top-ranking British generals sounded as good in their ears as in our own.

For tea we stopped at Steenvoorde, where Captain Wood, son of Field Marshal Sir Evelyn Wood, was AO. Here no introduction was needed, as all were old friends. Then back to HQ where we were invited to dine with General Holman at his mess. All in all a wonderful day. A very busy major general had thought it important enough to take a whole day to show another general this new department of the Army.

We Vote

France

12–12–17

Dearest:

Today I cast my vote. Had to go up to [Boeschepe]. Canadians were arriving from all directions. They are scattered through every Imperial unit. I took Colonel Pritchard and Colonel Campbell along from [Poperinghe]. I will send the car down to the 15th Casualty Clearing Station to take those two Canadian Nursing Sisters over to vote. Great pains are being taken to give every voter a chance.

Every chance for everyone to vote. Sure they wanted lots of votes. When they finished voting the live ones, they took the ballot box and voted the dead ones. Row on row of crosses voted. Was there ever a more corrupt election held in Canada, or rather in Canadian history? Perhaps some was only hearsay, but let us relate what we saw with our own eyes, heard with our own ears.

We knew what constituency we belonged to and also the name of the man we were voting for. As it happened our vote was lost, that is, our candidate did not win. And remember this, he was the only Unionist not elected from the Lakes to the Pacific. Next in line to us was a young lad, only eighteen. When asked what constituency he came from, he said he did not know. Asked if he knew the names of the candidates running in his constituency, he again replied, "no."

Asked, "of course you want to vote for conscription."

He replied, "Yes, of course."

"Then just sign your name and number on this line."

He did. "That is all," he was told.

This Canadian, voting in Belgium, had handed those in charge of the election a vote that could be used in any constituency in Canada. Was it any wonder that the Government was returned to power? The Returning Officer quite blandly told us how it was operating. As we said before, our candidate Jim Holden was defeated. It was explained to us after we came home that a mistake was made. Billy Griesbach in Edmonton received a thousand unnecessary votes that had been intended for Jim Holden of Vegreville. Of this latter, we can only say it was gossip—maybe true, maybe not. But we do know that the arrangement for such an event was developed there in a little village in Belgium before our eyes.[52]

Ironically, to blot out this blotch on our Canadian democracy, the next day the Germans blew to smithereens that house wherein we had voted.

Items From Here and There

France

22–1–18

Dearest:

Just in from a long trip. Had lunch with Billy Wilkin, who is Area Commandant at Theimbonne. One of the Corps Agriculture Officers lives with Wilkin. This chap, Captain Bloxham, is also a Canadian. I believe Wilkin is the most rabid Canadian I ever met. He has no use for the English man or his methods. [He is an Englishman.] He proposes as a solution of this problem for which we are fighting today that all decent Englishmen and Frenchmen leave Europe and go to America and leave the entire Europe to the Hun. He is a Canadian first last and all the time.

Colonel Hind, one of the Corps Agricultural Officers has left a note on my desk saying he is in town and asking that I dine with him at the hotel.

Later. Had a very enjoyable dinner at the Savage. Colonel Hind, Lieut. Colonel Frazer and myself.

France

30–1–18

Dearest:

Just a line before turning in. It's now midnight and my desk is piled high with reports, memos, requests and orders. Looks like the most hopeless confusion and I must wade through it somehow as every day the pile is growing. I have been out since early morning issuing plows, harrows and attending to conferences and trying to get a hundred and one details arranged. I had no idea when I started here that this would lead up to such large proportions. The Agricultural Director is coming Friday and we must make a showing to substantiate our claim to being the most forward army in the B.E.F. in so far as farming is concerned. I don't mind the work, am willing to go till I drop if I can do any good. Sergeant Major Matt Brimacombe is with me and has charge of a farm. He made a good impression at Headquarters.

France

17–1–18

Dearest:

This morning I was away early as I had to go down to [St. Omer] to meet an old French gentleman who is giving us the use of ten acres of vegetable land along the St. Omer marshes. This is famous vegetable land, but just now, on account of the lack of labour, much of it is uncultivated. This gentleman wanted us [Major Wheatley, Serg. Major Brimacombe and self] to examine the land. So we went a short distance in the car, then walked a bit, then got into a boat and were poled around the canals. These plots, that vary from an acre to four acres, are each surrounded by ditches or canals. Sometimes when the water is low there is hardly enough water to float a boat, but just now the water is higher than for twenty years and the land is nowhere more than two feet above the level of the water and in places is flooded, but this may be gone in a few days. Here you see cabbage, brussel sprouts and turnips growing for the winter market. A boat will have to be used in places to take the horses and plows from field to field. I may often row along these canals this summer, it is very pretty in places. Some nice farmers' cottages out on these little farms. All the communication is by boat. You would see the peasant women rowing into market with their boat piled high with baskets of vegetables. [Remember this is mid-winter.] We stopped at what appeared to be the nicest cottage and had some refreshments. This was owned by the gentleman we were with, a sort of summer cottage and shooting box. They get some wild ducks on these canals. This land adjoins about eight acres we are getting from another gentleman. Matt Brimacombe will be in charge. I am very keen on this farm, as being such a famous vegetable land it ought to produce two to one against the other farms up forward. There are no trenches to fill or shell holes, and no dud shells to worry about, or no chance of Fritz shelling some foggy day.

But Hun aeroplanes came over many times and once gave the farm a heavy strafing. Fortunately most of the bombs landed in the ditches, but we had three men wounded.

Have been talking to General Cooke over the phone. He seems pleased with Major Rowan, the Canadian I sent to Corps. Mr. Monod [interpreter] also likes him. I was also talking to Major Simmons. He tells me his engagement appeared in yesterday's Times. Also talked to Major Howe, who transferred to the Flying Corps.

We must tell about fertilizer for these famous vegetable acres that in peace time furnish many thousands of tons of green vegetables for the Paris market. We watched this very special operation. But first, let us go back to what our schoolmarm at Caestre said about sanitation. Not having sewers, most of the homes in town or village have cesspools. These are emptied from time to time by suction pumps which pump the refuse into big wooden tanks on wheels. Note: the day the pump comes to your house, best go for a picnic. Maybe the effluvium may have subsided by the time you get home.

Now for our gardens. These tanks unload into boats on the canals. We watched. At a distance. The boats are then rowed to the plot where fertilizer is needed. We followed, again at a distance. The rowers wore long rubber boots and needed them. Again we watched, but changed our viewpoint so as to be upwind from the boat. Water was then dipped from the canal and the whole mess thoroughly mixed. Then some sort of hydrometer was used. Evidently the consistency was still too strong, for more water

On the back of this WWI postcard are two typewritten lines: "On the water wagon" and "Smile, you beggar, smile, even it has come to this!" but no names, date, or place. It is assumed that these men worked on one of John's farms, possibly watering the vegetables. The man on the left is wearing leather leggings typical of those worn by cavalry troops (John is wearing similar leggings in the photograph on page 12), indicating he may have originally enlisted in a mounted unit.

was poured in and again mixed. This seemed to satisfy our workers, Frenchmen, who then proceeded to carry the rich fluid in pails and distribute it along the rows of young plants. Results—marvelous. Suppose you try it if you are not getting good returns from your garden.

There is one main canal through these flats, and along this main canal is a wide, well-paved highway. Six months after the writing of the above we often watched long convoys of lorries loading vegetables that would be welcome food for the men of the British Army. The farm was an outstanding success. Many generals, whose men had enjoyed the good food, came to see our Army vegetable farm and were impressed, not only with the wonderful crop but with the man in charge, Sergeant Major Matt Brimacombe. In fact, Brimacombe was recommended for his commission by General Lord Radnor, the Earl of Folkestone. Unfortunately it took too long to get this recommendation through the War Office in London and then to Ottawa, and it was not consummated until too late—Armistice and the end of the war came. The British Expeditionary Force in France and Belgium owed much to the quiet-spoken, one-time mayor of a Western Canadian town. So here let us tell another story about Matt Brimacombe. Two in fact.

First: during recruiting days for C Company 151st Battalion, the orderly room clerk in making out a man's enlistment papers had to put down what church the man belonged to. Perhaps out west more people have drifted away from the church of their fathers than back east. So when a man was asked "What church?", too often he said he had none. So our orderly room clerk (maybe he was an Anglican) put on his papers 'C of E' (Church of England). One day, noticing this, we decided to have some fun with our Sergeant Major, who was always a staunch pillar of the Presbyterian Church.

"Matt," we said, "how is it that so few Presbyterians are coming forward to their country's call?"

Matt, quick to the defence of his church, exclaimed, "What do you mean, Sir?"

"Why, just look at our muster roll. C of Es outnumber Presbyterians eight to one."

Matt snatched up the roll book. Sure enough, two-thirds of all names had 'C of E' attached. "Why, the lousy rascals," he exclaimed. "This one is no churchman. I have known him for years. Hasn't been in a church in a decade. And this one, and this one." Then with a smile as he saw the joke. "Well Sir, if all these backsliders have joined the church, then your Company has started a revival that bests anything ever held in Alberta. Anyway, I am going to be around when the next recruit signs. The Presbyterian church might as well have their share of these new church-men." Matt as usual was as good as his word, and from then on the Anglican and Presbyterian churches shared recruits who had no church leanings.

Second: we were on the train. Destination unknown. But we were on the way to glory or....

We noticed that Matt was wearing a service ribbon for the first time.

"Why Matt," we exclaimed, "when did you see service?"

"The Riel Rebellion, Sir."

"Then why have you not worn your service ribbon before this?"

"Think a bit, Sir. Do you think the doctors or others would have let me be on a train bound for overseas if they saw this ribbon?"

We had admired this man from the first day we met him. Now we were to appreciate him even more. Matt had been a soldier before we were born. Yet he had hidden his age so as to once more serve his King and Country.

Finally, a little incident, not recorded, unfortunately for myself. Fritz had given a certain spot, close behind our lines, a heavy dose of gas shells. It was a good field of wheat. A question arose—should this crop be harvested? What about the gas? Would it be harmful to humans when the wheat was made into flour?

The Army gas expert and myself were instructed to investigate. The gas expert's report read as follows:

> Have inspected gas-shelled field of wheat. The grain from this field will not be harmful for French civilian consumption. The straw must not be used for British Army horses.

We had sniffed a lot of small shell holes. We wonder, did that sniffing have anything to do with our frequent trips to the hospital in later years with pneumonia? No record.

On the Roads of Flanders and Nord

France
5–1–18

Dearest:
One of the officers at mess last night said, "Hughes seems to try and see how far away from HQ he can have lunch each day." And it looks like it. Today I am intending to have lunch with the 1st Army Agricultural Officer. Major J. Hughes,[53] 52nd Canadians then will swing south to that city [Péronne] where I have been twice during the last month. Again a question of plows.

Yesterday we had a long fast run. I had to go five miles out of my way to pick up Colonel Campbell.

We arrived at this, the largest city destroyed by war, at twelve o'clock, arranged to get our plows, and were then invited by the French officers to lunch with them. I was glad, as this was one more new experience for Colonel Campbell [lunching in a French officers' mess].

This was a sample of our day's work. Actually our field work was from the Belgian Army in the north to the 1st British Army in the south. From the front line then resting on a line two miles east of Ypres and Armentieres back to Boulogne and Calais. The British Army had substantially occu-

France.

31. 12. 17.

Dearest Girlie

This will be my last letter to you for this year. The last half of the year has slipped away very fast. because I was busy I suppose. And with present prospects I will be even busier next year. I am likely to leave here and go down to the Somme district working from G.H.Q. I don't like leaving here a little bit. as here I am very comfortable and know the officers of Corps and Army and I have a free hand. go where I like. when I like. as my letters of late have shown you I travel all over Northern France and have opportunity to see the country as but few men in the B.E.F. have. Today I was down at the ancient city of —— seeing about land for gardens. this is a famous district for vegetables and in peace times many trains leave there every day laden with fresh vegetables for Paris and other large cities. I had a new experience as I had lunch in the home of a real French gentleman a splendid home. I would like to describe it to you. as you have noticed through all my letters I have often said these French people know but little about real comfort. and in spite of this mans evident wealth his home lacks that touch of ease and comfort which is brought to its highest pitch in the English country home. well this house shows nothing but a plain outer wall to the street. but inside shows both taste and a full purse. a marble hall. (cold) many stained glass doors. large rooms. high ceilings. rich old furniture much of it delicately carved. no doubt very valuable today. all of oak. The shelves and furniture loaded with ornaments

The first page of a six-page letter John wrote to Sara on New Year's Eve, 1917. It is typical of all his correspondence with her, rife with incomplete and run-on sentences, severely lacking in punctuation, and often without paragraph breaks. The complete letter is show in Appendix V with a transcription.

pied this area for three years. It almost seemed as if they were permanent residents. The front swayed back and forth a matter of a few rods one way or the other, but this did not affect the position of a great mass of the army. Here and there, a group who had been in one place many months thought of gardens and fresh vegetables. Remember that the French people are great gardeners.

Gradually the idea had spread until it was taken up by Headquarters of Divisions, Corps, Armies, and by the Commander-in-Chief himself, Sir Douglas Haig.

We had arrived at 4th Army Headquarters as this new surge came to a head. The Quartermaster General, General Holman, was ever one to take the lead. So we had a driver behind us, and we also like to drive, and given a free hand we were away out in front in this new wave of Army Agriculture. We liked the work. We had come overseas for an entirely different kind of work, but when this was denied us we took up the new work, work we were better trained to do than fighting. Although not in the line, we were under shell fire nearly every day more or less, and that took at least some of the sting away of not being with the boys. We had command of a department under the Quartermaster General and it was growing by leaps and bounds. We were now thinking in terms of thousands of acres being cultivated by British troops. We were allowed to recommend men for Division and Corps appointments, so just naturally whenever possible we named Canadians. Canadians who, for a time, thought they were unwanted.

We now had an office with two assistants, both of whom were far senior to ourself, and we had been allotted twelve French interpreters. In all, at one time, we had five thousand men under our direction. Direction, remember, not command.

Everywhere you went you saw soldiers working on the land, and this was good. God made man and placed him in a garden, the healthiest place on earth. Men, tired, weary, nerve-racked, hating war and longing for home and loved ones, found rest and comfort from delving in the soil and planting seeds. True, at times they had to leave their particular plot of ground and, coming back, found just another shell hole to fill, but all in all it was just a little bit like being home. All this needed direction. Fields had to be found that would warrant cultivation. Implements found and distributed. Horses, many of them blind, had to be brought from the sick horse lines. A team of two horses with a total of one good eye was quite all right. With a good driver, even without the one good eye, good work could be accomplished. Seed, seed, seed, everyone wanted seed. Paris, London, and elsewhere were sending seed. We were fortunate to find a commercial seed merchant in the army, and straight away he had a job. A hundred pounds of cabbage seed, a hundred bushels of peas, ditto beans, just as a sample. Our job was to see that all things worked smoothly. We had a good car, a Sunbeam, a good driver, and we drove thousands of miles up and down the roads of Flanders and the *département du Nord*.

France
8–1–18

Dearest:

My next book will be entitled "Touring France in a Motor Lorry, By Day and Night". Got in last night a few minutes to twelve, after nearly a hundred miles in a lorry. Cold and tired, but pleased that the trip was finished, and more pleased now this morning to find a furious snowstorm raging. I wrote to you from [Arras] where we stayed the night. Well, we had a comfortable night and breakfast. Started out being towed. Our car had motor trouble along that long straight road which I have described before [Bapaume to Amiens] and on which last time I had to be traffic control officer. We arrived at [Péronne], where my other two lorries were waiting, at eleven. Went to the dump where there are thousands of farm implements of every sort and description gathered from the abandoned areas. We loaded our lorries and ran back in to the ruins [Bapaume] and had lunch.

We got away soon after one. I rode in the car for a while, but I don't like being behind, so when we reached the city of the leaning statue [Albert] I got up in the forward lorry and rode there with the driver all the way home. One driver drives, the other sits behind and signals passing cars, etc. We reached [Amiens] at dark, and I went to the Town Major and asked for billets for the boys and Falicon and myself. He said that we could have the billets, but that if we wanted to get back to our units we had better keep going, as thaw precautions had been ordered to go into effect at midnight. So I went back to the Corporal and we decided to go on as far as possible. So on we

The War of 1914–1918.

Maj. J. McK. Hughes, Alberta Regiment

was mentioned in a Despatch from

Field Marshal Sir Douglas Haig, K.T. G.C.B. G.C.V.O. K.C.I.E.

dated the 8th November 1918

for gallant and distinguished services in the Field.
I have it in command from the King to record His Majesty's
high appreciation of the services rendered.

Winston S. Churchill

War Office
Whitehall, S.W.
1st March 1919.

Secretary of State for War.

A certificate issued in 1919 indicating that John was mentioned in a dispatch from Field Marshal Sir Douglas Haig on 8 December 1918. It is a preprinted form, to which the recipient's name is added by hand, so the "for gallantry and distinguished service in the Field" is not necessarily an accurate description of why some soldiers were mentioned in dispatches.

went through the night. Now, as the roads were fairly free from traffic, not many traffic control men on duty and the roads good, we sure hit the high spots. Those big cumbersome lorries can travel quite fast. Ten miles an hour is the regulation speed on the roads. I asked the Corporal what his car could do. He said eighteen was what they were supposed to do, and immediately proceeded to show me that his could do twenty or better. Now twenty miles in a good car is not very fast and does not impress one very much, but twenty in a big lumbering lorry at night is a sensation worth having. They rattle and bounce and shake and swing, and don't try it unless the roads are good. Remember, these lorries have hard rubber tires. We were not riding on air. About eight, we arrived at _____, where we parked and I *took the boys to a café and fed them a good supper. Then, feeling warmed and cheered, we rumbled away again into the night, pulling steadily northward. The trees on the sides of the road seemed to be advancing in endless procession to meet us. Our lorry was a bit the faster, so occasionally we had to stop and let the others catch up. Finally we arrived and climbed the long winding hill to our quarters [Cassel].*

Mother Willox at once prepared hot tea for Falicon and me. She never goes to bed till twelve o'clock if any of her guests, or "boys" as she calls us all, are out. Someday I will tell you more about my trips through France in a motor lorry.

Bye.

GHQ sent word that, considering the size of the work we have undertaken for this army, we will remain at Army. Apparently we had been slated to go to Field Marshal Haig's Headquarters. We were quite content. We had not been too pleased to leave Corps for Army, but now we were so firmly established we did not want to move. It is true, when we think of it now in later years, it would have been nice to say that we served on the staff of the Commander-in-Chief. Anyway, at least he had recognized that we were in France, as he included our name in his dispatches to the War Office.

France
11–1–18

Dearest:
Another note tonight, as I know that if I try more than a page I shall go to sleep over it. Out all day in the car makes me awfully sleepy. This morning went down to Meteren and picked up Monod and went to see General Cooke about a garden scheme for the Corps. The General was cheery as usual, but reminded me several times that I had not found enough Agricultural Officers for them. Then I took Monod back and went to see Colonels Pritchard and Campbell. Then went to see Captain Wood at Steenvoorde. He is leaving. A Colonel Lind is coming in his place. From there I went to see Major Rowan who is Area Commandant. I stayed there for

lunch. I want Rowan to take the 9th Corps position. Then back through HQ and away down to [Aire] eighteen miles south to see the Commandant of a large School of Instruction about a school garden. Had tea with him and his staff and talked gardens. This is quite a usual day's work, driving eighty miles. I am here, there and everywhere to get gardens. My present plans to date call for two thousand five hundred acres of gardens. Tomorrow I have a similar day planned. Will call at three Corps, HQ and two Area Commandants. But as I said to start, this driving makes me sleepy, so I am off to bed.

Bye.

We came or went almost at will. Anywhere from Ostend to Paris, the sea to the front line. A good car and a good driver. We interviewed generals and Tommies, mayors of towns and governors of provinces, and the humble farmer clinging to partly shell-shattered homes. Yet with all that, our thoughts were always, "What chance to get in the line with our boys from Alberta?"

Am off in the morning, south for more plows. Am taking Colonel Campbell along. He is always ready to go anywhere that he has not been before.

Having a car of our own, or rather an Army car at our disposal, we have had opportunities to see such things as had few Canadians. So whenever possible we picked up our fellow Canadians. It was enjoyable for them, and we enjoyed their company.

Just in from a hundred-mile trip. Had a good trip, only got stuck in the snow once. No cars passed us, and we passed all in sight. We have a good car, a skillful and daring driver. He objects to passing other cars, except on hills. There is where this Sunbeam shines. It makes the drivers of Vauxhalls and Rolls Royces very cross for a Sunbeam to pull past. We delivered Major Bromley-Martin at the boat. Had lunch, then went up to #2 Canadian Hospital to call on nursing sister Nellie McRae, but found she was away on sick leave.

Quite often our trips took us through the town of Bailleul, where we liked to stop and talk to the Town Major, Colonel Sir Parry Price. He was really a farmer and wanted to be out on the land, so he had some good gardens around the town. Also there was a good officers' mess in the town, so it was a good place to stop for lunch. One day we sat near a couple of major generals, strangers to us. We could hear their talk quite clearly.

Said one major general to the other major general, "How do you classify the various divisions of our army?"

Said the other major general, "Well of course there is only one first. The Guards Division. Second I would place the 51st Highland Yeomanry Division. Then third, fourth, fifth, and sixth I would give to the Canadians."

"Yes," said the first major general, "I agree. You know, it is remarkable the discipline of those civilian soldiers."

"A fine soldier, this chap Currie."[54]

"Marvelous in fact, for a civilian," said the other.

Don't think I am bragging or one-sided expressions when I say that our Canadian boys are held to be the very pick of the British Army. I get it often from men who do not know they are speaking to a Canadian. I get it on every hand, even from other Colonials, given grudgingly but nevertheless sincerely. Not only as to their high fighting qualities, but also their splendid discipline, their unvarying cheerfulness and willingness to do anything or go anywhere, just to be courteous and uphold the honour of Canada.

Lurking in the back of our mind at all times was the query, "Are you playing the game?" We had been in the militia for nine years before enlisting for overseas. We had personally enlisted first a platoon, then a company of our fellow men and had trained them. That is, trained them in the accepted methods of the day, although how far outdated we did not know. Then here we were, not in the trenches as should have been, but in a cushy job on staff. Usually we slept in a comfortable bed, messed with interesting gentlemen we would never have met if we had been allowed to go with the boys. Had a motor car for our own use, was seeing France and Belgium as few, even much senior officers, even generals, ever had a chance to see these countries. While nearly every day there was a chance that a shell would get us, still our chance of survival was infinitely better than others of our now extinct battalion. In such times as this it was a great uplift when a letter arrived from the woman at home. So we gave thanks.

France

13–1–18

Dearest:

A pleasant surprise today when I received another letter from you, this dated Dec. 16. And Dearie I thank you very much for the inspiration and encouragement it contains. Your words make me see clearly that this opportunity open to me means that I am doing something really worth while. Something that is being recognized more and more every day as of vital importance. At a stroke of the pen yesterday my scope of work and size of command was more than doubled. I am a sort of visiting Director just now. Imperative orders have gone out to formations and units from the largest to smallest in the Army that this work must be done, so I am going from place to place. To Corps, Divisions, Brigades, Schools and other places telling what line they must take, what to do and how to do it. Getting gardeners appointed. Selecting and inspecting land, and many other things. There is no use me considering taking leave for quite a long time. All this organization must be put in motion before I go away for a day. This is my chance to satisfy myself that I am as much use here as I could be fighting in the trenches.

A Ton of Garden Seed

REMEMBER, 2240 pounds, not 2000 pounds. Usually the difference is not noticed by Canadians, but when it means an extra 240 pounds of such seed as carrots, cabbage, cauliflower, beets, and leeks it is a lot. We sent a lorry to Paris for most of this seed, as it was deemed wise to use French seed on French land. Our plans called for five million cabbages, just as a sample, and most of the seed for these plants was in the ground late in February. In spite of it being warmer as a whole in northern France than in Western Canada, most vegetables would not ripen more than at home. For instance, tomatoes would not ripen outdoors, nor corn. We were even planting gardens up in the actual front areas, where we could only spade the land by hand and in the dark of the night. The Germans had done a lot of this on Messines Ridge while they held it. When our troops took this land they reaped what the Hun had sown, but reaped it within machine-gun range. Imagine going out to gather carrots in a machine gun-swept field. Yet they did just that. We were finding out just how important fresh vegetables were to man. When we had time to pause and think, we remembered that our earliest history of man was when the Almighty placed him in a garden.

We were finding that our Canadian officers were much better fitted for this type of work than the Englishman. Our type of life, our very existence in taming Canada had developed a race of drivers. The old country man took all things at an easier tempo. Sometimes it made us boil when we found plows and teams idle. Often it was our duty to strafe a colonel or lieutenant colonel or maybe a nobleman, but being gentlemen they took it in good part. Every evening whenever possible Major Cotton and ourself had a conference. Cotton would just laugh when we unloaded our troubles, but he himself was a driver. A driver in more ways than one. A motor salesman at home, he was as excited as a boy at the arrival of our first two farm tractors and plows. International Harvester Company Moguls. The plows were made in Canada. The English spell it ploughs, always. General Lord Radnor came to see us every week, then spent much of his time telling AOs in the other Armies what we were doing, and this created a race to see who could plow the most acres.

General Radnor himself as the Earl of Folkestone was a large farmer in England. He had two thousand acres under cultivation. As is usual, this land was rented and divided into many farms.

France
27–2–18

Dearest:
Yesterday I was out at Army Farm A when the General and Cotton rolled up. Had to go around the farm with them. We reached there at an unlucky hour, as we found two tractors stuck in a mud hole as they were crossing from one field to another. A shell had just spoiled the bridge. So we all had to give a lift, and soon they were out and started once more on the new field. We found Doctor Monkman's grave near the centre of one of the farms [Captain Monkman,[55]* *3rd CMRs, buried on Hill 63]. So you see we are farming on historic ground [Ploegsteert]. In one of the old gardens of a farmstead that has disappeared to the last brick, I found a lot of bulbs just bursting through the ground, and a strawberry bed still struggling to live among the grass, old tins, shell cases, barbed wire and all the debris of battle. It will be fine if we can restore one or two of these old gardens. What a joy it would be to come back to restored farms and gardens even if the buildings are all gone.*

Just now I have on one farm a Scotch Labour Company. I had lunch with them today. The Captain is a very jolly chap and, as usual, has a wonderful idea of the ability of his Scotties to do any sort of job, from building rail-ways to stealing, no, securing things of interest as souvenirs. His definition of a good Scotchman is a man who takes cheerfully what God gives him, and everything else he can lay hands on.

Pigs

YES, PIGS OF COURSE. It is just natural to have pigs on a farm. Therefore pigs it is. We were thankful that this was not our particular chore. Just overall supervision and help where needed. GHQ had decided to imitate the enemy, who were making quite a success in raising pigs with feed from the leavings of the army messes. So here was work for still another Canadian. Major Grieve,[56] 110 Bn., arrived at our headquarters to take charge of this operation. Grieve is a stock breeder from Guelph and he has been commissioned to look into the idea of the Army raising five thousand pigs a year. Some job, but if the Army wants this done they have gone the right way about it by putting a Canadian in charge.

With March had come an uneasy feeling. It was well known that the enemy was building up for one more grand offensive. When and where the attack would come was anyone's guess. We thought we were ready and capable of holding, strike where he might. How badly we were deceived.

France

1–3–18

Dearest:

Tonight there is a steady roar and rumble from the line. The heaviest we have heard for months and all the horizon is lit with star shells. Maybe a

This was very fine, but we hoped we would all be home in Canada before the fruit trees came into bearing once more. General Plumer had put new life into the Italian Army and now, supported by a few British troops, the revived Army of Italy was steadily pushing the Austrians up and over the Alps. In fact it was not to be long before the first real break in the war was to come with Austria suing for peace terms.

Once more the 2nd Army was taking over the northern flank of the British Armies and the 4th Army was being disbanded. But even that was not to be for long. Under the 4th Army, with General Holman as Quartermaster General, the Agriculture Department had made great strides and was now firmly established. We were to miss our good friend Major Cotton, but we found that the man who took his place was also keenly interested in having fresh vegetables to feed the troops. We were therefore to receive the same whole-hearted support from Major Guerney, who took Cotton's place.

France

8–2–18

Dearest:

Tomorrow I am going to GHQ with Major Grieve, he to discuss pigs and I agriculture. Hope it is a nice day as it is quite a long run. About sixty miles there, then if possible have lunch at the Canadian Base Depot.

I notice in a Canadian paper that hogs are worth about eighteen cents a pound live weight. Well, here in France they are selling for forty cents a pound. So if Major Grieve can raise fifteen thousand pigs as the Quartermaster

Peasant house at sunset—A French postcard that John purchased in early 1918. On the back of it he has written, "Not an unusual scene in these parts" and dated it 24–2–18, at which time he was stationed in Cassel, France.

General thinks he can, from the waste from the troops, he will be making a big saving.

We expected to have Horatio Bottomley[57] [of John Bull] to lunch with us on Sunday, but his lecture has been postponed. He ought to be a very interesting person. He is a great power in England just now.

France
10–3–18

Dearest:
I wish I could tell you of all I saw and felt and thought, in and of this day's journey. This afternoon I stood at Dr. Monkman's grave side. I had told Lieutenant Monod [Interpreter] about where it was and he located it and, finding it in a deplorable condition, he took two men up and cut away the weeds and grass, banked up the grave and planted some bulbs. Now the snowdrops are forming a white coverlet. Was that not thoughtful of Monod? Beside the Doctor lie Sergeant Major Bloomer, Sergeant McCarthy and Trumpeter Bumford, and four or five other 3rd CMR boys all killed the

same day. A great shell had destroyed the next graves, missing those of the Doctor and his comrades by only two feet. And while I stood there this afternoon, four Australian boys were buried only a few yards away. And every few minutes the earth would rock as a monster, but a few rods away, hurled death and destruction into the Hun lines. We were so close to this gun we felt the blast, being directly in front. Over a bit, a steady rain of Hun shells were bursting. It was not a health resort by any means. Just the same, I am going to have that Canadian Cemetery put in order if I have to do it myself.

But enough of the horrors of war. Let me paint yet another story. Sunday it is today and not two miles from the last scene is a very pretty village, knocked about a bit, but still the people live there. Men, women and children. These people carry on as if the Hun was a hundred miles away instead of four. Today everyone is dressed in their Sunday best, and well dressed. Kiddies played about on the street or grass. Boys were playing marbles, girls skipping or wheeling dolls, older girls chatting with English, Australian and American soldiers. Women were sitting out in front of their homes in groups visiting neighbours. A few French and Belgian soldiers [no doubt on leave] walking arm in arm or with arm around the waist of their lady love. Laughter and song everywhere. Can you imagine such a contrast? This is the land where the distance is very short between peace and war, birth and death, horror and happiness, the song of children at play and the whistle of death-dealing shrapnel. May the time soon come when the pleasant side will always be uppermost and the other side disappear forever.

Goodnight Dearie.

Before the Storm

AN UNEASY CALM had settled over the land. The weather was good and crops were growing apace. There was a clamour for seed. We were thinking of seed instead of shells. Everyone wanted to plant at once, so the office was busy weighing out seed. Ten thousand packets were being packaged as fast as two experienced men could handle the requests.

Meanwhile, something kept urging us to get up near the front line. We talked to Corps Commanders and those of Division and Brigade. We talked of gardens, as that was our excuse for being far forward, but inevitably the talk turned to the coming offensive. We knew it was coming, but where?

Another trip south along the Bapaume Road and through Albert. There was something fascinating about driving past the cathedral and under the leaning Virgin Tower. We were not Catholic, nevertheless we were tempted to make the sign of the cross as we passed underneath. We hoped that the belief of those who were Catholic would hold good. As long as the Virgin could reach out to give her blessing, all was well with France.

Our Major Wheatley had been Town Major of Albert for near two years and never had a casualty among soldiers in all that time. The Hun was methodical in his shelling. A certain section of the town one day, then

119

passing to another section the following day. Wheatley had studied the pattern of the shelling, and no soldier was quartered in the section to be shelled that day. For this fine work he was awarded the Distinguished Service Order.

France

15–3–18

Dearest:

Have been out all day as usual, visiting Corps farms up forward. One Corps [10th] has a lovely garden for forcing beds. It is in an old walled garden belonging to a fine old chateau. The wall is intact, built of bricks, ten feet high and about one hundred and fifty yards square. This garden has run wild for three years and was a mass of weeds and rubbish. It has now been cleaned out, dug and made into beds, hotbeds made, fruit trees pruned and strawberry beds weeded. In fact, a wonderful transformation has taken place. A month has made a great change. You know, it is a great pleasure to help restore these old gardens. They are nicely laid out and you know I always did love a well-kept garden. I look forward to seeing these old places in full bloom once more. The men who are in charge of this garden were very proud when showing me around, and it certainly is a credit to them. They are two old Englishmen. [This was Col. Pritchard's work.] At another Corps garden I saw some fine hotbeds with cabbage plants coming on fine. These gardens are where plants will be grown to distribute around among hundreds of gardens in each Corps and for each Corps farm. Then I have big nursery beds on the Army farms. The original intention was that I should have all the forcing beds at one place, but when the demand for plants mounted up into the millions and I got studying the transportation ques-tion I decided it was the wrong idea, so then decided to get around and encourage and help others to start beds.

And very lucky we did just that, as the next few weeks demonstrated.

I have a fine lot of gardeners and farmers among my men, over a Company of them now, drawn from various units and attached for the season. My next effort will be to have these all transferred to one company under my

Canadian Cavalry ploughing and harrowing ground on Vimy Ridge where potatoes and other crops are to be planted, April 1918. Source: Library and Archives Canada, PA–003811.

charge and called an Agriculture Company, with one of my officers in command. You may not understand, but I am not a Commanding Officer. I have no power to discipline any man. I only administrate. I give general directions to all agriculturists in the Army, assist in every way and lay down the policy to be followed, but the executive power lies with the officers of the unit. Army Headquarters is a group of heads of departments, many with similar powers, some more, some less.

France
19–3–18

Dearest:
Yesterday I had tea with my old friends Colonel Harrison DSO, and Captain Brown [116 Bn.]. They had a great time at Nice. Brown got into a little card game with some Monte Carlo card sharps and cleaned them to the tune of six thousand francs, so after having a real good time he came home six hundred dollars to the good.

Wheatley sits across at his table facing me and seems always to be talking on the phone. He seems to delight in work, and can get things from Ordnance and the Royal Engineers and everyone else in a most surprising fashion. He blesses and curses people of all ranks in the same breath and no one ever takes offence or refuses his requests. I could never do what he does in his line, and he is quite content to sit at his desk all day.

Yesterday I had to take shelter [a shell hole] when one of the farms and one of our tractors had a close call. Shrapnel dented the fenders.

I am trying to write, and listen to two people talking, answer telephone calls, and the typewriter is clicking, so if there are many mistakes you will know the reason. We get all sorts of advice on agriculture and each expects we will follow his directions. But I set tight and watch the French farmer, he ought to know. Now I will close, having given all the news and that is not much.

Bye. John.

The Storm

France
23–3–18

Dearest:
Just a line this evening, although I am hardly in the right mood for writing, as I have just come in from the land of hell and destruction, and some of the sights are enough to make one too sad to write.

The worst of all are the little children, their scared faces seem to haunt me, and the drawn haggard faces of the mothers tramping along a road, a babe in arms, another clinging to her skirts, and her worldly goods tied up in a bundle. Or maybe she pushes a wheel barrow piled high with her treasures and a baby on top. A straggling line of women, children and old men wandering along a road, back maybe out of danger line, but with nowhere seeming to go. Dull, listless, heavy-eyed, looking back towards homes they have clung to through nearly four years of Hell and have to leave them after all. Sad, so sad. Oh, how glad I am that you and our boys are far, far away from this land that is so beautiful one day and a wilderness the next. One thing I noticed that made me glad, that was our Tommies helping the women and children. I saw them carrying babies, bundles, and laughing and chatting and trying to cheer the poor beings. Such things as these will not be forgotten easily. Oh, how these people have suffered. They have given their husbands and sons and now their homes. Yet they try to smile through their tears and they will find new homes and start anew without a grumble. But they will never forget or forgive the Hun, they or their children or their children's children.

Now I must close for tonight. Bye Bye Love. Kiss Daddy's boys for him and keep them safe and pray that they may never hear the rumble of cannon rolling along paved roads, or the break of shrapnel, or any of the sad things I have seen today.

With Love.

Alas, our prayers were not answered, at least not as we hoped. Our three sons, and one not yet born, were to hear the rumble of guns over the cobblestones of Europe. Yes, and drive their tanks over those self same roads and fly an aeroplane and drop deadly bombs. Now we can only pray that their sons never hear the rumble of guns over cobblestones.

The 23 of March 1918 will long be remembered even in a land that has seen war for generations. At last the great German offensive[58] had been launched, and maybe at the weakest point of the whole line that stretched from Ostend to the Alps. Right at the junction of the British and French Armies. We know now what their orders were, and no doubt they were good. "Smash a hole in the Allied line, cut the French from the English, and never stop until you have the Channel ports." And oh, how close those Hun Divisions came to reaching their objective.

For our own part we only saw the ruck of war as it affected the civilian population. It was not one grand smash and go through. British and French troops went back, it is true, back before overwhelming odds. But back stubbornly and steadily, fighting every inch of the way, and the Allies were not parted. Back they went, yet took time to push the civilian population back behind them. Hardly a civilian was taken, but their homes were gone. That which they had clung to through more than three hellish years was gone. Homes, possessions, treasures, stock, and crops. This was to be our first, but not our last, experience of whole peoples driven from their homes.

Before the Hun advance was stopped, the British 5th Army was nearly annihilated, never to be re-organized. General Lord Rawlinson was recalled from Paris, and when the line was re-established it was as the 4th Army, and a British Army Commander went home discredited. We who were at Headquarters mostly disagree with the general verdict as to who was to blame.

In the ten days that followed, we in the north were to see one continual column of troops moving southward. Every available unit—divisions, brigades, and battalions—was sent to help the hard-stricken southern Army. We knew only too well that in the north we were holding the line with a corporals' guard and artillery. Thank God for the guns and the shells that Winston Churchill with his amazing driving power had made available to us. Without those guns, our part of the line could have been pierced at any point the Hun launched an attack. But also thanks to our gallant air force—more than fifty per cent Canadian—they kept the Hun from knowing just how far-stretched our men were along our side of the line.

But the guns were not all on our side. Fritz had them and apparently unlimited shells and big ones. The depth of the shelling had increased greatly, and roads that had been comparatively safe were now a hazard. The reason, as we well knew, was to keep down movement of troops. Our farm supervising fell off, yet all were busy. Mayor Guerney found many duties that took us to all points along the line. There were just not enough dispatch riders available to carry all the increased number of messages, so we were detailed for this work. You see, our work had given us a knowledge of the country, the main roads, and the byways as had few officers in the Army, so in time of need we were used and used freely. Nothing could have pleased us better. We were seeing the staff work at its best. The shifting of hundreds of thousands of troops, guns, batteries by the score, food convoys and ammunition columns crowding every available road, and all working smoothly. And we were helping. For the moment we were not farmers, we were soldiers and oft-times under fire. We learned to jump for the ditch and did not look for a dry one, just anywhere below ordinary ground level.

The work still went on at Army Farm A up on Messines Ridge, but would it last? Would our part of the line hold? Seed potatoes were arriving. A whole train load came up. Would we unload? Yes. Seed time and harvest await not the wishes of man. Five hundred acres were ready for planting. Planting underneath a rain of hell fire such as had never before filled the sky anywhere on earth.

France
26–3–18

Dearest:
Well, by all appearances the war has at last commenced after nearly four years preliminary canter. How I wish I could write all I would like at a time like this when one might be able to make a letter worth reading, if allowed a free hand and could give opinions on various subjects. I sit down thinking and feeling like writing. Then I must remember that I am honour bound to say nothing on military subjects, and everything is military. So while the climax of the greatest drama in history is being enacted within sight and hearing, I must write and give the old greeting. I am well. Hope you are well.

Goodbye.

We had a hard day that had started at midnight, and we hoped to have lunch at Bailleul at the Officers' Mess. A military policeman stopped us as we neared the main square.

"Best not go through the centre of town, Sir. The Hun is giving it hell."

Actually we were in sight of the Town Hall, that stately old structure that was credited to the Spanish time of occupation of Flanders. A magnificent building that had withstood the winds and storms of centuries. Fierce overhead, and not very high overhead, screamed a shell and buried itself in the very centre of the wall of that ancient building, another, and still another. A landmark of generations crumbled before our very eyes in a vast cloud of dust. We did not envy Sir Parry Price his job of Town Major.

We found the road again and drove the two miles to Meteren, where Colonel Burbeck was Area Commandant. We had lived in this old village for three months and were worried about old friends. We found them carrying on as if the war was a hundred miles away. We were back in our own billet for tea when Majors Wilkin and Bloxom came along. They had been spending a few days with their old battalion, now turned into the 8th Canadian Railway Troops and under the command of that old pioneer and builder, Colonel Jim Cornwall.[59] What Jim Cornwall did not know about military drill would fill many volumes, but on the other side of the ledger, no man anywhere knew more about the job he was at than that old scout, trader, pioneer, and builder from the Peace River country.

France

27–3–18

Dearest:

The signal to take cover is going. But the best thing I always think is to keep working. Inside a building only a direct hit will get one, and few of these cellars would protect from a direct hit. Of course if they should shell us heavy, I would go to a dugout or leave town. Best thing is to have duty elsewhere. I can always find something to do up the line, and these days up the line is safer than in the back town areas.

I must admit, when I hear shrapnel whizzing, my hair stands on end, and how these inhabitants stand it is a wonder to me. While I feel like ducking, they stand quietly at their doors, children continue to play at their games while Mothers discuss where the last shell fell. How would you like our boys to be playing on the latest brick dust pile, which was but a few hours ago a house, while you wait for the next shell to burst?

Bye.

The Portuguese Ran Away and Saved the British Army

France
9–4–18

Dearest:
This is a dull heavy day with a light ground fog, rather bad as our airmen will not be able to watch the Hun during his attack. It is not far from us this time but maybe only a local affair, but the guns are making a fearful noise. They opened up with a crash at six this morning and are hard at it yet. Was down quite close, but could get no information. More than this I cannot say, although it would be interesting to you.

Thirty and eight years have passed and although we are a voluminous reader, we have yet to see the story in print of what we failed to tell our wife of that morning's drive. Yet it was one of the most dramatic events of World War I.

Let us lay the background before we tell the story.

The great German offensive of the spring of '18 was still in progress. The German Army had not broken the Allied line, although that line was stretched to the uttermost. Away south of the Somme, the British and

French Armies were struggling desperately to hold contact with each other. They had been forced back and back until the ancient city of Amiens was nearly in the front line. Still, Generalissimo Foch[60] refused to commit all the French reserves and thereby, as history afterwards revealed, proved his right to be called a great general. The burden of holding the bulging line fell on the British Armies. The northern armies, the 2nd and 1st, Plumer's and Horne's, had been depleted until a battalion was holding a brigade frontage, a division a corps frontage. All available troops of every description were hurried southward to help stabilize the southern bulge. Even all these might not have been enough, except for something that the English press passed without hardly a word. Why, we have often wondered. Perhaps the reason could be grasped if one studied a little incident, a short dialogue, that took place within K Mess of 2nd Army Headquarters there on that round hill on Flanders fields in the town of Cassel. We as a member of that mess had listened to many interesting discussions between the various mess members who were gathered from the far-flung parts of the Empire.

Breakfast was early. We were nearly finished when the Hun barrage opened with a roar that startled us, although miles away. We knew and had discussed the orders of the day. The 2nd Army was to take over a large slice of the 1st Army frontage. The 1st Army was to sidestep southward to take care of the extended line caused by the great bulge that now rested on Amiens. General Plumer had issued certain orders for the withdrawal of certain troops and this was under discussion. Keep in mind, we were Army. We knew ahead of time about movements of formations, knew even before the orders reached Corps or Division generals.

Said one officer, "General Plumer knew better than to trust part of his line to those cowardly Portuguese."

Another officer, a major from the Indian Army, was on his feet at once. "You have no right to accuse England's oldest ally[61] of being cowardly." Then they went at it hammer and tongs. This was the only row we ever saw in an English Army mess. In fact, these two officers never again were friends.

England's oldest ally. This was true. This in fact was the reason of Portugal's army being on the Western Front.

We took no part in this discussion, yet we were to be the only one of that group that saw with our own eyes the climax of the argument that parted old friends. That evening we were to tell our comrades the dramatic story. The first officer who had spoken might well have said, "I told you so," but he was a gentleman.

Hardly was this argument over when we had a call from Q: "Hughes, we have lost contact with the 10th Heavy Lorry Park. They are somewhere down Merville way. Get down there and try to locate them. We need them to move ammunition from X point to Y point. Report in by phone when you locate them."

On the hilltop the visibility was fair, down on the plain it was next to nil. Yet we crept southward. Somewhere east of Hazebrouck we ran out of the fog and into the Portuguese Army. Army? No, that is not the right word, just say Portuguese. Have any of you ever seen an army in flight, on the run? No? Again, run is not the word, they were walking. And again, it was not an army, it was just men walking across country. They were not following the roads. Their eyes were looking westwards, towards the sea. They had no rifles. They had thrown them away, no doubt they hampered this cross-country walk.

"Look," said my driver. We looked. We saw two officers riding one mule, one small mule. As far as we could see, the land was covered with men of the Portuguese one-time Army. It is something we hope never to see again, an army broken and in flight. We were to see another army, our own British Army, in retreat the very next day, but oh, what a difference. Never is the British Army more magnificent, more dangerous to the enemy, than when in retreat, but that is another chapter.

We found our lorries. They were not lost. They were just played out and had pulled to the side of the road for a few hours to rest and sleep. They had been on the move for a full week without a moment's respite. They were loading ammunition when we left them. Then, again, we ran through the remnants of an army in flight. Whether it is true or not, we were told that the British Cavalry were used to round them up and guide them to a camp between Boulogne and Calais. This may have been only a rumour, but we do know that we later passed this camp, a barbed wire-enclosed camp, and we were sorry. Nevertheless, let us tell more of the story. All did not run. Certain units of this same Portuguese Army stayed and died to a man, rather than disgrace their country's flag. Once more, let us add, the English press did not carry this story, for you see Portugal was England's oldest ally.

What is the real story behind this, we do not know. We only know that the Portuguese were to be withdrawn from the line that day. We also know that troops are at their lowest ebb at the moment of withdrawal. After a long period of extreme tension when facing the enemy, the orders came to withdraw. Man had lived through a hell, now he was going for a rest. At that moment he is not dependable, he has done his stint of fighting, he has earned a respite, let's get moving.

Now turn back to the heading of this chapter.

This statement was made by a general on General Plumer's staff, the day this happened. Keep in mind that at that time he was more or less guessing, the battle was still in full swing, and no one knew the outcome. This general gave his reasoning in this manner.

Prince Rupprecht of Bavaria, General-in-Chief of the German Armies of the north, had gathered every available division of his army that he could spare, to send south to make the final grand push and capture the Channel ports. Somehow from somewhere he got word that the Portuguese would be withdrawn on the early morning of April 9th. He knew what we have said about the condition of troops about to leave the line. He turned every gun for miles up and down the line on that small sector. The Portuguese did not wait for their replacements in the front line. They just left, and left in a hurry. A hole, four miles wide, was left in our line. Prince Rupprecht of Bavaria saw a chance to do for himself what other German generals had failed to do. He poured all these divisions, that should have gone south, through this hole. Our general used the old slogan, "United we stand, divided we fall." Then he went on, "We can close this gap. We can hold him. Our Army in the south just could not have withstood those extra twenty Hun divisions. The Portuguese have run away, we are safe."[62]

We are not a historian. We do not know the facts. All we report is the day-to-day happenings as memories are revived by old, now mouse-eaten letters.

Refugees

France
12–4–18

Dearest:
My pencil is too weak to tell you all I have seen and heard the last thirty-six hours. Weeks before this reaches you, you will know.

14–4–18

I just started to write a note to you two days ago when I was called to carry dispatches, and this is the first quiet moment I have had since. Things are a little more settled, although the Great Battle is still raging now only a few miles away. From my window I watch the flash of guns. The flashes run up and down the line without ceasing. From my present billet window I can see fifteen miles of the line. But to go back to the first day of the fight, as I know you like to follow me from day to day. I will tell all I can leaving out names, places and units. The morning of the 9th, when the great show for us opened, dawned with a heavy fog over all the land. Just the wrong sort of day for us, as our planes could not work. All day the fog hung heavy, and the guns roared all day from early dawn. Although not yet on our Army *front, we were anxious, because we knew it was on the one weak place on the Northern line. Reports were coming slow, though by evening we knew there was a big dent in the line. I had duty down that way, and got down near the swaying line. On account of the fog we could not know whether it was a local thrust, or a main offensive to draw our troops from the South. And no doubt not till the war is over will we know what took place behind the Hun line. There is no doubt his troops were massed to attack miles further south and then, on account of his initial success in the fog, suddenly decided to shift his offensive Northward, or was it all arranged beforehand? We each give our own opinion on the subject, but many a day will pass before we are sure what happened. We only know that the pressure got stronger and stronger and certain units had to fall back to close the gap made by certain people retiring.*

As has been told, it was the Portuguese army that (to give it the best face possible) "retired."

Early in the morning of the 10th I started for the Army farm. As you know, it is only a few miles from the old front line, to be exact it is three miles. Going up, I stopped at my old billet in [Meteren] to see Colonel Burbeck, Area Commandant. He told me that Major Bromley-Martin, Major Rowan and the staffs of the Corps and Army farms had just passed through. They had left at one a.m. and marched all night. All non-combatant troops had been ordered to retire. I turned in the direction they were marching, met them and went on with them to where they were to billet. Then, taking two of the tractor drivers in the car with me, we turned about and made back for the farm. On account of the heavy shell fire we had to go by a round about route. Reaching one side of the farm, we had to leave the car in a quiet sector and go forward on foot. The shells were coming fairly fast, but we found a road that we thought was fairly safe to use and got to within five hundred yards of the tractors, but no further. Fritz must have spotted the tractors and thought them guns, as he was churning the ground all around them. I saw it was useless to try and remove them, so we went back and tried to reach the camp, but it was also being shelled. So all our implements, tools and seeds were left, and are still there.

We could see the big pile of seed potatoes, and at that moment the German troops had not reached them but they were just across the road, as we were soon to know. We started back, our car driver, our two tractor drivers and ourself. There were two roads not far apart and these were receiving a perfect hail of shells, so we kept to a path we knew near the centre of the field. We had not gone far when Bothwick said, "Look over to the left, Sir." We looked. Not more than five hundred yards away was a line of grey-coated soldiers, travelling parallel to ourself. "To the right, Sir." Again the same sight. Lucky for us the path we were following was along the low marshy land by the Douve River, for had those grey-coated lines met we would have gone to Germany. Lucky also for us, about that time the New Zealanders came up. For a few minutes we were in no-man's-land. Then the men from Down Under charged. We did not see the end of the fight, but later we were to know that gallant New Zealanders not only held that line all day but pushed the Hun back.

There the line, although bent back a bit, still holds and the farm tonight is still in our hands. That night was anxious again, but what must it have been for the poor civilians turned out of their homes by the advancing foe. In no case were any of them allowed to be captured. All were given warning to get away, and made to get away. Much of this was our work.

We came to one farm home and the lady flatly refused to move, although the front was even then only a half mile away. She was determined she would stay. In the first weeks of the war the German cavalry had swept through this area and according to her had done little damage. A GS wagon was brought up and she was ordered to get the children loaded. Still she protested. "I slept with a German in 1914 and I can do it again," and she smiled at a fair-headed little boy of three who clung to her skirts. No more time was wasted, time was running out, troops were already in her fields. She and her children and nothing else were placed in the GS wagon, and her long trek to a less wrathful land had begun. Looking back from the next rise she saw her house, her barns, and all she possessed in flames. Our doing or that of the Hun, we do not know, but we do know we left a scorched land behind.

We had managed to get back to our car unscathed, but would we get it out of the pocket in which it was hidden without being seen? We did. Just ten minutes later, a shell landed right there.

Right near was a battery of 60-pounders. We stopped to speak to the captain in charge. We were telling about the great pile of seed potatoes that the Germans could now use for food.

"Can you pinpoint that pile of potatoes on the map?" he asked.

"Yes," we replied, and did.

Came a few quick snapping orders and that battery was hurling shells eastwards. After a few minutes came the order, "Cease firing."

"There you are," said the battery commander. "If the Huns want to use those potatoes, they are already mashed."

Still the fog hung low and the pressure grew heavier and heavier. The 11th I spent mostly in getting our men placed on some farms further back and helping refugees. Some of our men helped in digging new trenches and some loading ammunition. Bromley-Martin and ten men are to run a refugee camp.

At a railhead near Hazebrouck we placed twenty thousand refugees on trains in twenty-four hours. A train would back into the siding and we herded the people aboard, women and younger children inside the coaches, or more often freight cars, older children and men on top of cars. Packed like sardines, with all the gear they had rescued piled in with them. Then the train pulled out and another backed in. All day and all night this went on. Where they were going we did not know.

Oh, Dearie, the sights I saw that day and every day since are too sad to write about. The roads for miles were crowded with the poor people, mostly women and children and old men. The blind, the halt and the lame, men and women tottering with old age, children everywhere, wagons, carts, traps, wheelbarrows, baby carriages, piled high with all these poor people could save. Cattle, hogs and poultry, every road lined with them. Oh, the poor wretches, women with eyes that showed that they had not slept for days, but dry-eyed and brave. Not looking back much. They knew their homes were gone forever. They had come out of a perfect hell of shells, gas and smoke, and a wall of fire behind told of the work of a lifetime gone in a few short hours. That was our most anxious night. The next morning, our troops pouring forward told us the line must hold no matter how bad the dent. Unless Fritz can break our line, cut our communications and drive us out of France, he cannot win. Mere ground or trenches have ceased to be of vital importance. This is the final battle, the test of giants. He who can keep his reserves till the other is weak, wins.

Generalissimo Foch did just that, and won. All, or nearly all, of Army Headquarters went back to a safer zone.

I remained here to attend to forward work and to do anything the Army wanted of me. It was three in the morning when I got to bed. Lucky I was to be able to have a bed, when so many thousands have known no bed or sleep for days. That evening at dark found me just at the city of ruins [Ypres], where I had to go on my rounds to see how the Corps chaps were preparing to retire. All was quiet as yet on that sector. Coming back I worked south, and ran almost into the ruck of battle.

We were told that our new line was only a hundred yards away. This was near Dickebusch and they were already burning the Signal Training School at Ouderdorm. Thousands of signal rockets were being destroyed, and they lit up the sky in the most wonderful display of coloured lights we ever saw. Anything fired off by cities as fireworks we have ever seen was a mere drop in the bucket in comparison to that wonderful display. We wondered what Fritz thought.

I was stopped by a Medical Officer and asked to take a poor old paralyzed man of 88 years away. The village had just been forcibly evacuated, and this old man had apparently been forgotten. Naturally I could not do otherwise than as requested. The MO told me to turn the old man over to the hospital in the next village. That was an hour I never forgot. The crowds of poor refugees on the roads, guns and men coming up, a village in flames behind us, and creeping along a bad third-class road with this poor old paralyzed man in the car.

First, just outside the village we came to a block in the road. We were halted and an officer came forward wanting to know how in hell an Army car could be in the front line.

"What front line?" we asked.

"This is the new front line," he replied.

Yes. It was Winston Churchill's new front line. Guns, guns, guns, and more guns. Eighteen-pounders locked wheel to wheel, and a second line of guns with noses poked between the guns in front. A solid line of steel as far on either side of the road as we could see through the gloam. Every gun loaded and sighted for point-blank range. Later we learned that this line stretched for miles. They had taken the Guards' slogan, "They shall not pass." They did not pass.

At the next village I found the hospital all packed up and on the move, and I must again work backward along the crowded road to the next village, where I was told the next Casualty Clearing Station would take in the old man, only to find the CCS also on the move. Now we were on a wide road and clear to the thick of the refugees. At the next town [Steenvoorde] I was to see the only mean, disgraceful thing I have seen done by these people of France. It was now late at night and I went to the police [civilian] office to see who would care for our passenger. They took me around to the Mayor's office and house. The Mayor was in bed and the policeman dare not waken him, but I did. I rang his bell as it had never been rung before, and this brought the Mayor to the window, but he refused to let us in. Said it was too late. Now my French consists of about a dozen words, but I told that man what I thought of him in language he understood. I even threatened to sit the old man on his doorstep to lie there until he took charge of him, but the policeman, who was a gentleman, said he would try and get the old man taken in at one of the estaminets.[63] After a couple of tries we found a kind old couple who gladly undertook to look after the old cripple. I left him sitting before a glowing fire. I hope that town will escape bombardment, but if it does not, my hope is that a fifteen-inch shell lands first crack on that Mayor's house and blows it to atoms. Remember, this is the only instance like this I have seen. I have seen thousands of poor refugees crowding back. The people of every home in the safe areas welcome them in, and every house is crowded to the limit.

After I got back here I had something to eat, then going into the square I found a lot of wounded who had been able to walk that far back. Every man who can walk although wounded in a time like this, walks as far as he can after receiving first aid and dressing. Some were in an exhausted condition, so I rang for the car again and until two o'clock drove wounded men to the CCS[64] four miles further back. They all told the same story as has been told in the newspapers every day of late. How the Boche came on in wave after wave, and how they were mown down by rifle shells and machine gun fire. Yet still other waves came on, sheer weight of numbers. How long can he pay such an awful cost? He plays our game by this destroying himself without gaining any material advantage for himself.

One lad in the car going to the CCS was very sick. He seemed to be trying to throw his insides out. We asked him where he was wounded. He said he was not wounded, only sick. "I have killed so many men this day I am sick with the blood I have spilled. They came on in waves," he said. "We mowed them down. There was a great pile of them in front of our machine guns. We had to fall back and get a new position. Again and again they came on. They died, oh how they died by the hundreds. Oh my God, I will never forget those dead," and he was sick again.

At the CCS the surgeons were working by the light of barn lanterns. Their once-white coveralls were as gory as a butcher's in a slaughter house. They were near dead on their feet, still they carried on. The CCS had been moved three times in twenty-four hours. We laid the men in rows and they could watch the surgeons operating on tables that dripped blood. The smell of human blood is sickening. A lad with a shattered arm was told by an orderly to come to the operating table, and the orderly offered him a cigarette. "Give it to Doc," said the lad, "he needs it more than I do."

We had sent a detail of six men and a GS wagon to help at #15 CCS down near Hazebrouck. We went down to see how they were faring. The corporal in charge came to us with tears in his eyes and begged to be relieved of his work. "Sir," he said, "it is not so bad hauling dead men out and burying them. But this hauling wagon loads of arms and legs is horrible."

We managed to get our boys relieved. Yet we knew someone had to do this gruesome work. Thousands passed through this CCS during those dark dismal days.

The morning of the 12th I was on duty in Q Office at seven-thirty, then carried dispatches till after dark. I covered the frontage twice over. Sometimes up on roads that were under heavy shell fire, then back to meet units coming up. My last duty was to go twelve miles to intercept a lorry column moving from [Lumbres] to [Merville], turn thirty lorries about and take them back six miles to unload a train of ammunition and start a reserve dump.

Another day and five thousand bushels of seed potatoes would have been unloaded at Army Farm A and lost. Today I got track of the trucks and found them well back in safety. One set of Corps tools and Army farm tools are lost. The remainder were brought back and are now on a quiet front. I am the only one of our mess remaining here at [Cassel].

No officer in the Army knew this land better than we ourself. We had crossed and criss-crossed it a hundred times, by car on the roads, by horse-back on the byways and lanes, on foot across fields and ditches. We knew the towns and villages and, more than that, we knew the people. Scores we could call by name and we were welcome everywhere. But now we had to tell these friends to go. Go, leave your homes, not tomorrow, but right now. A low-flying shell would whistle over, lending emphasis to our words. They went, and we thanked God that this was not Canada.

The Guards Come Up

WE HAD SEEN A COUNTRY ON FIRE. Many times we have seen prairie fires that stretched for miles. Also in our early days in the West during threshing season the usual practice was to burn the straw piles as soon as the threshing machine left the setting. At night a circle of fires would light the whole horizon. It was just straw burning, yet it was a spectacle to watch, but nothing to worry about. During those first two weeks in April 1918 we watched a whole countryside on fire. From our Headquarters on Cassel hill we had a wonderful view of the surrounding Flanders plain. Flanders stretches far south into France. From our view-point we could count three cities, ten towns, innumerable villages, and hundreds of farm homes on fire. We did not know if we had burnt them, or the Hun, all we knew was that they were in flames. From the break-through point south of Armentières, the German thrust had seemed to be headed for Hazebrouck. They reached Merville and still came on. Our numbers were just too few to stop them. Then the Guards came up.

The Guards Division and the First Australian Division formed a line right across the German main line of advance. The line was one we had travelled many, many times, that second-class road between Vieux Berquin and Neuf Berquin, about three miles east of Hazebrouck. There the

Guards planted their banner, "They shall not pass." Alongside this, the oldest division of the British Army, came one of the youngest, the First Australian. The battle flags of the Guards list names for two hundred years; the Division from down under was winning their first. The Guards said, "They shall not pass." The Aussies said, "That means us too." The proudest and steadiest battalions with an age-long record held one part of that old road, the other part was held by one of the most daring, yet most irresponsible, unpredictable group of battalions in the British Army. What the Guards could do, the Aussies said they could do, and they did it.

The whole might of the oncoming, seemingly irresistible German Army was hurled at that line between an old and a new village, and hurled in vain. All day and all night, and all day and all night, wave after wave was hurled at our line. The waves came on but they did not recede, they died. At last there were no more divisions that Prince Rupprecht of Bavaria could hurl at those Aussies and the Guards. Rupprecht had failed, just as the other German generals had failed. Would the other German generals have won had Rupprecht sent his divisions south? We did not know, all we knew was that our line held. Then they brought the Guards and Aussies back. They went in as divisions and came out as weak brigades. Of the Guards, the Irish had fared the worst—their battalions came out as platoons. The newest of the Guards, yet the proudest, few though they were.

Maybe what interested us the most was that this titanic battle was fought on one of our farms. A farm sixteen miles back from the front line, a farm we never gave a thought to as being unsafe. Yet a farm enriched by the blood of thousands of brave men—Australians, Germans, British.

From the point of the breakthrough of our line, the German Army had come near sixteen miles. The line that for over two years ran roughly from Lens through La Bassee, Armentières, and Warneton to Passchendaele, was now pierced and at the extreme apex was not far from Hazebrouck, which had been evacuated. This meant that the whole line south from Ypres had to be swung back, so now our new line meant much of the land we had worked on and worked to help the civilians with was now on the German side. From Vieux Berquin north to a point between Flêtre and Meteren to Berthen. From there north our old line held, and this saved near a thousand acres of our farms around Poperinghe and Ypres, up to Poelcappelle and beyond. The rich land around Bailleul, Meteren, Strazeele, Steenwerck, the big army farm on Messines Ridge, and all around Kemmel Hill was all in German hands. But even worse than being in German hands, it was under our own shellfire.

We have said that we were holding the line with guns, not men. This was literally true. More and more guns came up. Not the real big stuff, but eighty- and sixty-pounders. These guns never stopped firing. Before this the artillery fire had been spasmodic, sometimes heavy, sometimes light. Now it never ceased. Day and night, fog or sunshine. After four months, we were to go over the ground we had lost and then regained. For miles and miles it was one mass of shell holes, not large ones, but shell holes by the hundreds on every acre of ground. German prisoners told us—and we could see with our own eyes—that they, the Germans, were never able to dig new trenches. They just clung to a series of shell holes. We let them cling and hammered them unceasingly.

This was the richest and most fertile land in all France. In this triangle of land we had had ten Canadian officers looking after farms. Now they were back and on poorer land. Yet they went right ahead and found otherwise uncultivated fields and within days were clamouring for seeds, seed potatoes. We could not now hope to fill our objective of vegetables and potatoes for a million men, but we came close to supplying the full need of the Army of the North just the same. In manpower we were less than half what we were when General Holman gave us our objective. Our brigades and our divisions were further south. Churchill's guns and shells were holding our end of the line in the north.

A Rather Delicate Job

MANY AND VARIOUS were the jobs handed to us by our Quartermaster General, some of which had nothing to do with farming. We were called into conference one evening.

"Hughes," said our General, "I have a rather delicate job I would like you to handle. Do you happen to know Colonel Brown-Smythe (not his real name), Gun Park Commandant down near Aire?"

"Yes, Sir."

"Well, it appears that he has a lady love and during these late moves he has been seen with her in his car, or so it is reported. Now you know it is against Army Regulations for an officer to have females in an Army vehicle. Actually Brown-Smythe ranks rather high in the social world back home and we don't want any undue publicity. Now would you go and see him and warn him that this must stop."

So we had a new job. As our General said, a delicate job. Right early next morning we arrived at Colonel Brown-Smythe's new billet.

If one of England's social leaders was surprised at a young Canadian taking him to task on a question of his actions with the ladies he at least showed no annoyance. He calmly made the statement that he had known this French lady for a long time and that during the German push he had gone out of his way to give her a lift back to a safer zone. Naturally he would see to it that this did not happen again.

143

"I will report accordingly," we said. "We can now consider the incident closed," and we rose to leave.

"*Bonjour, messieurs.*" A beautiful and charming young lady had just come out of the adjoining bedroom. She was easy to look at, only it was ungallant to look too long or closely at one wearing only the flimsiest of silk negligees.

"Ah, now *messieurs*. You are just in time for coffee. May I?" And she rang the bell. A servant, a British Tommy, came in with coffee, cream, and sugar.

We drank coffee and were charmed by the wit and the gay laughing remarks of a lovely French lady.

Later we reported Colonel Brown-Smythe's statement to our General and he heaved a sigh of relief. His young Canadian had handled a delicate situation with discretion.

Remember, we were dealing with the breaking of Army Orders on Transport, not with anything really serious.

It had been a pleasant morning. She was nice to look at, we hope we did not stare.

Farming in the Front Line

On Active Duty
April 9, 1918

Colonel Pritchard and Captain Trombly [110 Bn] were in for tea. They are
coming to join our mess. The Colonel's farms are still in our hands, but in
too hot a place to work at present. Captain Trombly was Area Commandant
at Kemmel Hill. He lost all his kit when the Hun arrived.

Thinking back over the years we realize how contemptuous we were
of danger in those days.

Colonel Pritchard was one of Canada's unwanted senior officers. He
had given up his business, left his home in Ontario, raised a battalion of
his friends and neighbours, trained them to the best of his ability and
knowledge, and taken them to where they could smell gunpowder. Then
he was told he could go home, he was no longer wanted. What would
they call him at home? Even that was not the main point. His boys
(every officer worth his salt thought of his men as "his boys") were going
up to the land of hell and destruction, he could go the ease and safety of
his home.

Colonel Pritchard was not made that way. He grasped at the first opportunity to go where his boys had gone, humble though the position might be. If those in charge would not let Pritchard lead his men into battle, well and good, then he would feed them. In the Good Book, the Master said "Feed my people."

Pritchard's garden was near St. Julian, where our First Division won undying glory and saved the Channel Forts. Soldiers from the British Isles, Australia, Canada, and New Zealand were amazed when trudging back up the line beyond Poperinghe even to the outskirts of Ypres, to see land that only Dante could describe being turned into a garden.

One day, visiting this garden, we found the Colonel very annoyed. Some heavy shells had exploded close to his prize cabbage patch. A piece of a horse, several days dead, had been thrown among his plants. The worms, white, were not the kind a gardener loves, also the effluvium was not pleasing. The Colonel had repaired several dugouts so when the shrapnel became very heavy he and his assistants could take shelter.

You men of Ontario are famous for your gardens. If, when you dig, you turn up an arm, a leg, or part of a thigh bone, would you use it for the marker at the end of a row of carrots? I think you would. You are of the same breed as that man Pritchard.

France
9–5–18

Dearest:
I doubt if you can find the place on the map where we live now. It is called Longuenesse [one mile west of St. Omer]. My Meteren billet is now out in no-man's-land. Our farm which was on the slope of Messines Ridge is all in the Boche lines. Dr. Monkman's grave on Hill 63 was the South East corner of the farm. Another farm we still hold runs right up to the South west side of Ypres. Another has and is still seeing some bitter fighting. That's the one at Dickebusch. We still work the one at Elverdinghe. Another we lost was east of Merville. That went the first day of the push. Wonder when we will get them back. We will some day.

It was mid-August when we went back. We did not know the country. Much of what had been a pleasant country of good homes was a wilderness of shell holes. All farmers look forward towards harvest and we were already wondering about the harvest time. The Hun drive had created a new strip of land behind the front line, about six miles in depth and thirty miles in length that was producing a fine crop for our army. Wheat, oats, barley and potatoes. Who would do the harvesting?

I wrote to Davie Tomlinson [9th Reserve] asking him to come over and work with me here. But he had just got a position as Orderly Officer to the Brigadier at Bramshott. Now the Brigade is broken up and he is without a job and wants to come. If I had known before this push I could have arranged it, but not now.

We last saw Davie in Calgary, where he is a successful business man and one of Canada's outstanding Red Cross organizers. As well, he went on to command the Calgary Highlanders. Davie had already done his share at the front and was wounded, but still he did not want to go home to Canada. He wanted to stay and see the finish.

France
11–5–18

Dearest:
Today I had a visit from three high-up French Military officials connected with Agriculture. After the loss of so much of our farms it was proposed by some to disband our agriculture work, but the French are working tooth and nail not only to prevent that, but to increase our size and scope of work. I believe that will happen. I have been busy all day drawing up a scheme for handling the situation under the changed conditions both in France and Belgium. I took it to the Quartermaster General before dinner. He approved of the scheme and will forward it to GHQ. What we want to do is to save all these thousands of acres of crops in the evacuated areas. No matter where the line may be at harvest time, there will always be an area four to six miles in depth the whole length of the line, on which crops are

growing and which cannot be gathered by civilians. The question: Can we save this crop? Just consider what a large undertaking this is to harvest this crop within range of the enemy guns. I am the only one of course who has to do with Belgium as well as France. I saw the Chief of the Belgian mission today and he is very keen that we should help.

A few weeks later Generalissimo Foch called a conference of his Army Commanders and their staffs. As was reported to us direct, Foch said, "France is woefully short of wheat. There is a danger of actual hunger. This last German push has placed thousands of acres of wheat in the evacuated areas. Also our farmers are very short of labour even where the civilians still are. Now I propose to demobilize twenty thousand of our older soldiers, men with agriculture experience, and send them home to help harvest the crops."

We have no means of knowing, nor do we know with any certainty that Field Marshal Haig had read the plan that we had submitted to the Quartermaster General 2nd Army on this subject, but from our informant we knew what was our Commander-in-Chief's reply: "No. Very definitely no, General Foch. The spy situation is terrible as it is. We just could not handle this problem if we had thousands of new men coming into our Army area. No. Instead of that, in so far as the British Army areas are concerned, *we* will harvest the crop."

We had a new job. As big a one as growing vegetables and potatoes for a million men. This one we completed as well as completing our farm operations on the fields the Hun did not get.

Parcels from Home

France
10–5–18

Dearest:
You must not work too hard at knitting. I think a hundred pairs of men's sox too much for one pair of hands. Especially when they are so filled looking after three husky boys [aged four, six and eight]. I know they are very capable hands, but don't overdo it Dearie.

We know our readers will forgive the little personal touch here and there. What soldier did not long for the personal touch? Wife and kiddies at home, or mother or sister were often in our minds. Regularly once a month a parcel came to France. A cake now and then, but mostly sox. Warm, hand-knit wool sox. Many an English soldier was to bless a woman back in Canada when we handed him a pair of those warm sox. In spite of good boots, feet got damp and sore and holes came often in those Army sox, so what a treat it was to get an unexpected gift of well-knit wool sox. We were proud to be able to say, "Just a pair my wife knit and sent to me to give where needed." We never kept track of how many of those parcels came, usually with ten pairs of sox, but we know we must have

A photograph of Sara, taken in 1915, that John carried throughout the war. The original image is about 30 mm wide and 125 mm high, and was glued into a small leather case, rather like a fancy bookmark.

received four hundred pairs. The one hundred pairs were extra; they were knit for the Canadian Red Cross.

Of the cakes, that was another story. Usually fruit cakes baked in a tin the size of a shoe box. Placed in the shoe box while quite warm, and iced. Then wrapped in stiff paper and sewn into a cover of table oilcloth. On several occasions these cakes arrived in France without even a crack in the icing. We used this same piece of oilcloth to wrap a gift from France and it was then used a second time to bring a cake from home.

We enjoyed placing these cakes on the messroom dining table. More than once the toast was drunk "To the cook back home in Canada."

Yankees and Other Neighbours

NOT REALLY YANKEES, but men from New York. Most people think of American participation in World War I in terms of their front line midway in the French sector and their desperate resistance and victory at Château-Thierry.

We have seen few references to the time they were brigaded with our Scottish Highlanders in the filthiest spot on all our British Army line, Dickebusch. We at 2nd Army were to know the 30th New York Division. We had a couple of their officers attached to our mess. This division came to learn the how and wherefore of trench warfare. Where better could they learn than with our Scotties? We understand the 30th still point proudly to the fact that they alone of all the American divisions fought in Belgium.

They came to learn. There was no bombast, no "we know it all," about them. As we had it from the American major who was with us all the time this division was in Belgium, the training was in this manner. First time in the trenches it was Yankee, Scottie, Yankee, Scottie. The second time it was Yankee platoon, Scottie platoon; the third time Yankee company, Scottie company, and that day was when they had their baptism of fire. The Hun came over to take those trenches. Most of them stayed there and the Yankees helped to bury them. Then it was Yankee battalion and Scottie battalion. The Scotties slapped the Yanks on the back and said,

"You are a fine braw bunch of soldiers." When a Highlander slaps you on the back, you know you are alright.

Another neighbour of ours was Billy Bishop's squadron of the Royal Flying Corps (RFC). We had tea one day with three of Bishop's men. Young lads, all under nineteen. Canadians like Bishop. These lads had great admiration for Bishop, but said that he was a lousy airman. Said he crashed more planes than all the rest of the squadron together. This was the day that Bishop was ordered back to England so that the RFC would have the benefit of his experience. Bishop did not want to become an instructor. So, angered by the order to return to England, he hopped into his plane and single-handedly sent to the ground every Hun plane he could find in the air. Then, according to these lads, busted up his own plane on landing.

France

19–5–18

Dearest:

The Duchess of Sutherland has just been here, but she would not stay for tea as she said she was having a tea party at the hospital. Her place is right alongside of ours. We have a standing invitation to come and see her any time.

After writing last night, Captain Heyer and I went to call on the Duchess of Sutherland. She is most charming, very pleasant, and everyone calls her Sister, just as all the other nurses are called. This is the Dowager Duchess. She is a fine looking woman, I would judge her to be near fifty.

In a Monastery Garden

GENERAL LORD RADNOR'S OFFICIAL RANKING was Director of Agriculture for British Armies in France. The general was one of England's outstanding agriculturists, and now there was a rumour that we were to lose him. The British government was considering sending him to Mesopotamia on an agricultural mission. We were asked if we would go as his assistant. Naturally our answer was "yes." As it happened this mission was delayed until after the Armistice and this spoiled our chance to see the Middle East. The Director was attached directly to Army Headquarters, so quite often we found ourself in that walled city of Montreuil, GHQ for so long. Coming back from GHQ one day we took the coast road to Boulogne and there we visited #2 Canadian Hospital. Here we met our old friend Captain Forester, who was chaplain back in England. We could give him information about a score or more of the senior officers he had known back in the 9th Reserve at Bramshott.

We had moved our Headquarters back to an old house that had in more recent years replaced a monastery. They told us that these monks had been a teaching order and had gone all over the world. The Abbot had charged his men that wherever they were in any country they were to consider the trees. If they saw a tree not grown in France they were to procure a slip and send it home. The result was that there were ten acres of trees and shrubs gathered from all quarters of the world. Once before, we mentioned that our assistant, Major Wheatley, was the son of the Warden of the Royal Parks of England. Therefore he had been brought up in the atmosphere of forestry. Yet even he did not know the names of all these trees.

We had known the sugar maple and the Manitoba maple, but we were to learn that there were actually scores of different maples and many were represented in this old monastery garden. Roses there were by hundreds. We gathered one, pressed it and sent it home to our Dearest in Alberta. It has lost its scent, but we hold it in our hand today as we write these lines, thirty-eight years after it was plucked from the edge of a bomb crater.

France
10–7–18

Dearest:
We have just had a shower of rain, and now the setting sun is shining on the trees and making them all glorious in their fresh-washed foliage. How I wish I was an artist so as to preserve this picture I see from my window so that others might see and marvel at the wonderful colouring, only no mere man could ever reproduce this work of the great Architect of the Universe. Well, I will try to describe the colouring. Just the trees in the immediate foreground surrounding the lawn in front of the house.

On the left overshadowing the gate a fine tall lime tree in full bloom, all the top yellow as gold. Next, low down, a hazel thicket, overtopped by a row of Manitoba maples, a bright green, again overtopped by the dark green of a spruce alongside of which is a wonderful Copper Beech, every limb of which shines like a bar of gold hung with copper leaves. Again further along a high poplar, light green, showing above an eyleane, wide spreading below which is the dark green of a fine mulberry tree. Again right in the centre, a wonderful tulip tree, with every blossom showing as a cup of gold. Next a thicket of Acadia overtopped by a fine Yew tree. Then again a dark green Weeping Birch, whose branches hang like great cascades of falling water. Alongside a light green Split Leaf Lime alive with golden blossoms. Then the beauty of the whole garden, in my eyes, a wonderful tall and stately Copper

Beech, under whose boughs you can keep as dry as in a tent in a heavy rain. Next a Cherry tree, with red cherries showing in the sunlight, alongside of which is another Tulip tree. Next a Judas or Pain Leaf tree overtopped by a Tamarack, or Larch as they call it here. Then a wide spreading Slit Leaf Maple that must be very old. Then, last on the right, a wide spreading chestnut tree, one of the beauties of the place. Not since I passed down the Messeapedia Valley in September have I seen such a riot of colour, and all within fifty feet of my window. But now the light is fading, tint by tint disappearing. God has just shown us what a beautiful world he has placed us in, to contrast in our minds what a hell we can make of the beauty spots he gave us. Just a few short miles and there are no trees, and the setting sun shines on heaped up ridges of dirty clay and chalk, rusty brown rows of tangled wire, great rents in the lands, dirty white bone which once was man or horse, and that is what thousands have to gaze on this evening. A few of us have had a chance to see how beautiful this world is when unspoiled by man.

Now Dearie it grows dark, and after dark comes the Dawn, which signifies that after war comes peace. When I will away to my loved ones in a land to me fairer and more beautiful than France ever will be, Our Canada.

Goodnight Sweetheart.

The Harvest of '18

MAYBE WE SHOULD WRITE the story in our own language today, but when we read the letters written those days in the harvest fields in France and Belgium, we realize that our pen cannot capture the atmosphere of those long-past days.

France
3–8–18

Dearest:
It is interesting to wander over the evacuated country where this time last year it was all peace and quiet. Men and women worked in every field, children played on the roads or in the school yards and only the rumble of guns and the tramp of marching men by day and aeroplanes by night told how close the war was. But the people got used to these things after three years, and they thought that they at least were safe.

How different today, no civilians work in those fields from early morn till late at night. The schools are mostly in ruins, some but piles of brick dust, and the children are scattered far and wide over France. Only Khaki-clad men inhabit this land. Yet in spite of all the damage caused by a vast army of sometimes careless men, in spite of guns by the hundreds, trenches by

*the hundreds of miles, wire by the thousands of tons, there waves a nearly
ripe harvest. The result of the patient toil of those French peasants among
whom I spent many pleasant days last year. Now soldiers from all parts of
the British Empire will try to gather this harvest, not for themselves, but for
the French people directly and the individual owners indirectly. The harvest
will be gathered in bulk, without attention to boundaries of farms, and all
will be stacked together and threshed together and consigned to the French
Government. Someday the individual will be paid from the "fait de guerre"
funds, which are intended to recompense those who have lost their all by
enemy action.*

This is no doubt how we would have arranged it, but not the French.
We had a visit from the Governor of the *département du Nord.* Now it seems
that in France the people are very jealous of their civilian rights. Too
often in their history the military had overrun civilian rights, and now
no matter how much danger existed for the State, the person was supreme.
Now we were to understand that some way, somehow, each farmer's right
and ownership to the crop must be assured. This indeed was a problem.
Farmsteads had been blown away, fences in ruins, roads, many of them
new, made by British troops. Just how could we identify any certain farmer's
field? We think the answer was given by Captain Stubbs, 69th Battalion,
who said, "Why not use the aerial photographic branch of the RAF?"

This was a lead, and we turned the matter over to our assistant, Major
Wheatley. Within the hour, Wheatley had it all arranged, and it worked
just fine. The planes flew low over the fields and took pictures. These were
developed and turned over to us. Captain Stubbs took these photos, numbered every field, be it ever so small, then an NCO or officer kept a record
based on these maps and listed his estimate of what grain was harvested
from each numbered field. These were then turned in to the government,
and from these maps and records we understand that each owner was
paid for the crop he planted and British Tommies harvested.

*It is good to see the Australians at work in the harvest. They go at it as if
working their own land at home. I used to see the same thing last spring on
the Army farm. I would have nothing else but Australians if I could.*

Next week our boys try night harvest work. Grain must be cut up forward for military reasons, and after cutting must the very same night be carted back, miles away to safe places for threshing, not a bomb-proof job by any means. I was watching a binder working up as far as we dare go with an outfit. A Hun plane came over, swooped around several times in spite of a deluge of shells, and went away.

In a very short time a shell came over and landed in that field. Fortunately the binder was at the other side of the field. Another came over and again the binder was not on that side. But this was getting a little warm. Did the driver quit? Not by a long shot. He just moved over to the next field. We asked him about this little byplay between himself and the Hun gunner miles away. He said that this happened nearly every clear day. "Made a mess of things," he said. "Those damn shell holes are spoiling my nice field of wheat." Think of it, "spoiling my nice field of wheat." He said nothing about what would happen if the shell landed under his binder.

Two days later we saw what did happen, not to this binder but to one a mile away. A shell landed right under the binder. The horses were killed, the driver went to hospital. We did not even try to repair that Massey Harris binder.

In the Dark of the Moon

France
5–8–18

Dearest:

Today I have looked down on miles of the front line. It was a bit hazy and we could not see as clearly as we might have done, but on the other hand we were able to stand in the open on quite a high hill and look for miles across the plain. We were up to see the ground which our boys are harvesting at night. Think of cutting a thousand acres of grain after dark with scythes, binding by hand and hauling four miles back. Everything cut that night must be back before daylight. That is what one of our harvesting platoons has ahead of it. No, not all ahead. One trainload of twenty-two trucks is behind them. That is, safely delivered at the dump where it will be stooked for a while, then stacked and threshed. The General is very interested and is coming up some night to see them work. I hope we never have another harvest under such conditions. One casualty last week, but only slight.

Goodnight, or rather Good Morning, Dearie.

159

We cut that French harvest with binders, with old-fashioned reapers, with mowing machines, with old-fashioned cradles, with scythes, with hand reaping hooks, and we pulled the heads of ripe grain off the stalks by hand right up to our front line trenches. We carried the grain back to where it could be loaded onto sleds (wheels made too much noise), then loaded it on to GS wagons and hauled it back to light railway yards. These railways hauled it ten miles back, where it was stooked for drying. Remember, wheat was worth six dollars a bushel in France and, more than that, France was in danger of going hungry.

France
12–8–18

Dearest:
Just in from a long drive with the General. Next book I write will be entitled "The Earl at the Wheel or the Speed Maniac." We broke every rule of the road twenty times over. My hair was perpendicular for hours. You see he will not allow anyone else to drive. He has a special permit to drive. [This was given to few.] He is no doubt a splendid driver, but he takes too many chances. We passed cars, lorries, caterpillars, horses and men by inches every minute. We whipsnapped between converging lorries midst curses of lorry drivers. We took the Cassel Hill curves at thirty miles an hour, and they look like this ⌣⌢⌣⌢⌣. I had to tell him to drive slower several times when we were under observation from Kemmel Hill, that had German batteries on top, so as not to raise a cloud of dust, as Fritz has a habit of popping a bit of shrapnel over dusty roads. Then when he gets to the forward area and we have to walk, it is hard to get him to wear a steel helmet or carry a gas mask, and he wants to wander right up into the front line. I don't mind taking this chance myself, but feel a bit responsible when I have a General who is an Earl in tow, but he wants to see everything. We have now covered the whole 2nd Army front line.

The Earl took us back to GHQ for a conference. Driving miles south of our Army lines we passed miles of cavalry moving south. This bothered us, and no doubt it showed on our face.

"What's bothering you, Hughes?" asked the Earl.

"Well Sir, these regiments are going the wrong way. They should be headed north."

The Earl looked at us very intently for a moment. "So you have not been told. You don't know where our big offensive is to be launched?"

"Why certainly. Up north near Ypres."

"Why do you say that?"

"Well, you see troops are concentrating there by the thousands every day, and moreover the Canadians are coming up."

We wonder if the Earl hesitated a moment. If he did, we did not notice at the time, but then he went on and told us something that made us very proud. "Yes, the Canadians are going north. Going north by day and south by night. We are counting that the Hun will think that the Canadians will be used as the spearhead of our offensive. Every endeavour has been made to lead him to believe that the Canadians are moving up to the 2nd Army in Belgium. Actually, moving mostly by night, the Canadians are now down nearly to our extreme right. The big offensive will be right over the ground of the Hun offensive this last spring."[65]

France

29–8–18

Dearest:

Just a few lines tonight, as I am rather tired. I have driven ninety miles today and over bad roads, right up in front, and have walked I don't know how far. Other work in the back areas has kept me out of the forward harvest fields for two days, and there was a lot of things that needed attention in widely scattered places. So I was running in and out following the main road right along our entire front and even up among our brave Belgians. The Belgian Army of today is nothing like the Belgian of even a year ago. Today he is sure and confident. He is a match and more for the Boche and now he is continually worrying Jerry instead of the other way about, as in the past.

Everyone is again talking about the wonderful work of our Canadian Corps. One side in particular I hear, that is what might be called the Q side. You see, I deal altogether with Q of the Army and the men I deal with are those I hear talking. Q deals with supplies, rations, ammunition, transport and moves. What these men talk about is General Currie's wonderful organi-

zation. How first he so secretly withdrew his Corps from one front, trans-
ported it miles and miles away to our extreme right without anyone
knowing what was happening. Then fighting for ten long days and nights
and again secretly withdrawing his corps back to his old stamping ground
and striking again within an hour of arrival, with Divisions up to full
strength. Here, they call it a marvel of discipline and organization. Naturally
we are proud to hear these things, and remember, Currie is only a civilian
soldier like ourself.

We do not know how true these lines are to the actual facts, but they are as observed and told by men who knew what they were talking about, and recorded by us for our wife's eyes.

At this point we want to tell a little story, although it was not told to us 'til months after the happening.

When we officers of the 19th Alberta Dragoons offered ourself to Colonel McKinery when he was forming the 151st Battalion, a neighbour of ours from Vegreville, one Lieutenant Ted Clarke, and ourself went up together and were accepted as foot-slugger lieutenants. Ted, known as Tubby (but not to be confused with another famous Tubby Clarke of Edmonton), went overseas with the 66th. This battalion was one of the early units to be broken up for reinforcements, and Ted went to the 1st Canadian Mounted Rifles Battalion. This is the story he told us when we met him back in England in the spring of '19.

The 1st CMR battalion was the extreme right-hand unit of the Canadian Corps, and the Canadians were on the extreme right of the British Army. Ted was now a major and second-in-command of the battalion and there-fore on the extreme right-hand side of the battalion when in line and advancing, and thus the extreme right-hand man of the British Army. All went well during the early part of that day that marked the begin-ning of the end for Germany's hopes. During the afternoon they were held up by Hun machine-gun fire. The machine gunners were in pill-boxes and the battalion could not flank them. Now remember that Ted was an Englishman, very much an Englishman, although resident in Canada. Here were his words:

"I called on the English gunners for artillery fire to dislodge those blooming machine guns. Do you know what happened? It was four o'clock in the afternoon and those bloody gunners were having afternoon tea. Could I hurry them? Not by a damn sight. I had to call on the French gunners to our right. They dislodged the Hun damn quick."

Major Ted Clarke MC and two bars. Canadian.

We Give the Heir to a Dukedom Permission to Marry

MORE THAN THAT, we actively helped in the noble romance. We had a new AO who had replaced Captain Wood at Steenvoorde. He was Captain Lord Beauclerk,[66] brother and heir to the Duke of St. Albans. A direct descendant of King Charles and Nell Gwyne. The captain was a keen farmer and took his duties very seriously. A pleasant chap to meet, and he liked us to arrange our visits so as to have lunch with him. As he had been in France more than six months without leave, he asked for and received his fourteen days leave. On his return we asked him if he had enjoyed his trip home. Rather noncommittally he replied that he had. Then he went on to say that he had become engaged while on leave. The lady was an old friend who, according to the captain, he had asked to marry him on numerous occasions, and one rather gathered that he was somewhat surprised when she said "yes." He said that the marriage was arranged for a month hence and he would be asking for leave. The lady was the Marchioness of Waterford, daughter of Lord Roseberry, one-time Prime Minister of England and the richest nobleman in the Kingdom.

In due course the announcement of the wedding appeared in the social columns of the English papers. It was to be the social event of the year. The captain put in his request for permission to marry, and we were happy to grant his request. (Something we little thought we would be doing when we enlisted for overseas.) Then he made application for leave to go home for his wedding. Again we were happy to recommend this and sent it on to the Army. Promptly it came back:

Leave refused. This officer had leave one month ago. Signed Plumer.

Captain Beauclerk came to our Headquarters in great haste and very much disturbed. As he explained, this would upset the whole social world in England. Even the King would be represented. What should he do?

Our suggestion was that he make another application setting out the situation, but to make it short. (The captain had a habit of writing extra-long letters to us on any old subject.) In the request we suggested that he ask that this be referred to the Commander-in-Chief, whom we understood he knew personally. Then and there the captain sat down at our desk and wrote out the application for special leave. Again we endorsed the application, and made the notation, "Attention of the Commander-in-Chief" and sent it off by special runner. Knowing that the captain would be of little use at his own post, we suggested he stay at headquarters until a reply was received. It came within twenty-four hours:

Three days special leave granted. Signed Haig.

We had saved the situation, all was well in the social circles of England.

Now what we should have done was save that paper signed "Haig" and send it home to the wife in Canada. It would have been a memento worth having.

Binders in Shell Holes

France
14–8–18

Dearest:
I have had a long trying day and it has been very hot. Work is going on very well all along the line, but there are many difficulties. Our binders fall in shell holes, or get tied up in barbed wire, or the horses fall into old trenches, or crazy horses break the binders. Every Divisional officer wants to butt in and give the most ridiculous orders. Men who do not know wheat from potatoes give orders contrary to mine, and I am sort of trouble man and have to go around and straighten things out. When my officers, who are experts at their jobs, tell a high-up Staff Officer that he is a bally fool, or words to that effect, I have to go round and smooth things out. Now I guess I have unloaded my day's troubles so will stop grumbling.

Pleasant dreams.

When we felt real grumpy we used to go around and have a talk with Major Coe, 151st Bn. Coe had D Company when we had C Company. Now he had a company in the 10th Railway Troops. Said always that he would like to change jobs with us. When we were there he always called in his Quartermaster Sergeant, Bert Pilkie of Vermilion. Pilkie had been our own company QM and a good one, best scrounger in the army. Now somewhere in the Dominion Immigration Department. This day in particular we had just sat down to lunch when Fritz started throwing shells into camp. It got very warm and there was a hasty order to move camp. As it was they lost several horses and mules. This was not a very salubrious spot, there just outside Elverdinghe. In fact it smelled. It was not to be wondered at. There were more dead horses to the square rod than anywhere else on the Western Front. Ever see a horse that has been dead for forty-eight hours? His four legs gradually turn until they stick straight up in the air, and his body...well, don't be near if a chunk of shrapnel cuts the belly open. You won't mind the shrapnel, in fact you will forget that bit of steel, but you won't forget the—shall we say—aroma.

France
24–8–18

Dearest:
Just in after a tour of the fields with the French officers from their GHQ and the Ministry at Paris. They are coming again next Tuesday. They want to see with their own eyes what we are doing. As they made no suggestions that I should hurry or change my arrangements, I judge they are satisfied, and they again provided a most excellent lunch, this time at the hotel in St. Omer.

We did not know for months after if they were satisfied. Then we received a letter and a small box from the War Office. We were notified that the Republic of France had made us an *Officier de l'Ordre du mérite agricole*[67] (Officer of the Order of Merit in Agriculture). The decoration, or medal, is much more elaborate than an English medal. We do not know if any other Canadian received this award.

Little by little the line was being pushed back. No great battles were fought along our front. Just the day-in, day-out, night-in, night-out hammering. Churchill's shells were making a hell that even the stout German soldiers could not take. Never for one single moment for months on end did those guns stop roaring. This made things a bit easier for us. No longer

The l'Ordre du mérite agricole medal (front) awarded to John McKendrick Hughes in 1918.

were our forward area farmers under machine-gun fire. Stop and think of that: our soldier farmers heaved a sigh of relief—no machine-gun fire, only shell fire.

We went forward to find what had happened to the village of Meteren where we were billeted for several months. We climbed through tangled wire over bits of trenches, around shell holes, over piles of brick dust. Then we happened to look back. There on a half-wall left standing were the letters METEREN. All that was left of as pleasant a village as could be found in all France. Where was the big old church? Over there to the right. Yes, that bigger heap of broken brick. Where was the lovely *château*? There to the south. We walked, or rather crawled, over to see. Again dust, bits of burnt timber, all that was left of a once happy home. But no, what was that up on top of the heap?

We clawed our way up. There, of all things, we found a warming pan. It hangs in front of our big stone fireplace today. Many people have asked us what it is. Here in our dry climate the housewife does not have to worry about damp sheets before ushering guests into the guestroom for the night. It is different over there. A brass pan, covered, with a live charcoal fire in it, passed between the sheets makes a bed ready for any guest. Now a question: how did that old, very old, hand-made brass warming pan escape destruction when everything else about that old *château* was blown to very small pieces? We wonder, is there a history behind this old hammered brass pan?

To London for Binder Twine

Mid-Channel
27–7–18

Dearest:
A beautiful day and the boat rides smooth, and so far I feel no desire to feed the fishes.

Not so another officer we saw on the boat. We were leaving from Boulogne, a major came aboard, walked across the deck and fed the fishes on the far side. We were talking to a ship's mate and he told us that this was a regular occurrence. This officer was a King's messenger. He crossed the Channel regularly twice a week and also regularly he was seasick the moment his foot hit the planking of the ship's deck. We looked with admiration at this man. Duty first, last, and all the time in spite of bodily pains. An honoured position, the King's Messenger.

We left Boulogne harbour and were not out ten minutes, then turned around and went back. We all wondered who had been late arriving, that had caused this about-face. Then four little destroyers streaked past, out into the channel. There were great geysers of water thrown into the air. Depth charges we understood. Then we turned about and proceeded on our way to England. We often wondered, was there actually a Hun sub lurking there, or was it all a false alarm?

Had it been a Hun sub and had it scored a direct hit, in Germany it would have been hailed as a great victory. Aboard that boat were a number of VIPs. We stood in a group and talked, at first little realizing with whom we were speaking. An English major informed us (on the side). One was Austin Chamberlain,[68] one the Rajah of Bapore, another a member of the French Cabinet. The centre of the next group was the Prince of Wales.[69] We think that had that sub commander made a hit, he would have had more than an Iron Cross.

I will actually be out of France fifty hours, as I left late afternoon Thursday and this is Saturday. I will be in France in time for dinner, that is if all goes well, and we are used to things going well on these trips. The coast of France ahead, behind us England. I wonder when it will be that I will be leaving the other coast of England and sailing west instead of east. I stayed two nights at Charing Cross. Most of yesterday I spent at the War Office.

Now just what did all this mean? It meant that we had gone to England for binder twine. To the farmer, binder twine is a very important item, that is when a big crop of grain is to be harvested. We had a very big harvest ready for cutting, and no twine.

We went to GHQ to see the Director and he admitted ruefully that his requisitions so far had produced no twine. Shells were more important, or so we considered the War Office had decided. What would we do? The grain was ready for the harvest. We just naturally suggested that the general slip across to England, see the War Office, and get the twine.

"Good Lord, Hughes, you cannot do things like that in the Army. Why, I would get scragged. They would throw me out of the army. We have just got to wait."

Western farmers are not in the habit of waiting when the grain is ripe. We offered a solution to our problem. "If you can't go General, then send me. I am too unimportant to throw out."

"Would you go?"

"Sure. Glad to."

John most likely purchased this postcard of Westminster Abbey on one of his trips into London. It was not used to convey a message until 1960, when one of his grandchildren mailed it to the Editor's brother.

Up spoke Major Addie, Welshman, professional soldier and the general's Aide. "You know General, Hughes just might pull this off. You or I could not, but these Canadians can do things we cannot. Let him try."

So it was arranged. We were not being sent. We were not the representative of General Lord Radnor, Director of Agriculture, British Armies in France. We were just a Canadian, temporary Staff Lieutenant, AO, 2nd Army. We did not know army red tape.

In due course we entered the portals of the War Office. Also in due course, after many enquiries, we found ourself facing a general behind a big oaken desk. We stated our reason for being there; the wheat was ripe and we needed binder twine so as to start harvesting.

The general's face grew red. He all but exploded. He did explode, that is in words. "Did I not know that there was a proper way to get anything in the Army? Had I never read standing orders on requisitions? Had I not done this, did I not know that?"

Then he stopped, wiped his forehead and looked at the word on my shoulders—CANADA. He heaved a sigh, his face was an open book. "Oh, you Canadians, you ignorant Colonials."

Turning, he snapped out some orders to his aide at the adjoining desk, then reached for a cigar. He offered us one, put his feet up, and said, "Tell us about Canada."

When we arrived back in France, the binder twine was there ahead of us.

France
10–7–18

Dearest:
Just a few minutes while waiting for a party of thirty-two harvesters to turn up. These will be furnished with horses, wagons, etc., etc. and sent forward to reap what the farmer left behind early in the spring. I sent one party out yesterday and have to secure and organize, equip and send out twenty such sections. This extra and over our own farms. Then they will receive help from fighting units on the ground. The wheat harvest should be good. All winter wheat. The early sown oats are also good. Our potato crop is turning out well, where we have started to dig. The French farmers who said "no bon" when we started work are now studying our operations very closely. Also they are on the lookout to secure some of our seed for next year's planting. Where our seed [imported from Scotland] was sown side by side with French seed, and on poorer land, our potatoes are showing away the best.

We did not want to sell any of our potatoes. We needed them all, but we did arrange to exchange so that the French farmer would have the improved seed.

Had we been able to carry our farm scheme through as we started, it would have been an immense success financially and otherwise. Now others are already urging me to prepare for next year. Needless to say, I have been silently preparing all along.

Preparing, yet hoping it would not be needed. Now we had some good reason to hope. Germany had made her last (at least we hoped) desperate attempt to wrest victory from defeat and failed.

A Dead Fritz in a Shell Hole

THE FRENCH GOVERNMENT was evidently so pleased with our harvest work that they wanted to show the people of France what the British Army was doing. Something to pep up a sagging morale. They arranged to send an official photographer to take pictures of our operations. We were allowed to say where. Just naturally we picked the section officered by a Canadian, Captain Stubbs,[70] 69th Bn., who had for his principal assistant Sergeant Harry Compton of Vermilion. Pictures were taken in progressive stages. Back where binders were comparatively safe. Then where the old-fashioned reapers were at work. Then closer up where the wheat was being cut with scythe and sickle. As he could not take a picture of harvesting in the dark of the moon, he had to use his imagination at least a little bit. We did take him up where he heard the whistle of machine gun bullets. Finally the photographer wanted a picture of this harvest group sitting around the edge of a shell hole eating their lunch. This was done. Then our quiet unassuming sergeant from Vermilion made a suggestion.

"Let's change our position. Let's go over to that shell hole there. The picture would be more realistic. There is a dead Fritzie in the bottom of the hole."

We did not doubt Harry's word. We could smell Fritzie. But as we wanted to retain our lunch we decided not to move.

France

15–7–18

Dearest:

The Director had called a meeting of all Agricultural Officers in the Armies, at Headquarters, and I had to go down. It is about a two-hour run. I went by way of Thérouanne and took Major Billy Wilkin and Bloxham[71] with me. He is one of our outstanding AOs. The meeting was to discuss ways and means of harvesting the crop under fire. I have most of my arrangements already made and my sections at work. I find the best way to work out these problems is to send out small parties to start the work early and then by practical experience, in a week, they will be able to tell more about what must be done and how to do it. This is better than a month of study in an office or holding conferences. Every part of the front has its own difficulties and must be handled in a different manner. Some land is flat and the enemy can see all we do. Other places are quite the reverse. Some parts there is high land and big farms where machines of all sorts can be used, while in other parts the fields are so small and there are so many ditches, hedges, trenches and balls of barbed wire that all the work must be done by hand. So instead of waiting for my sections to be made up to strength [130 men, 25 horses], I am starting a nucleus section to plan and start. Ten or fifteen thousand acres to cut and stack on the open prairie, with plenty of men and horses at one's disposal would not be a task that would daunt one with experience. The same amount under the eyes of the Hun and under all sorts of strange conditions is quite a different story. How much we will eventually save remains to be seen.

We saved practically all. We cut, stooked, stacked, and threshed it all, and as we threshed French lorries were there to take away the grain and English lorries there to take away the baled straw. Canadian officers and Canadian men were running most of the threshing machines.

Captain Bloxham told me yesterday that he had just bought a 640-acre farm in Northern Alberta through Major Billy Wilkin and intends farming when he goes home. He was a Bell telephone expert before the war, but from his work with us has decided to be a farmer.

Last night I had a call on the phone. I knew the voice at once and nearly dropped the receiver. It was Major Duncan McRae. He had just arrived in France and is awaiting posting to a flying squadron.

Duncan and ourself had applied for transfer to the RFC the same day soon after our arrival in England. Both of us were overage. We were refused as we were married. Duncan was a bachelor. Duncan was quartered only six miles from our headquarters, so it was arranged and later carried out that we should pick him up some day and go to Boulogne, where his sister Nellie was nursing in our Canadian hospital on the hill. We did this and as well took Nursing Sister Miller (Edmonton) and drove to Calais. There at Number ___ Hospital we had lunch with Nursing Sister Happy Acton, also of Edmonton. A pleasant day, a nice drive far away from war, except at night, when the Hun liked to come over and turn a pleasant land into hell.

Only a Ford Could Do It

France
2–9–18

Dearest:

I promised to tell you about my trip up in the recent taken areas and will try to do so. If incomplete it will be because certain things as you know of which I must not write. What I have seen I have since seen described by a War Correspondent in today's Times. He travelled the same road as I did and on the same day, but then he knows how to give expression to his thoughts and to tell what he saw. I started out about eight thirty to go up forward to see what was the crop situation. Up forward where we had planned to plant when our scheme first started. We had nearly reached the limit beyond which I had considered it too dangerous to send our men to cut grain, either by day or night. Then the Boche retired. Not driven back by our infantry but, as I will show, blown back by our guns. I wanted to know first hand how much grain remained between our forward work and the old line and even behind the old Boche line. I found that we had still at least a two-mile depth along the whole front, a strip of fairly good grain. Not badly trampled, and this I hope we will be able to harvest. Behind the Boche line there is nothing. Not because he harvested it, our guns did that. Where he had put one shell hole in the fields on our side, we put fifty to one hundred on

his side. We went first to the village of Strazeele, which is all destroyed. Then
to Vieux Berquin, which was either in Boche hands or no man's land. This
place consisted of one long street of nice houses, today one long pile of
broken brick. Then, turning north, we went to Outersteene. Our Ford was
the first car to get through, and only a Ford could have made the journey.
Over shell holes, shells, timbers, broken-down houses, dead horses, parts of
wagons, guns, and all the debris of a destroyed country. Then we saw what
sort of a hell the Hun has lived through in the last few months. How he
stayed there at all is what I cannot understand. He was given no rest day or
night. Our guns obliterated his trenches or wire as fast as he made them.
The whole country stinks with dead men and horses. Every last vestige of a
house or shelter is blown away, trees uprooted or shot away. His dead lie
unburied, have been unburied for weeks. Half-decomposed men lie in every
ditch and by heaps in shell holes. No one who has not been there can
conceive the utter desolation, absolute Hell that existed there. For weeks
and months we have listened to our guns firing night and day, now we
know the result.

Few Canadians saw this stretch of country after the Germans went
back. They had known this area in more pleasant days, but now they were
on their way up by another route. From Amiens once more, along the
great wide Arras-Cambrai road towards Bapaume, to Roye, and on to the
Hindenburg line.[72] We believe that we were the first Canadian to follow
up the advance in this sector south of the road that leads to Bailleul and
on to Armentières. Our Sunbeam car had worn out and now we had a
Ford. For this work the only car that could or did get through.

The whole French line from the sea to the Alps was vile with the
stench of dead horses and dead men, but nowhere else along the line
had men in uncounted hundreds lain unburied for weeks on end. Had
Goethe seen this hell on earth his story would have been more realistic.
Any of us who were up in the front line saw dead men, our own and our
foe, but over this stretch of country two miles in depth and ten in length
there had not been a burial in many weeks. And remember this was in
the heat of summer. Not only had the bodies not been buried, they had
been tossed about by continual succeeding shells, and now it was no
longer a body, but a stinking worm-filled chunk of what had once been

a man. Churn up a hundred men and strew them across an acre of land, and have those acres stretch for miles and miles, and only then can one realize what hell on earth really meant.

I got into what used to be no-man's-land with the car and had an awful time. We went through a road that has not been used since the advance. We were five and a quarter hours going two miles, and believe me that Ford went over roads as bad as ever travelled by a car anywhere anytime. We were stuck fourteen times. We took eight iron gates from various farms to make roadways. Over shell and mine holes we used innumerable boxes, shell cases, duck boards, etc. to fill holes. We had to use long poles as levers. We carried, it seemed, thousands of bricks. We climbed trunks of trees across the road, and finally we were stuck. Yet got assistance from an artillery horse and went on.

We knew we could not make it back the same road so took a side road and ran right into a line of troops along the roadway. We were on the road and between the troops and we knew not what. An officer came up to the car and wanted to know what in blankety-blank-blank we thought we were doing. We tried to tell him, and asked if we could make it over the next rise of land.

"Oh sure," he said sarcastically, "Fritz is over there and he would be most delighted to see you." We decided not to call on Fritz that day seeing as we were all mud and dirt. We would wait. We did, until we met him in Germany.

Actually our Ford was ahead of our front line for the moment. We waited until our front line moved past us and then made our way home. We found a road the field artillery had cleared coming up, and by dark we were out of the worst of the land of destruction. One last item, maybe a bit gruesome-seeming today, but casual for that day. It was growing dark and we were too close up to use lamps. We went bump-bump, as over broken cobblestones. Eason, our driver, stopped and used his flashlight on the road. Then, with a resigned sigh, drove on. "Only dead Fritzies," he said.

During those years in Belgium and France we covered nearly the entire Belgian and British line, and some of the French, yet nowhere did we see the utter destruction we saw in the area east of Hazebrouck to Armentières.

And remember, this was not done over years of shelling such as was in the Ypres section, but between mid-April and the first of September, 1918. And again not so much by big guns, it was mostly eighteen-pounders. As we said before, this line was not held by the infantry but by Churchill's shells.

That was a story of what a Ford could do. Now let us tell a story about a Singer sewing machine and a German steel helmet. One of those nice homes in Vieux Berquin was absolutely blown away, only the tile floor of the kitchen was left. On this tile floor was standing a Singer sewing machine, intact. Except for the belt being missing, we believe it would have operated perfectly. What we wished for was a camera. We believe we would have sold the picture of that machine for a good sum to the Singer Company. Against the stand of the machine rested a German steel helmet. We picked up the helmet and out rolled part of the head it was supposed to protect. We dropped the helmet, and our own rose inches from our head. Then, gritting our teeth, we again picked up the German helmet. Today it rests in our library.

Romance

OUR TALES ARE GRIM and usually tell only what men are doing in this land of destruction. We have a couple of tales, one very sad, the other with a happy ending, in fact a bit of romance.

France
25–9–18

Dearest:
I was in town this morning and went into the little shop where I usually buy post cards and papers. I noticed the little girl who usually serves me was very depressed, not having her usual sunny smile. I asked her what was wrong. She burst into tears and then handed me a letter. It was from an Australian boy and in mixed French and English he told her quite a common tale out here. How his comrade had been shot dead while dressing the wounds of a Hun prisoner. This lad was engaged to this girl. What could I say to her? Nothing, only time will heal. I wonder what will happen to the next Boche prisoners taken by that Australian Battalion. A sad tale.
Let me tell you one, sad in a way, but with a pleasant ending. A romance of this war. Pte. Sandy McClosky belonged to one of Scotland's proudest Battalions. He fought at Mons those terrible days when we were falling

steadily back before overwhelming odds. Today Sandy is a B class man. Forty-one years of age, nearly deaf as a door post. He is in charge of my sanitary section and keeps the grounds and buildings of our HQ in beautiful condition. Sandy asked for leave. It was granted and he asked to go to the south of France. This being unusual in such a man, a few questions and a story told by a pal brought to light a real romance.

One day Sandy's battalion was fighting a stubborn rear-guard action. They had just left a village as the Hun entered the other side. A woman ran out of a house, she was shot dead then brutally bayoneted and stabbed. Another young woman, a daughter of the first, ran out and attacked her mother's murderers with her hands. She was promptly shot, the bullet going right through her breast. The Hun was about to bayonet her also. This was too much for Sandy. He rushed back, bayoneted one Hun and shot another and, picking up the girl, carried her to a place of safety. She recovered under the care of the Battalion Doctor, and Sandy was able to restore her to her Grandmother and other relatives. Sandy is now out of the fighting line for life, twice wounded, but he no longer takes his leave in old Scotland. Soon I am to be asked for my consent to another Franco-British wedding, which I will do with pleasure. There now, when you write your next novel you can use this story. It is true. No doubt there are many similar stories.

We wished Sandy and his bride long life and happiness.

Hughes's Dragoons

THE COLONEL who was director of the Remount Service was a busy man these days. The casualties among army horses were terrific. It is that way when an advance is on. Horses are then in the open by day moving up supplies. It was reported to us that during the war the British Army used half a million horses and mules, and a hundred thousand were killed. We do not give this as authentic, but we know the number was very large.

France
5–10–18

Dearest:
I have not written for three days. I have been away on a trip, taking remounts, horses and mules, from Calais to the divisions in the front line. Some trip it was. I hope never to take such another. Our Director of Remounts was hard up for someone who had men, and he asked us to help him. So as many of our men as possible were gathered and sent by lorry and I decided to go myself in charge. It would have been laughable if it had not been so serious. I did not realize there were so many men anywhere who did not understand horses. I had a hundred men, two hundred horses and one hundred mules. Two-thirds of these men had never even laid a hand on a horse before in their lives.

We arrived at a little village just outside Calais where we had billets for the night, then moved a mile to where the horses were supposed to be. Sure enough, there they were—with not a single bit of equipment except their halters. A remount section had brought them out from Calais, then promptly left. They were ours, do what you like with them. There were neither bridles, blankets, nor saddles. For a few minutes we were really stumped. What could we do? Cry quits? Say the job was too big for us? We looked around. One of our men, wearing Lance Jack's stripes, was carrying a saddle. We had our own.

"Corporal," we said, "you at least seem to know what you came here to do. Do you know how to ride?"

"Yes, Sir."

"Where did you learn?"

"On Pat Burns's[73] ranch, outside of Calgary."

"Corporal, all I can say is thank God you are here. I promote you now, on the spot, to the rank of Sergeant."

"Thank you, Sir. But may I say, Sir, that you have one hell of a job on your hands."

"I know that, Sergeant, but by the gods of war if we two Canadians can't lick this job, then nobody can." We did.

We had one hundred men, three hundred animals. Mount one and lead two. Mount a man on a horse, a man who had never even touched a horse before. The sergeant and ourself were from Western Canada, where every man was more or less a horseman. These men were from factories of Leeds and Sheffield. They were frightened even to approach a horse. A man with shaking hand would grasp a lead rope and with chattering teeth say, "Will he bite, Sir?"

Yes, they would bite. Do you know anything more apt to bite than an army mule?

The sergeant and ourself made bridles by putting the tie rope in the horse's mouth as a bit and using the rest of the rope as bridle reins. Each man had his blanket. This we tied on a horse's back with a bit of rope as a saddle. Then we were ready to mount. Our old cavalry drill came to our mind. "Prepare to mount. Mount!" The only trouble was that we had no cavalrymen. So the sergeant and ourself shoved the men up onto the horses one by one.

Imagine me lifting these poor trembling chaps up onto the back of restive horses and mules. They were thrown head over heels, into ditches and hedges. They were tramped on and bitten. They were kicked clear across the road times without number. But like true soldiers uttered not a complaint. I was off my horse at least a hundred times picking up men, or hats or coats, or blankets or odds and ends of equipment. Those poor boys [some past the prime of life] will not be able to sit down for a week. I herded up and down the line trying to keep them on the right side of the road, and picking up the fallen and cheering the fainthearted. I laughed and swore and talked and blarneyed them till I was hoarse. Then when we stopped at night they did not even know how to tie up a horse or put on a nose bag. Some of the officers still laugh and joke about Hughes's Dragoons, but we got there and delivered our charges.

If those men suffered the first day, they suffered more the second day, when broken blisters stuck their shirts and pants to their skin. Some were so tired and sick that they did not eat any supper, but revived during the night and were even able to crack jokes about "The Major's Cavalry." Many of them even managed to mount without help—that is, they did as we did when boys: lead the horse up to a fence, mount the fence, and thence onto the horse's back.

The second day out on the Wormhoudt-Poperinghe road we passed two regiments of Belgian cavalry. Splendid horsemen, very fine horses, a joy for any cavalryman to behold. As an ex-cavalryman we admired them. They did not admire us, yet they gazed in wonderment. When we called a command, "Heads up, boys," our horsemen from Leeds and Sheffield held their heads high. We were not ashamed of our horsemen.

We delivered those horses and mules to the waiting remount detail in Poperinghe square. Within minutes we were surrounded by a laughing, jeering, cheering crowd of Tommies. The Director of Remounts came up and looked on in wonder. "Do you mean to tell me, Hughes, that you brought all those horses and mules all the way from Calais without a single bridle or saddle?"

"We did that, Sir, save that the sergeant and I had our own bridles and saddles."

"Wonder of wonders," he said, then he addressed the men in terms of highest praise for doing something far beyond what should have been asked. He went on to say that this was a great help. And further, if any of our men wanted to continue to help, that he personally would see that they had the equipment that they should have had these last two days.

We turned to our men. "You have heard what the Director of Remounts has said. If any one of you is willing to volunteer for Remount Service, take one step forward."

As one man, one hundred men took one step forward. We were proud of our Squadron of Cavalry.

Now our one great regret is that the mice have destroyed the letter giving our sergeant's name. Our one great hope is that he may see this account of two hectic days and call us on the phone, R105 Flatbush, Alberta.

This stunt was talked about in the whole army. One general made the remark that there was only one comparable event during the whole war. That was when a battalion of Highlanders in kilts took six hundred horses from the base at Étaples up to the Somme. Well, we doubt if even the Scotties had as many blisters as Hughes's Dragoons.

Plumer's Cows

THE ARMY was on the move, forward. What a relief from the mud and dirt and stink and rats of the trenches. We knew that the forward movement might be slow and also for a time we would be in a land denuded of food of all sorts. We knew that the German was desperate for food and that he would strip the already cleaned-out farms. General Plumer, Army Commander, sent for us.

He said it was expected that for some considerable time the Army would be in areas where there were no cows, where no milk or cream could be bought. Then he suggested that, as the Army AO was the only man with ready cash available, we buy some cows and take them along with us so as to supply milk and cream to the army messes. He said to charge a good stiff price, so that a profit on the enterprise could be made and that there would be no chance of anyone saying that the officers were scrounging on the men's Fat Fund.

We sent Major Wheatley out on a purchasing mission around the country. Now it was not easy to buy good milk cows and no doubt we paid twice their value, about five to six hundred dollars per cow. We bought twenty cows, made one of our men who had dairy experience Sergeant Herdsman, and gave him a couple of helpers. Actually this was a financial success. As the Army moved forward, lorries were available to move our herd. The first big move was to Roubaix, near Lille.

187

France

29–10–18

Dearest:

I wanted a dairy farm. I found what I wanted right where I wanted it. The lady at the farm told how before the war they had twenty milk cows. The Boche appropriated them all, but sold one back to her at five times its value, even at present high prices; 5000 francs in fact. When the Boche was leaving they took this cow also. Also their horses and chickens and all the produce on the farm, and left her and her children to be fed by the American Red Cross. How thankful she was for a loaf of bread, a can of jam and a little milk for her kiddies.

By successive stages we took our herd all the way to the Rhine. They were still there and paying well when we left for home in April 1919. A photographer came and took pictures of our cows and we still have a clipping cut from an English newspaper.

The Army Commander wanted milk. We bought cows, sent them fifty miles by lorry with feed, cowmen, utensils, and were supplying milk forty-eight hours after we were asked to undertake the job.

General Plumer was pleased.

The English Press

APPARENTLY the work of the AOs of the British Army had been noted in our Canadian press.

France
5–10–18

Dearest:
On my return here I found your letter of the fourth enclosing clipping about an Agricultural Officer. This chap's name is Washington, a very nice capable fellow. He is a Corps man. He does not come under me, but under Captain Davidson of the 1st Army. I have five Corps officers doing like work, but none on the scale of this Canadian. They lead all others both in amount and quality of work. Wish they were with us. Canadian writers are apt to write as if these things and many other things are only done in the Canadian Corps. Now, we know they lead in most things, yet they should give others at least credit of being good followers. When Englishmen see these things [often printed in English papers] it sometimes makes a little hard feelings. I have found the Englishman ever ready to praise the other fellow and keep quiet about what he does himself. The Canadians and others from various parts of the Empire who are over here all realize this and now are the first

to resent these screeds about what our own particular boys do. Of course we lead. We ought to, we are composed of the pick of the red blood of Britain and other parts of the world. Our troops are the Storm Troops of the Army, they build more railways, cut more timber, dig more potatoes than any others. Yet there are others.

Our Canadian Railway builders are marvels at pushing the light railways forward. Jim Cornwall [8th CRT] from Northern Alberta holds several records.

I Am a Socialist

"I AM A SOCIALIST."

The words were not mine. In fact, I was startled when I heard them. We were in France and the election of 1918 was coming up in Great Britain. Naturally politics were to the fore. Quite casually I had asked my Commanding Officer, a General and a Peer of the Realm, "I suppose you are a Conservative," and the above was his answer.

Again I stumbled. I said, unthinking, "I suppose you will be going home to vote."

"Oh no," he replied, "you see I am what you Canadians call 'on the Indian list,' as a member of the House of Lords I cannot vote." Then he went on, "They have asked my wife to stand as the Conservative candidate in our constituency."

Now was this a case of man and wife with different political views, or was there a paradox here, a Socialist and a Conservative in one and the same person? I learned a great lesson that day, a lesson unassumingly taught by a fine gentleman.

My general went on to talk about socialism and socialistic problems, not about the Socialist Party. From time to time he quoted from our great book, The Bible, to strengthen his theories and reasoning. He told of work to be done, not as charity but work by the whole body of people, working together for the common good. His plans were no doubt advanced

191

socialism, at least for that day, nearly forty years ago. I was learning, at least I hope I was learning, and from that day on I felt that if a Peer of the Realm was not ashamed to be called a socialist, then I, a young man from the backwoods of Canada, could be one also.

One of my good friends not long ago laughed at me and said, "So you call yourself a socialist because it is fashionable." To show that this was not quite fair I am going to make a bold statement: No one should be ashamed to call himself a Communist. What I want to point out is our false way of thinking and talking today.

My friend and OC used "socialist" in its true form and not in the degraded manner it is used today.

Today we class all persons who belong to the Socialist Party as social-ists. No such thing. A very large percentage are just self-seekers, just like any other political party. We class all who belong to our Co-operatives as co-operators. No such thing. They support the Co-operative because it means dollars and cents to them. Not thinking, or if thinking not believing, that co-operation means helping the other fellow first. Just so the same with Communism. A body of evil, wicked men have corrupted a good word. Communism even in its clean, pure sense is not practical today. But that does not say that the ideal of everyone sharing alike is wrong. Bad men have corrupted the word and put their own evil meaning into common-day use, so we are afraid to say, "I believe in Communism" and stand up and defend our belief. We are afraid of the unthinking mob who just naturally would brand you as a Red. Communism and Socialism just never should have become political parties. Both are ideals. Clean, pure ideals taken from the teaching of Christ, and now unfortunately muddied by men who grasp at a slogan to gain power for themselves.

Unfortunately also, we who believe in true socialism have allowed these people to brand those not willing to join their party as capitalists. Another word twisted until its true meaning has been lost. Let us no longer be blinded by false interpretations of straightforward English words. Let us face the fact, for fact it is, that we have as many socialists in the Liberal or Conservative or Social Credit parties as in the Socialist Party. Now if my reasoning be wrong and you or Louis St. Laurent[74] hear me saying "I am a Socialist" and hear I voted for George Drew,[75] don't blame me. Blame my old commanding officer, General Lord Radnor, Earl of Folkestone.

The Navy Comes for a Visit

GENERAL LORD RADNOR had his son, Commander Radnor of the British Navy, for a visit. He had just added new lustre to the grand old name by his daring feat in blocking the port of Ostend. We were honoured in that wanting to show his son something of the Army front he brought him up to the 2nd Army and asked us to be his guide for the day. Naturally this young man wanted to see something of his father's work. We spent the day driving over farms where men cultivated potatoes but had dugouts in which to take shelter when the Hun shells came close and fast. Up where men were harvesting wheat within machine-gun range of the front line. Eager to get up to Ypres, we ran out from behind the camouflage on an open road in full sight of German gunners on Kemmel Hill. A shell passed close above and buried itself a hundred yards away, throwing chunks of earth over the car. Another and another. One of our traffic control men from behind a clump of trees cursed us one and all, not minding that the driver of the car was a general. We have said that Lord Radnor was a splendid driver. Never did a driver get his car turned around more quickly on a narrow road than he did, and we ran the gauntlet once more. A dozen shells, no hits.

Within days those gunners left Kemmel Hill. All along the line they were going back. Straightening their line, so it was announced by their press. Well, we were happy. None wanted to fight another great battle over that wasteland that had seen battle for four long bloody years.

France
8–10–18

Dearest:

Yesterday the General and I were up over the farm we had to leave in such a hurry last April. I did not have time to go up to the graveyard where Dr. Monkman and so many other brave lads of the 3rd CMRs are buried. The whole country for miles and miles is one vast waste. It is hard to describe. As the General said, "I wish we could bring all the people of Britain over here to see only what we have seen today, and they would go home and fall on their knees and give thanks that the British Isles were kept from the spoilers' hands."

German Army Farms

WE WERE TO LEARN that we had been slow to adopt agriculture as part and parcel of army life. The Germans started army farms within months of the stabilizing of the front line.[76]

We were still in charge of the entire 2nd Army farm system, but a new phase had been added. The Quartermaster General had called us in and outlined the situation. First he commended our work both in producing vegetables and potatoes for the army and for the way we had carried out the harvest under the most difficult conditions ever experienced by harvesters. Then he went on, "Hughes, I think that you have your department so well organized that it will pretty well run itself. Now, we have new work for you. We are advancing and hope we will continue until the war is over. We do not know what food supplies the enemy will be forced to abandon. Your new job will be to follow very closely behind our front-line troops. Search the country, locate food supplies, if any, and also we understand that the Germans have established army farms just as we have. Locate these and take them over in the name of the British Army. We know that this will keep you nearly in the front line, but we understand you have been there a good deal of the time anyway. Organize your work back here to carry on without constant supervision, then take on this new work."

A page from John's Soldier's Own Diary showing the address for several of his friends, including Major Bromley-Martin.

Nothing the General could have said would have pleased us more. We had watched trench warfare as long as we wanted. Now we wanted to see war of movement. More than that, we were to be up there among the first to see liberated France and Belgium. We were to see new country, new cities (some the oldest in Europe), meet new people, and when the end came our chance of going right through to Germany would be good. From the city of Roubaix we wrote to our wife back in Canada.

France

3–11–18

Dearest:

A few lines tonight before dinner. Our new mess consists of Majors Bromley-Martin, Grieve, Captain Robinson, and self. The remainder of our party are still back at our delightful old place. But they will be here in a few days, just cleaning up our work there. I will be going back in a couple of days. Wheatley is in charge of the back work. It is very interesting up here and we have just as nice a place as our last for our HQ. Bromley-Martin and I have been looking for Boche Army farms and so far have found five. But the largest and best is just across our line in another Army Area and unless I can get the Army boundary swung south about a mile I am afraid that I will have to go and tell my colleague in this other Army where this farm is located. At present we are squatting on the place and issuing vegetables as fast as we can.

We kept right on issuing under Bromley-Martin's direction and never knew if our hint to an Army Commander was carried out or not. We can hardly consider General Plumer, Commanding 2nd Army, going to General Horne, Commanding 1st Army, and saying, "Horne, how about you side-stepping a mile south and letting us take over a mile of your present frontage? You see, there is a nice little Hun vegetable garden down your way and we need it."

We can hear Horne's reply. "Not by a damn sight. You stole the Canadians from us. Now you want to steal our garden. No Sir." This of course is all fantasy.

This farm is only a short distance from the line and within easy shell range. The Boche went in strong for agriculture in his Army. At this one farm the Boche Agricultural Officer was stationed there for nearly three years, working the place with prisoners. All hand labour, it appears, at the last, as they had very few horses left of any kind.

At a farm near Roubaix we had a long talk with the owner. It appears that he and his wife were allowed to stay in the basement and had to act as caretakers. There was just one German officer and one sergeant. The chief gardener and all the foremen were English farmer prisoners. The labourers were Russian prisoners. According to the owner, the English foremen were treated very well and had many privileges. On the other hand the Russians were driven like slaves, with a whip, and their food was vegetables unfit for the troops.

One of the principal things grown was cabbage. Much of it was made into sauerkraut. A large dye factory near here was converted into a kraut

factory. They left about five hundred tons of kraut in the vats. This of course
will be wasted as neither ourselves or the French eat this stuff.

When we entered this factory many of the big vats were fermenting and running over onto the floor. It smelled like a brewery. We sent a recommendation to the Army that this kraut be used for one of two things: feeding the German prisoners or putting on the land as fertilizer. We had brought up our herd of cows and we made good use of a lot of the cabbage as cow food.

We have the only cows in the whole country. Not a civilian has a cow left,
the Boche took them all. We will reap what the enemy sowed and we must
admit that he did the job well or rather made others do it well. He was a
hard taskmaster, made everyone work, gave no pay and only enough food
to live on.

At the outskirts of Roubaix we found a food cache that the Germans had not burned. Actually they took a more diabolic way to cause damage to their oncoming enemy. Here was an immense warehouse stored with thousands of tons of food for man and beast. Dried vegetables, peas, beans, oats, hay, and straw. We were congratulating ourself on this find when our motor driver, Eason, called to us, "Major, come up here." He was up on one of the bins of food. He had noticed burns in some of the bags of food. Looking closer he found a couple of broken bottles. On one was the inscription "Caustic Acid." What did this mean? Was the food poisoned, and deliberately?

We wasted no time trying to find the answer. A battalion of the Hampshires were at the moment in the warehouse yard. It seemed that they were telling off parties to go in and secure some of this extra food. We quickly got in touch with the Officer Commanding, told him the situation, and asked him to surround the warehouse and prevent anyone taking anything until it could be examined by competent authorities. We then went right back to Army HQ and reported the incident. We did not follow up the investigation and do not know what was the result. But we did see those broken acid bottles with our own eyes. We still wonder, was that the reason no match was set to that warehouse?

The War Is Over

ALL DAY OF THE 10TH we at Army were on the *qui-vive*. We knew the hour and the place of the meeting of the German delegates with Generalissimo Foch. We felt sure that the terms would be accepted. Then came the flash, "Terms Accepted." The war was over. For us there was no outburst of joy, rather it seemed like a letdown. Few talked, we wrote.

France

11–11–18

Dearest:

So the old war is over at last. What a finish. The boldest prophet did not speak of such a quick end six months ago. Peace should come quickly as no doubt our terms are all arranged and must be accepted. The great question now is, when shall we get home. All is quiet back here as yet. I don't know what it is like in the cities and towns. Am leaving for the front as soon as the car is ready, but something is wrong with the magneto and it won't start. Paris and London will be gay places tonight. Would like to be in either place just to see how the people take it. In the Army, I think, it will be taken very quietly. We have known that it was coming and were unconcerned whether the Delegates signed or not, as the Army is confident of being able

This studio portrait of Sara, William, Charles Edward, and Paul, was taken at Christmas, 1918 and sent to John. Paul's hair is cut even shorter than normal as he had recently managed to pick up a case of ringworm on his scalp.

to dictate their demands in Berlin if necessary. Our men were never in better form, better clothed, better fed, better disciplined. So all will be well in the Army. Now I will close as I hear the car coming. And soon I am coming, coming.

Home soon to Sweethearts.

France
13–11–18

Dearest:
Today is one of the finest days we have had this year. Clear bright sun, no wind, but the tang in the air makes it feel good. Not even the distant boom of guns, hardly a plane up. Last night the stars were brilliant, the moon bright, it was almost like day. An ideal bombing night. But every light was lit, every window seemed open. What a relief, no fear of bombs, no dread

aircraft alarm. Peace. What a wonderful word it is, how we have talked about it all these years. What we would do, where we should go. Just now there is only one thing to do, one place to go. HOME.

Just at the moment we are wondering who will be selected to go forward to the Rhine. That name, the Rhine, how we have played with it. Many despaired of ever reaching it. Now we [some of us] will likely be there in a few weeks. I would like to go as far as the Rhine, then right about for Canada.

It was nearly a month before we rolled into Cologne on the Rhine. We were nearly the first of Army Headquarters. In fact we—that is, Captain Heyer and ourself—were there to arrange for the billeting of the Headquarters of the Army of Occupation in Germany.

Turkeys for Christmas

France
18–11–18

Dearest:
I am on my way to see General Radnor back at the coast, about a five-hour
drive. Of my command here, Wheatley and I and a few clerks and maybe
Major Grieve will be the only ones going forward, all the rest will remain in
this area. The General wanted us all to remain, but both Wheatley and I
want to see the new country, then get our discharge as soon as possible.

As usual there was much behind these few lines, things we did not write about. Our little group was going to the Rhine. Naturally we would not go unless our Army, the 2nd, was going. It was soon known that only one of our British Armies would go forward into Germany as Army of Occupation. Which would it be? We understand there was some furious discussion on this point. It was generally assumed that the honour would go to the 1st Army. But remember, seniority is very, very important in the British Army. General Plumer was the senior Army Commander on the Western front. We understand that he insisted on his seniority in this dispute. Therefore General Plumer was given command of the force going to the Rhine. Naturally he took his own Army and we were part of his Army.

We had two duties to perform. First we had to see our Director, General Lord Radnor, and arrange for someone to carry on our work. Second, we were instructed to buy turkeys for our Christmas dinner.

We saw our friend, the Earl of Folkestone, and with deep regret we said goodbye. It had been something more than just pleasure to work under this fine Christian gentleman. We hope we learned many lessons from his kindly talks.

Then we went north along the coast road to Boulogne on our mission to buy turkeys. It was thought unlikely that we could buy turkeys in Germany anyway, so we were taking no chance on this important project. In cases like this we always let our assistant, Major Wheatley, do the bargaining. He could outbargain any produce vendor in France. Our turkeys were bought and, to make sure of delivery, we had our lorry ready. We saw our load of one ton of Christmas dinner on its way to cold storage at Roubaix. There was to be an interval before the army moved, so we thought it a chance for leave in England.

Russell Hotel, London
27–11–18

Dearest:
Well I wish you could have been with me last night to see Roxana. Doris Keane is certainly fine. It is a laughable play right through and I enjoyed it fine. Just behind me was sitting Colonel Hamilton who I knew quite well in the old 9th Corps and also in the 5th Army. I expect to meet him again when I get back to Roubaix where I left our HQ. They will be moving on in a few days but not till I get back. I am not sure if we will stop at Namur or go right through to Cologne or Bonn. The Canadians are coming to our Army and I may see a lot of old friends. Coming out the other day I came from Roubaix through Lille, Armentières, Bailleul, Meteren, Flêtre, Cassel, St. Omer to Boulogne. Can you follow that road on the map?

The Canadians were going as part of the Army of Occupation. Once more honoured above others. Why not the Australians, or the New

Zealanders, or the South Africans, or the Newfoundlanders? We wonder, does history say why?

> I have taken my ticket to Aberystwyth.[77] It is on the coast in centre Wales. I
> am going to have a look at the home of my forefathers.

Naturally we enjoyed our few days in the place where the name Hughes is as common as Smith is in Canada. We were amused when some of our new acquaintances said that we still had the Welsh accent. We are only fourth-generation Canadian.

On the Road to the Rhine

2nd Army HQ
12–12–18

Dearest:
Not much news today but I must write to you just the same. It always seems
I have left undone some of my work if I have not written to you. I hope long
before this that the awful flu has left the West. You seem to have had it
worse than over here.

We who were in the British Armies, who had seen and lived with death for years, were escaping a worse harvest of death than anything we had seen on the battlefield—the flu.[78] We were in the safest place on earth, from the wave of destruction that swept to the far corners of the world.

How was that, you ask. The entire army had moved forward at, for us, a very opportune time. Our hospitals had been emptied, the patients evacuated to England. We had doctors aplenty, nurses asking for work, medicine chests full, and empty hospital beds. At the first sign of flu a doctor was there, a nurse to take over, and a bed ready. We had losses, but very few by comparison. While all this time it was the reverse in England. There the hospitals were already crowded, the doctors few, and nurses working around the clock. Had the Almighty Power called a halt to war to give war-weary men a chance against a still-greater killer? We still wonder.

When censor regulations were relaxed I thought I could write reams of letters, but everything seems flat and tame now. Anyway we are away back here miles and miles from the front with but little to do as we have handed over to the Fifth Army. We will be moving on Sunday and I hope to be able to write and tell you about the country we pass through. I don't know who goes by train and who by road. Of course, I intend to go by road myself if nothing hinders. There will be ten or a dozen cars so we will be quite a little party. We will likely be about three days on the trip. We do not know the country we will be travelling so we will not run after dark. We must always be armed when in Germany and one person must not go out alone, always in couples.

The Army order was to the effect that while in Germany, all other ranks when not on duty must be in parties of at least four and carry sidearms, officers must be in pairs and carry their revolvers.

General Plumer showed a mark of genius when, within twenty-four hours of our arrival in Cologne, he countermanded this order and instead issued this order;

No officer or other ranks will carry revolvers or sidearms when not on duty.

We, an Army of Occupation in a hostile country and unarmed.

The very fact that we went unarmed gave us greater protection than if we all bristled with guns and knives. We gained something greater than arms, we gained respect. The German honours the man who is unafraid.

Hôtel de Poste
Brussels
14–12–18

Dearest:
Well here we are, so far on our way to Germany. Captain Heyer and I are travelling together in Heyer's car. Wheatley and Lidden [Heyer's assistant]

will come on last in my car. This car is an open Sunbeam and for these lovely days much the nicer. Heyer and I are an advance party to prepare billets, horse room and mess. Major Grieve is coming in charge of the train. We expect to reach the Rhine a day ahead of the rest of the party. Yesterday, when we started out, it was intended that we should go right through to Leuven at least. But we reached here at four o'clock and it is such a wonderful place I wanted to stay for the evening and night. I may never get another chance to see this which has the reputation of being the gayest city in Europe.

The sun was shining when we drove into the Grand Plaza and it was a wonderful sight. Every building in the square is covered with gilt that shines like burnished gold. Heyer had been telling me about this place and he said it was worth a day's journey to see. He said that it should be seen at three different times. When the sun is shining, when the moon was full, and in the electric light. We saw it in the sunshine. We decided to see it by moonlight and electric light. So we looked for a hotel. Or rather Heyer led us to this hotel.

Captain Heyer stayed at this hotel thirty eight years ago, then a boy of thirteen and going to school. If you knew him now you would not take him to be any older than myself if as old. He talks French, German, Flemish, Italian and a smattering of others. The shops are full here, but everything is very very expensive.

If we have good luck tomorrow we will lunch in Liège and stay the night in Aix-la-Chapelle [Aachen].

Brussels was worth staying over to see. First we were taken to see the statue of Edith Cavell.[79] This was only two weeks after the German Army had given up Belgium's capital city, yet already a large monument was there for everyone to see. It was a beautiful thing, very life-like, and cast in some sort of plaster. Later the people told us it would be made in everlasting marble. This was the first thing these liberated citizens did, even as the Hun was leaving their gates. Erect a memorial to an English woman who had given her all for freedom.

We said to Captain Heyer, "we should see the Peeing Manikin."[80]

The famous Manikin Pis fountain in Brussels, Belgium, as it looked in 1995. It probably looked the same when John saw it in late 1918.

Hardly were the words out of our mouth than an urchin of about eight said, "Me show you. Me show you." He led us down a narrow street and there at the corner was the life-size statue of a small boy peeing on a cabbage leaf. It is on a rather obscure corner on a narrow street, yet this is the prized emblem of Brussels.

The streets of Brussels, how to describe them at night? The wave of joy at liberation was still flowing high. Bands played in the streets. Men and women danced in the centres of the roadways, blocking all traffic. Laughter and song and dance, and an English soldier in their midst only made the gaiety more gay. We were hugged and kissed and made to dance, then come in and have a glass of wine. We went to the theatre and met a Belgian gentleman who was a newspaper proprietor and he told us tales of the underground resistance, some sad, some gay, and all courageous. In the wee small hours of the morning we went to bed, and a dance was going on in the middle of the street under our window.

Grand Hotel, Liège
15–12–18

Dearest:

Do you remember those days of suspense, the first ten days of August 1914? When all eyes were turned to a then but little known town in Belgium. Where King Albert's little army under General Léman held up the rush of the whole German Army. Well, here tonight I write you from that very spot. We decided to stay here tonight instead of going on to Aix-la-Chapelle and try and get right through to Cologne tomorrow. This is a big city and well kept but lacks a brightness and cheerfulness of Brussels. The crowd is very dead. This partly accounted for from the presence of thousands of returning prisoners all who show very evident signs of hardship and starvation.

These returning prisoners of war were streaming down from Germany. Under the Armistice terms Germany agreed to turn all prisoners loose, and supply them with transportation and food till they reached Allied lines. They were turned loose, that is all. Footsore, weary and hungry these men had walked, some of them several hundred miles, begging food where they could. Our transports were coming up loaded with food and here in Liège they were fed. But they came in long streams and even our supply ran low. Our soldiers, our Tommies, willingly and gladly went without meals so these poor hungry men could eat.

The Rhine

THE RHINE AT LAST. Did we make a mistake when we stopped just ten miles east of this German river? Twenty-two years later the answer was yes. At the time we said no. We were glad to stop and this was a pleasant land after more than four years of trenches and mud and rats.

The cavalry came up first, crossed the river at Cologne, Bonn, Koblenz, and Mannheim. Belgian, British, American, and French cavalry had taken up bridgehead defence positions in arcs of a radius of ten miles out from each of these cities. The infantry and artillery followed, and two days after we arrived in Cologne the cavalry gave over their positions to the infantry and retired across the Rhine.

Captain Heyer was Chief of the Requisition Department of the 2nd Army, now the Army of Occupation. According to the Armistice terms, Germany agreed to furnish many things for the use of the Allied Armies, including housing for troops of occupation. This was Captain Heyer's immediate work, find billets for Army Headquarters Staff and a division of the Guards in the city of Cologne. We were acting as his assistant. Army headquarters was still back at Namur, but would be up in two days' time. We were to receive a lesson in German discipline and order. We walked into the office of the Mayor (burgomaster) of Cologne and told him what we wanted. Rooms and offices for two hundred and fifty officers, rooms for a staff of five hundred other ranks, and billets for ten thousand troops.

The Mayor received this order without batting an eye. "Very well gentlemen," he said, "if you will come back in say half an hour, I will have a list of rooms and billets ready for you."

Half an hour to arrange the billeting of eleven thousand men. Very definitely being burgomaster of a German city was quite different than being the Mayor of an English city. The burgomaster had his list ready at the stated time and handed us a typewritten list of the billets. Also he stated that guides would stand by at his office, day and night, to guide parties to their respective billets. No fuss, no worrying, no quibbling; efficiency exemplified.

Captain Heyer and ourself then made a tour of the centre of the city. The finest hotel, on the Grand Plaza and close to the Cathedral, caught our eye. Said Heyer, "That's the place for the senior officers of the Army." "Fine," we said, "let's go in and take it over." We did. We walked into the manager's office, stated our qualifications and orders. We told him to turn out all his guests and discharge his staff within twenty-four hours, as we were taking over the entire hotel in the name of the British Army.

He protested, stating that a Swiss company, not a German, owned the hotel, therefore it did not come under the Armistice terms. His English was good, so Captain Heyer did not need to use his German and we could follow. This ruse got the manager nowhere. He was told to take it up with Berlin, but in the meantime the British Army was taking over the hotel in the stated time. Seeing that we were not arguing with him, he immediately allotted us rooms for ourself and the rest of our party who had just rolled in.

An hour later the manager came to our room with a proposition. He proposed that he maintain his entire staff—clerks, waiters, chambermaids, chefs and helpers. That he would continue as hotel manager and run the establishment. We would be like usual guests. He said that his cooks were among the best in Germany, his waiters carefully trained, and he would assure the comfort of all officers just like as if they were paying guests. Heyer looked at us, we looked at Heyer and nodded our approval. Heyer accepted at once in the name of the Army, and appointed one of his staff to act as co-ordinator between manager and Army. This plan had the approval of General Plumer and worked splendidly. In the four months we were to stay, there was not a single complaint. We were guests in the finest hotel on the Rhine.

Opera

THE DUTY FOR THE DAY BEING OVER, Heyer said, "Now for some pleasure. Let's go to the opera."

"Opera," we said. "Never been to an opera in my life. Don't know one note of music from another."

"That does not matter," replied our friend, "just come along to the opera for this once and you will change your mind."

We did. The opera house at Cologne was one of the Royal Operas of Germany and was a magnificent place. The attendant asked us if we would like a box. The price in the already depreciated German currency was actually very low, so we took a box. The next box on the right to the Royal Box of Emperor Wilhelm. Some class for an English captain and a Canadian major.

As we said, we did not know one note of music from another. We did not need to. Music, good music, does not need an education in music to charm. We sat enthralled. Captain Heyer, a linguist and a musician, knew the story of every good opera on record and from time to time at intervals told us the story. When, after three hours of delightful music and song, our friend suggested taking a box for a week, we agreed. A box for four. We knew that others of our party would be glad to attend. When the manager told us the price, we increased our time to a month. Our party—one major, one captain and two lieutenants—took the box next to the Emperor's for one month. Remember, we had promised ourself to be on our way to Canada after a week in Germany. We renewed our lease twice after that. We took in the whole season of opera.

That first night there was just a handful of men in khaki in the audience. The next night a hundred, and within the week a thousand. Finally the manager was worried. It looked as if the civilians would be crowded out altogether, so he proposed that a thousand seats be allotted to army personnel and the remainder to the people. This was agreed, and all units of the Army of Occupation were given a chance to see and hear opera. There was never a night when there were vacant seats. English troops, Englishmen, and Canadians crowded that place. Then why has opera never been a success in England?

The second night, the play was *Tannhäuser*, one of Wagner's best. Captain Heyer wrote out the story for our benefit before the show, and this was a great help. The next night, there were requests for copies, so our friend had several copies made. This night, the Army Commander, General Plumer, and his Chief of Staff, General Percy, occupied the Royal Box. General Percy,[81] who had been kind to us the first day we, an unwanted Canadian officer, came to 9th Corps looking for anything to do and whom we had met on many occasions at Army Headquarters, noted us reading the score of the play. "Hughes," he said, "what's that story you are reading?"

We handed him the sheet, telling how our friend had made the play more agreeable. The two generals studied the written story and were more than pleased.

Next morning, Heyer had a call from the Army Commander. When he returned, he said that he had been asked to write out the story of the coming evening's opera and that the army would mimeograph a goodly number for the benefit of army personnel attending the opera. This was a great success and our friend had a new job for every day, or rather twelve days every two weeks. Finally the manager of the opera, noting these leaflets, suggested that he himself write out the story of the day's opera in English and these would be available at two pence a copy. This was agreed and took considerable work off our friend. Today we look at these booklets. The English grammar, not good but very understandable. *The Flying Dutchman, Mastersingers of Nuremberg, Last Rose of Summer,* and many, many others, a reminder of a winter season of opera at one of the finest opera houses in Europe. A magnificent house of music that charmed thousands who knew nothing about music. A son of ours, still unborn at that time, helped to blow that home of music to rubble and dust some twenty-six years later.

Christmas 1918

Cologne, Germany
Christmas Eve

Dearest:
I wonder what you are doing this evening. Here one day is the same as another. Sunday, Monday, Christmas or any day. To be sure there is an effort being made to give the men an extra dinner. A turkey dinner they would not have had except for Wheatley and I. We bought turkeys in Boulogne for all HQ messes. And by car, lorry and train delivered them here. While the EFC [Expeditionary Force Canteen] people went to Paris and spent two million francs on turkeys and they have not turned up yet, and that is two weeks ago. Am afraid they will be a bit high when they do arrive.

Actually the turkeys were green when a week after New Year's they arrived. They were unloaded with shovels. We had watched anxiously for those turkeys, as it would create a bad impression if we officers had roast turkey and our men had none. The whole matter was in the hands of Major Wheatley, Captain Heyer, and ourself, as we were more or less the overall mess committee. It was left to ourself to decide. The day before Christmas and still no EFC turkeys. We called the mess committee of the men and told them to arrange among themselves for the distribution of the officers' turkeys. Perhaps for an hour we were the most disliked officer on General Plumer's staff, but as soon as the circumstances were explained, every last officer said, of course, this was the only thing that could be done. The officers had roast beef.

We have two new members of our Mess. Lord Devenport,[82] *late food controller of England, and Commander Benn,*[83] *R.N., M.P. for a London division. Both are very interesting men who are out seeing conditions at first hand. Benn tells great tales of the Navy and is a great talker on any subject. Very nice meeting such interesting men, leaders in their walks of life.*

Another new messmate was Captain Ramsay, brother of Commander Ramsay who was marrying Princess Patricia. Captain Ramsay, as the best man, went home for the wedding. When he returned, we asked him how it went off and was he himself soon going to marry. He said he enjoyed it fine and had fallen in love with the Princess Royal, but as he had not a penny to his name he had better forget it. He was very interested in Western Canada and suggested we go into partnership and buy a ranch. We understand that after the war he got a position as manager of a very large estate in Scotland, so we did not see him in the West.

The Guards' Colours

Cologne, Germany
7–1–19

Dearest

*I have just come from witnessing a historic sight. The arrival of the Guards'
colours in Cologne. Just think of it, all the colours of a Guards Division here
on the Rhine, and thousands and thousands of German people crowding to
see the event. They showed no displeasure or annoyance. Those in uniform
came to salute, and those in civilian clothes took off their hats as each pair
of colours came past. Would we do the same if the Prussian Guards were
marching through Edmonton or London? I cannot understand it. It made
one proud just to watch those Guards. Each colour party fifty strong, everyone
a picked man, tall upstanding chaps. The pick of the Empire's fighting force.
Each regiment had their drums and all the bands were going together as
they swung down through the square under the shadow of Germany's
greatest Gothic structure, the Cologne Cathedral. Not a sound but the
drums. Not a cheer. Will it help bring home to these people that they were
beaten? What was the main thought in the minds of these thousands of
people?*

where General Plumer Stood

KÖLN a. Rhein. Hohenzollernbrücke

*A postcard of the Hohenzollernbrücke in Cologne (Köln a Rhein). John has made a
marginal notation of where General Plumer stood, possibly to review a unit of the
British Army of Occupation as it arrived in Germany in late 1918 or early 1919. Like
many of John's WWI letters, the card was nibbled upon by the mice before it was
rescued from the attic of John and Sara's house in the mid-1950s.*

> *Today at lunch an officer came and sat at the next table to ours. It was
> Captain Brick, 202 Bn. He is now Camp Commandant Canadian Corps at Bonn.
> He is from Fort Saskatchewan. You know he bought the next farm to our own.*

Captain Brick's granddaughter now teaches in our village school.

The Prince of Wales

Cologne, Germany
9–1–19 .

Dearest:
What shall I tell you about today? Oh yes, I know. I saw the Prince. Many others saw and passed our future King. A quiet unassuming young lad. Military rank, Major. Our own boys passed him on the street and in the usual careless manner forgot to salute. He was only an officer, and why be saluting all the time? To these civilians, he was but another British officer. But to a few of us who knew, he was far more. I would no doubt have passed him like the others, only I was watching for him.

We were standing in the rotunda of our Headquarters hotel and the Sergeant of the Guard, at the door, came to us.

"Sir," he said, "have you seen the Prince about?"

"No Sergeant. Are you expecting him?"

"I had a tip, Sir, that he was in the city, and it would be terrible if we did not give him a salute, for he is Honourary Colonel of our Regiment." The sergeant was in the Grenadier Guards, this was a General's guard, and there the Present was given only to generals or above. The Prince was Royal.

"I will try and find out for you, Sergeant," we replied. Going over to our friend Lieutenant Ledden, son of a nobleman, we asked him if he had seen the Prince.

"No," he replied, "is he expected?"

We told him what the Sergeant of the Guard had said. Ledden looked around. "There he is," he said, "over there at the news stand buying picture post cards."

We went quietly over to the sergeant and told him where the Prince was. In a few minutes, the Prince and his companion, having bought their post cards, strolled slowly past and out the hotel door.

"Guard...PRESENT...ARMS!!" You could have heard this ringing order clear across the Grand Square of Cologne. The Guard came smartly to the Present. The sergeant was rewarded by one of the Prince's winning smiles as he returned the salute.

> He had no escort. Just his chum and he strolled unconcerned about these streets, no swank, no blaring of trumpets. He did not even wear his red staff cap, just his Guards badge. Everyone in the Army admires him very much. Maybe a careless gay youth at times, but a very manly boy. And his free mixing with his people will in the end make him a better ruler when his time comes. All he needs is a good English wife.

What made us write that last line that day in Germany? Would that our wish had come true.

> I wonder had it been known who was here, how many thousands of people would have thronged the square. I have only seen the King once, and that was while passing in a car, back in France nearly a year ago. Then it would have been a serious offence to have written to say I saw him. It was one of his flying trips when things looked none too good for us. He came over to see for himself and to cheer his Army. Always the trouble was to keep him out of the danger zone. He was so keen to see the actual fighting line and to cheer the boys under fire. One day he was at Watou, and hardly had he left than the Boche started shelling the town with H.E. Did they know, I wonder? I was there an hour later and saw how accurate was their range. In St. Omer I had lunch and tea in the same house as the King used to stay

at. A fine old French gentleman was his host and very proud of having entertained our King.

Another little story about our Prince: While stationed at Flêtre in mid-1917, we often saw, in the early morning, a young man in shorts out for a run. Just shorts and running shoes. We paid no attention to him. If he wanted to run, then it was alright with us, we would walk.

We would have paid more attention to the runner if we had known that he was Prince Eddie—Edward Prince of Wales. This young man's idea of keeping fit was to eat sparingly and exercise freely. He was a Corps Ammunition Officer. The only trouble was that he wanted to personally carry the ammunition right into the front line.

One day we stopped to inspect a garden belonging to an Artillery unit. We were talking to a young Captain we knew. They had been having a sports day and I knew that this chap hoped to win the one-mile horse race.

"Well Captain, how did the races go? Did you win?"

"No such luck, but my horse did."

"Just what do you mean?"

"Well it was this way. Along came the Prince of Wales and he saw my horse. He said, 'who owns this little beauty of a grey mare? I would like to ride her myself if I was in this unit.' Well, naturally there was nothing I could do but step forward and ask him to ride my horse. He did, and won."

Many tales were told about the Prince's reckless riding and his many spills. Is it any wonder when, at a moment's notice, he was ready to ride a horse without previous knowledge of that horse or saddle. He was absolutely without fear.

The Armistice Commission

Cologne, Germany
21–1–19

Dearest:
Just a few lines this morning before I go out to count agricultural machinery
in stock and to find out the capacity of the factories engaged in the manu-
facture of such implements. I don't know, but I suppose it has to do with
these new Armistice terms where the Boche must hand back to France and
Belgium fifty-eight thousand agricultural implements. I think the Boche is
being let down very lightly in this matter, as I am sure he stole or destroyed
twice this amount. I am trying to get relieved so I can come home in a few
weeks.

How far we were out in our wish to get on our way home. General
Chichester,[84] Quartermaster General, called us in and told us that we had
been appointed the British Army Agricultural Representative on the
Armistice Commission, and that we were to report to General Green[85] at
Spa, France. What did this mean? We did not know, neither did the general.
This had come from GHQ.

Cologne, Germany

23–1–19

Dearest:

Just a few lines this evening. No word about my relief orders and worse still I have to go to GHQ tomorrow morning where I am appointed to represent the Army on a Commission to see that the Boche hand over all those farm implements called for in the last Armistice terms.[86] How long this will take I haven't the foggiest notion or if once at the job I can stop when Major Grieve is appointed to take over my post. But orders are orders and must be obeyed. Especially when they come from GHQ.

It was nearly a hundred-mile drive to Spa, down near the Luxembourg border, but it was mostly through new country to us and quite enjoyable, a rolling, tree-covered country, a pleasant land.

At Spa we reported to General Green and sat in at a meeting of one section of the Armistice Commission. This was an interesting group—English, French, American, and Belgian officers. We soon learned what our work was to be. Under the terms of the Armistice, Germany was to send to France and Belgium farm implements for those stolen or destroyed. The value of these was to be counted in the reparation payment. England did not want any of these implements, but the value of these would be considered when the Allies totalled up their shares of these reparation payments. Therefore our work was to check and see if the values and invoices that came with the shipments of implements corresponded with the actual implements received. We would be expected to visit each railway receiving point along the Rhine and from time to time inspect the actual shipments and check the invoices.

One of the English officers present expressed our situation fully; "Hughes, you lucky chap, here you are handed *carte blanche* instructions to go where you like, when you like, all up and down the Rhine. Wish I could go as your assistant."

Another English officer warned us that we must watch very carefully, as the Boche would be trying to slip things over on us and send faulty or only partly equipped machines.

An elderly Belgian officer, in faultless English, said this was wrong, and went on to explain. "Germany lost the war. Now she is out to win the peace. She will send the very best machines she can make so that we will send repeat orders to her factories. I predict that Major Hughes's work will be very easy."

Nothing could have been more correct. The implements were all new, right from the factories. Instructions for their use were carefully printed in English, French, and Flemish. Also, all railway officials no doubt had been instructed to give us every possible help in our work. Yes, Germany was out to win the peace.

General Green asked us to lunch with him personally, and we expected more detailed instructions about our work. These instructions consisted of questions about farming in Western Canada. We remember General Green for this enjoyable lunch and his always courteous manner.

So there we had it. Take your time, go sight-seeing up and down the Rhine, with only token work at all the railway crossings leading to France and Belgium. In the Belgian area at Crefeld near Düsseldorf, British at Cologne, Canadian at Bonn, American at Koblenz, and French at Mannheim. A car, a driver, and take friends along with you if you like. Truly, war is terrible, especially when we could so often arrange it so as to get back to Cologne in time for the opera.

Army Cows on the Rhine

Cologne
22–2–19

Dearest:
Last night a Canadian Chaplain drifted in here, quite lost, but I was able to fix him up. He is staying for three days. He was Presbyterian minister at Tofield, Alberta and enlisted in the ranks. McColl is his name, a jolly little chap.

I am taking the little Canadian padre out to the farm this afternoon just for a run. From what the papers say and print you would think our dairy farm supplied all the milk and butter for the Army of Occupation instead of a favoured few who happen to be connected with Army Headquarters. The boys have been buying up copies of the papers to send home to their relatives.

We have before us clippings from the *Daily Mail*, February 21st 1919, showing cuts of our men making butter and showing off our cows. When General Plumer asked us to buy cows to supply milk and cream for Army Headquarters messes, we did not think that within a few months we would have these cows foraging on a German dairy farm on the Rhine and that Germany would be footing the cost of their feed.

Fokker-Kampfeinsitzer (Dreidecker) D.R.I.

John probably purchased this postcard of a Fokker Tri-plane in Germany in early 1919. On the back is a note to his youngest son: "Dear Billy, This is a picture of the wonderful three deck fast climbing plane the Germans used against us. It was very hard to catch. With love, Daddy. Cologne, Germany, 11–2–19" The card must have been enclosed with a letter to Sara as the note runs across the entire back, and there is no address or stamp on it.

> *Evening and my letter not finished. A Colonel just strolled into our office and wanted to know where we could buy a thousand cows, two thousand pigs and five thousand hens. Some order. I told him I would produce the articles named if he would give me a bank balance of a million dollars. He is to try and arrange this. Hope he does not arrange this until Major Grieve gets back. I don't want the job. They would have to be bought in England, as France would not allow us to export that number. They need them all themselves.*

We do not know if this ambitious order was ever carried out or not. But we do know that our cows were all milking fine when we left the army. Nearly every day German farmers would come around and try to buy our cows, offering twice what we had paid for them back near Cassel, France. All in all, it was a highly profitable venture, as they had already paid back into the Fat Fund more than their cost.

We Decide Not to Requisition the Cologne Cathedral

WE HAD ONE VERY JOLLY CHAP in our mess at Cologne. He was the Senior Roman Catholic Chaplain of the Army of Occupation. He was very broad-minded in many things. Also he was a good poker player. He would play up until 12 p.m. Saturday, but not a minute after, until he had said High Mass on Sunday. This also applied to his drinks.

We were, for a few weeks, acting Requisition Officer for the Army, taking the place of Captain Heyer, then on leave. One day during this time the Padre came to us in quite a heat.

"Hughes," he said, "I want you to requisition the Cologne Cathedral for the use of the British Army."

"Well now, Padre," we said, "what do you mean?"

"It is this way. The Archbishop of Cologne refuses to allow me to conduct services for our troops in the Cathedral, so I want you to turn him out and let me use it for the Army."

"Now Padre, let us study this. I doubt if the Army Commander would want to get embroiled with Rome. Let me suggest something. You go and pull a good Canadian bluff on the Archbishop. Tell him that you have consulted the Army Requisition Officer and that he has agreed to requisition the Cathedral unless he gives you permission to use a part of it for British troops."

The Padre actually was a Canadian and, knowing his ability to bluff when the jackpot was loaded, we felt sure he could out-bluff the Archbishop. He did. He came back an hour later all smiles and reported that our bluff had worked. He was to use the West Nave.

We felt relieved. Of course we would not have acted without personally consulting General Plumer. Anyway, we had avoided any dispute with Rome.

Hotel Manager

Cologne
or Coln or Koln
23–2–19

Dearest:

This job of hotel manager is not detailed in Kings Regulations and Orders. You see, when we came to Cologne we took over the finest hotel in the city. We kept all the civilian help and turned out the civilian visitors. Ground floor is for messes and anterooms, next two for offices, and next two for officers billets. Then part of the top floor for servants quarters and my clerks, as you see it has always been run from my office. We keep ten rooms for casual visitors of a few days. This means constant changes other than the usual changes in Army Staff. Then we have a visitors mess where we feed all these chaps. Lucky one of my corporals who runs all this is an A1 chap so takes most of the load. He also draws rations for all messes, divides the rations and keeps the accounts. Just one of the side shows one gets pushed into in the Army. Of course someone must do these things and our Quartermaster [General Chichester] has found us capable of expansion in many directions and just sort of passes these jobs onto us as a matter of course. So you may see me looking for a job as a hotel manager when I get

back home. I guess not. I am waiting in the office now for a couple of
Generals who want looking after for the night.

Then it was decided to move GHQ up from Namur and even this big hotel did not have enough rooms. So the Quartermaster told us to enlarge our quarters. Another smaller hotel joined this one, so we walked in and told the manager to turn out his guests and be ready for Army personnel within forty-eight hours. He made quite a protest, but we were used to this and paid no attention. Maybe we were a bit arrogant. Some of his guests were quite indignant at being turned out on short notice, especially some of the women. One woman was very eager to stay. She even offered to share her room with an officer. We saw that this lady (?) left within the hour.

Touring the Rhine

Cologne

18–3–19

Dearest:

A few lines tonight, but not the news I hoped to send you as Major Grieve has not turned up to take my place. He must be sick in England. Tomorrow I go to Duisburg and Dusseldorf. I would like to cross into the main part of these cities but they are in the neutral zone and as there is considerable trouble going on between the local government and the strikers we are not allowed to cross the Rhine there. Then I must go to Mainz and Frankfurt-on-Main, returning by way of Spa [to report to General Green]. This is a three day trip at least.

19–3–19

Well I have had a full day. Leaving early we drove north to Dusseldorf. The Belgian guard would not let us cross the river so we kept on up between Duisburg and Crefeld where we are receiving agricultural machinery from the Boche, then back to Crefeld for lunch.

Crefeld was Belgian Headquarters and here we were to see the difference in the way the British Army treated their late enemies and the way the Belgians did the trick. In Cologne and Bonn and all other places, our men of all ranks gave full and equal rights to all Germans. They were courteous and as correct as if they were tourists in peace time. German police kept order and kept it well. A British soldier always gave his seat to a German woman in a street car. We sat together at the opera, at the theatre, and in the cafés. Not so the Belgian.

We got out of our car and happened to follow three Belgian officers walking abreast down the sidewalk. They took up the whole width of the walk. When they met civilians, men or women, the civilians stepped aside into the gutter or street. This was a sample of their behaviour. The Germans were sullen and their looks showed hatred. Belgian police ruled the town. We thought, how much easier our way—we let the Germans run their town and we go to the opera.

Leaving Crefeld we arrived back in Cologne in time to make a report and then go to the opera. It was the first part of the Ring [Rhine Gold]. This was Wagner's masterpiece and of course the star turn in German opera. I am afraid I will not be able to see the other three parts.

We were to go south and see how we Canadians and our American cousins and the French treated their late enemies. As we always had the excuse that we must inspect shipments of agricultural implements from Germany, we could go anywhere along the Rhine.

Cologne
15–3–19

Dearest:
Yesterday Wheatley, Liebert and I took a holiday and went joy riding to Coblenz. The American HQ. It was a delightful trip and many times during the day I wished you could be with us. I know you would have appreciated and enjoyed it very much. Of course we went by car and the car ran well and never a puncture the whole trip. We started at 1000 hours [new army way of writing time and means ten o'clock]. The famous Rhine vineyards

are on the slopes of the hillsides on the right bank, as that side gets the
most sun. These vineyards are terraced into the hillsides and are really quite
small. Soon we were in the American zone and ran for miles along their
piquet line, Americans on all sides of you. It is remarkable how much of our
equipment and arms they have adopted. We eventually arrived at Coblenz
at 1230 hours and crossed the Moselle River just in the town. After winding
around many crooked streets we found the American Officers club where
we had been directed to have lunch. An American Captain stepped up to us
and introduced himself and asked if he might act as our host and insisted
on sharing a bottle of wine. Nothing stronger is allowed.

Do you know the white Rhine wine? If not, go easy. It goes down very easy, but be careful, it has the kick of an Army mule. We saw what it would do to the uninitiated. An American officer came in and sat at a nearby table. He ordered a bottle of wine. He drank it as a man might a bottle of beer on a hot day. Soon his eyes grew glassy, he slowly stiffened and oh so slowly slid under the tables. The waiters, apparently used to the effect of their very potent vintage, took this as quite normal and saw to the comfort of the officer who, for the moment, was *hors de combat*.

We had early learned to watch our English or—better still—our French comrades when using wine at the table. A little incident comes to mind. Months before this incident we were dining with Colonel Count de Jourdains, Chief of the French Army Interpreter Staff. We were his guest. He was talking most interestingly when just casually he raised his glass of wine to his lips. Actually he did not taste the wine. A look of disgust, then anger, came over his face and excitedly he called the headwaiter. We did not need to know French to follow his tirade; "Swine, pig swill. What did he mean by insulting his guests. Take it away. Throw it down the gutter, bring us wine!"

The headwaiter was most apologetic. He had not noticed that a French gentleman was ordering. Just give him a moment to rectify his mistake. He sent one of his men on the run for the wine cellar. A bottle came, still covered with cobwebs. Carefully the headwaiter handed it to Count de Jourdains, who looked at the label and date, then handed it back for opening. Fresh glasses were brought and carefully filled by the headwaiter himself. Our host lifted his glass and sniffed. Remember that: sniff first, not taste. Count de Jourdains was all smiles, the headwaiter was forgiven, and we learned what wine, real wine, tasted like. What we had first been served was quite alright for ordinary folk, Canadian or American.

We had lunch, then out again to see the city. We crossed the Rhine on the Bridge of Boats [pontoons placed side by side and planked, it had been used for many years]. Then we climbed up and up and up the winding road to the Fortress Castle that far overlooks all the surrounding country. There we had a wonderful view of the Rhine and the Moselle.

On the way back, at Bonn, we stopped at the Officers club of the 10 Corps. Lieberts old corps. He Is our Paymaster.

This trip came of Liebert saying, "Hughes, I am fed up with the office, what can I do to get some fresh air?"

Incidentally, we inspected and reported on recent arrivals of plows and tractors straight from German factories.

Going Home

WE HAD NOT EXPECTED to be in Germany for more than a few weeks.

Cologne

23–1–19

Dearest:

I am coming HOME. Soon, very soon. We have been recalled and I expect to be on my way within the next two weeks. Home Dearest to you and the boys and Mother and Dad.

But it was exactly two months later when we wrote:

Cologne

23–3–19

Dearest:

Just a note to tell you that I leave here on the early morning train. What luck after that remains to be seen. Anyway it will be a start homewards. Just at the moment I am on G duty. Rather curious that after escaping Day & Night duty at Q for nearly a year and a half I should be caught on the last day of my stay. You see, one officer must stay during breakfast and dinner and lunch, on duty, to answer for the whole Army. Same at night; no hardship as one goes to bed as usual with the phone at one's head. Well in a way I am sorry to leave the boys here, because I have been very well treated all the time I have been here. Have had many chances that one not wearing CANADA on his shoulder would not have had. Now for Home, and my loved ones.

Cologne-Boulogne Express,
Between Verviers & Namur, Belgium

Dearest:
Well here I am on my way to you. I was setting reading the paper when I looked out of the window and saw we were in a very pretty part of the country and at once thought I ought to write Dearest. Somehow it is always like that. I see something interesting and I think, how Dearest would like to see this, and as she cannot, why I must write to her.

Our train consists of hospital coaches, converted first class English day coaches and kitchen cars. The hospital coaches are like our American cars, all one compartment with three tier stretcher beds along the sides. The day coaches have been made so one seat only remains in each small compart-ment and two in the larger. No one below the rank of Lieut. Colonel may use one of these compartments and they are usually filled with Generals. But I happen to have one to myself, because I had a friend at court, or in other words, Captain Morgan, one of our mess, who has charge of trains and appointed me OC train. So once more I am favoured. I am afraid I have been spoiled by the Imperials and will get a rude awakening when I get back to our own force.

It is nearly eleven o'clock and I am going to turn in pretty soon and try and sleep and hope to wake up in Boulogne. So Goodnight. I am coming to you just as fast as I can.

John.

Russia and the Foreign Office

ONE LAST STORY we feel must be told, because we believe that we are the only one who can tell the tale to the end.

We were in the 9th Reserve Battalion, Bramshott, England, in early 1917, waiting and hoping for a chance to go to France. One day we had a new roommate—Lieutenant Nels McKela.[87] We had known Nels as a boy back in Fort Saskatchewan days. As a lad he worked in the local furniture store, then he had gone to university. He had enlisted for overseas in the Western University Battalion, and when this was broken up like so many other battalions, he had been sent to military school and obtained his commission.

In May 1919 we were at Ryl, Wales, awaiting return to Canada. Again one day we had a new roommate—Lieutenant Nels McKela. Nels had joined the air force and naturally we expected to hear tales of the air. As it was, Nels was rather reluctant to tell of his experiences. Then at last he told his story.

"Major, you may not believe what I tell you. Not a single person has believed my story and I had decided not to tell it again, but you have known me for years and maybe.... After you went to France I was called up to London and was sent to the Foreign Office. There I met the Honourable Arthur Balfour,[88] Minister of Foreign Affairs. He questioned me about my family history and then asked if I would be willing to go on a Secret Service. I said yes. You may not know, but actually I am a Finnlander. My father was a Colonel in the Russian army. He was accused of plotting for the overthrow of Russian control of Finland. They could not prove anything against him, but he was told that the best thing he could do was to leave Russia for life. He brought his family to Canada and we settled near Redwater, Alberta. From there on you have known me. I think you also know my mother. My father is dead. Now you know that after the Russian revolution it was nearly impossible to get any information out of that country. What Arthur Balfour asked me to do was go to Russia and observe and report. Of course I accepted. I could speak Finnish and our family still had many connections over there. I was told to go back to my unit and await instructions. A month later I was called again and there in London I entered a room and was startled at what I saw. It was as if I was looking into a mirror. An officer, a lieutenant, who was so like what I saw every day in my mirror, was facing me. My exact double. I was told that this man would take my place in the air force squadron as Nels McKela, so that no one would know that I was not there myself. We lived together for a month. He learned to speak like myself, learned my every action, learned to imitate my writing, learned all my family and social life. He actually wrote letters to my mother. Then he went to the squadron and I went to Russia. I was accredited to General Kerensky[89] and he was the only one who knew that I was not a Russian. I managed to get information out by way of submarines to England. I was on the Russian front in the Carpathian mountains and was wounded twice. I saw the massacre of the Russian officers in the Grand Square in St. Petersburg and narrowly escaped a like fate. Finally after months of service all over Russia, I managed to get away on the last submarine that left St. Petersburg. After returning to England my double was withdrawn and I went back to the RAF." That was his story.

Then he went on, "No one believes my story. I was laughed at, some even think I am a bit cracked. After all, why should they believe me? Nels McKela never left his Canadian unit or the RAF."

For some reason we believed Nels's story, or maybe it was just sympathy for a young friend in trouble, who, if his story was true, had done much for his adopted country, Canada.

When later we left for Canada we were OC draft going home. We had 600 men and four officers, one of whom was Nels McKela. We carried the pay cheques and army records of those whose destination was Edmonton. We were to hand these over to the Army Commandant there. Our curiosity was so great that we opened the parcel of records and there we read, "Lieutenant Nels McKela, Seconded to the Imperial Foreign Office" from such a date to such a date—the exact time my friend said he was away.

Our own army record reads, "Seconded to the War Office." We know that we were not with our Canadian Army during that time. Our last report of Nels McKela was that he was on his way to join the Finnish Air Force at the invitation of an old friend of his father's, Marshal Mannerheim of Finland.

The Happiest Girl in the World

WAR IN THE PAST has mostly been a man's story and is apt to be grim, nevertheless war in all times has produced romance, so here near our close let us have a bit of romance.

We were in Ripon Camp in Yorkshire waiting so impatiently to go home. A month from the day we left Germany. We had as a roommate one Billy Benn[90] from Medicine Hat in Alberta. We had known Billy in the old days in Sarcee Camp when he was in the 175th Battalion. A fine upstanding chap who had joined the air force. We watched Billy one day, from our cot where we were lounging.

"What's wrong, Billy? Sick?"

"No."

"Well what is it? You look as cheerful as a man going into the trenches for the umpteenth time."

Billy looked our way, he wanted to talk but seemed afraid, then it all came with a rush. "Here I am billed to go home to Canada on Monday and I am leaving behind the loveliest, sweetest girl in all England. I wish... I wish I wasn't going."

"Well then, why don't you take her with you? Won't she go?"

"She would go alright, but you see I cannot afford to marry her now. I will have to go home and get a job and work for a year and save enough money to send for her."

240

"Tell me Billy. Do you really truly intend to send for her when you can afford to do so?"

"Certainly!" He was very emphatic.

"Well then Billy, is it not a case that you cannot afford *not* to marry her now?'

"What do you mean?" Billy was sitting up on his cot, eyes wide open.

"Why just think. Marry her now and she will get free transportation home to Canada. Also she will draw Separation Allowance until you are discharged and for six months afterwards."

Billy stared unblinking and so slowly said, "Are you sure, Major?"

"Certainly. Tell you what we will do, let's go to the Orderly Room and talk to the Adjutant."

Billy needed no urging. We went. Our story was confirmed. Back we went to our room. Then doubt for a moment assailed our young friend. He was going home to Canada on Monday and this was Friday. He was in the north of England, the girl in the south. Maybe we helped.

"You say you want her, Billy. Send her a telegram and see if she really wants you."

We did not see what actually went into that telegram, but when it was on its way we had a nervous, high-strung lad on our hands.

Unicorn Hotel
Ripon, Yorks
26–4–19

Dearest:
I am waiting here for a Bride and Groom to come. Then we will have a wedding dinner. The groom is my room-mate, a Lieut. Billy Benn, 175 Bn from Medicine Hat. This is a hurry wedding as they did not intend to get married for six months yet. In a way I am an aider and abettor in the plot, because it was myself who pointed out to Benn that by getting married here instead of having the lady come to him in Canada six months hence, he would save her passage money and he or rather she would receive separation allowance along with his six months gratuity. And moreover it is much nicer for a woman to be coming all those thousands of miles to her husband than to be coming just to her lover.

We are sure that Billy did not sleep much that night and he was up early, waiting. At last came a messenger boy with a telegram. Billy's hands were shaking when he opened it. Then over his face came a wide happy smile. He thrust the glad tidings into our hands. We can read that telegram today after all these years.

She must be a plucky girl to come on the moment all alone as she did. Her telegram in answer to his telling her to come was typical of a woman.

> *Happiest girl in the world.*
> *Coming on the double.*
> *Love always, Mona.*

and addressed to Lieutenant Billy Benn. How is that for romance.

She was coming. Now we had a busy day. We just could not wash our hands to this, now that we had started something really rolling. So we became the groom-to-be's advisor and guide. First we had to get the colonel's consent. That was easy. He was busy all day giving consents. Then a license. We had heard about special licenses. They cost a pound. We got one. Then a room at the hotel for the girl, who would arrive at night. Here, fortunately, we had help. Lieutenant Stillman, also with the 175th Bn, was here with his wife, and in a case like this truly a woman was needed. We had our reward. We were kissed and called the Fairy Godfather by a bride who was brimming with happiness.

Can we tell the end of the story? No, for we hope the end is still far away, but we can give interim reports.

At Christmas 1919, we had a card from Mona and Billy.

At Christmas a year later, a card from Peter, Mona, and Billy.

At Christmas two years later, a card from Mabs, Peter, Mona, and Billy.

At Christmas seven years later, a card from Issie, Mabs, Peter, Mona, and Billy. In between there were letters that told of a happy and busy married life in their new home in Leaside Toronto.

Then came World War II, and two of our sons found a ready welcome in the home that we had had a wee bit in making, when they were training in the East.

Many of our readers have seen pictures of the youngest of this family, a continent-wide favourite as a model. We saw her picture along with other famous models and Eleanor Roosevelt in McCalls Magazine.

If you read this war romance, you will know that Mona and Billy were willing to share their happiness with you all.

Our Last Camp Overseas and Home

OF KINMEL PARK, Rhyl,[91] we will say little, although here was our forefathers' home. A great-grandfather had sailed from here to PEI, then an English colony. One hundred and thirty years later, we sailed in the same direction, only we went on and on, three thousand miles further west.

There on the station platform in Edmonton we met the Dearest of our letters, and still Dearest after forty-six years of married life. We would have taken off our uniform for good and shaved the moustache we had favoured for nearly four years, but our Dearest said no. "You have three sons waiting at Vegreville and they are expecting Daddy, a soldier Daddy in uniform. You must at least wear the King's uniform for one more day."

They were babies when we went away, now they were boys and looked with awe at their soldier Daddy. Little did we know that they, and another to come, would some day come home from another war, soldiers of the King.

Coming across the Atlantic on the SS Regina, we had won ten pounds at poker. On the train from Halifax to Edmonton, we lost fifty dollars at the same game. To us, this was a sign—leave poker alone. We did, and tried a much more hazardous game, farming. A farmer at peace, at war, and again at peace.

CANADIAN EXPEDITIONARY FORCE

J.T. 11-33.
R.A.P.

Certificate of Service

ISSUED TO OFFICERS AND NURSING SISTERS

This is to Certify that (Rank) Major

(Name in full) John McKendrick HUGHES,

Enlisted in 66th Battalion,

CANADIAN EXPEDITIONARY FORCE, on the xxxxxxxxxxxxxxxxxxxxxxxxxxxxxxxxxxxxxxxxxxx

day of xxxxxxxxxxxxxxxxxxxxxxxx 191xxx AND WAS APPOINTED to COMMISSIONED RANK

in 66th Battalion,

CANADIAN EXPEDITIONARY FORCE on the Twenty Ninth day

of June 191.5

He SERVED in CANADA, England and France with the 66th Battalion,

151st Battalion, 9th Reserve Battalion, Alberta Regt'l Depot., & 21st Reserve Battalion.

and was STRUCK OFF THE STRENGTH on the Fourth day

of June 191 9 by reason of General Demobilization

Dated at Ottawa, this Eleventh day

of March 19X 1920.

Appointed as Staff Lieutenant, 1st Class, 13-7-17.
Seconded to War Office and attached for duty with 2nd & 4th Army H.Q.
from 13-7-17 to 27-3-19.
Mentioned in Despatches, L.G. No. 31089, 31-12-18.

for _____ Lt. Col.
Director of Personal Services.

M. F. W. 2618
30m.—4-19.
1772-39-1428.

A Certificate of Service is a standard document that was issued to all officers and nursing sisters who served in WWI, indicating their rank, starting and ending dates of service, places where they served, and any special notes, such as being mentioned in dispatches.

We, the Unwanted, Go Home

WE, PERSONALLY, came home to Canada in charge of six hundred men. Men who had seen service in France and Belgium and Germany. We could and did talk to these men as an equal. We had seen France and Belgium and gone on to the Rhine. We had been in the trenches, if only for a short time. We may not have shot a German but we had shot and killed a rat, and somehow the men would sooner talk about rats than Boche. We had been under shellfire, had a bit of gas, and been bombed many times. We knew the roads and ditches and the barbed wire, and we had seen more than most of our men. We could talk about duckwalks, *estaminets*, and the stench of dead men and horses. We had seen French and Flemish women, been entertained in their kitchens, drunk their coffee and their wine, known their sorrows and their joys. We had been kissed by French women and kiddies of all ages, and by bearded men, young and old, on New Year's Day. We had been there. Just so had hundreds of the unwanted senior officers of Canadian battalions that should have gone overseas as reinforcement units, not complete battalions.

Early in our story we said that this more or less just had to be the story of one man, but we know that our story could be repeated over and over again, and if our story can but arouse others to put their story on paper, we could weave them all together and have a page of Canadian history as yet not completely compiled.

CANADA

HMS
ADDRESS REPLY TO
THE DEPUTY MINISTER

Ottawa, Canada

May 20th, 1930.

RECORD OF SERVICE
Canadian Expeditionary Force

Lt. John McKendrick HUGHES.

1. Appointed Lieutenant, 66th Battalion, 29-6-15

2. Transferred to 151st Battalion, 31-12-15

3. Promoted Captain, 17-7-16

4. Promoted Major, 31-8-16

5. Embarked for England, 3-10-16

6. Transferred from 151st Battalion, to General List and attached 9th Battalion, 13-10-16

7. Transferred to 9th Reserve Battalion, 25-1-17

8. Attached Temporary to 29th Battalion, France, for instruction, 24-12-16

9. Ceases to be attached 29th Battalion on return to England, 5-1-17

10. Graded for pay as Staff Lieutenant, 1st Class, and seconded to Imperial Forces, 13-7-17

11. Taken on strength, General List, France, and attached for duty to H.Q. 2nd Army, 13-7-17

12. Ceases to graded for pay as Staff Lieutenant, 1st Class, but remains seconded, 18-10-18

13. To be specially employed and to remain seconded to Directorate of Agricultural Production, 19-10-18

14. Graded for purposes of pay Class F.F. 19-10-18

15. Graded for pay under S.P. Class 21, 19-10-18

16. Ceases to be seconded for duty with War Office, 25-3-19

17. Posted to 21st Reserve Battalion, 8-4-19

18. Struck off strength O.M.F. of C. on transfer to C.E.F. in Canada, 20-5-19

19. Struck off strength C.E.F. in Canada on General Demobilization, 4-6-19

20. HONOURS and AWARDS.

Mentioned in Despatches.
(Auth. London Gazette dated, 31-12-18)
Ordre du Merite Agricole "Officier"

A Record of Service detailing the major events of John's Army service, from his enlistment in the 66th Bn. in 1915 to his discharge in June 1919.

Is it possible that for some reason or other we were favoured more than most? We struck France at the top of the wave that swept the whole English people, at home and abroad. The desire that is inherent in our race, to dig in the soil, to plant and to hoe, and to be a farmer's boy. We know it swept all England, and Englishmen weary of war, even in the midst of war, turned to nature and the soil. Three outstanding men gave us the work they themselves longed to do: General Cooke, Quartermaster General 9th Corps; Major-General Holman, Quartermaster General 4th Army; and General Lord Radnor, Earl of Folkestone. Everything possible was placed in our hands. Assistants, more capable than ourself, served willingly and gladly, and quibbled not at rank or seniority. We had one asset many of them did not have. We had CANADA on our shoulders. Whenever possible we brought fellow Canadians into the work, but this was pure selfishness on our part. We knew that they knew the work and they took an immense load off our shoulders. In return, whenever we could, we tried to give them the opportunity to see places and people that was only possible when a motor car was available. Somehow our predecessor at Army Headquarters had got an order through Army that the AO rated a car to himself, and this order was never rescinded. We reaped the benefit. Our work, not being laid down in Army Regulations and Orders, had to be improvised all the time. We had no red tape to follow and moreover we soon found that every general in the British Army had one common longing—to retire to a farm and get his hands into the soil, to raise potatoes and roses. This gave us an entry to the top level. We saw Generalissimo Foch, knew Field Marshal Haig at least by sight, and talked freely with General Plumer, General Lord Radnor, and General Birdwood of Australia. We had seen our King in France and brushed shoulders with our Prince. We had helped to feed a million men and had helped harvest enough wheat to feed two million French. We had a wee bit to do with the Armistice Commission and, last but not least, we had a season of opera.

[signed] J. McK. Hughes, Lieut. Col.

Appendices

Appendix I
Review of the Agricultural Work

IN LATE 1917 Major James Aubrey-Smith, the AO for the 2nd Army, wrote a report on his agricultural activities, although who it was intended for is not known. At some point it was translated into French, and what follows is a back-translation of that document. It appears that whoever translated the original report into French phrased it in French terms, as far as names of departments and titles of personnel are concerned. In some places it has proven impossible to do anything more than guess at what is meant by some of these references, and these guesses are indicated by translator's notes in [ ] square brackets. There are also some typos, such as the reference to the 3rd Army in the title of the document; these are marked in the same way. JRH

Review of the Agricultural Work

done by British Troops in the IIIrd [sic—should read IInd?] Army Area
by Major S.J. Aubrey-Smith, Army Agricultural Officer

THE ORGANIZING of this work was undertaken by this Army's Agricultural Officer at the beginning of April 1917. At that time, the farmers were not getting very much help, and the help was being given in a disorganized manner, by fits and starts. Requests for manpower found a very cold reception and we ourselves were coolly received when we tried to get the manpower they were asking for. A lot of effort was required to convince people of the great value of the work undertaken. The farmers themselves were at first very suspicious and showed some reserve in accepting our offer of help. It was difficult to break through this reserve until they began receiving information about the work that had already been done. For all that, things improved, and towards the end of April the work began to progress. The whole Area was visited and the Mayors of communes were asked to take down the names of farmers wanting help. Whenever possible, only men with experience in agricultural work were sent. They were billeted on the farms and soon convinced the farmers of the value of their contribution. The men received their rations and they got their pay, so the farmers found themselves being helped by skilled workers at absolutely no cost.

The requests for manpower soon exceeded our means and we had to be careful to properly allocate the men at our disposal.

We also looked after farm implements and repaired them free of charge.

In May, on average, there were 120 experienced men working on the Area's farms. In June, this number dropped as a result of military operations that required all the available men. In July came an order that almost put an end to the whole undertaking: all P.B. (temporarily unfit) men who had been working on farms were ordered to return to England [P.B. indicated a soldier was not fit for front-line duty] and, as a result of that order, 161 men who had at various times been placed at the disposal of French farms were sent to England. The situation appeared serious, since harvest time was approaching, but, owing to the efforts of the Corps Agricultural Officers, a remedy was found and adequate arrangements were made for harvesting the crops. All units that could contribute to this goal were solicited, and people's opinions as to the value of this work had changed so much that many offers of assistance were received. The fact that an Army Corps was in its Rear Area rest camps at the time made things much easier. The Agricultural Officers and their interpreters were asked to make this harvesting operation their main project for the year. The following figures show how successful they were in this endeavour:

May	120 men	
June	100 "	
July	88 "	(161 sent to England)
August	4,605 "	and 56 horses
September	1,900 "	and 44 horses

The harvesting work is now almost completed and the number of men employed in this work has gradually declined. At the time of writing this report, it still employs 600 men.

A new problem arose because of the inadequate number of threshing machines. The Central Purchase Board has two threshers, but they are in permanent use in the Rear Area and are not available for the more exposed Forward Area. There are a number of French machines, but because of the shortage of manpower many of these cannot be used. Some are being used by their owners. At present, we are trying to get some of those that are standing idle. We are going about this as follows: the farmers in a district are being encouraged to form a pool to purchase one of these machines. Fuel and oil are supplied C.O.D. and teams of men are set up to operate the machine. This has already been done in two cases, but the farmers are loath to spend money to put the system in motion. Once they have made up their mind to go ahead, they find the proposal so advantageous that they are delighted with it. Now that the idea has been floated, it should spread quickly. It has been proved that the threshing can be done, and all that remains is to pick up the pace.

The hops crop was brought in mainly by means of the casual help provided by Units billeted near the hop fields.

Characteristic of all this agricultural work was the readiness with which the troops billeted in the various locations helped those who had already been detailed for that work.

British Soldiers

employed in Agricultural Work in France

(Source. Directions for the future.)

THE AGRICULTURAL WORK began with a very small number of men supplied by the Divisions, to which were added some men who were temporarily unfit (P.B. men). The latter, having been absorbed by various Labour Companies, are no longer available, and, owing to military requirements, it is difficult to obtain the former.

The necessary manpower was recruited as follows:

a) A set number of men provided by the Corps from among those who needed rest after the hardships of the trenches.

b) Men from Evacuation Hospitals who were strong enough to leave hospital, but not strong enough to return to the front.

In some cases, which did not occur in this Army, labour units supplied men, but, given the urgent nature of the work done by those units, they cannot be considered a regular source of manpower.

Concerning source a): This method of recruiting agricultural workers is the best by far. The Corps Agricultural Officer knows exactly how many men he can count on and when he can have them. The Nth [sic—should read 9th?] Corps, which carries out its duties on a permanent basis [sic]. The Agricultural Officer therefore has this solid core of 75 men for his sector's operations and, of course, he is often able to add to it plenty of casual reinforcements.

A valuable feature of this type of assistance is that the Army derives great benefit from it. Exhausted men from the trenches are put on farms for a while, where they find a complete change of occupation and surroundings and make a remarkable recovery. If all the Corps were to adopt this means of not only assisting the French farmers, but also helping war-weary men, they would be amply rewarded by the results.

Concerning source b): With regard to men who can be pulled from Evacuation Hospitals, who are not fit to return to the front but are strong enough to leave hospital, it is customary in some Corps to make them available to the Agricultural Officer for a fixed period, generally one month.

At the end of that period, the men are sent back directly to their Units. This procedure has only been used for a short time, but it has been very satisfactory from every point of view.

————

In addition to the above means of obtaining a definite number of workers, there are vast resources of casual manpower, provided that the Agricultural Officers are careful to use them effectively. The troops in Rear Area rest camps are always willing to help out when asked to do so. Usually the difficult thing is to make the best use of this manpower. The Agricultural Officers must keep a record of their sector's needs, so that if they receive offers of assistance from the troops at rest, they will be able to allocate men immediately. Any delay is fatal, as the troops usually do not stay very long in their rest camps.

For this harvest, the 2nd Army was fortunate to have the Nth [sic— should read 2nd?] ANZAC at rest. Thousands of agricultural workers volunteered for the work, with the result that harvesting was done faster than in peace time. At the end of September, the cereal crops had been harvested, while the picking of hops and the digging of potatoes were well under way.

Agricultural Officers

AGRICULTURAL WORK in the 2nd Army is carried out under the direction of

1. an Agricultural Officer for the Army;
2. an Agricultural Officer for each Army Corps;
3. an interpreter from the French Military Mission is attached to each of these Officers. [sic]

The Corps Agricultural Officers provide the Army with a report every 10 days (every 5 days during harvest season). These reports are summarized by the Army Agricultural Officer, who provides a consolidated report.

The interpreters provide reports at Corps level to the French Mission, which forwards them to the S.D.S. of the Army [editor's note: unable to verify the abbreviation S.D.S.], where they are put together in a consolidated report that is sent to the Quartermaster Branch ("Q" Branch) of the Army.

In this way, each set of these reports is controlled by the other.

The value of the work depends entirely on the Officer. All have worked well, as shown by the outcome, but more effort is still required.

The Nth [sic—should read 9th?] Corps has always particularly stood out, mainly owing to the interest shown in this work by Brigadier General **B.H. COOKE**, who has generously contributed in every way. This Corps has also been well served by its Agricultural Officers: Captain **G.H. GASKEL** [sic—should read Gaskell], a very capable and energetic Officer, who has been succeeded by Major **J.M.C.K. HUGHES** [sic—should read J. McK. Hughes], who also gives cause for satisfaction in every respect. It is entirely owing to this latter's initiative that the farmers of his sector were organized for the purpose of buying threshers that were standing idle and putting them into operation.

Other Officers have also distinguished themselves by the results they have obtained. They are: Captain **A.H. WOOD**, who stayed behind in the Army's sector when his Army Corps left, and Lieutenant **JAQUES**, officer of an A.N.Z.A.C. corps.

The ideal Officer for this kind of work is one who is so interested in it that he communicates his enthusiasm to others, and whose physical energy allows him to pay frequent visits to all parts of his sector.

Our Aims

IN THIS AGRICULTURAL WORK, our essential aim is to be of assistance to French farmers who are suffering from the severe shortage of manpower produced by mobilization of the French Army. It is important always to bear in mind that the more food we produce in FRANCE, and the more resources the British Army finds in FRANCE, the more purchasing power it has there. Therefore, the farmers must be helped not only to meet their own needs, but even to make the land yield everything it possibly can.

Another aspect of the question is that, by providing judicious assistance, we are also improving our relationships with those from whom we are obliged to seek billets. It does not take much thought to realize that this obligation to billet troops continuously, month after month, puts a severe strain on the farmers' good nature.

A further point to consider is all the benefit that can be derived for our own troops from organizing this work. After a long spell in the trenches, a month of peaceful work on a farm, with good food and a good bed works wonders on our men's health. The whole system depends on the ability of the Agricultural Officers. It is quite interesting to visit farmers all over the place and hear the way they speak about these Officers. These Officers are welcome everywhere and, in some places, they are called upon as agricultural advisers.

Note for Corps Agricultural Officers

TRY TO PREVENT military manpower from being used in routine farm work. Farmers must make every effort to operate their farms with civilian manpower; they should not rely solely on military manpower, which is always bound to be uncertain and must be reserved for particularly busy times (seeding, harvesting) or times of real hardship when there are really no more men on the farm.

(signed) J. AUBREY-SMITH
Major, Agricultural Officer 2nd Army
October 1917

Appendix II
Letter to The Secretary, War Office, from Travers Clark, MG for Field Marshal Haig

PRO/WO/95/36
App.XII.120
10,367 (Q.C.)

From Field Marshal in France
To The Secretary, War Office. 'General Headquarters,
25th December, 1917.

Sir, With reference to War Office letter No. 121/France/1459 (D.Q.M.G.) dated 21/12/17, and in continuation of my reply thereto No. 10,367 (Q.C.) dated 24/12/17, I have the honour to report that I have selected the following Officers to fill the establishments approved of in your above quoted letter: -

- *Assistant Director ... Major (Temp. Lt.Col) L.H. THORNTON, D.S.O., r.p. now A.Q.M.G., X Corps*
- *D. Asst. Director ... Major L.M. WEBBER, Royal Artillery, R. of O.*
- *Staff Captain ... Captain A.H. DILLON, Oxfordshire Yeomanry.*

Major WEBBER is an officer who has a good knowledge of agriculture and is a specialist in Tractor Working and machinery.

Captain DILLON farms two properties in England and after serving two years in an Agricultural College, worked on the Westminster Estates under Mr. Cecil Parker.

I understand that the Assistant Director will be graded as an A.Q.M.G., and the D.A.D. as a D.A.Q.M.G., and that Captain DILLON will be graded as a Staff Captain.

In addition to the staff, I have selected three officers to control Areas of about 5,000 acres each. Two of these are Canadian Officers, Major H.J. HUGHES, 52nd Canadian Infantry Battalion, and Major W. HUGHES [sic— should be Major J. McK. Hughes], 151st Canadian Infantry Battalion, and have experience of agriculture on a large scale, and a third is Captain HOWARD WHITE, 6th Cavalry who for some time past has been employed as Agricultural Officer with the Cavalry Corps.

Pending the arrival of the Director to be selected by you, Lieut-Colonel L.H. THORNTON, D.S.O., will at once start the office, and deal with the maps which are being prepared by Armies, so that the French can be approached at the earliest possible moment.

With regard to the units suggested by Dr. KEEBLE as suitable for dealing with an area of 5,000 acres I submit the following as an amendment, after careful consideration with the best known Agricultural Officers out here :-

1 Officer.
4 N.C.Os. (1 with knowledge of machinery.
    1 with knowledge of Agriculture.
    1 with knowledge of Horticulture.
    1 with knowledge of accounts.)
20 tractors.
20 ploughs.
1 water cart fitted for tractor haulage.
40 tractor drivers.
1 N.C.O. and 3 mechanics.
1 carpenter.
4 ploughmen.
3 blacksmiths.

I hope to be able to arrange the personnel required form sources in France, but I would ask you to send out early 3 N.C.Os. with a knowledge of Agriculture and the 3 N.C.Os. with a knowledge of Horticulture and 40 Tractor drivers, and I hope to be able to train other tractor drivers in this country.

In order that no delay may take place, I would also request that the following machinery should be earmarked at once and despatched to this country as opportunity occurs:-

30 Cultivators,
50 Harrows,
150 Double Mould Board Ploughs,
50 Large Grain Drills,
25 Large Iron Rollers.

As the scheme develops and areas of 5,000 acres are established, it will be necessary to increase the Directorate's Staff by at least 2 Deputies for inspectional work. These Officers will be able to supervise the work of several areas as well as the vegetable growing which Armies and L. of C. Area are now undertaking.

I have the honour to,
Sir, Your obedient Servant, [in ink] sd.

Travers Clarke,
MG for Field Marshal,
Commanding-in-Chief, British Armies in France.

Appendix III

Excerpt from a Letter to Lieutenant Saubot from Lt-Col Reynaud, DS

This is part of a longer document, originally in French, dated 7-2-18, from a Lt-Col Reynaud, DS, to Lieutenant Saubot, head of Agricultural Services at Peronne, S/C S.D.S. 3rd Army. The file number is Archives de l'Armée de Terre, Château de Vincennes, 17/N/446.

> *British kitchen-gardens in the vicinity of Saint Omer. 4th Army gardens.*
> *At the end of December 1917, I indicated to the 4th Army that, on the Saint Momelin road, about 1 kilometre from St. Omer, 25 hectares of land belonging to the Dambricourt family were abandoned. At the request of Major Hughes, I negotiated the transfer of these lands to the 4th Army, which is now organizing their cultivation. This Army will also be cultivating other lands I have told it about that remain idle in the areas surrounding those mentioned above. Lastly, I indicated to the 4th Army many abandoned lands at Coulomby (Pas-de-Calais). These lands would be particularly suited to the growing of potatoes.*
>
> *St. Omer Base gardens.*
> *Following several meetings, the Base suggested to me that I should be part of a committee charged with organizing the Base's gardens, a committee that would also include four officers of the British Army.*

I began by visiting the owners of lands lying idle in the St. Omer marshes. Those owners agreed to put their lands at the disposal of the British Army at no charge for the first year of cultivation, and to give that army the option of continuing to cultivate them in the following years and until the end of the war in exchange for payment of the pre-war rental price.

Accompanied, on a rotational basis, by a member of the committee, I visited all the COs of units capable of cultivating Military Gardens: 26 units agreed to cultivate parcels of land obtained under the above-noted conditions, the total area of which is 24 hectares.

Means of transport. Since most of these lands are accessible only by boat, I negotiated the purchase of 4 boats and the rental of one, or several if necessary.

Farm implements. I obtained the loan of 5 plows belonging to various farmers, and found on site 106 spades, 6 scythes, and about 20 forks, which were purchased by the Base.

Fertilizer. Veterinary Hospital 23, where there are between 1500 and 2000 horses, was selling its manure to a contractor who was paying 1 F/100 horses for it. That contract has been terminated and the manure from the Veterinary Hospital is being reserved for the Base's gardens.

Pig barn. A pig barn that can house between 40 and 60 pigs is currently under construction.

Vegetable nursery.

St. Omer's Société des Jardins Ouvriers currently has 2 hectares 25 acres [sic] of land earmarked for use in creating a vegetable nursery.

Appendix IV
John McKendrick Hughes
—A Biography

John R. Hughes

The Early Years

JOHN MCKENDRICK HUGHES was born on the family farm near Richibucto, Kent County, New Brunswick, on 15 August 1882. The second of three boys born to Charles Edward Hughes and Catherine Mattock McKendrick, he was named after his maternal grandfather. The Hughes and McKendrick families had been farmers in New Brunswick and Prince Edward Island for well over 100 years, and despite the wide range of activities he was involved in during his long life, John was a farmer, first and foremost, until the day he died.

The land along the Richibucto River southwest of Kingston is very rough and making a living at farming was hard work. There was not a

Note: *Due to the repeated use of the name "John" in the Hughes family, John McK Hughes is referred to simply as John; his second son, John Paul Hughes, is referred to as Paul; and his grandson, John Richard Hughes, is referred to as JRH.*

lot of other work in New Brunswick at the time, so many farmers went west each summer to work in the grain fields of the prairies to supplement the income from their small Maritime farms. Others moved south to the United States. The Hughes family did both.

In about 1960, John wrote a brief history of the Hughes and McKendrick families, in the form of a letter to his grandchildren:

My Dear Grandchildren:

No doubt in time to come someone will ask you "from whence come ye, and when."

As I grow old and after me there will be no one to answer these questions for you I have decided to put down on paper the answers as far as they have been handed down to me by your Forefathers.

We are an old family as far as British people are concerned. As each man or woman marries a new family tree comes into the picture but as to this story I will only relate what I know about the two family names I bear, McKendrick and Hughes.

The McKendrick, which also may be spelt MacKendrick, appears first in my name and was the first to settle in Canada, although it is possible the Hughes came to Canada's shores first, but did not at that time make it their permanent home.

The MacKendricks were among the first shipload of British people to land and stay in Prince Edward Island. This was in the year 1770, very nearly two hundred years ago.[1] There are many of our family name still on the Island. Your great-great-grandfather, John McKendrick, left the Island and came to Bass River, New Brunswick about 1810. Your great-grandmother, Catherine McKendrick, married Charles Edward Hughes in Kingston, N.B. on January 28, 1880, and that makes the union between the Hughes and the McKendrick family. One more item before I go on with the Hughes family. Your great-great-grandmother McKendrick's maiden name was Mattock. An Irish family also very early settlers on P.E.I.

Your great-great-great-grandfather was a Ships Captain sailing out of Llandudno or Aberystywyth in North Wales. It is told that he made several trips across the Atlantic to what was then known as Arcadia ports. Late in life about 1790 he came to Canada and also settled on Prince Edward Island. Somewhere about 1800 or 1810 he crossed over and settled near or in

Memramcook, New Brunswick. Here your great-great-grandfather William Hughes was born about 1813 or 1814. When your great-great-grandfather was a very small boy the family moved north to the Richibucto River and took land at Kingston, Kent County. (The name Kingston was in later days changed to Rexton.) These are little items told to me in my youth which still linger in my memory. These may or may not be exactly correct but I pass them on to you, my grandchildren.

Your great-great-grandfather William Hughes was widely known as Red Headed Bill Hughes. He was the strongest man in the County of Kent. He was at one time Deputy Sheriff and is said to have put the fear of god into many of the turbulent characters in that small seaport village. One story I would pass on to you, told to me as true but may or may not be the exact truth. A sailing schooner from a foreign port put Into Kingston harbour with a mixed cargo which was exchanged for a shipload of hand hewn timbers. When this ship was ready to leave for home the sailors had imbibed too freely of the rum which was available at every dock side grog shop. They refused to go aboard their ship. The Deputy Sheriff, your great-great-grand-father, Red Headed Bill Hughes was called. He was told that there were eight drunken sailors who refused duty. Your great-great-grandfather went to the nearest Grog shop where a wild time was going on. Apparently the inmates were waiting for him. They made a rush to throw him out, they did not know they were tackling the strongest man in all North Eastern New Brunswick. Your great-great-grandfather grabbed the first two that came at him by the scruff of their necks, lifted them off the floor and banged their heads together, then chucked them into the corner, grabbed two more, one in each hand and literally dragged them across the dock to the ships side, giving them a great heave he threw them into the ships deck and called out "One." Back he went to the Grog shop, grabbed two more and dragged them also across the dock and hurled them aboard ship, and shouted "Two." Back again and two more were hurled aboard and he shouted "Three." This went on and on, "Four," "Five," "Six." He was not heeding what was being said by the Captain and the Mate aboard the ship. "Seven." Then the last two "Eight." But the ships Captain had enough men and more and had set the sails and the ship was twenty feet away from the dockside and the last two, your great-great-grandfather's "Eight" landed in the water. It looked as if they could not swim and would be drowned so there was nothing for if but Red Headed Bill Hughes had to jump into the river just as he was and bring them safe to shore.

Now that might have been the last of this story but next morning it was found that the eight foreign sailors were still in port, but curious as it may seem fourteen of the toughest most notorious characters of the village had been shanghaied by the Deputy Sheriff and sent to foreign parts. It is said that some of these did not arrive back home for over two years, sadder if not wiser men. Now maybe that is not what may be called family history but it does show from what sort of breed you come. Your great-great-grandfather was respected and loved by all that knew him. How much education he had I do not know but it was said of him that he knew his bible off by heart.

A stroke of lightning took him on his seventy-third birthday[2] as he and I lay abed only a few feet apart.

Grandfather married Sarah Hutchinson and they had eight children.[3] Fanny, Sarah, John, Fanny, Charles (my father), Abraham, Jonathan and Jennie. Why two Fannys, the first was burned to death as a baby and the fourth child given the name of the first.

It was told to me that the village of Rexton of present day was partly on your great-great-great-grandfather's homestead. Also that he built and operated a ferry over the Richibucto River before the first bridge was built.

Of this bridge I would tell a story. My own story and a true one. Our farm, my Father's farm, was a mile up river on the north side from Kingston. My first school days, I must have been six years old, I went to the school in Kingston. The school was on the south side of the river. On times when school was out for the day, a ship was to be seen coming upstream with the tide. (Kingston is six miles from the ocean and the tide ebbs and flows several miles up past our farm.) To pass the bridge the ship must pass through the drawbridge. When we kids saw a ship just about to reach the bridge we were in no hurry, we loitered (kids have that habit, you know) when the bridge gate opened we were in a desperate hurry. Down we rushed and watched the ship pass through, then when the drawbridge was closed we went home. When Mother asked why we were so late coming home we had a perfectly valid answer. "Oh, we could not cross the bridge, a ship was coming through." Did Mother know? Of course she did.

Now I must tell you about my Father, your great-grandfather, for with him the Hughes family came West. The day I was born, August 15, 1882, my Father came into Winnipeg. He had left his family, my Mother and my brother William, back home in New Brunswick. Dad came on a harvest excursion train and while he did not stay all the time in the West, from then on it was only a matter of a few years until we were of the West, Westerns. Our first western home was near the Red River three hundred miles south of Winnipeg. From there when I was sixteen Dad came to Edmonton, Alberta and bought a farm at Fort Saskatchewan, just a mile east from where now is the Sherritt Gordon Enterprises.

Let us now go back to those first days of our Family in Canada. The McKendricks came from Scotland as settlers for the new Province of Prince Edward Island. No provision had been made to take care of these newcomers. In those days governments did not think it their duty as they do today, to look after people. They must do it all themselves. There were no houses, no roads, and no stores. They had very little food and practically no money. There were a few French settlers from whom they bought some wheat which they ground in homemade mills for flour. But this was soon used up. Having no money they traded their clothes for food, any kind of food, mostly potatoes. Then the French ran short of food. Some fish they caught but they had no good boats to go out far from land. The French people told them that up along the coast there was a place where Sea Cows came in on to the sands. This is just at the north end of Prince Edward Island. So your people made hand sleds and with these tramped sixty miles through the woods or along the shore through knee deep snow. They found the sea cows and with clubs killed many of them and on the flesh of these managed to live through the winter.

Your great-grandmother's brother Neil was a Doctor. He went to Newfoundland to live. He never married. He spent his life among the poor fisher people along the coast. By dog team and boats he attended to his patients along a barren shore. He was an elder in the Presbyterian Church, but the Roman Catholic Archbishop of Newfoundland said High Mass in the Cathedral at St. Johns for his soul when he died.

These few items about our family I pass on to you of a younger generation. You came of a hardy breed, it is up to you to pass this on to those who come after you.

John's formal schooling ended after grade four, by which time he had mastered the basics of reading and writing; these two passions stayed with him until the day he died. When he was about nine, the family moved to Massachusetts, where Charles managed a sawmill for a short time. It may have been close to Boston, as Paul remembers John saying they sold vegetables in the Boston farmers' market. Then they farmed near Barnsville, Minnesota, for about eight years, before deciding in 1898 to move to Alberta.

It was decided that Charles, Catherine, their youngest son, Robert, and Catherine's niece Anna Campbell[4] would travel west in the spring as soon as the crop was in, to find land and start building a new home. John, however, was left behind with one of his uncles[5] to harvest and sell the crop, then travel (alone) to Alberta by train, carrying the proceeds of the sale of that last crop. Although many 17-year-old boys would have been intimidated by the magnitude of this task, Paul figures John looked at the whole thing as a huge adventure: "Dad was always willing to try new things."

John described the move west in a long story, *Tales of the Trails Out of Edmonton*, of which this is a short excerpt:

> From early days I was an avid reader, so now more than ever I looked for books that told about the home I was going to, come the spring of 1899. But in this I was sadly mistaken. It was decided to raise one more crop on our Red River farm. Dad, Mother, sister, and brother would go north in the spring to build a house and clear and break land on both his and his brother's new farms. While I would stay with my uncle and under his super-vision would plant and harvest the year's crop. All through the summer and early autumn I dreamed of life on the Victoria Trail, then having harvested and sold our 1899 crop, I started north. I was on my own, 17 years of age, I was on my first long trip by myself, with $800 in cash, sewn into a cotton belt and worn next to my skin. I still wonder just why my uncle had not obtained bank or express vouchers instead of letting a very green farm lad carry a wad of money that just might have tempted someone who needed cash.
>
> Of that long train ride there were a couple of episodes that still linger in my mind. We were on the bleak Saskatchewan plains (Assiniboia Plains, I

should say, as this was before Canada gained two new provinces). Our train
pulled into a siding to let a special train go past. On this train were nothing
but soldiers, volunteers for Canada's first great contribution to the defence
of the British Empire. They were on their way to South Africa. Forgotten was
the lure of the Victoria Trail, the old pathway of the fur traders. Gladly
would I have changed trains, gladly gone East instead of West, forgetting
that around my waist I carried the work of a year, the returns from two cars
of golden wheat. But it was not to be; sadly I watched men in Queen's uniform
disappear along an iron trail that had usurped that made by generations of
red men. I would never have the chance to wear a soldier's uniform; how
badly I was mistaken.

When the Hughes family took up farming near Fort Saskatchewan, the North West Mounted Police were policing the area. John was always very interested in the Mounties, and at one time both he and Rob apparently considered joining the force.[6]

For the next few years, the Hughes family worked on the farm at Fort Saskatchewan, but by 1904, John and Rob wanted farms of their own. There was no homestead land to be had in the area, so that December, Rob filed for homestead on the SE quarter of Section 2, Township 52, Range 8, West of the 4th Meridian (SE 2–52–8–W4), just to the northeast of Mannville, about 140 km ESE of the Fort. John appears to have worked on the homestead with him.[7] Apparently the farm at Fort Saskatchewan was not exactly what Charles wanted either, as he homestead on a quarter-section just to the west of Rob and John's land, SW 4–52–8–W4 in July 1909.

Charles, John, and Rob apparently did not stay on their homesteads any more than absolutely necessary, as they also continued to work on the farm at Fort Saskatchewan. They usually travelled back and forth by train, as the roads were very poor, often not much more than a string of pot-holes tied together. (Even in the late 1920s the road between Vegreville and Edmonton was dirt—not gravel—and went around hills and lakes, unlike today's highways that flatten and/or fill in everything in their path.) Patents for the Mannville farms were granted to Charles in September 1909 and Rob in October 1909.[8]

John probably did not plan to live on the farm at Mannville for long, because in September 1908, he had met a young woman by the name of Sara Paul. It was by far the most important event of his life.

Sara

SARAH MARIA PURDY PAUL was born on 6 August 1890 in Bonnie Bridge, Stirling, Scotland, the youngest daughter of John Paul, a Scottish tailor, and his wife, Alice Eliza Ann Cook. She detested that final "h" on Sarah, and never used it. In 1903 John Paul and his son John Jr. left Britain and came to Winnipeg, MB. On 3 March 1904, Eliza and the rest of the family came to Canada. They stayed in Winnipeg about two years, then moved to Fort Saskatchewan as Eliza could not stand the cold winters in Winnipeg, having been born in British Guyana.

Sara graduated from high school when she was 17, went to Normal School in Edmonton for about a year, and received her provisional teaching certificate on 8 August 1908, just two days after her eighteenth birthday. It gave her the authority to teach in Pleasant View School District 663, about five kilometres east-north-east of Fort Saskatchewan, from 2 July to 31 December 1908. At least one of her pupils in her first class was older than she was. In her second year of teaching she worked at Deep Creek School, some 16 kilometres north-east of the Fort. Both of these were relatively new one-room school houses; Pleasant View had been built in 1902, and Deep Creek in 1895, although it had been rebuilt in 1906.

After a long-distance, two-year courtship (John was alternating between his farm near Mannville and his father's farm at the Fort, Sara was teaching school in Pleasant View and Deep Creek) that was complicated by the fact that Sara seems to have considered both John and Rob, John and Sara were married on 20 January 1910. John used his share from the sale of the Mannville homestead to buy land near Lavoy. He and Sara farmed there for the next five years, during which time three of their four sons were born: Charles Edward on 16 December 1910, John Paul on 20 November 1912, and William on 24 January 1915. Their fourth son, Neil McKendrick, was born on 21 August 1920, while John and Sara were farming south of Vegreville.

JOHN'S INTEREST in law and order did not wane with his marriage, and on 1 May 1906 he joined the Canadian Mounted Rifles (CMR), a militia unit, as an enlisted man. In June 1909 he was promoted to Lieutenant, and stayed at that rank for several years. He spent the winter of 1912–13 at Ft. Osborne Barracks, Winnipeg, Manitoba, and was promoted to Captain. John remained a member of the unit (by then called the Alberta Mounted Rifles) until 1 April 1934, by which time he was living in Athabina. In early 1936 the AMR was absorbed into the 19th Alberta Dragoons, and the following December John (then 53 years old) was transferred to the Reserve of Officers.

John did not hesitate to volunteer for the army in the early days of WWI, despite the fact that he had three small children, and was therefore exempt from active service. He enlisted in the 66th Battalion on 29 June 1915, with the rank of Lieutenant. His Medical History Sheet notes that he was 33 years old, 5 feet 8 inches tall, of slight build, weighed 133 pounds, and had a mole on the left side of his head. John transferred to the 151st Battalion on 31 December and spent the next six months recruiting men in the Vegreville/Vermilion area.

He and Sara rented out the farm at Lavoy early in 1916. On 4 June the 151st was transferred to Sarcee Camp in Calgary, where John was promoted to Captain on 17 July, and to Major on 31 August. When he left for England in October, Sara and the three boys moved in with John's parents at Saddle Lake, where Charles was the Indian Agent. Over the next two years she and Catherine knitted between 400 and 500 pairs of wool socks as their contribution to the war effort. These were sent to John and he gave them to the men working on his farms. Ted, Paul, and Bill had to wind the skeins of wool into balls—that was their war effort.

Despite the huge amount of work he was doing as an AO, John still found time to write to Sara every day, sometimes more than once a day. His hastily written letters often had no paragraph breaks, only minimal punctuation, and some rather dubious spelling and grammar. Here are two paragraphs from a six-page letter dated 31/12/17:

The last half of the year has slipped away very fast, because I was busy I suppose. And with present prospects I will be even busier next year. I am likely to leave here and go down to the Somme district working from GHQ. I don't like leaving here one little bit, as here I am very comfortable and know the Officers of the corps and Army and I have a free hand, go where I like, when I like. As my letters of late have shown you I travel all over Northern France and have opportunities to see the country as but few men in the BEF have. Today I was down at the ancient city of _____ seeing about land for gardens.

Later Nearly midnight and very cold but was just thinking that I am not near as uncomfortable as I was this time last year, for then I was down in that wet muddy trench or crawling out through the gloom and mud and wire and corruption to visit the listening posts. And being my first experience my hair was naturally on end, in fact I think it was lifting my steel helmet well clear of my head. I had a Mills bomb in my hand and another in my pocket.

Naturally, a lot of his letters concerned agricultural matters, although there were significant differences between farming at Lavoy and farming in France, as explained in this excerpt from a four-page letter written on 18–2–18:

...Am sending a lorry to Paris tomorrow to bring up our seeds and am busy on several farms getting ready for forcing plants. On Brimacombes farm we are building a small greenhouse for early plants, to be used later to grow vegetables that have to have glass. In spite of it being warmer here than at home there are very few more vegetables that will ripen than at home. Onions do not do well. Tomatoes do not ripen in the open, nor corn, altho quite a bit is grown for fodder.... Our line is potatoes, cabbage, carrots, turnips, sweeds, beets, and lettuce and small quantities of peas, beans, radish, brussell sprouts and cauliflower. Potatoes over fifty percent, these will be planted on all heavy or sod land not fit for smaller vegetables. Many of our plots will be small around Camps in back areas and other small plots up among the shell holes on land not fit to plough but which can be dug by hand. The Hun did a lot of this sort of work a year ago along the Ridge and our Boys reaped the harvest. Sometimes as the units were coming out of the line to

support trenches they would gather turnips or cabbages as they came along or if the vegetables were in exposed positions they would send up parties at night to gather them. Just fancy going out onto a machine-gun swept spot to pull carrots.

On 10 September 1918, John wrote to Sara twice; in the second letter he gave his recollections of their early courtship.

France
10–9–18

Dearest Girl,
Just about ten years ago on a Sunday like this, Mrs. Berry invited Rob and I to dinner one day. And there I met a girl. We were not introduced. Everyone took it as a matter of course that having lived near each other for three years or more, we ought to know each other. What sort of dinner did we have? I do not know. No doubt it was good, Mrs. Berry's dinners were usually good. I do not think I talked much. What I remember thinking is what a charming young woman had developed from a big eyed, long legged chit of a girl I had sometimes seen on the streets or about her father's shop. She could talk well, she was cheerful and good to look at; I am sure no thought of any future entered my head that day. Then there is an interval. Mother came up to care for us Boys who were harvesting. Then I remember a night when I was told we were to have a party at our house. Who started it I do not know. Who was there I forget; I think I took but little part. Rob was more the host. But what I remember was that this same girl managed the whole show. She showed tact and skill and kept a party of ignoramaces on the move. She was master of the situation right through, as unlike as daylight and dark in comparison with the rest of the guests. Another interval. Rob had gone back to the homestead; Mother was leaving by the morning train. I took her to the train and sat with her, this girl came to say goodbye. I was surprised. I think Mother also, but more than pleased. Did Mother dream of a future with her life and that girl's. I wonder! That little act of thoughtfulness and courtesy touched me very deeply. I remember the train whistled and we had to make a hurried departure, and girlie made a nearly fatal jump from that train. Another interval and then several events

happened in a few short days or weeks and today I have difficulty placing them in their proper order. Each incident is clear enough but which first and which last I cannot now say. A night when a dance was held over at a neighbors to the North. As a dance it was a awful failure to me there was only one girl there and full of mischief as a schoolgirl not as a sedate schoolmistress should have been, and she turned the sleeves of my overcoat inside out and did various other tricks so I had to make a fearful struggle when I went to get my coat in a hurry when I saw this girl was leaving. Was that the oldest Thorne girl going to walk home with you? Anyway she did not; was I over bold when I tucked your arm under mine. I never remember having done that to a girl before, and you did not protest nor did you attempt to remove it. Of what did we talk that night? I know not. Then another night; I was alone, just finishing clearing up after having my supper, I heard a whistle, very bold little girl to whistle like that; was I slow about being ready to go for a walk? I think not! That was a wonderful walk over the fields to Robert's, back again and not fast, into your abode where everyone was busy preparing chickens for market; out for another walk. Meeting Mr. Doze who seemed to consider it a great joke for some reason or other. Over the fields again. Leaning over the fence watching the moon. And there, I believe came the thought to me, how nice it would be to have this girl for a companion for always and always. But I said to myself, she is but a girl, a mere school-girl. You chattered gaily on never noticing that I was silent, dreaming of what might be but what seemed so far away. Another night which I think was before the last when you came bounding into the barn where I was, as only a young girl would, startling me at first and asking if I would go as far as Thornes or was it to those other people near the school. It matters not; did I make any excuse for not going? I don't think so. Yet again when to please you I took a load of country youths to your home and where first I met your family as a family. Most of that drive and night has slipped from my memory except the last hour. How we dropped our load one by one rather clever on my part that and prearranged as far as I was concerned. And those last two miles home, while others were there you were able to keep on your own seat without assistance, then why did you not object when I found it necessary to use one arm to keep you safe on your seat; which said arm should have been used for driving. Did you ever think that those last two miles took as long to travel as the former five, I don't remember *hearing you ask me to hurry. Were we having consideration for the horses? Or the night of the Thanksgiving supper. Mrs. Berry, wise woman, made no comment when it <u>happened</u> that you went home in my rig instead of hers, but her eyes said very much. And you did not object when it was necessary for me to put my arm around you to keep the robe up and protect you from the cold. And the night of the election what happened anyway? did you go into town with me, I really forget that, but remember giving you the gloves in payment of a bet. I often wondered if you told at home about wining those on a bet or how you accounted for them, all I know it was a pleasure to me to buy them for you. And the night which followed the big supper, how I invited yourself, Mrs Berry and Anna to dinner with me. Mrs Berry could not come, but you and Anna did. How Anna opened her eyes when I called you 'Sara,' a name sweet to my ears then and now. Did you enjoy that dinner in that bare kitchen with few dishes, but much fun and laughter? And that walk again to Robert's. That was a brainwave having Jake there. Were Anna's eyes opened to their full. I guess so. Was that the night we tried to dance on the concave floor to mouth organ music and try to eat impossible sandwiches and cakes in a stuffy upstairs room. From what queer things did we extract enjoyment; mine was your company. I wonder what your thoughts were at that stage of our acquaintance. Then a few nights later I said goodbye to you, there was no tender leave taking, the world might have looked on and thought but the most casual friends parting, to you it was maybe no more, to myself I know not. My thoughts of you had hardly crystallized to such a stage as I dared to hope that there was any use or chance of you caring for me. In all it was only a few short weeks. I really think it was among the silent moments when alone on my homestead and I dreamed again of those wonderful hours, those wonderful drives and more wonderful walks that I realized that you had stolen my heart, that you were the one and only girl for me. Life was very empty during those weeks till Christmas. Did I write once, twice or how often. Your answer or answers were not long but between the lines my fancies read many messages which perhaps you little dreamed were there. Rob had a letter from you and showed it to me, but my letters from you were for my eyes alone. How many dozens of letters I have had from you since. And how many more I have written. I know not why I have written about these things today, I wrote you this morning my usual letter of everyday events. Now the day* *has gone, and beautiful moon and bright stars make it almost like day. Such a night as some of those nights I have been dreaming of. Many nights and days, months and years have passed since then, many happy times we have had together, many weary miles I have travelled, many temptations, many fights, some wins and many falls. But come what may or will these memories can never be blotted out; their like only happens once in a man's lifetime, never more, they could not; each impression each thought must be the first.*

Good night Sweetheart
Good night my little Sweethearts
Sweet Dreams, Sara, My Love
John

John ceased to be seconded to the War Office on 25 March 1919, returned to England, was posted to the 21st Reserve Battalion on 8 April, and struck off strength on 20 May, when he boarded ship in Liverpool. Eight days later he landed in Halifax, after being overseas for two years, seven months, and 17 days. On 4 June he was officially retired from active service as part of general demobilization. His military service awards included the British War Medal,[9] Victory Medal,[10] and *Officier de l'Ordre du merite agricole*. He was also mentioned in dispatches by Field Marshal Haig, with the official notice appearing in the *London Gazette* on 31 December 1918. Some time after 1930 he was awarded the Canadian Efficiency Decoration.[11]

When John arrived back in Alberta, Sara travelled from Saddle Lake to Edmonton to meet him. The next day, Charles, Catherine, and the three boys drove to Vegreville to meet them. As they drove down the street, the boys saw their mother standing on the balcony of the Alberta Hotel with a strange man—none of them recognized their own father.

When they got back to Saddle Lake, each of the boys received a couple of gifts from John. One was a napkin ring made from a short length of a 50mm anti-aircraft shell. Each one had the coat of arms of a European city on it. Sarah immediately confiscated them all, otherwise they would have probably been lost in a matter of days. She gave them back after the boys were old enough to appreciate them. Next was a gift that the boys were much more interested in—jack-knives.

"We went out by the garden to play with our knives," Paul says, "and the first thing I did was cut a great slice into my left thumb, almost to the bone. I was bleeding like a stuck pig. They wrapped my hand in a couple of towels and drove to the hospital in Vegreville. I got stitched up and they might have even kept me overnight." And he never saw his jack-knife again. Sara probably confiscated it, too.

During his time overseas, John got a whiff or two of poison gas and it affected his health for the rest of his life. Any time he caught a cold it took him a long time to get over it, and he had several bouts of pneumonia over the years. The gasses used in WWI were heavier than air, so they pooled in low-lying areas and were absorbed into the soil. Pretty much everyone who served in or near the trenches was affected, and John had spent a lot of time checking land immediately behind the front lines for suitable garden spots.

The Farm at Vegreville

AS SOON AS HE GOT HOME from France, John went looking for land. The man who had rented the farm at Lavoy would not pay the rent but would not get off the land, either. John had been a farmer before the war, during the war, and he was determined to be a farmer after the war. The Soldiers Settlement Board assisted him in finding and buying a 320-acre farm south-west of Vegreville and a nearby 80-acre hay field. The Vermilion river ran across the south-east corner of the farm. It was very crooked, and not very deep, but a great playground for John and Sara's boys. In dry years they could jump across it, but in wet years it flooded half of the farm.

For the next 10-plus years, John and Sara farmed south of Vegreville. He continued to be an active member of the community, including renewing his military connection to the AMR. He was promoted to Major on 6 May 1929 and to Lieutenant Colonel on 3 July 1930, before being transferred to the Reserve of Officers on 17 September 1936. Until he died over 30 years later, he was called "the Colonel" by most people who knew him.

In true military fashion, discipline was strict on the farm. "We did what we were told to, when we were told," says Paul, "or we got a whack on the butt." And it was John, not Sara, who doled out the punishments. "When we were going to school, if we were bad the teachers let Dad and Mother know, and when we got home we got worse from Dad. I don't remember Mother ever slapping us, it was always Dad." Neil has a slightly different memory of the situation; "I don't remember either of them spanking me," although he admits he probably deserved it at times.

Because John had been a staff officer during the War, he had his own horse, saddle, etc. When he was ordered home from Germany, he put his saddle, bridle, blanket, helmet, 45-calibre Webley revolver,[12] a German helmet, and a German gas mask in a great big gunny sack, labeled it with his home address, and turned it in to Stores. Two years later it arrived at the Vegreville farm. Paul learned to ride a horse using John's English flat saddle, and Ted carried the Webley in WWII.

Paul joined the AMR, John's militia outfit, as a Trooper in about 1928. He went to several camps at Sarcee (Calgary) and also Innisfree, and was promoted to Sergeant in March 1930. In September 1931 he was promoted to Second Lieutenant. John objected to Paul becoming an officer since he was the regimental commander, and felt the promotion might be viewed as favouritism. Major Frank Fane[13] and John had a real set to over Paul going for commissioned rank. In the end Frank told John to either give way or he would resign. John gave in. But he had made it plain that his sons could not expect an easy ride just because he was the CO. In fact, he demanded more of them than of others.

Diversification

IN THE 1920S AND 1930S many farmers on the prairies raised wheat and nothing else. But John had a bit of everything—a variety of grains, potatoes, carrots, turnips, beets, cattle, and poultry, as well as sunflowers and corn for cattle feed. The feed crops were harvested using a corn binder that cut and bundled the stalks. The bundles of sunflowers were often three metres long and took two men to handle. John had a wooden silo (about five metres across and ten high) built and into it were tossed all kinds of organic scraps, as well as the sunflowers and corn. Carrot and beet tops, undersized vegetables, excess spuds, and anything else that would otherwise go to waste went into the silo. In the winter the boys would have to crawl inside, hack the frozen feed loose, and toss it down a chute for the cattle.

John even planted a variety of tree types in his windbreaks. In later years he experimented with many types of trees at Athabina. He got seedlings from the Experimental Farm at Morden, Manitoba, and others, and religiously reported his results to them. The researchers said that most of the trees would not grow, or if they did grow they would not do well, that he was too far north, the soil was the wrong type, and so on. That just gave John a challenge, and he usually proved them wrong on all points.

John experimented with machinery too. He was the first person in the Vegreville area to use a combine. It was "borrowed" from the local machinery dealer who was looking for a large field in which to demonstrate the operation of this new-fangled device. John had the largest field, so his crop was used as the example. The machine was drawn by 12 horses, needed two men to handle the horses, one to stand on the cutter to keep the wheat from bunching up, and another who stood on top of the whole thing. Paul says he never saw another one like it.

Starting shortly after his arrival in Alberta and continuing until the early 1960s, John was involved in the formation and operation of dozens of co-operative organizations, both official and unofficial. For example, he was a member of the Dairy Pool from 1928 and its Secretary from about 1938 until 1953. His battle cry was "Co-operate" and he had a way of talking that made people happy to do so. His prime motivation in all these co-op activities was to ensure the farmers received the best possible price for what they produced.

Some time in the late 1930s or early 1940s, John started corresponding with Walter Norman Smith,[14] the editor of *The Western Farm Leader*, an agricultural newspaper published out of Calgary. Their letters are concerned primarily with farm and co-op organizations. John appears to have acted as an unpaid correspondent to the paper for several years, supplying reports on the activities of various co-ops and articles on everything from how to increase co-operation on the farm in wartime, to growing flowers in Alberta. In January 1953 Smith wrote to John, asking him to "send a few lines about yourself and your long connection with the movement, which we could use in a boxed item of your own to go with your article."

John gave a very detailed answer, probably much more than Smith was looking for or could use.

As to personal history along co-operative lines, it is hard to say just where to start as the start is a long long way back. I will just give you some running comments and you may use what seems best to yourself.

Coming to Alberta in 1899 we settled twenty miles east of Edmonton at Fort Saskatchewan. Our nearest market was Edmonton and hauling wheat twenty miles with horses and getting forty cents a bushel for it left little with which to buy groceries or overalls. So in 1902 we, a group of farmers, formed a company and built a flour mill. This I believe was the first co-operative flour mill in Alberta, maybe in the West. We had no co-operative laws, in fact we did not even know the name, co-operative. It was just a farmer's mill. After two years it burnt down. No insurance. A total loss? No. After adding it all up we found that after allowing for loss of what the mill had cost us we still had made fifty percent more than if it had been sold in Edmonton and likewise saved us those long hauls.

That was the start on the co-operative road, the end is not yet in sight. The Society of Equity formed, we were in it. Our mill was not on track and news of the farmer movement building elevators was in the papers. Moving to Lavoy after I was married, we needed an elevator for our grain, and helped build and was Chairman of the Board of the Lavoy Local.

Along came the war. Four years in the Army, a long spell out of one man's life. Yet my sons did more in the second war. Four of them gave five years each.

We came home. Farmers were growing politically minded. So we took our turn as Secretary and President of the Vegreville Constituency Association (Dominion) while the wife was Secretary of the Provincial.

Co-operatives again. We formed a co-operative hatchery. That brought us into the Poultry Pool where I served two years as President. That along with the new Northern Alberta Dairy Pool where I spent twenty-four years as director and fifteen as Secretary, retiring last March. We had moved in 1930 to our home here at Flatbush and were experimenting with growing forage crop seeds. We needed a better market. No use doing the work and letting the other fellow have all the profit. We formed the Central Seed Growers Association. That was 1938. In 1941 we merged this into the Alberta Seed Growers Co-operative and as Chairman of the small concern I became a Director of the larger and Secretary. And still hold these two positions. We have seen this small co-operative become Canada's largest seed handling organization. We found that we were competing with Seed Co-operatives in Manitoba and Saskatchewan. We soon stopped that. We formed the Northern Canadian Seed Sales. This has been interesting work. We have two directors from each province and it is fine to sit on a Board with men like Bill Parker, President of the Manitoba Wheat Pool, and Howard Braken, organizer of the White Fox Alfalfa Growers Co-operative of Saskatchewan.

Then just to top things off we needed a seed cleaning plant where farmers could do a better job than with the old Fanning mill. So four years ago we built the Westlock Municipal Seed Cleaning plant; that takes a day a month but is well worth while.

Let's run over them:

Farmers Mill, Fort Saskatchewan	*1902*
Farmers Meat Packing, Fort Saskatchewan	*1904*
Society of Equity, Fort Saskatchewan	*1905*
Alberta Farmers Elevator, Lavoy	*1913*
Co-operative Hatchery, Vegreville	*1918[15]*
Co-operative Livestock, Vegreville	*1928*
Co-op Store, Vegreville	*1928*
Northern Alberta Dairy Pool, Edmonton	*1928*
Alberta Poultry Pool, Edmonton	*1929*
Canadian Poultry Pool, Winnipeg	*1930*
Central Seed Growers, Westlock	*1938*
Alberta Seed Growers Co-op, Edmonton	*1941*
Northern Canadian Seed Sales, Winnipeg	*1943*
Municipal Seed Cleaning, Westlock	*1948*

Just think what a lot of interesting men and women one has met in those years, then chuck in twenty-nine years of militia and active military service and there have been few idle periods.

In addition to running a farm and doing all the co-op work, John found time to become a Master of the Masonic Lodge and a Patron of the Eastern Star. He was also a lifetime member of both the Farmers Union of Alberta and the Alberta Old Timers and Pioneers Association, and was well known in Conservative political circles.

John had only attended school through grade four, then went to work to keep food on the table. Paul says the military would have had a fit if they had known of his lack of formal schooling. "He wouldn't have made Corporal with just a grade-four education; as it was, he made Lt. Colonel." He read constantly and to a large extent was self-taught. All his co-op business letters were written in pencil, then Sara checked the spelling and grammar. "She insisted that words be *á la* the dictionary. She more than anyone else got him to the top," says Paul.

The Move to Athabina

BY THE LATE 1920S, the Vegreville farm was not doing at all well— in the previous five years it had been flooded once, dried out twice, grasshoppered once, and caterpillared once. It was heavily mortgaged and John and Sara were broke. In the fall of 1929, John spoke with a neighbour, Fred Richardson, about the idea of homesteading again. Fred and some other men had been moose hunting in Athabina (about 160 kilometres north-north-west of Edmonton) the winter before. They liked the area and had filed on several quarter sections. So John and his family decided to homestead close to the Richardsons.

During the winter of 1929–30, Paul and seven cousins and friends lived in a one-room shack on their new land. All that winter they cut logs for buildings and for lumber. Fred Richardson had worked in logging and road construction in Ontario before moving to Vegreville in 1907, and he was the teacher when it came to building everything from houses and barns to roads. Once enough logs were cut, the men started putting up houses for their families. As there was only one team of horses, everyone worked endless hours every day.

It took almost three years for the two families to complete the move to Athabina. In the summer of 1930 the first four wagon loads of equipment and supplies were moved from Vegreville to Athabina, with more following in the spring of 1931 and again in 1932. Some of the larger machinery was moved by train. In 1933 Bill and Paul drove a herd of cattle and 10 horses to the new farm. At that time the railway bridge at Fort Saskatchewan had a roadway under the rail tracks which was barely wide enough for two vehicles to pass. "The hayrack had to be rubbing the right-side girders to allow a car to pass," says Paul. "We started across the river at 4 A.M. to avoid meeting any traffic, but had a terrible time getting those damn cows started onto the bridge."

All through this drawn-out move, of course, the Vegreville farm had to keep running, with dwindling livestock and equipment, and minimal manpower. By the summer of 1933, however, John and family had completely shifted operations to Athabina, having moved all their furniture, quite a bit of machinery, about 40 head of cattle, 24 horses, six pigs, as well as numerous chickens and turkeys. The bank repossessed the Vegreville farm and several years later sold it to the son of the man John had bought it from in 1919.

Although a small log house was ready and waiting for Sara and John when they got to the new farm, he had already started building a larger home, of his own design. During the war John had stayed in a French chateau that had one wing for cattle in and another for people. The connecting section was for machinery and grain, with a mix of hay loft and sleeping quarters upstairs. John did not adhere too tightly to this mix, but with four sons, he was looking at providing housing for an expanding family.

Virtually all the materials used in the entire structure were either hand-made or salvaged; only the window glass, nails, door hinges, and a few other items were purchased. Even the door handles were second-hand, rescued from an old car. Due to the ongoing need to develop the homestead, it took over two years to complete The Barracks, as it was called.

The Barracks was 20' wide and two stories high. The south wing was 60' long with a 12' veranda on the west end, the north wing was 48' long, and the center wing 22' long. To "prove up" a homestead, a person had to tell the Government land office how many acres of land had been cleared, how many of these were in crop, how much land had been fenced, the number and size of all the barns, the size of the house, and so on. When

John filed all this information, the land office people demanded a recount on the house, as he had stated it was 20' wide, two stories high, and 130' long. John sent back the same figures. Presently an inspector arrived to do his own count. John's figures were confirmed.

While The Barracks was the Hughes family home it was also, for a long time, the district meeting place. Church meetings and Athletic Association meetings were held there, as well as dances, all types of social gatherings, even casual gatherings. The huge stone fireplace was a must for many of these events. Many neighbours were in the habit of bringing their guests over for a look-see. John and Sara were the best of hosts and The Barracks became known far and wide.

Sara and Edna Richardson used to divide up the bachelor neighbours for Christmas and other festivities, and there would often be 20-some people around the dinner table at each household. John would stand to say the blessing, wave the carving knife about for a moment, and promptly start telling a story. "Everyone would be sitting there waiting for him to carve up the turkey, the younger members of the family almost falling out of their chairs, but he'd be oblivious to all, telling his story," says Paul.

John did everything possible to bring ministers to the district. In the early 1940s he (an Anglican), Fred Richardson (United Church), Stan Kasawski (Ukrainian Catholic), and Georg Proels (German Lutheran) got a non-denominational church going in Flatbush after the Catholic and Lutheran churches had given up and left town. The other church buildings were still there, but the church authorities refused to allow anyone else to take them over, so John, Fred, Stan, and George built a new one—a truly united church.

John also got a branch of the Canadian Legion started in Flatbush. To get a quorum he enlisted Dan Richardson, Ted, and Paul, all of whom were members of the 19th Alberta Dragoons. John was the secretary of the first School Board in Athabina and pushed for a lot of community projects, such as the first telephone exchange in the area. He was also an active member in the Athabina Athletic Association (AAA), although he never held an office in it. At first the AAA was strictly as a sports club, but it soon branched out, and was used to run the community hall, school, the phone system, and a variety of community activities. The AAA meeting was held on the first Saturday of each month, regardless of the weather, usually at The Barracks. "Everyone came to these meetings," says Neil. "It was the social event of the month. That was probably more important than what was discussed at the meeting."

When it came time to establish a cemetery, a place was found easily enough, but who was going to manage it? "Well," said someone, "we use the Athletic Association as a forum to run the district business, why not the cemetery?" Paul says the government balked at first, but "we persisted and eventually they gave way."

Over the years John's farm became something of a horticultural showplace as he grew dozens of exotic trees, flowers, and shrubs as well as the usual fruits, vegetables, and grains. His raspberry patch yielded mass quantities of fruit. One year he tried bottling the juice. For some reason, however, he did not fully understand that sweet juice not only ferments, it expands. He learned this the hard way when his bottles of juice started to explode in the basement. The Barracks smelled like a distillery for a while. The irony of this is that John and Sara were both teetotalers. At army dinners John carefully poured his drink into his neighbour's glass as the toasts were being given, when everyone was watching the speaker, not him.

The Storyteller

JOHN WAS A STORYTELLER at heart; he wrote scores of short stories and several full-length novels. They were written in longhand on any piece of paper that was at hand when time allowed and/or inspiration struck. John used the backs of the hundreds of notices, minutes of meetings, financial statements, and so on that he received from the many agricultural organizations of which he was an active member, in addition to the occasional purchased writing pad. The range and variety of his stories would be a credit to any writer:

> *Muttnick*, a science-fiction story about a Russian satellite that crash lands in northern Alberta and sets off an explosion in an underground gas field.

A Household God, a story about how, during the retreat of the South
Korean people in the face of the North Korean invasion in 1950,
two people who had never met before acquired an instant family
of about a dozen orphaned children, then got married with
the assistance of a trio of Canadians—a Catholic, a Methodist, and
a Jew—all within a matter of a few days.

Red Fife, a novel based on the life of David Fife, who planted some
wheat seeds sent to him by a friend in Scotland, thus trans-
forming Canadian agriculture.

The Escalator, a story of love at first sight, aided and abetted by the
escalator in Eaton's new store in Edmonton, a Negro stockboy
by the name of Joe White (a subtle bit of humour, perhaps?), and
a jaunty red hat adorned by a Scotch thistle broach.

The White Cross, the story of two Canadians, a nurse and an army
Sergeant, who meet on a battlefield in the midst of an artillery
barrage which they doubt they will survive, then again six months
later, as she is being reprimanded for being six-months pregnant.

Co-operators Make Neighbours, an utterly over-the-top story of how a
rather grumpy go-it-alone farmer is all-too-quickly won over to
the virtues of a wide variety of co-ops.

John's female characters are almost always stronger than the men
and usually a lot smarter. They know they are going to get that certain
man, often before he even knows of the woman's existence (let alone her
intentions), although the man usually remains convinced to the end
that it was all his idea. Faith (both of a religious nature, and of humanity
in general), honour, nationalism (sometimes to the point of jingoism),
and love (very often at first sight) are central themes to virtually all John's
stories. As far as is known, none of John's fiction was ever published,
although he wrote many articles dealing with agriculture and co-ops
that were published in the 1940s and 1950s.

In about 1955 or 1956 John found all the letters he had written to Sara
while he was overseas during WWI, used them to refresh his memory, and
reconstructed the day-to-day details of his war-time experiences. And
although he called the book *The Unwanted*, he did not dwell on the disap-
pointment of not being able to stay with the men he had enlisted and

trained, but instead focused on the challenges and joys of being in charge of the biggest vegetable gardens in Europe.

Apart from *The Unwanted*, few of his stories were auto-biographical, but sometimes he revealed snippets of information about himself, such as in this introduction to *Red Fife*:

A not unusual question asked a writer is, what is the background for your story?

One of my earliest recollections is seeing barrels of seed potatoes, grown on my father's farm in New Brunswick and shipped to Massachusetts where our family, like many Maritime families, was living. Early, seed was imprinted on my mind. When I was nine we moved to Minnesota and settled on a farm not far from the Red River of the North. Again, seed was imprinted on my mind. My father sent to Manitoba for seed wheat. Red Fife wheat.[16]

When I was sixteen, my father took his family back to Canada. A new home not far from Edmonton, just east of Fort Saskatchewan and close to where stands one of Canada's greatest chemical factories, on land that at that date was untouched by the plow.

Seed. Seed wheat, again it was Red Fife. We raised some wonderful crops on that deep deep black soil but always it was a race between ripe seed and Jack Frost. We needed an earlier wheat and my father was always reaching for better, earlier seed. My mother taught me the love of flowers and the gathering and care of seed, always the best was kept for seed.

During World War 1, I had an experience not usually connected with war. I became an Agricultural Officer for the Second British Army in France and Belgium. In my book, The Unwanted, *I tell how the British Army saved an immense amount of wheat, for seed and flour, under hazardous conditions perhaps never before experienced by men in any age. The Republic of France made me an Officer of the Order of Merit in Agriculture. I believe I was the only Canadian so decorated during that war.*

Coming home, I began raising registered seed wheat, oats and barley. I became a member of the Canadian Seed Growers Association.

In the spring of 1941 a group of seed men met in Edmonton and under the chairmanship of Howard Wright, President of the Canadian Seed Growers Association, formed the Alberta Seed Growers Co-operative. From the very first meeting I became the Board secretary and with the exception of two years when I held the President's position, I remained secretary until the co-operative merged with the Alberta Wheat Pool.

During those fifteen years I wrote hundreds and hundreds of minutes, briefs, letters and directives all about seed, seed of all kinds grown in Western Canada.

One day I reread a bit of Canadian history. It was the story of how a man in Glasgow, Scotland, filled a Scotch bonnet with hard red wheat that had come from the port of Danzig on the Baltic and sent it to a friend in Canada. That friend's name was Fife. He was known as Red Fife. From that bonnet of wheat came the seed that turned the prairies of the West from a grazing ground for buffalo to the finest wheat field in the whole world.

Then the thought came to me that our meeting of seed growers in Edmonton had been held exactly one hundred years from the date when a Scotchman sent a bonnet of hard red wheat to a friend in Canada who went by the name of Red Fife.

Such is the background for my story, Red Fife.

World War II

In WWI JOHN HAD NOT HESITATED to enlist in the army and he tried again when WWII broke out, despite the fact that he was 57 years old. He wrote to someone by the name of Scott, asking to "get involved"; Scott's full name is not shown on the letter, nor is there any indication of where he lived or what he did, although it is quite likely he was associated with the Department of National Defence in Ottawa.

I wonder if you could place my application for a place in the National Defence force. I have been a soldier nearly all my life, and now in this last crisis I would like again to take part. I started serving in 1906, joining the unit which later became the 19th Alberta Dragoons. I received my commission in 1909. I enlisted in the 66th Battalion C.E.F. in June 1915 and served until June 1919. My rank was then Major. In 1928 I reorganized the Alberta Mounted Rifles and finally went on the reserve in 1936. In 1917 while in France I was placed on Staff, serving under General Plumer at Second Army H.Q. After Armistice I went with the Army of Occupation to Germany and *was appointed to work on the Armistice commission under General Green. My duty there was to work with the French and Belgian Officers who were checking and receiving the agricultural implements that the Armistice terms gave to France and Belgium in lieu of the implements stolen by Germany.*

The next paragraph briefly describes his work as an AO in France, then, near the end he says:

I have told you this to show that I have had a great deal of organization work of a military nature and I would like to get back in harness once more. I am willing to take any job any place at any time. I can leave at a moment's notice.

Unfortunately, the reply has been lost. So John stayed home and raised crops as his contribution to the war, much the same as he did in France 20 years earlier, just on a smaller scale.

Of course he did not try to stop any of his four sons from volunteering. Ted and Paul were already officers in the AMR, and they stayed in the Army, though not in the cavalry. Bill went into the Forestry Corp and Neil joined the Air Force. John, Sara, and Selma (Bill's wife) kept the farm going as best they could while the four "boys" went overseas.

For much of the time the boys were overseas, John and Sara probably did not hear from them all that often. "We went off into a different world and pretty much forgot about the homestead," says Paul. He wrote to his parents, but not often. There was also the problem of censorship; it was an offence under military law to divulge information that might be of use to the enemy. In one letter, Paul told John that, "the mud is just as sticky as when you were here." Thus John and Sara knew Paul was stationed on the Salisbury Plain, in the south of England.

As they had done in WWI, Sara and Catherine knitted socks and sent them to the troops overseas. They also sent cigarettes to the boys, as these were in scarce supply in England, and made excellent trade goods.

Not surprisingly, John redoubled his efforts to produce more and more food. By mid-1942 he was seriously concerned about the depletion of manpower from the farms of Western Canada, as more and more men were drafted or volunteered for military service, just as his own sons had done. He sent this article to *The Western Farm Leader* in July of that year. It was titled *Wartime Co-operation on the Farm*:

We on the farms of Canada are faced with three facts: First, we are asked to produce more farm produce (barring wheat), than ever before in our history; Second, we must do all this with a greatly reduced manpower; Third, our manpower is being and will be still further reduced by voluntary enlistment and compulsory service in the armed services.

Under the Mobilization Act, farm labour is in the preferred classes and we are assured that farm labourers who can show that they are needed at home, will not be drafted for military service. Nevertheless, great numbers of our young men feel that they are needed in the army and will enlist as they come of age, thereby still further reducing our available supply of farm labour.

Then we must be careful that we do not arouse a feeling in Canada that farmers are, as a whole, not willing to do their full share of shouldering the military burden.

Now with those facts before us, what can we farmers do to help solve this problem of producing more with less help.

The answer is, more co-operation among farmers; *the next question is* how to bring this about. *Our people must be aroused to the seriousness of the situation, then to the possibility of ensuring the situation through systemic, sustained, organized co-operation.*

A nation-wide appeal should be made to farmers by Government, press and radio. Farm Co-operation Associations should be asked to take an active interest in the movement.

We suggest the following, as a brief outlining plans for such a campaign, this brief to be submitted to the Dominion Government, our Provincial government, Municipalities, the Press, especially farm papers, The Alberta Federation of Labour, all the larger Farm Co-operatives and that this Association take the lead in presenting this problem to Canada.

How to Release more men for National Service and Produce More by Co-operation on the farm.

Many surveys have been made to determine how much waste of labour and machines takes place every year on the farms of Western Canada through the fact that labour is not used to the best advantage and machinery lies idle more hours than it works. The results of these surveys have been published and all agree that the waste is very great. Therefore, to overcome these disadvantages it is proposed to initiate a programme of co-operation on the farms with the object of producing more with less labour and with the machinery already on the farms. To bring this about, it is suggested that the organization take the initiative and by every means in its power awake the farmers to the real need of producing more with what help and machines we have. Let us ask *every farm paper to give their support by publishing articles showing how savings can be made.* Let us ask *every active co-oper-ative to bring this problem before its members and ask that co-operators everywhere talk this subject over with their neighbours.* Let us ask *the Western Provincial Governments to take an active interest in this problem and to lend the assistance of their field staffs in organizing co-operative groups everywhere.* Let us appeal *to municipalities that every Municipal Councillor consider it his duty to organize groups to work together in his particular district.* Let us ask *the Dominion Minister of Agriculture to give his support by radio and the press and any other means in his power.* The hay, grain, seed and potato harvest will be on us in a few weeks. Let us appeal *to the men who are strong, to pitch hay and stook and thresh, thinking only of the greatest amount of work they can do.* Let us appeal to our women to go out to the barns and gardens and relieve the men folk, of all the little chores possible so that more hours may be spent in the fields by their men folk. Let us say *to owners of good machinery, use the best machines you have and use them long hours. Leave your neighbours worn-out, hay-wire outfits in the yard and cut your neighbour's crop, while he in return stooks and hauls and stacks yours. Organize your haying and threshing gangs from among your neighbours. Start all idle tractors with plows to follow right behind the threshing outfits. You women feed those men well and you strong girls get out and show the boys how to run a tractor or pitch bundles. But in all this be fair, be just, give just a little better than you expect to receive. Don't shirk or lie down on the job, especially when working on your neighbour's crop. Remember that the man with good machinery has a heavy investment, for which he has had to or will have to pay a big price; be fair when settling up; if you are working with your hands, give good measure pressed down and running over. Co-operate and we can handle all our crops with what machinery we have and for years to come.*

*Co-operate so that there will be no lack of food for our boys in the army,
our industrial workers, and much to send to all free nations. Co-operate to
win the war and then stay co-operative and win the peace.*

Bill was the first of the boys to come home from the war and Neil was second, arriving in August 1945. Paul arrived in Edmonton at the end of December. The last one to get home was Ted: he was in an active unit at the end of the war and was assigned the task of organizing drivers and equipment to take several hundred surplus trucks east to Czechoslovakia, where they were given to the government, so he did not arrive home until January 1946. The safe return of their four boys was probably the best Christmas present John and Sara ever got.

The Post-War Years

"FOR THE FIRST three or four years after the war, Bill and I were working in various sawmills. We were gone most of the week, so Dad was doing all the chores," says Neil. "But he didn't do any field work after the war. He did the garden and that was a wonder to behold. He'd work for an hour or so, go into The Barracks for a nap for 20 minutes or so, then go back and work some more."

Even though he was 63 years old at the end of WWII, John continued to attend dozens of meetings, sit on Boards, write letters, and talk about co-ops to anyone who would listen, throughout the late 1940s and early 1950s. "Dad would be asked to say a few words at a meeting, and those of us who knew him well would look bored," says Paul. "He could go on and on. Never said a bad word about anyone, though."

In 1952, John and Sara sponsored a Dutch family, Jim and Hilly Terpstra and their three girls, so they could emigrate to Canada. They lived in a small house to the south of The Barracks and worked as hired hands on the farm for two years. In the early 1960s the house was rented by the University of Alberta, and grad students spent their summers studying the incredible variety of bugs that also lived on the farm. These students, be they black or white, Dutch, Australian, Indian, or Canadian, male or female, were made welcome by John and Sara, and often invited to join

Sara and John in their flower garden on the west side of The Barracks (near Flatbush, in northern Alberta) in about 1960.

in family gatherings. At one Hughes birthday party in 1965, there were guests from six countries.

By the late 1950s, both John and Sara were slowing down; John was in his mid-70s, Sara in her late 60s. Neil and his family were doing 99% of the work on the farm, but John still kept an eye on things, and he and Sara helped out as and where they could. John took care of the chickens, offered advice, and worked in his garden. Sara still hosted family gatherings and seemed to spend endless hours in her kitchen. Summer evenings would often find the whole family sitting around a bonfire, roasting weenies and marshmallows. In colder weather a fire roared in the huge stone fireplace in the living room of The Barracks, and although the children were not allowed to run about as much as they could outside, a good time was always had by all.

In January 1960, John and Sara celebrated their 50th wedding anniversary. As was typical of the times, the event was recorded in the local papers, and even the Edmonton Journal covered it. A photo shows both of them standing straight and tall, in front of a rather lavish cake.

John and Sara with their four sons at the district reunion in August 1962. Left to right: Paul, Neil, Sara, John, Bill, and Ted.

In August 1962 an Athabina district reunion was held at The Barracks. Typically, John was "the big push behind the reunion," says Neil. "He really spruced up the farm. It was a beautiful day and Dad was as happy as a lark to have everybody there to talk to." Well over 100 people attended, with many coming from as far away as British Columbia and Saskatchewan. Several people commented that they had to drive through heavy rainfall to get to the farm, but all that afternoon the sun shone on the gathering. The next day, after all the guests had gone home, it rained on The Barracks.

Ever since John was a young man, he had had a mole on his left cheek. In the early 1960s it was found to be cancerous and had to be removed. The cancer had already begun to spread, however, and the surgeons took out his left eye at the same time. As was all too common in those days, they did not get all the cancer and it began to spread through his body. A few years later, he had to be operated on again, this time losing much of his stomach and lower intestine. Despite this, John did his best to keep going much as he had in the past, working in his garden and flowerbeds, doing what he could around the farm, enjoying his grandchildren and great-grandchildren, and continuing to write whenever he had a spare moment.

He also continued to delight in showing visitors around the countryside, giving the local history, and pointing out all the crops, trees, and gardens of interest. The only scary part of this was that he did it while he was driving along the gravel roads, weaving from side to side. "He was no hell of a driver anyway," says Paul, "and after a while it was agreed that one of us would do the driving." Sara had never learned to drive.

John and Sara spent their last few winters in the relative warmth of Sidney on Vancouver Island. Their only income was their Old Age Pension, so they could not afford much, but they must have figured a wet winter in British Columbia was better than a cold winter in Alberta.

In the summer of 1966, Sara had a stroke and was hospitalized for a short time before dying on 16 July 1966. Her death took the heart out of John, says Paul; "he got quieter and seemed to shrink." They had been just as much in love then as the day they were married, and his health obviously suffered.

Several months after Sara died, Paul and his wife, Helen, drove out to Vancouver Island for a holiday, and John went with them. He sat in the back seat of the car all the way out to the coast and hardly said a word. The three of them spent a week or so visiting with Helen's sister Jose and her family in Sidney. Jose's son-in-law was a real estate agent, and he showed Helen and Paul an old house in the Deep Cove area that was about to come on the market. They liked it so much they decided to buy it.

"The Deep Cove house got Dad going again," says Paul. "He wanted to set to work on the shrubbery and flowerbeds right then and there, and we had to hold him back, as we didn't take possession until the following May." Despite this caution, John found a long-neglected grape vine near the north-west corner of the house. After Paul and Helen moved out to the coast, they built a trellis for it and harvested several excellent crops of grapes, most of which were turned into a wonderful wine called "Granddad's Discovery."

John chose not to return to Edmonton with Paul and Helen. For a time he stayed with a cousin, Peg Watt, but the cancer was spreading again, and he took the train back to Edmonton in late October. A few weeks later, he was operated on for the third and final time. This time, however, the doctors said the cancer was too wide-spread and there was nothing they could do. John was told he had at most a few weeks to live. In typical style, however, he said he would not spoil his family's holiday season, and would hang on until after Christmas. And he did just that; he died in the Colonel Mewburn Pavilion on 12 January 1967.

The funeral was held in the simple wood-frame church in Flatbush that John had helped build some 25 years earlier. The temperature was around -40°, the church was unheated, and the bugler's lips nearly froze to his trumpet as he sounded *The Last Post* at John's graveside. John and Sara are buried side by side in the Athabina Cemetery, probably the only cemetery in Alberta to have been owned and operated by an Athletic Association, which the two of them had helped to found, over 30 years earlier.

The Saddle Lake Trail

AS NOTED EARLIER, few of John's stories are truly auto-biographical, as he often tended to mix fact and fiction in a way that is difficult to separate. One story that has a firm basis in truth and does tell some of his personal history is *The Saddle Lake Trail*, although how much of the detail is 100% accurate is impossible to say. It is typical of his stories, however, and is a good illustration of both his character and Sara's.

> One last story about an Alberta Trail we would write. In this case we must leave our maximum date of 1905, even though this trail is one of the oldest in the West. The lands, the lakes and the rivers that centre roughly around Saddle Lake were once one of the richest beaver lands on all of the Hudson Bay's Empire. Lac la Biche, Whitefish Lake and Heart Lake were Indian Reserves when in 1911 my father, Charles Edward Hughes, became the resident Indian Agent at Saddle Lake.
>
> Here again we run into that friend of those needing assistance, Frank Fane, ex-Mounted Police Staff Sergeant, homesteader, farmer, and Homestead Inspector. Frank Fane had been my father's friend from the early days back in 1898 when Dad first settled astride the old Victoria Trail not far from Fort Saskatchewan. Through the years they had met at each other's homes, at

Masonic meetings, and especially at Conservative rallies, for both took their politics seriously. Now Frank Fane found a ready welcome whenever he passed through Saddle Lake on his duties as Homestead Inspector. The idea always existed that a homestead inspector's duty was to see that all homesteaders lived up to the letter of the law and saw that no one shirked on his new land-breaking requirements or the building of the necessary house and barns. No such thing. The homestead inspector was the all-out friend of the man who had bet ten dollars with the government of the day that he could live for three years on his one hundred and sixty acres and not starve to death. True, somewhere in the regulations it said that a man must break and culti-vate thirty acres of land, build a habitable house and barn. From personal experience I can say with confidence that a good inspector could stretch a five-acre field so that even in your own imagination it looked like fifteen and you were ready to swear to the fact. But the homestead inspector was much more than that. He was guide and councillor, instructor in the growing of wheat and in the raising of cows, pigs and chickens and then finding a market for them. Nowhere in the west was friend and guide needed more badly among Alberta's new Canadians; call them what you will, Galatians, Poles, Bukovinians, Romanians, or as so many did, just Bohunks.

Congenial friends just naturally gather together and it was just natural that their co-friend, Dr. Herbert Monkman, medical advisor to the Saddle Lake Indian Reserve, often made a trio for an evening at the Agency. The Agency house was large enough and Mother was delighted to have friends stay for the evening and a bed was always ready.

I have mentioned these three for a basis of a story still in the making. 1911–12–13 were peaceful years, so also was 1914 until one day in August. The world has not known the real meaning of peace since that date.

But let us go back a bit. Canada had a Militia and some of us played at being soldiers. Frank Fane, Herb Monkman and the writer spent the winter of 1912 at Fort Osborne Barracks, Winnipeg. There, in forty-below weather, we chased the enemy (he carried a red flag so we would know him) clear out of the Red River valley and out onto the Portage Plains. Presumably he froze to death out there. It was an overwhelming victory. All three of us were promoted to Captains in the 19th Alberta Dragoons. We were soldiers capable of meeting the Kaiser's Dragoons, or so we thought. Of course there was no chance that we would ever use our cold-won military knowledge.

The scene changes. The trail had been long and costly. One of the trio was no longer a soldier. Yes he was, he had been buried on the field of battle. Another was a soldier tried and proven on the field of battle and had, much against his will, been compelled to take the long trail back to his home in Alberta. There he hoped to recuperate and once more be ready for the battle. The other was still a soldier in the making.

The day was dull with low-hanging clouds that only seemed to bring the thunder of the great shells passing overhead that much closer. Steadily and sullenly the enemy was searching for one of our own great guns hidden in a nearby grove of stumps that had once been trees. We paid little attention to those sullen outbursts, only when exploding nearby the shells had the effect of giving one a slap on his bottom as the earth heaved.

We, a French officer and the writer, were looking for Herb Monkman's grave there on Hill 63 near to where once stood a prosperous little village called Plough Streets. We found it. The only white cross standing and it with a bullet hole exactly in the centre of the cross. All the other crosses were smashed nearly beyond recognition although we were able to reconstruct those of our old friends Sergeant Major Munson and Sergeant MacGarry.

Looking over the ground and lining up where had been the all-too-shallow trenches, we tried to reconstruct the story of the day when the 3rd Canadian Mounted Rifles had been cut to pieces by overwhelming odds but still refused to go back. I had been told the story as to how my old friend Major Fane, sore wounded, even threatened with his revolver any stretcher bearer who tried to take him out until his last wounded boy had been cared for. How Herb Monkman (a medical man who never should have been a combat officer) wounded unto death crawled on his hands and knees saving lives. His own he could not save.

Sadly, reverently this French interpreter officer helped me reconstruct my friends' graves and there we left them, murmuring as a prayer the immortal words of Sir John Moore at La Coruña.

"Little he'll reek if they let him sleep on in a grave where Britons hath laid him."

Just at his side while we stood there with heads bared a party of Australians buried two of their dead. I am back at my billet at Second Army H.Q. and have a duty to perform. I must interview a boy charged with illegal enlistment in the Canadian Expeditionary Force.

On my desk are two official letters. Curiously enough, one is from my father as Resident Indian Agent at Saddle Lake, Alberta, Canada. A certain Indian boy was supposed to have falsely given his age as eighteen before a recruiting officer when he was actually only fourteen. His parents were demanding that he return to the reserve at once. Did I know anything about this case? Another letter from the Provost Marshal stating that a certain Indian soldier had been found who answered to the description of the boy mentioned in my father's letter. Would I interview this soldier, who would report to me, and write a report to be forwarded to Canadian H.Q., London, England.

The lad came in, a fine strapping soldier taller than myself. Then I grew humble. On his arm he wore three wound stripes. I had none. He was a veteran, I was not. How could I break down that reserve, a reserve traditional of his people. On my desk was a letter from my wife and in it some pictures of her and our three small sons Ted, Paul, and Billy taken as they played in running water near a fish trap on the Saddle Lake Reserve. My wife and little ones were staying with my father and mother for the summer.

I took the snapshots and handed them to the man I was supposed to interview. "Did you ever happen to see my kiddies at Saddle Lake?"

Ever build a mud dam in a small creek as a boy and see it all washed away in a moment when the waters backed up behind? That was how my Indian lad's reserve went out at the sight of three small boys playing in the water.

An experienced stenographer would have had hard work to catch all the words that flowed in the next half hour. I did not even try. So now, fifty years later, I must reconstruct the story to the best of my ability, using first-person singular as my Indian lad used it so long ago.

"My mother had three sons, all died but me. I was always big and strong. Mother said I would be a great warrior some day but as I grew older I knew that the days of warriors among our people were gone forever. We Crees were no longer warriors, we were no longer guides for the white men who would know the lands beyond the horizon, we would no longer blaze new trails into the unknown. We were not even great hunters, the white man shot most of the deer and moose. We just carried them out to where wagons could take them away. We were Treaty Indians and my father received five dollars a year for each member of the family.

"Still our fathers sat in council and smoked the peace pipe and talked about the old times when we Crees ruled the land from the waters to the East to the Athabasca.

"We small boys played at being warriors and we sat in solemn council and smoked a peace pipe we had found behind a deserted house the white man had built but which we red men refused to use.

"We Indian boys did not play with the Indian girls. Yet there was one girl I watched for often, she was very beautiful. Her hair was jet black and she always had it carefully combed. One day we boys sat in solemn council. My back was to a willow bush. I knew this girl was behind the willow bush listening and watching. When my friends got tired of playing warriors they went away to catch gophers with their strings. I sat still as a warrior of old. The girl waited. Then I said, 'Come.'

"She came and sat at my side. For a long time we did not talk. I knew her name was Mary Wolfrib. I did not like the name. I said, 'Your name is Dawn.'

"'Dawn,' she said, then as if afraid she got up and ran away.

"Again we boys played at being warriors and again they tired and went away to catch gophers. Again I said, 'Come,' and out of the shadows came the girl.

"This time she did not, as at first, sit by my side. From among her own black hair she took out a small black feather and, putting it in my hair, said, 'You are a great warrior. You are black Feather.' Then she was gone.

"Black Feather, that was a good name. Many years before one of my family had that name. He had travelled with Thompson, the great white trail blazer, all over the west. I was only a boy, if I used that name my father would be angry. I hid that black duck feather in the spruce tree near the fish pond you see in this snapshot of your wife and boys. Many times I sat alone and Dawn would come to me and we would talk. I would never touch her. We are not like white boys and girls who played together.

"Then came the war. I wanted to go away to be a soldier. My father was very angry. My mother said I should be spanked for wanting to go away from home. Many months passed. Your wife and little boys came to live at Saddle Lake. Many time I watched them as they climbed the trees and waded in the creek at the fish trap.

"One day after your boys went home Dawn came to me. 'Why do you not go and be a soldier? You are of a line of warriors.'

John and Sara's first three
children—Bill, Paul, and Ted—
doing what all little boys love to
do: play in the mud and water
until they look like walking
mudballs. The photo was taken
on Saddle Lake Indian Reserve in
1917, where Sara and the boys
lived with John's parents when
John went overseas in 1916.

"'My mother says I should be spanked for thinking about going away
and that I will be killed.'

"'In the old days did a young warrior ask his mother if he could go on
the warpath?'

"'No.'

"The next day Dawn came again and she was excited. 'Twenty young
men are going out to work in the harvest fields. If one young man went
and got a job on a farm all by himself no one would notice if some day he
was not there. That young man could go to Edmonton or Calgary and
become a soldier.' Then she was gone.

"It was hard to make my father and mother think that I was old enough
to go away from home and work but I was big for my age and tall, and
then they said 'yes.' I worked one day for a man near Vegreville then I walked
all the way to Edmonton. The recruiting officer said I was too young. The
boy ahead of me had a letter from his father saying he could go, but he did
not need the letter and left it on the table. Next day I went to another
recruiting office and the boy's letter, that he had left behind, was all that I

needed. Before dark, I was in uniform. My battalion was nearly ready for overseas. Soon I was on the train, on a big ship, in England. I just sent one postcard home. It was a scene of a wheatfield where men were working. It went to Dawn's mother. She never knew why and she never noticed a very small black feather printed at one corner. Dawn's mother wondered who John Smith was but did not see some wee small numbers as if they were a post mark put on by some postmaster. It was my military number.

"Soon we came over to France. Three times I've been over the top. I have been here for more than a year." So far his story had been dispassionate, then his voice grew bitter. "Now they are going to send me home to the reserve. I am a small boy who needs spanking."

Three times over the top. Three times with fixed bayonet he had faced the enemy. I could imagine the war whoop that chilled the blood of those stern-faced Huns who seldom went back.

What could I say? Among those snapshots was one of my father as he watched his grandsons at play. A big six-foot man, a kindly man. I had my answer.

"Black Feather. I like that name. Once I wrote a story and my hero was an Indian chief named Broken Feather. I am a Canadian. My people have been Canadians for one hundred and fifty years. In all those years my family has lived in close proximity to the native Americans. So maybe I know your people just a little better than some. Now my wife and little ones are living right among your people. I have followed many of the trails of the west that your people have made over the ages. So now listen to me, not as an officer, but as a friend.

"You are not going home as a bad boy for his mother to spank. You are going home as a soldier of our King who needs a long rest. You are going home wearing your uniform."

"Wearing my uniform?" and there was a new sparkle in the lad's eyes, an added lift to the shoulders.

"Yes, you will go home in uniform. Now remember, don't take it off until your mother and the small boys and girls see you, and especially Dawn. See to it that your uniform is in perfect order. Then you will be wearing ribbons no member of your family of Crees wore."

"Me wearing ribbons?"

"Yes. You will have the 1914–15 Star, the General Service Medal, and the Victory Medal.

"Now remember this, you are not going to be discharged. You, if my recommendation is observed, will just be on reserve until you are eighteen years of age."

"Then I can come back here to my regiment again?"

My voice, my eyes said "Yes." My inner soul said, "No, pray god, no. No, not two more years of this land of dead and stinking men and horses and rats and mud, hell by night and shells by day, no, no, not two more years!"

"Yes, of course you will be back again. Remember even your mother can't say no when you are eighteen. Now you won't get many orders. You may even think that you are being pushed around. But don't mind that. Just remember that you are a soldier. The last real warrior of your tribe returning from a long trail. You will go to England and from there you will go onto one of the big ships that the German subs are always looking for. You will come to Halifax. Just try to imagine for a while that you are David Thompson, the great trail blazer your father's father knew, coming to a land where there were few roads but many trails. Then you will be at Montreal. Look down at the river, then shut your eyes and see the brigade of York boats ready for the two thousand mile-long paddle and portage, paddle and portage, all the way to the McKenzie. You will come to Winnipeg. It's not Winnipeg, it's Fort Garry, the headquarters, the starting place for the Assiniboia Trail, the Qu'Appelle Trail, the Blue Quill Trail, the Battleford Trail, and finally, for you, the Saddle Lake Trail. Then you will come to Vegreville and now is your testing time, for you are among people you know. Try to get your uniform cleaned and pressed because you have the honour of your regiment to uphold. Then you leave the railway and go on that old, old trail to Saddle Lake, Whitefish Lake, Lac la Biche, and Heart Lake.

"Joe Saint Pierre, the stage driver, will come dashing up to the hotel, his horses on the run, blowing his brass horn to tell everyone to make way for His Majesty's Mail. He will spit tobacco juice clear to his horses' ears to try and make everyone think he is a hell of a man when really he is one of the very finest. He will make room for you on the front seat with him so everyone will see that he has a passenger, a soldier who has been to war. Then you will dash away north along that winding trail all the way to

Brosseau on the Saskatchewan River. There Johnny Borwick[17] will be waiting for you with the fine team of grey geldings that my father uses when he goes on his inspection trips. Tell Johnny stories about the war. I sent him a postcard showing two big six-inch naval guns in action. I wrote on the card, 'How about me bringing a couple of these home and we could go duck shooting with them.'

"You will come to the Agency and my father will be standing at the door of his office to welcome you. Johnny Borwick will bring the team up with a flourish and you will step down, come to attention and salute my father, for remember, he is the King's representative at Saddle Lake Indian Reserve. My father will shake hands with you and then you will be among your own people. Black Feather, that may be your hardest test. You ran away from home a boy. You are returning a soldier and a veteran. Don't act like a boy ashamed to come home, but above all don't strut about like a turkey gobbler. Show you are glad to be home, home among your own people but from the first let it be known that when the time comes you will go again.

"No doubt Dawn will be there and her eyes will show she is proud of you. I do not know the customs of your people as between boys and girls of your age, but for two years you have lived among other people, other customs. Maybe if you walked over to Dawn and spoke to her openly as a special friend it would do more to bring home to your people that now you are a man, not a boy, than anything else could do."

There was no saluting, we shook hands as friends.

Two years? No, thanks be, Black Feather did not come back to France, Belgium, or Germany. The war was over and it was my turn to take the long trail back to my loved ones.

My wife met me in Edmonton. Early the next morning I said to her, "Now the first things to do are shave off this mustache and discard this uniform forever."

"No. You are going to do no such thing. Back home on Saddle Lake Indian Reserve are three small boys. They are anxiously waiting for Daddy, and their Daddy has a mustache and wears the King's uniform."

Appendix V
Two Letters to Sara

THESE TWO LETTERS are the only known examples of John's voluminous correspondence with Sara; all the other letters that she kept and he
referred to when writing *The Unwanted* have been lost.

If one compares these letters to the examples John quotes in *The Unwanted*,
it is obvious that his original spelling and punctuation was cleaned up
when the book was written in 1956. Many of the letters were probably
written quickly, most likely late at night, after a hard day's work, much
of it carried out in dangerous circumstances. No one working under
those conditions is going to produce textbook-perfect English.

It must also be remembered that John had only completed Grade
Four before he dropped out of school—in about 1892, at about age 10—
and went to work on the family farm. This was typical for working-class
people in that day and age; going to school was not compulsory and there
were no truant officers to hunt down children who were not in class.
Despite this, John read widely throughout his life and wrote hundreds
of short stories, going far beyond what a Grade Four education would
support. He must have received some sort of home schooling, as both his
written vocabulary and range of interests are indicative of a much higher
level of education.

Virtually all the credit for the readability of John's later writings must be given to Sara; she was a school teacher and always—always!—insisted that her children, grandchildren, and pretty much anyone else who came within her sphere of influence, speak, write, and behave properly. I can clearly remember her informing me one day that there was a 'd' in 'grandmother' and that it was *not* to be slurred over. And although she may have been a bit more up-front about such things with her grandchildren than she was with John, her influence is obvious, if one is able to see the original documents. That is why these transcriptions are as true to the originals as possible.

France

31.12.17

Dearest Girlie,

This will be my last letter to you for this year. The last half of the year has slipped away very fast, because I was busy, I suppose. And with present prospects I will be even busier next year. I am likely to leave here and go down to the Somme district working from G.H.Q. I don't like leaving here a little bit, as here I am very comfortable and know the officers of Corps and Army and I have a free hand, go where I like when I like, as my letters of late have shown you I travel all over Northern France and have opportunities to see the country as but few men in the B.E.F. have. Today I down at the ancient city of _____ seeing about land for gardens. This is a famous district for vegetables and in peace times many trains leave there every day laden with fresh vegetables for Paris and other large cities. I had a new experience as had lunch in the home of a real French gentleman, a splendid home. I would like to describe it to you, as you have noticed through all my letters I have often said these French people know but little about real comfort, and in spite of this mans evident wealth his home lacks that touch of ease and comfort which is brought to its highest pitch in the English country home. Well this house shows nothing but a plain outer wall to the street, but once inside shows both taste and a full purse. A marble hall (cold), many stained glass doors, large rooms, high ceilings, rich old furniture, much of it delicately carved, no doubt very valuable today, all of oak, the shelves and furniture loaded with ornament, old bronze statuets, heavy silver, bright and shining brass, fine old pottery. To much for an English house but seeming not out of place there. The table laid with fine linen cloth and napkins, old china and silver, thin wine glasses a fine old pewtar jug for beer. The table was set for five Mosieur Lardevs Madame (his sister) his son (a lad home from school in Paris) Lieut Falicon and myself. Now there may be a shortage of food in France (which I doubt) but there was none here. Soup, (the French certainly excel in soup making) baked bacon with sauce, eaten with bread, first course. Mutton chops, and potatoes, (and here's a wrinkle for you to try some day, at the end of the bone from the chop wrap a bit of tin-foil so as to hold without getting the fingers greasy) second course, Pressed meat with jelly third course, baked apples, (and I would like to know how they were done, in England they pride themselves on their baked apples but never have I tasted the like of these, they broke apart and were so light and mealy as a real good Canadian potatoe) (potatoes on this side of the pond are always soggy) then thin cakes, sweets, coffee (I can drink coffee like a native now), cigarettes, not to bad for a plain ordinary everyday lunch. Then in the course of our travels we were in two other fine homes, one which is the residence of our King when here, splendid homes but like the first very plain outside, but show wealth and taste when once within the heavy doors. This is rather a disjointed sort of description but you may get dome idea from it. I wish I was good on descriptions as I see so much of interest. How some would revel in just describing these narrow winding streets, these old old buildings dating back for hundreds of years, the two cathedrals, one in good condition, the other burnt down during the French Revolution and never repaired, the square of Grand Plaza crowded on market day with open booths, the farmers mostly women and girls selling eggs, butter, fowls, vegetables, and ever other manner of things, not forgetting the paper flowers and the crowds of civilians and soldiers of all nationalities, all mixed together and the best of fellowship being shown on all sides, and our English traffic police directing all move-ment of traffic, never see a French policeman, and to watch the traffic through these old streets. First a big five ton lorry, then and old donkey cart with a little donkey about the size of a big dog, then a great Catipiller engine drawing a big long naval gun or a twelve inch howitzer. Then a push cart with one two or three dogs hitched underneath, and how those dogs can pull! The a big Rolls-Royce motor car, then a farm cart loaded high with straw, one or two horses. I told you about the farm carts how they had no pole to steer by, and all this medeldy of old and new, great and small along these streets that have been there for a thousand years. What a chance for for one with imagination and power to transfer that imagination to paper, by paint or pen picture. Twice today the brige was up and we had to wait while the slow moving barges went through and I noticed two officers making sketches and was wishing I could sketch. At least in the future when I see sketches and pictures of Northern France I will be able to say whether they are true to life or not. I remember I often doubted some of the peasant scenes but now know they are mainly true.

Later *Nearly midnight and very cold*, but was just thinking that I am not nearly as uncomfortable as I was this time last year, for then I was down in that wet muddy trench or crawling out through the gloom and mud and wire and corruption to visit the listening posts, and being my first experience my hair was naturally on end, in fact I think it was lifting my steel hat well clear of my head. I had a Mills bomb in my hand and another in my pocket. As this year is better than last I hope next will be better than this. Two letters from you this week but both older than one the previous week. These dated the 5th and 7th. The one a very descriptive account of the invasion of the Hughes tribe and connections, I think you hit them all off pretty well. Am very glad our Boys "played the game" while the visitors were there, as it is such a satisfaction and takes a load off ones mind when expecting visitor when you know the kiddies will help instead of hinder. Mother also speaks of how well the Boys acted. She takes as much pride in our Boys as we do ourselves. I hope they may always live up to such a record, so one may always depend on them. I believe they will, and will be mainly due to their Mothers training.

I rather expected that Aunt Sarah and Uncle Abe would tell about what the USA is going to do. It is easy enough for them with their hundred or more millions and unlimited wealth to do big things, but when compared in the true light they can never do what our few people have done. If you want to hear what Canada has done just ask an Englishman, he is unstinted in his praise and for some reason or other we are much more popular than any of the other colonials. Maybe they know us better. One thing is that long ago that idea of the undisciplined Canadians disappeared, died a natural death, and today people speak of the wonderful discipline in the

Canadian troops, which they never do of the Australians. I know these latter bunch, as I mix with them every day. Remember I get on with them just fine and if I want anything or have some work wanted doing I always go to the Anzac Corps in preference to any other because they do things and talk about it afterwards. Yet the men lack the discipline and smartness of the Canadian or English soldiers. We are using them now on the farm for plowing, ect., not right today as it is frozen up but were up till last week and hope to next week again. I prefer the Australians to the New Zealanders. I have never run across the Newfoundlanders yet, except when at their reserve base last winter. They are a smart snappy lot, but being only few in number naturally have not been able to make such a name for themselves as others.

Now midnight will soon be here. My light is going out and it is getting very cold so I am going to bed to get warm. So will close Hoping that this time next years we will be in our own little home and watch the old year out and the New Year in together.

With love always to my Sweethearts.
John
11.45 PM 31.12.17

France.
31. 12. 17.

Dearest Girlie
　　　　This will be my last letter to you for
this year. The last half of the year has slipped away very
fast, because I was busy I suppose. And with present
prospects I will be even busier next year. I am likely to leave
here and go down to the Somme district working from G.H.Q.
I dont like leaving here a little bit, as here I am very comfortable
and know the officers of Corps and Army and I have a free
hand. go where I like, when I like, as my letters of late have
shown you I travel all over Nothern France and have opportunities
to see the country as but few men in the B.E.F. have. Today
I was down at the ancient city of ――― seeing about land
for gardens. this is a famous district for vegetables and
in peace times many trains leave there every day laden with
fresh vegetables for Paris and other large cities. I had a new
experience as I had lunch in the home of a real French gentleman
a splendid home. I would like to describe it to you, as you
have noticed through all my letters I have often said these French
people know but little about real comfort. and in spite of this
mans evident wealth his home lacks that touch of ease
and comfort which is brought to its highest pitch in the
English country home. well this house shows nothing but
a plain outer wall to the street; but inside shows both taste
and a full purse. a marble hall. (cold) many stained glass
doors. large rooms. high ceilings, rich old furniture much
of it delicately carved. no doubt very valuable today.
all of oak. the shelves and furniture loaded with ornament

2.

old bronze statuets, heavy silver, bright and shining brass,
fine old pottery. too much for an English house but seeming
not out of place there. The table laid with fine linen cloth
and napkins, old china and silver, thin wine glasses
a fine old pewter jug for beer. The table was set for five
Mosieur Lardeur Madame (his Sister) his Son (a lad home from
school in Paris) Lieut Falke on and myself. Now there may
be a shortage of food in France (which I doubt) but there was
none there. Soup. (the French certainly excell in soup making)
baked bacon with sauce. eaten with bread, first course. Mutton
chops. and potatoes, (and here is a wrinkle for you to try some
day. at the end of the bone from the chop wrap a bit of
tin-foil so as to hold without getting the fingers greassy)
Second course. Pressed meat with jelly third course. baked
apples. (and I would like to know how they were done. in
England they pride themselves on their baked apples but
never have I tasted any like these. they broke apart and
were as light and mealy as a real good Canadian potatoes
(potatoes on this side of the pond are always soggy)
then thin cakes. Sweets coffee (I can drink coffee like
a native now). cigarettes. not so bad for a plain ordinary
everyday lunch. then in the course of our travels we
were in two other fine homes. one which is the residence
of our King when here. splendid homes but like the
first. very plain outside. but show wealth and taste
when once within the heavy doors. This is rather
a disjointed sort of description but you may get some idea.

from it. I wish I was good on descriptions as I see so much
of intrest. How some would revel in just describing those
narrow winding streets, those old old buildings dating back
for hundreds of years the two cathedrals, one in good condition
the other burnt during the French Revolution and never repaired
the Square or Grand Place crowded on market day with open
booths, the farmers mostly women and girls selling eggs,
butter, fowls, vegetables and every other manner of things
not forgetting the paper flowers. and the crowds of civileans,
and soldiers of all nationalities, all mixed together and the
best of fellowship being shown on all sides, and our English
traffic police directing all movement. never see a French
policeman. and to watch the traffic through these old old
streets, first a big five ton Lorry. then and old donkey cart
with a little donkey about the size of a big dog. then a great
Catipiller engine drawing a big long naval gun or a twelve
inch howitzer. then a push cart with one two or three
dogs hitched underneath. ar how those dogs pull! then a
big Rolls-Royce motor car. then a farm cart loaded high
with straw. one or two horses. told you about the farm carts
how they had no pole to steer by. and all this medeldy
of old and new great and small along these streets that
have been there for a thousand years. what a chance for
one with imagination and power to transfer that imagination
to paper. by paint or pen picture. twice to day the buge was
up and we had to wait while the slow moving barges
went through and I noticed two officers making sketches

4.

and was wishing I could sketch. at least in the future when I see sketches and pictures of Northern France I will be able to say wether they are true to life or not. I remember I often doubted some of the peasant scenes but now I know they were mainly true.

Later Nearly midnight and very cold. but was just thinking that I am not near as uncomfortable as I was this time last year. for then I was down in that wet muddy trench or crawling out through the gloom and mud and wire and corruption to visit the listening posts. and being my first experience my hair was naturally on end. in fact I think it was lifting my steel hat well clear of my head. I had a Mills bomb in my hand and another in my pocket. As this year is better than last I hope next will be better than this. Two letters from you this week but both older than one the previous week. these dated the 5th and 7th. The one a very descriptive account of the invasion of the Hughes tribe and connection I think you hit them all off pretty well. am very glad our Boys "played the game" while the visitors were there. It is such a satisfaction and takes a load off ones mind when expecting visitors when you know the Kiddies will help instead of hinder. Mother also speaks of how well the Boys acted. She takes as much pride in our Boys as we do ourselves. I hope they may always live up to such a record, so one may always depend on them, I believe they will. and will be mainly due to their Mothers training.

I rather expected that Aunt Sarah and Uncle Abe would tell about what the USA were going to do. It is easy enough for them with their hundred or more millions and unlimited wealth to do big things. but when compared in the true light they can never do what our few people have done. If you want to hear what Canada has done just ask an Englishman. He is unstinted in his praise and for some reason or other we are much more popular than any of the other colonies. Maybe they know us better. One thing is that long ago that idea of the undisciplined Canadian disappeared. died a natural death. And to day people speak of the wonderful discipline in the Canadian troops, which they never do of the Australian. I know these latter bunch, as I mix with them every day. Remember I get on with them fine and if I want anything or have some work wanted doing I always go to the "Anzac corps" in preference to any other because they do things and talk about it afterwards. yet the men lack the discipline and smartness of the Canadian or English soldiers. We are using them now on the farm for plowing etc. not right to day as it is frozen up but were up till last week and hope to next week again. I prefer the Australians to the New Zealanders. I have never run across the Newfoundlanders yet except when at their reserve base last winter. They are a smart snappy lot, but being only few in number naturally have not been able to make such a name for themselves as other

<u>6.</u>

Now midnight will soon be here. My light is going out and it is getting very cold so I am going to bed to get warm. So will close Hoping that this time next year we will be in our own little home and watch the old year out and the New year in together

With Love always to my Sweetheart's

John

11.45 P.M. 31.12.17

France

18.2.18

Dearest Girlie,

Another fine clear day but with quite a heavy frost during the nights, three nights now we have had frost. Some thought we were having summer all at once and wanted to start planting seeds right away and it was lucky our seeds had not arrived or they would have put them in and had their plants all frozen. And the local inhabitants all say they nearly always have frosts until mid March. Am sending a lorry to Paris tomorrow to bring up our seeds and am very busy on several farms getting beds ready for forcing plants. On Brimacombes farm we are building a small greenhouse for early plants to be used later to grow vegetables that have to have glass. In spite of it being warmer here than at home there are very few more vegetables that will ripen than at home. Onions do not do well. Tomatoes do not ripen in the open, nor corn, although quite a bit is grown but only for fodder. Our Army gardeners who are drawn from the four quarters of the globe would each like to try the vegetables that he grew on his own particular garden. But we are holding them down to standard varieties that are known to do well in these parts and if these gardeners like to try any fancy sorts they are quite welcome but at their own expense. Our line is potatoes, cabbage, carrots, turnips, sweeds, beets and lettuce and small quantities of peas, beans, radish, brussell sprouts and cauliflower. Potatoes over fifty percent, these will be planted on all heavy or sod land not fit for smaller vegetables. Many of our plots will be small around Camps in back areas, and other small plots up among the shell holes on land not fit to plough but which can be dug by hand. The Hun did a lot of this sort of work a year ago along the Ridge and our Boys reaped the harvest. Sometimes as the units were coming out of the line to support trenches they would gather up turnips or cabbage as the came along or if the vegetables were in exposed positions they would send up parties at night to gather them. Just fancy going out onto a machine-gun swept spot to pull carrots. Was up again yesterday watching our tractors work. Cotton was with me and he was not satisfied until he had tried driving on around the field. In civil life he is a motor car merchant so understands gas engines. These tractors run on either gas or coal oil, best and cheapest on the latter. I am always wondering what would happen to the driver in case the plow struck and exploded a six inch dud. I think the makers of these tractors the International would give a big sum for some pictures of these tractors plowing among the old trenches, shell holes, barbed wire entanglements, gun pits and broken down dugouts. I hope that when the official photographer comes around again he will think it worth while to give us an hour or so, it would be fine to have some records of this work. Of course you know that it is a Court Martial offence to even have a camera in ones possession let alone to take pictures. I have a few souvineers gathered up which I hope they will allow me to take home when the war is over. Just now they also are forbidden. Many a Lad gets interesting things gathered up and packs them around for months in hope of getting them home then gets a blighty and loses them all as he is often carried out and never sees his pack again. Am sending you a little bell made by Mr. Monod, this is not a forbidden object. Monod and Rowan are going up forward today to take charge of the Australian five hundred acre farm.

Now Bye Bye Sweetheart Mine
John

297   France.

18. 2. 18

Dearest Girlie.
                Another fine clear day
but with quite a heavy frost during the night
three nights now we have had frost. Some
thought we were having summer all at
once and wanted to start planting seeds
right away. and it was lucky our seeds
had not arrived. or they would have put
them in and had their plants all frozen.
And the local inhabitants all say they
nearly always have frosts until mid march.
Am sending a Lorry to Paris tomorrow
to bring up our seeds. and am busy on
several farms getting beds ready for
forcing plants. On Brimacombes farm
we are building a small green house
for early plants. to be used later to
grow vegetables that have to have glass
In spite of it being warmer here than at
home there are very few more vegetables
that will ripen than at home. Onions

do not do well. Tomatoes do not ripen
in the open, nor corn, altho quite a bit
is grown but only for fodder. Our Army
Gardeners who are drawn from the four
quarters of the globe would each like to
try the vegetables that he grew in his
own paticular garden. But we are holding
them down to standard varieties that are
known to do well in these parts and if
these gardeners like to try any fancy
sorts they are quite welcome but at their
own expense. Our line is potatoes, cabbage,
carrots, turnips, sweeds, beets and lettuce,
and small quantities of peas, beans,
radish, brussell sprouts and cauliflower.
Potatoes over fifty percent, these will be
planted on all heavy or sod land not
fit for smaller vegetables. Many of our
plots will be small around camps
in back areas, and other small plots
up among the shell holes on land not
fit to plough but which can be dug by
hand. The Hun did a lot of this sort

3

of work a year ago along the Ridge and
our Boys reaped the harvest. Sometimes
as the units were coming out of the line
to support trenches they would gather turnips
or cabbage as the came along or if the
vegetables were in exposed positions they
would send up parties at night to gather
them. Just fancy going out onto a machine
gun swept spot to pull carrots. Was
up again yesterday watching our tractors
work. Cotton was with me and he was not
satisfied until he had tried driving on
around the field. In civil life he is a motor
car merchant so understands gas engines
these tractors run on either gas or coal oil.
best and cheapest on the latter. I am always
wondering what would happen to the
driver in case the plow struck and
exploded a six inch dud. I think the
makers of these tractors the International
would give a big sum for some pictures
of these tractors plowing among old trench
shell holes. barbed wire entanglements.

4)

gun pits, and broken down dug outs.
I hope that when the official photographer
comes around again he will think it
worth while to give us an hour or so.
it would be fine to have some records
of this work. Of course you know that
it is a Court Martial offence to even
have a camera in ones possession over
here. let alone to take pictures. I have
a few souveniers gathered up which
I hope they will allow me to take home
when the war is over. just now. they also
are forbidden. Many a Lad gets intresting
things gathered up and packs them
around for months in hope of getting them
home then gets a blighty and loses them
all as he is often carried out and never
sees his pack again. Am sending you
a little bell made by Mr Monod. this is
not a forbidden object. Monod and Rowan
are going up forward today to take charge
of the Australian five hundred acre farm.
Now Bye Bye Sweetheart Mine
John.

Abbreviations

ADC	Aide de Camp
ANZAC	Australian and New Zealand Army Corps
AO	Agricultural Officer
AQMG	Assistant Quartermaster General
BEF	British Expeditionary Force
BNA	British North America
CAMC	Canadian Army Medical Corps
CB	Companion of the Order of the Bath
CCS	Casualty Clearing Station
CEF	Canadian Expeditionary Force
CMG	Companion of the Order of Saint Michael and Saint George
CMR	Canadian Mounted Rifles
CO	Commanding Officer
DAQMG	Deputy Assistant Quartermaster General
DCM	Distinguished Conduct Medal
DFC	Distinguished Flying Cross
DSO	Distinguished Service Order
FO	Foreign Office
GRO	General Routine Order(s)
GHQ	General Headquarters
HE	High Explosive(s)
HQ	Headquarters

KCMG	Knight Commander of the Order of Saint Michael and Saint George
MC	Military Cross
MGGS	Major General General Staff (the official title for the Chief of Staff of an Army)
MM	Military Medal
MP	Member of Parliament; Military Police
NATO	North Atlantic Treaty Organization
NCO	Non-Commissioned Officer
OC	Officer Commanding
OMFC	Overseas Military Forces Canada
PM	Prime Minister
POW	Prisoner of War
PPCLI	Princess Patricia's Canadian Light Infantry
QMG	Quartermaster General
RAF	Royal Air Force
RCAF	Royal Canadian Air Force
RFC	Royal Flying Corps
RSM	Regimental Sergeant Major
VC	Victoria Cross
WO	War Office
WWI	World War One

Notes to Text

1. **rats**—a plague to most soldiers in WWI, they ate anything that did not move and many things that did. One British private, J. Bowles, noted in his diary just before the Battle of Messines, that the rats "go about in swarms and at night they are all over us. And they eat every mortal thing they can get at." By 1916 the British were losing so much food to rats that at least one Rat Officer was appointed to control the pests. Philip Gosse, the grandson of English naturalist P. H. Gosse, was a keen naturalist and qualified doctor who served with the Royal Army Medical Corps in France and Belgium in 1915–1917 and India in 1917–1918. In March 1934 he published *Memoirs of a Camp Follower* (reissued in 1942 as *A Naturalist Goes to War*), which describes his war-time experiences, including his activities as the official Rat Officer for the 2nd Army. His job was to control the rat population (a difficult task) and/or make it more difficult for the rats to damage food and equipment.

2. **Herbert Campbell Holman (1869–1949)**—4th Army QMG in mid-1917. He attended Sandhurst, joined the Devonshire Regiment in 1889, served in Burma (where he was wounded in action and mentioned in dispatches), then was transferred to the Indian Army in 1892 and posted to the 16th Bengal Lancers. Holman qualified as a first-class interpreter in Russian and French, studied at the Staff College, and was appointed adjutant of his regiment in 1899. In 1900 he served as

Staff Officer in China during the Boxer Rebellion, then returned to India briefly, then worked in the Intelligence Branch in Whitehall (London) for several years. He was attached to the Russian Army in Manchuria during the Russo-Japanese War and finally got back to his regiment in 1906. When the Indian Army was moved to France in 1914, Holman was attached to its staff in the Intelligence section. In early 1915 he became the AQMG of the 1st Army, then QMG of 11th Corps, and by the end of year he was QMG of the 4th Army, a post he held until the end of the war. In early 1919 he was appointed Chief of the British Mission in South Russia, for which he was knighted in April 1920. Holman was awarded the DSO, CMG, and *Commandeur de l'Ordre du mérite agricole* (see Note 67). He returned to India in 1921, where he stayed until he retired in 1928, with the rank of Lt. General.

3. **Ypres**—a municipality in Flanders, one of the three regions of Belgium, in the Flemish province of West Flanders. During the Middle Ages it was a centre for the cloth and weaving trade. Today the municipality comprises the city of Ypres (Ieper in Flemish or Dutch, Ypern in German, often referred to as Wipers by WWI Allied soldiers, although the correct pronunciation is 'eeps') and the towns of Boezinge, Dickebusch, Elverdinghe, Vlamertinghe, Voormezeele, Zillebeke, and Zuidschote. Ypres was a principal town in the British lines in WWI and the area was the site of three major battles, during which the town was completely destroyed. In the First Battle of Ypres (31 October to 22 November 1914) the British captured the town from the Germans. In the Second Battle of Ypres (22 April to 25 May 1915) the Germans used poison gas for the first time on the Western Front and captured the high ground to the east of the town. In the Third Battle of Ypres (21 July to 6 November 1917), also known as the Battle of Passchendaele (see Note 41), the British recaptured the ridge, but only at a terrible cost in lives. After the war the town was rebuilt in its original style.

4. **Messines Ridge**—a natural stronghold southeast of Ypres, and a small salient (a battlefield feature that projects into enemy territory) that the Germans had captured during the First Battle of Ypres. It was by attacked on 7 June 1917 by nine Allied divisions under the command of British General Herbert Plumer (see Note 38), as the opening maneuver in the much larger Third Battle of Ypres. The Messines attack was planned with great care and, most unusually, achieved all its objectives quickly and at a fraction of the usual cost. For over a year

before the attack, British, Canadian, and Australian Tunnelling Companies dug 21 tunnels—up to 600 metres long and as much as 30 metres deep—under the German lines. One was discovered by the Germans and blocked, but the other 20 were undetected, and they were packed with over 600 tons of high explosives. The day before the attack, Plumer said to his staff, "Gentlemen, we may not make history tomorrow, but we shall certainly change the geography." At 0310, 19 of the remaining 20 mines were detonated, creating what was said to be the loudest man-made noise up to that time; Lloyd-George is reported to have heard the explosions in Downing Street, and people as much as 50 kilometres behind the front lines said it felt like an earthquake. Approximately 10,000 Germans were killed by the explosions, which were followed by an artillery barrage laid down by over 2200 guns and an attack by 12 divisions of infantry; total German casualties were in the range of 25,000. By noon the ridge was in British hands, at a cost of some 17,000 men, most of whom were hit by artillery fire while digging in after the German troops had fled.

5. **British Labour Corps**—the initial need for labour units during WWI was met when some 38 Labour Battalions were established in 18 different infantry regiments. There were also a large number of Labour Companies from other infantry regiments, the Royal Engineers, and the Army Service Corps. The Labour Corps, initially a non-combatant organization, was formed in April 1917, absorbing the earlier infantry labour battalions and companies. It was split into Labour Companies, Area Employment Companies, Area Employment (Artisan) Companies, Divisional Employment Companies, and Agricultural Companies. They carried out a wide range of defence duties in the UK and overseas, especially in France and Flanders, including building and repairing roads and railways, moving ammunition and stores, loading and unloading ships and trains, burial duties, and agriculture and forestry duties. In general, men in the labour companies had a reduced medical category, due to wounds or disease, but were still capable of physical labour and able to serve in rear areas in operational theatres. By the end of the war, the Labour Corps had strength of about 380,000 men stationed in the UK, France and Flanders, Italy, Egypt, and Salonika. In fact the Corps reached its greatest size—almost 400,000 men—in January 1919. This included about 240 Labour Companies in France and Flanders, with about 30 to 50 companies allocated to each of the five Armies, plus a few kept aside as Lines of Communication

units. After the end of the war, labour battalions were involved in salvage work, grave and burial registration, and as prisoner-of-war guards, until the Corps was disbanded in late 1919. The Pioneer Corps of WWII is the successor to the Labour Corps. (See Note 33 for information on foreign Labour Corps.)

6. **H.T. Cotton (?–?)**—staff officer with 4th Army Headquarters in 1917. Cotton graduated from the Royal Military College in 1898 and was appointed a Second Lieutenant with the Prince of Wales Volunteers (South Lancashire Reg.). He was promoted to Lieutenant in 1900, seconded for service in South Africa in 1902, and was a Captain in the 3rd Battalion by 1909. In October 1913 he became the regiment's adjutant, but gave up this position in January 1915 to rejoin his regiment, which was then posted to the front lines near Messines Ridge. He was promoted to Major in February, and to temporary Lt. Colonel in June. He relinquished the temporary rank in September 1916, however, and took on a new Staff position—adjutant to General Holman.

7. **Agricultural Officers**—army officers who were initially charged with assisting French farmers on their farms, and later, with growing crops for the use of the British Army. The first indication that the British military had any agricultural thoughts appears in GRO 740, issued in April 1915, which stated that commanding officers were to assist French farmers in restoring fields that had been damaged by activities of British troops. There is little evidence of wide-spread, effective assistance at this time, although individual soldiers and units provided some aid on an as-possible basis. The main reason is that the British did not have men to spare for agricultural efforts until much later in the war. By 1916, the policy makers in London realized that the BEF had to be more proactive in raising some portion of its own food and forage, if only because horse fodder was taking up a huge amount of space in cross-Channel shipping. Some 500 hectares of vegetable gardens were planted behind the front lines shortly after the Somme offensive, but this seems to have been the exception, not the norm. Beginning in January 1917, AOs were appointed to Army and Corps headquarters. Working with French interpreters and other experts, they were to determine who amongst the French civilian population needed what help, and ensure it was supplied. To maintain continuity within their areas, some AOs were not moved when their regiments were moved. Under Brigadier-General Cooke (see Note 35), 9th Corps established a permanent pool of 75 men from which the AO could

draw (for which Cooke was awarded the *Commandeur l'Ordre du mérite agricole*—see Note 67). By late 1917 the British government was pushing the BEF to get more directly involved in agricultural operations, and in December the War Office appointed General Lord Radnor (see Note 48) Director of Agricultural Production. He arrived in France on 2 January 1918 and promptly proposed that British troops undertake large-scale gardening on abandoned land immediately behind the front lines.

8. **The *California*—**a passenger ship built for the Anchor Line in 1907 by D&W. Henderson Ltd., Glasgow. She had a gross weight of 8662 tons, was 470 feet long, just over 58' across at the beam, had two funnels, two masts, twin screws, a top speed of 16 knots, and could accommodate 232 First Class passengers, 248 Second Class, and 734 Third Class. She worked the Glasgow-Liverpool-New York run for the Cunard-Anchor joint service until 7 February 1917, when she was torpedoed by a German submarine some 60 kilometres southwest of Fastnet Island, Ireland, and sank with the loss of 43 lives.

9. **U-53—**a German submarine, commissioned in April 1916. It made 13 patrols during the war, probed the eastern seaboard of the USA in September 1916, returned to British waters in October, and was the first German sub to sink an American warship, the Tucker-class destroyer *USS Jacob Jones*, on 6 December 1917. Its first commander, Lt-Commander Hans Rose, displayed an interesting combination of ruthlessness and humanity, sinking about 90 ships, but often taking risks to ensure his victims' crews were rescued. According to a report in *The Times* on 19 October 1916, the U-53 sank a Dutch steamer, *Blommersdijk*, off the coast of Nantucket, Rhode Island, in the presence of an American destroyer, the USS *Benham*. The article quotes a letter from one of the *Benham*'s officers to his father, which says Rose attempted to sink the Dutch ship with a bomb; when that failed, he asked the Captain of the *Benham* to move away from the *Blommersdijk* so he could safely torpedo it. An official statement from Washington denied that this was the case, stating that the destroyer "stood by for purely humanitarian purposes." Rose ceased to command the U-53 in the summer of 1918, and a harder-hearted officer took over. The U-53 surrendered on 1 December 1918 and was broken up at Swansea in 1922.

10. The British Army had neither interest nor faith in Canadian militia officers; what it wanted—and got—was manpower. When Britain

accepted Canada's offer to send an infantry division in August 1914, most Canadians expected it would be created using some of the 60,000 members of the Canadian militia. Instead, Colonel Sam Hughes, Minister of Militia and Defence (see Note 19), decided to organize volunteers into new, consecutively numbered "draft-giving" battalions. This decision was made in preference to a scheme developed by the Chief of the General Staff, Major General Willoughby G. Gwatkin (a British regular officer who had been seconded to Canadian militia headquarters to provide expert advice to military and political officials concerning the mobilization of troops), who recommended organizing depots in Canada for receiving and training recruits, then sending them overseas in reinforcement drafts. Unfortunately, Hughes's plan produced an accumulation of senior officers in England who could not be given suitable employment when their units were absorbed into the reserve battalions. The authorities in Canada were reluctant to discontinue this system, however, for, as Gwatkin observed in June 1916, "Drafts, for administrative and financial reasons, are to be preferred; but the despatch of complete battalions would gratify the senior ranks and appeal to local sentiment." In December 1916 there were 7240 officers and 128,980 enlisted men of the CEF in Britain, up from 2467 and 49,379 a year earlier. By comparison, there were 2526 officers and 105,640 men in France.

11. **Albert Edward Pilkie (1877–?)**—Quartermaster Sergeant, 151st Bn. Pilkie was born in Lindsay, ON, although he apparently also lived in Montreal for some time before moving to Alberta, as he claimed militia experience in both the 45th Regiment in Lindsay and the 5th Royal Scots in Montreal. Several of his brothers moved west in 1904, put up a sod building in Vermilion (which was the hub of north-east Alberta), and opened the town's first general store. Pilkie and his family joined them in 1907, but within months his wife, Beatrice, died of typhoid, leaving him with a young daughter to raise. He enlisted in the CEF in December 1915.

12. **Vermilion**—a small town about 200 kilometres east of Edmonton, AB, first settled in 1899. John had homesteaded just north of Mannville, 20 kilometres west of Vermilion, in 1905, and was farming near Lavoy, another 60 kilometres west of there, when WWI broke out. He was an outgoing man, and probably knew most of the farmers in the sparsely populated land between Vermilion and Fort Saskatchewan, and this is

the area where he recruited men for 'C' Company, 151st Bn., in 1915–16.

13. **Sara Maria Purdy Paul (1890–1966)**—Sara was born in Scotland, the daughter of a tailor, and emigrated to Canada with her parents in 1904. They lived in Winnipeg, MB, for about two years, then moved to Fort Saskatchewan, AB. Sara graduated from high school in 1907, enrolled in Normal School in Edmonton, and received her provisional teaching certificate in August 1908. At least one of the pupils in her first class was older than she was. In the fall of 1908 she met a local farmer, John McKendrick Hughes; they were married in January 1910, and started farming near Lavoy, a small town to the east of Vegreville. By the time John enlisted in the army, they had three children; Charles Edward (1910–1986), John Paul (1912–2005), and William (1915–1997). Another son, Neil (1920–) was born after the war.

14. **Saxonia**—a 14,281 gross ton passenger ship, 580 feet long and 64 feet at the beam, with one funnel, four masts, twin screws, and a top speed of 15 knots. She could carry 164 passengers in First Class, 200 in Second Class, and 1600 in Third Class. Built by John Brown & Co., Glasgow, for the Cunard Line, she was launched in 1899, and sailed primarily between Liverpool, Queenstown (Ireland), and Boston until WWI broke out.

15. **Missanabie**—a 12,469 gross ton passenger ship, 500 feet long and 64 feet at the beam, with two funnels, two masts, twin screws, and a top speed of 15 knots. There was room for 520 passengers in Cabin Class and 1200 in Third Class. Built in 1914 by Barclay, Curle & Co, Glasgow, for Canadian Pacific, she sailed between Liverpool, Quebec, and Montreal throughout the war. On 9 September 1918 she was torpedoed and sunk by the U-87 about 80 kilometres from Cobh, Ireland, with the loss of 45 lives.

16. **Matthew Brimacombe (1866–1939)**—an early Alberta pioneer and soldier in several wars. He arrived in Breague, a small settlement to the east of Vermilion, in about 1902 and served as postmaster and government land agent there until 1905, when he moved to the new town of Vermilion. Brimacombe was elected the town's first Mayor in 1906, and was re-elected in '07, '08, and '13. He also served on the town council, was a member of the hospital board, led the first church choir, was bandmaster for several years, and took a leading role in the local drama society. He enlisted in December 1915 in Vegreville, at age 49.

The front page of the two-page Attestation Paper filled out by all enlisted men joining the CEF. Note that the officer who signed up Matt Brimacombe was his friend and neighbour, Lieutenant John McKendrick Hughes, OC, C Company, 151st Battalion.

Source: Library and Archives Canada, RG150, Box 1069–38.

17. **Shorncliffe**—a British Army camp on the coast of Kent. The Army purchased over 200 acres of land just west of the town of Folkestone in 1794, and built Shorncliffe Army Camp. Troops were stationed here before being sent off to fight in the Peninsular Wars (1820s). Throughout WWI it was the main embarkation point for thousands of soldiers leaving to fight in the trenches of France and Belgium. Due to space limitations, however, it could not be used as the main holding-point for Canadian reserve battalions after October 1916, and these units were sent to the new Bramshott Camp near Liphook, about 70 kilometres south-west of London. In his autobiography (*Slide Rule*), Nevil Shute says that at some point during WWI, Shorncliffe must have been used as an RAF instructional camp, as there were still several derelict aircraft in a hanger when he was posted there in December 1918.

18. According to the *Nominal Roll of Officers, Non-Commissioned Officers and Men of the 151st Battalion, CEF*, these officers would have been:

> Lt. Colonel John Wilson Arnott
> Major Allen Pardee Coe
> Major George Jonathan Dawson
> Major Alexander Cameron Grant
> Major John McKendrick Hughes
> Major James Robert Lowery
> Hon. Captain Christopher Carruthers
> Captain Wilson Henry T. Collinson
> Captain Robert John G. Dow
> Captain Roy McGregor Foster
> Hon. Captain Howard Percy H. Jones
> Captain Bernard Richard Mooney (CAMC)
> Hon. Captain Harold Moore
> Captain Charles Ernest Morrow
> Captain Louis Guthrie Scott
> Lieutenant Royden Coleman Ames
> Lieutenant Reginald Wemyss Chipman
> Lieutenant Brian Leroy Cooke
> Lieutenant Leslie Gordon H. Forhan
> Lieutenant Lorne Douglas Foster
> Lieutenant William Whitton Lowery
> Lieutenant Charles Frederick Lyall

Lieutenant Alexander Stuart Macullouch
Lieutenant William Tertius McCrum
Lieutenant Andrew Robert Mercer
Lieutenant Samuel Fleming Patterson
Lieutenant John Morrison Peterkin
Lieutenant Arnold Walter Tayler
Lieutenant Francis Austin Walker.

There are slight discrepancies between the number and ranks of officers John lists in the book, and that given in the Nominal Roll; the "Junior Major" may have been listed as a Captain, and perhaps John mis-remembered how many Lieutenants there were in the battalion.

19. **Sam Hughes (1853–1921)**—the Canadian Minister of Militia and Defence at the opening of WWI; the modern equivalent would be the Minister of National Defence. Sixty-one years old in 1914, Canadian-born of Irish parents, Hughes had been dreaming of leading Canadians into battle for most of his life. He joined the Canadian militia as a boy, fought the Fenian raiders in the 1860s and 1870s, was elected to Parliament in 1892, helped convince Prime Minister Wilfrid Laurier to send Canadian troops to fight in the Boer War (1899–1902), and in fact saw action there himself (although he claimed his British superior officers had deprived him of a VC). Prime Minister Borden appointed him Minister of Militia in 1911 with the aim of creating a distinctly Canadian Army. Hughes accomplished an incredible amount in the early days of WWI, building Camp Valcartier virtually overnight, and within weeks of the declaration of war, the first contingent of Canadian troops was ready to sail for England. The embarkation was a nightmare, however, and was a harbinger of problems to come. Hughes believed that the patriotic fervour and courage of new recruits would compensate for their lack of basic training; in fact it severely limited the manner in which the units could be used. Although the First Contingent went to France as a group, later shipments of volunteer battalions were broken up into "drafts" and assigned to Reserve Battalions, where they received advanced training before being sent to France as reinforcements for existing battalions. As time passed, it became obvious that Hughes was not only immune to persuasion and blind to ridicule, but increasingly out of control. He ignored the constraints placed on civilian ministers, created chaos within the

army, ignored Borden's wishes, and alienated the British. Borden finally fired him in late 1916.

20. **19th Alberta Dragoons**—a pre-WWI Canadian militia unit. Like many such units, its history is a confusing mess of renamings and amalgamations, many of them politically motivated. The Canadian Mounted Rifles were formed in 1901, with its headquarters in Winnipeg and squadrons in Calgary (G), Fort McLeod (H), and Medicine Hat (I). In 1905 the 15th Light Horse was formed in Calgary and the CMR reorganized to include squadrons in Edmonton (A), Strathcona (B), Fort Saskatchewan (C), and Medicine Hat (D). A second Edmonton squadron (E) was added in 1907, and the following year a regiment was formed in Edmonton from a number of CMR squadrons. It was named the 19th Alberta Mounted Rifles. The term "mounted rifles" indicated the unit was a cross between cavalry and infantry; the basic idea was that the troops would advance as far as possible on horse, then dismount and fight on foot. A "dragoon" is defined as a "mounted infantryman armed with a carbine" (Canadian Oxford Dictionary) which may explain why the name was changed to the 19th Alberta Dragoons in 1911. At the start of WWI many soldiers from the 19th joined up for active service as the 1st Divisional Cavalry Squadron of the CEF. After WWI the 19th continued as a militia unit. In 1936 it was amalgamated with another militia unit, the Alberta Mounted Rifles, although the name 19th Alberta Dragoons was retained.

21. **Frederick Charles Jamieson (1875–?)**—an Ontario-born barrister and solicitor, Jamieson was living and working in Edmonton, AB, when he enlisted in the army at Valcartier on 23 September 1914. He had served in the Boer War with the CMR and had been an officer in the 19th Alberta Dragoons since 1896. Lt. Colonel Jamieson went overseas with the First Contingent in 1914 as the CO of the Division Cavalry (later called the 1st Division Cavalry when additional cavalry units went overseas). He returned to Edmonton after the war, resumed his practice as a lawyer, and was elected to the Provincial Legislature in 1931.

22. **William Antrobus Griesbach (1878–1945)**—a successful lawyer and politician, as well as one of the most talented soldiers Canada produced in the first half of the 20th Century. He was born in Saskatchewan, the son of NWMP Lt.-Col. Arthur Henry Griesbach, the first man to be issued with a North West Mounted Police badge in 1873—Canada's first Mountie. The family arrived in Fort Saskatchewan in September 1883, and Griesbach considered Alberta to be his true home for the rest of

his life. He left in 1891 to attend an Anglican church school, St. John's College in Winnipeg, but returned to Edmonton in 1895 to study law. In 1899 he enlisted in the 2nd CMR to go to South Africa and spent two years there, fighting in the Boer War. He said that his experience there taught him "how not to do things," and turned down the offer of a commission and the chance for a career in the regular army, judging that it would be a dead-end move. In 1901 he began practicing law, with an office in the *Edmonton Bulletin* newspaper building. He stood for election as an alderman stood in 1903 and 1905, winning the second time, then served for a year as mayor in 1907, the youngest person to ever be elected to this office. He was, however, less successful in provincial politics. In 1908 he was commissioned as a lieutenant in the 19th Alberta Dragoons (see Note 20) and was a member of the regiment until WWI. When war broke out, the 19th Dragoons volunteered as a unit and Griesbach—by then a Major—was among the first to offer his services. In December 1914 he was named Commanding Officer of the 49th Battalion and started recruiting in January 1915. In a city of just 72,000, the drive for 1,000 men took only eight days—a recruitment record that still stands. The 49th—commonly known as the Loyal Edmonton Regiment—arrived in England in June 1915, embarked for France in the fall, and later took part in many notable battles, including the attack on Vimy Ridge, the defence of Arras, and operations at Passchendaele and Mons. Griesbach was promoted to Brigadier General in 1917, when he was just 39 years old, and left the 49th to command a brigade. He was awarded the DSO twice, made a CB and a CMG, and received the Victorian Decoration for long service. He retired in 1921, at which time he was promoted to Major General. In 1917 he was elected as Member of Parliament for Edmonton West, and in 1921 he was appointed to the Senate, a post he held until his death.

23. **John William Herbert McKinery (1878–?)**—an Irish-born engineering contractor who enlisted in the 66th Overseas Bn. in Edmonton on 14 April 1916, having served in the PPCLI. He served in France with the 66th and was awarded a DSO in 1918.

24. **Ross rifle**—Sam Hughes (see Note 19) insisted that Canadian soldiers use the Canadian-made Ross rifle, if only to thumb his nose at the British. The Ross had a straight-pull mechanism and high firing-chamber pressure, which meant it could be fired faster than a standard bolt-action rifle, such as the British Lee Enfield (which Hughes considered to be obsolete). It also had excellent range and accuracy, and a very flat

trajectory, which made it a superb rifle for snipers. Unfortunately, it was longer and heavier than a Lee Enfield, overheated and seized up under rapid-fire conditions, and jammed in muddy conditions, making it essentially useless for trench warfare. Moreover, the bayonet had a nasty habit of falling off at all the wrong time.

25. **Mills bomb**—a fragmentation grenade invented by William Mills (1856–1932) in the early part of WWI. Officially known as a No. 5 bomb, it weight 1.25 lbs. and had a serrated case wrapped around an explosive core. (A later version, the No. 36, was still in use in WWII and was sometimes called a "pineapple grenade" because of its oval shape and notched surface.) British troops used some 70,000,000 Mills bombs in WWI, along with some 35,000,000 other types of hand-thrown bombs. At least five variants were used during the war, but the basic design was the same. Mills was knighted for his services to the Crown in 1922.

26. **revert to Lieutenant**—On 26 May 1917 Canadian Routine Order 1535 required that all officers of rank higher than lieutenant who were surplus to establishment either revert to lieutenant's rank as a reinforcement or be returned to Canada. After this date, all officers accompanying battalions to England were considered to be draft-conducting officers, and could be retained in England or returned to Canada, at the discretion of Headquarters OMFC.

27. **William Lewis Wilkin (1875–?)**—a broker who joined the CEF in time to become one of The Unwanted. Wilkin was born in England and saw active service with Lord Strathcona's Horse in South Africa for a year. At the time he enlisted (22 June 1916), he was living in Edmonton and was a member of the 19th Alberta Dragoons (see Note 20). He was accepted into the 218th Bn. with the rank of "Provisional Lieutenant."

28. *charabanc*—a bus used on sightseeing tours, often lightweight with open sides and no centre aisle. From the French, *char-à-bancs*, literally "wagon with benches."

29. **James MacQueen (1891–?)**—another of The Unwanted. MacQueen was a surveyor, single, living in Edmonton, with six months experience in the 101st Edmonton Fusiliers militia unit when he enlisted on 3 July 1915.

30. Like other elements of the British army, the Canadian Corps was moved as needed. In April 1917, it was part of the 1st Army at Vimy Ridge; by October it was part of the 2nd Army at Passchendale.

31. **William Riddell Birdwood (1865–1951)**—commander of the ANZAC at Gallipoli and later in France, and commander of the British 4th Army

in the latter part of the war. Birdwood was educated at Clifton College, Bristol, and at the Royal Military College, Sandhurst. He spent most of the pre-war years in a number of cavalry units in the Indian Army, and served on Field Marshal Lord Kitchener's staff in India and during the Boer War, but had never commanded as much as a division when Kitchener appointed him to lead the ANZACs in 1914. He was not a great strategist or tactician, and generally left the day-to-day running of his forces to his Chief of Staff, General Bruendell White. Birdwood maintained command of the ANZAC forces through the end of the war, even after being given command of the 5th Army in May 1918. He was a genial man and had an indulgent style of leadership which endeared him to his men, to whom he was universally known as "Birdy." He was a regular visitor to the front line and was contemptuous of danger. In July 1917, he made a point of not moving his headquarters in order to escape shelling by a German 14" gun. None of this endeared him to Field Marshal Haig (see Note 42), however, and Birdwood did not improve things with his strong defence of ANZAC interests and occasional opposition to Haig's strategy. In his *Private Papers*, Haig stated "I spent some time to-day with the Canadians. They are really fine disciplined soldiers now and so smart and clean. I am sorry to say that the Australians are not nearly so efficient. I put this down to Birdwood, who, instead of facing the problems, has gone in for the easier way of saying everything is perfect and making himself as popular as possible."

32. *Mont Noir*—a 130-metre high hill about six kilometres north of the town of Bailleul, France, the fifth in a line of hills (locally known as the "Mounts of Flanders") that rise up from the surrounding plain. The name was apparently derived from the dark-coloured woods which once covered it. Mont Noir was captured by the British Cavalry Corps in October 1914 and held throughout the war. During the German offensive of March 1918 (see Note 58), the British used a windmill on the crest of the hill as an observation post until the German artillery destroyed it and the observers.

33. **foreign Labour Corps**—in 1917 the British recruited a Chinese Labour Corps from the province of Shantung. Estimates of their numbers run from a low of 92,000 to a high of 175,000. Other "foreign" Labour Corps were raised in Africa, India, and the West Indies, most of them for service in Europe, but also in East Africa, Cameroon, Salonika, Gallipoli, Sinai, Mesopotamia, and Russia. Many of these labourers

The Officers' Declaration Paper filled out by Robert Thomas Pritchard when he enlisted in March 1916. Source: Library and Archives Canada, RG150, Box 7995–43.

worked in skilled and semi-skilled jobs, while others built railway spurs, served as stretcher bearers and burial parties, moved supplies, and salvaged equipment. In Egypt, the British employed 23,000 men as camel drivers. An estimated 50,000 Chinese and Indian labourers died on the Western Front, where they worked within range of the German guns, and even in the front-line trenches. At the end of the war, there was a delay of at least six months in sending many of these men home, and rioting broke out in some of their camps. By the early 1920s, however, all had been repatriated.

34. **Robert Thomas Pritchard (1868–?)**—an Area Commandant and AO for the 10th Corps in August 1917. Pritchard was a 48-year-old farmer from Hespler, ON, when he enlisted in the 111th Bn. on 9 March 1916. He had been in the militia (30th Regiment) since 1893 and had held the rank of Captain since 1904. When his unit arrived in England, Pritchard was transferred to the 25th Reserve Bn., another of The Unwanted. He was made an *Officier de l'Ordre du mérite agricole* (see Note 67) in 1918.

35. **Bertram Hewett Hunter Cooke (1874–1946)**—Quartermaster General, 9th Corps, in 1917. A career Army officer from Buckinghamshire, Cooke was awarded the DSO in November 1916, the CMG in February 1918, and made a *Commandeur de l'Ordre du mérite agricole* (see Note 67) in May 1918.

36. About 14% of the total population of pre-WWI France was either killed or wounded during the war. These include approximately 1,376,000 dead, 4,266,000 wounded (of whom 1,500,000 were permanently disabled), 361,000 missing, and 176,000 taken prisoner; this is just over 73% of the 8,410,000 mobilized. The vast majority of them were young men (typically between 18 and 28), often unmarried, who would have contributed to both the population and the economic well-being of the country if not for the war.

Here are approximate casualty figures for a few other countries (published casualty figures vary wildly; these are averages of what was found):

	Killed	Wounded	Missing/POW	Mobilized
Great Britain	908,000	2,090,000	192,000	8,904,000
Canada	59,500	155,800	3,790	629,000
Germany	1,774,000	4,216,000	1,153,000	11,000,000

37. **James Aubrey-Smith (1877–1955)**—2nd Army AO, on the staff of General Plumer in 1917. Aubrey-Smith, a career Army officer, was a Lieutenant in the Welsh Regiment (14th Bn., Swansea) at the start of the war, and was promoted to Captain in December 1914. By 1917 he had transferred to the Labour Corps and held the rank of Lt.-Colonel. He was mentioned in dispatches twice, awarded the Legion of Honour, made a CMG, and received two French decorations—the *Croix de Guerre* and the *Officier de l'Ordre du mérite agricole* (see Note 67). He served as Inspector of the Army Educational Corps from 1921 until his retirement in 1937. In late 1917 he wrote a report on the activities of various AOs, which mentioned John by name; it is reproduced in the Appendix I.

38. **Herbert Charles Onslow Plumer (1857–1932)**—considered by many to be one of the best British generals of WWI. Plumer was educated at Eton, and entered the army in 1876 with a commission as a sub-lieutenant in the 65th Foot Regiment. He served in Sudan (1884) and led the army that relieved Mafeking during the Boer War. In May 1915 Plumer succeeded Smith-Dorien as commander of the 2nd Army, and served in Ypres for two years, culminating with the launch of the Messines Ridge offensive in June 1917 (see Note 4). Following the Messines success, he was appointed to salvage the disastrously unsuccessful Passchendaele campaign (see Note 41), which had been overseen by General Gough. Plumer was sent to Italy in November 1917 to take over the Allied force of six French and five British divisions, returned to France in early 1918 to lead the 2nd Army through the final battles of the war, and commanded the Army of Occupation on the Rhine until April 1919. Later he became Governor of Malta and then High Commissioner to Palestine. Plumer was popular among his men (if not with Field Marshal Haig, who disliked him and considered removing him on several occasions), a meticulous planner, cautious and impossible to fluster. He was widely known as "Plum" among his peers and as "Daddy" to the troops. Dudley Ryder, the 6th Earl of Harrowby, who served in the Royal Field Artillery and spent a great deal of time in the Ypres Salient, said that he and a few other irreverent junior officers often referred to Plumer as "Drip" due to his permanently runny nose. Because of Plumer's walrus moustache, beefy complexion, and rotund figure, British cartoonist David Low is reputed to have used him as the model for his character, Colonel Blimp.

39. In January 1917 the French Military Mission (*Mission Militaire Française attachée à l'Armé Britannique*) sent a list of 31 Agricultural Interpreters to be attached to the various British Armies and Corps, as well as the ANZAC and Canadian Corps. With one exception, this list does not show their ranks or given names, just their last names. The head interpreter for the 2nd Army was Falicon; under his "command" were three interpreters assigned to the 8th, 9th, and 10th Corps—Batier, Monod, and de Noblens—and one interpreter for the 2nd ANZAC Corps, Maurice Roze. There are several typing errors in the document (noticeable by the fact that letters are either over-typed or stroked out and followed by the correct letter), so it is possible that Roze—whom John says is the son of an English father and a French mother—should be Rose, as Roze is not exactly a common English name.

40. ***Mont des Cats***—a modest hill rising less than 100 metres above the flat plain of Flanders, immediately to the north of Meteren, France. *Cats* does not refer to felines (the singular would be *chat* (m) or *chatte* (f) in French, the plural *chats*), however, it refers to a tribe that resisted Caesar's Roman legions and were mentioned in *Caesar's Commentaries*. Two thousand years later, any features allowing improved observation of the surrounding plain were highly prized by both sides as observation points, making *Mont des Cats* and the other hills in the area of immense value, despite their modest height. *Mont des Cats* was captured by the British on 13 October 1914 and held throughout the war.

41. **Battle of Passchendaele (21 July to 15 November 1917)**—also known as the Third Battle of Ypres, one of the major battles of WWI, fought by British, ANZAC, and Canadian forces. Field Marshal Haig (see Note 42) decided in June 1917 that Passchendaele Ridge had to be taken, to increase pressure on Germany, which he believed was close to collapse. In four weeks of fighting during August, General Hubert Gough's 5th Army advanced less than three kilometres along a front of a few thousand metres, at the cost of 68,000 casualties. Haig wasted most of September (and its fine, dry weather) rearranging his armies. On 9 October torrential rain began to fall and rarely let up for the next month. The low-lying ground, already churned up by months of fighting, could not absorb the moisture, and turned into a deadly quagmire. When Plumer attacked that day, he lost 28,000 men. A few days later he lost 13,000 in a few hours. Conditions were so bad it often took six stretcher-bearers to carry one wounded man back to a casu-

alty clearing station. Trench foot and dysentery were rife. In early October, Haig informed General Currie (see Note 54) that the Canadians were to capture Passchendaele. Currie replied, "What's the good of it? Let the Germans have it—keep it—rot in the mud! It isn't worth a drop of blood." Haig pointed out that this was insubordination (a court-marital offence) and Currie replied that he could not help that. Haig was adamant, however, and although Currie had to accept the assignment, he insisted that his Corps fight as a united unit, and not under the command of General Gough, whose abilities he distrusted. Over the next two weeks, Currie planned an attack that would gain the most objective at the least cost. He decided on a series of small advances well within range of his supporting artillery, followed by a period of consolidation while the artillery was dragged forward. Currie estimated the battle would cost 16,000 men. In three assaults between 26 October and 6 November, the Canadian Corps succeeded in taking Passchendaele, at the cost of 15,654 casualties (approximately one-third dead, two-thirds wounded). Some units lost as much as 75% of their fighting strength. Finally, on 15 November Haig called a stop the battle, which had cost 300,000 men in less than four months. The following spring Plumer ordered a withdrawal from Passchendaele Ridge without a fight, to shorten his lines and forestall a fresh extension of the German offensive (see Note 58).

42. **Douglas Haig (1861–1928)**—commander-in-chief of the British forces in France for most of WWI, and the man most responsible for the senseless slaughter of Allied troops in one battle after another. The son of a wealthy Edinburgh whisky distiller, Haig graduated from the Royal Military Academy, Sandhurst, a cavalryman through and through. He fought in the Omdurman campaign (1897–1898) and the Boer War (1899–1902) before serving as Inspector General of Cavalry in India until 1906. After three years as Director of Military Training at the War Office, he returned to India as Chief of Staff of the Indian Army. In August 1914 he was one of the most experienced officers in the British Army, and was given command of the 1st Corps. At that time there were only two Corps, with a total of 90,000 men, organized into five divisions. By early 1915 Haig was commander of 1st Army, and in December 1915 he succeeded Sir John French as Commander in Chief of the BEF. Like many military commanders on both sides of WWI, however, Haig had no idea of how to fight a static war in which the primary considerations were trenches, barbed wire, mud, and

machine guns; all he really understood was mobility, and he searched for it all through the war. He also failed to learn that massed infantry could not attack entrenched machine guns, a weapon which he dismissed as being of no relevance. Starting in July 1916 he threw massed troops against the strongest German defences on the entire Western Front. On the first day of the Battle of the Somme, 20,000 men were killed and another 40,000 were wounded. By November, when the battle finally ground to a halt, it had cost the Allied armies some 620,000 casualties; the Germans lost about 465,000. Until the end of the war, Haig's tactics rarely changed, although in early August 1918 it entered a period of increased mobility, and Haig was at last able to demonstrate that he was a good general. He commonly signed documents "D.H.", and was also known as "The Chief," indicating the respect, tinged with fear, with which he was regarded. Haig has also attracted less salubrious nicknames, notably "Butcher" Haig, but this dates from the post-war period, when disillusionment with the war had set in. In the Introduction to *In Flanders Fields*, British historian— and former Major-General—J.C.F. Fuller said of Haig, "He lived and worked like a clock, every day he did the same thing at the same moment, his routine never varied. In character he was stubborn and intolerant, in speech inarticulate, in argument dumb." By contrast, Frank H. Simmons points out in *They Won The War*, that Haig "exemplified all that the British army prizes most highly." After the war, Haig received many honours and decorations, including an earldom, directorships of several large companies, and a parliamentary grant of £100,000, but he never again worked in any military or administrative capacity. The only contribution he was allowed to make was as head of the British Legion, a charitable group devoted to the well-being of the soldiers who managed to survive of the war.

43. **Henry Sinclair Horne (1861–1929)**—commander of the 1st Army for the latter half of WWI. Horne received his commission in 1880 and served in the Royal Artillery, with whom he saw action during the Boer War. For several years prior to WWI, he was Inspector of Artillery, gaining a reputation as a calm, conscientious, and efficient soldier. In 1914 he went to France in command of an artillery brigade with the 1st Corps. After a short stint in Egypt during 1915, he returned to Europe and took command of 15th Corps in January 1916. During the Battle of the Somme, Horne directed the first combat test of tanks at Flers. He was also one of the first British officers to make use of the "creeping

barrage" to support infantry attacks. He was knighted in 1916 and took over the 1st Army that September, the only artillery officer to command a British army during WWI. After the Battle of Vimy Ridge (April 1917), Horne called Currie's former division "the pride and wonder of the British Army" but a year later he complained to Haig that Currie (see Note 54) "is suffering from a swollen head." In 1919 he took the title Baron Horne of Stirkoke.

44. **Henry Seymore Rawlinson (1864–1925)**—commander of the 4th Army from 1916 to the end of the war. The son of a diplomat, he joined the King's Royal Rifles in 1884 and took part in campaigns in Burma and the Nile before serving in the Boer War. In 1914 Rawlinson was given command of 4th Corps and sent to assist the Belgians against the German siege of Antwerp. In 1916 he was appointed Lieutenant General of the 4th Army, and played a major part in the Battle of the Somme. In early August 1918 he commanded the Australian/Canadian/British/French forces that routed the Germans near Amiens, the first breakthrough of the final Allied offensive. Despite his involvement in the Somme fiasco, Rawlinson is generally regarded as having been a very competent field commander. He was made a Peer in 1919 and sent to command the British forces in India the following year, a position he held until his death.

45. **C.M. Wheatley (?–?)**—a career Army officer, Wheatley enlisted in the 3rd Bn., Essex Regiment, in the late 1800s as a Second Lieutenant, was promoted to Lieutenant on 3 January 1900, and to Captain on 20 March 1901. On 8 March 1901 he was seconded for service with the Remount Department, and sailed at least four times from South Africa to England (on *The Mongolian* between 8 May and 6 June 1901; on *The Hawarden Castle* between 18 September and 10 October 1901; on *The Plassy* between 23 January and 13 February 1902; and on *The Canada* departing Africa on 7 May 1902). On 15 April 1904 he was appointed Instructor of Musketry, a position which he held until 9 April 1907, when it appears he resigned from the army. On 6 October 1916 with the rank of Temporary Major, he was transferred to the General List, effective 8 July 1916. He was "graded for purposes of pay as a Staff Lt. 3rd Cl." as of 14 September 1917 (by which time he had been awarded a DSO) although the notice did not appear in *The London Gazette* until 18 December 1917. On 28 November 1918, under the heading of Special Appointments, a notice indicates he was increased from Class II to Class HH, effective 28 Nov 1917. [Took their jolly good time about that one, didn't they?] Finally, on 5 June 1923

Wheatley—identified as an "Hon. Maj., ret., Spec. Res., Hon. Capt. in Army" relinquished his commission "on completion of service." The only other reference to him is a note in a small Soldier's Own Diary carried by John, which gives Wheatley's address as "Windham Club 13 St. James Square London SW" (see page 79).

46. **Kemmel Hill**—another of the low hills rising up from the Flanders plain, much coveted by both sides as observation points, and much fought over. It was held by the Allies until being captured in the German offensive of March 1918 (see Note 58).

47. **Major Hogg**—probably William Hogg, a 29-year-old Scots-born steamfitter who was living in Toronto when he enlisted in Valcartier on 23 September 1914. He had been in the British Army (Imperial Service—R.O.S.B.) and the Canadian militia (48th Highlanders and 95th Sask. Rifles). There were several other Canadian officers named Hogg, but none of them appear (from their Attestation Papers) to have any qualifications for running an army workshop.

48. **Jacob Pleydell-Bouverie, Lord Radnor, Viscount Folkestone (1868–1930)**—a substantial landowner, Conservative MP, graduate of Harrow School and Cambridge University, and officer of the Wiltshire Regiment. Radnor served with the 4th [Militia] Battalion Wiltshire Regiment in the Boer War and became its CO in March 1903, a position he held until 1914, when the unit formed part of the 43rd (Wessex) Division, and was sent to India in October 1915. There the division was broken up and individual battalions were deployed on garrison duties to release Regular troops for service in France. In March 1915, Radnor was given command of Dehra Dun Brigade, a post he held until late 1917, when he was appointed Director of Agricultural Production, attached to Haig's GHQ in France. He arrived there in early January 1918, and immediately let it be known that he envisioned something much more proactive than simply providing assistance to farmers or suggesting agricultural activities but leaving the actual decisions up the individual commanding officers. He proposed that the BEF undertake widespread cultivation and gardening. GHQ would establish its own farm, and each Army was to do the same. And these were not to be small, scattered plots, but large farms totaling thousands of hectares. Unfortunately, there was little or no manpower to spare—the British armies were stretched to the breaking point, as they were in the process of taking over portions of the front previously held by the French. And the German offensive of March 1918 (see Note 58) overran

many of the farms which had been established. Some good work was accomplished, however. The Canadian Corps, which held the area around Vimy, was busy planting some 570 hectares when the Germans attacked (see photo, page 121). Despite this and other problems, such as the movement of large portions of the Corps, these farming operations continued through the end of the war. The 3rd Army managed to plant and harvest crops from between 400 and 500 hectares in the Somme region in the fall of 1918. And British, Canadian, and Australian soldiers helped French farmers take in their own harvests that autumn. It is likely that little of this would have happened without the energy and enthusiasm of Lord Radnor.

49. **Eliot George Bromley-Martin (1866–1946)**—a lawyer and gentleman of independent means. He joined the Queen's Own Worcestershire Hussars as a Second Lieutenant in 1891, while pursuing his occupation as a lawyer. He was given the temporary rank of Major in the Yeomanry of the Territorial Force in September 1914 and was confirmed in this rank in August 1917. At the end of the November 1918 Bromley-Martin relinquished his appointment and in April 1919 he resigned his commission, while retailing the rank of Major, and resumed his career as a businessman and lawyer.

50. **Harry Compton (1872–?)**—assistant to various AOs. A blacksmith from Vermilion, Harry was recruited for C Company, 151st Battalion, by his friend and neighbor, Lt. John McKendrick Hughes, and enlisted on 20 January 1916. He held the rank of Lance Corporal when the *California* sailed for England on 3 October 1916.

51. **William Richard Bird (1891–1984)**—a Nova Scotia-born writer of historical fiction and war stories. He enlisted in April 1916 and served as an enlisted man in France and Belgium from December 1916 to February 1919, including eight months with the 42nd Bn. (5th Royal Highlanders) in the Vimy Ridge sector. He was later posted to Hill 70, Passchendaele, Amiens, Arras, Cambrai, and Mons, where he was awarded the MM. His first stories appeared in a Halifax weekly, *The Sunday Leader*, in 1923. By the 1930s his stories were appearing in many Canadian papers and magazines, and also in the USA, Australia, and Europe. Many of his stories were about people from Yorkshire who settled in the Chignecto Isthmus on the Nova Scotia-New Brunswick border. Bird went back to France and Belgium in the fall of 1931 to revisit the front lines and write a series of articles for *Maclean's Magazine*. The articles were later expanded and published as a book, *Thirteen Years After*, in 1932. He

wrote several more books about his experiences in WWI. His only son, Stephen Stanley Bird, was killed in WWII.

52. **the election of 1917 and the battle over conscription in Canada—**"a gigantic gerrymander" (*The Road Past Vimy*, by D. J. Goodspeed). By early 1917 it was becoming obvious that Canada could not maintain four full-strength divisions in the field without resorting to conscription, which was violently opposed by most French Canadians, as well as many outside Quebec, including most farmers and many labour groups. Conservative PM Robert Borden tried to convince Liberal leader Wilfrid Laurier in May 1917 to join him in a coalition government to ensure the passage of the military service bill he felt was necessary (despite a 1914 promise that conscription would never be invoked), but Laurier declined, saying conscription should only be introduced if approved by a majority of voters in a federal election. A good deal of the slowdown in volunteer rates, especially in Quebec, can be laid squarely at the feet of Sam Hughes (see Note 19). He absolutely refused to allow the formation of a French-Canadian brigade, and in fact would not allow any militia unit to take part in religious processions of any sort. His plan of raising battalions (see Note 10) saw over 200 battalions recruited, sent to England, and broken up into reserve battalions without any concern as to religion, race, or language. A French-speaking brigade was organized at Valcartier in 1916 but it too was broken up, further increasing the reluctance of French-Canadians to enlist. In June 1917 Borden introduced the Military Service Bill, drafted by the austere, aloof Arthur Meighen, that made all male British subjects (Canada was not yet fully independent of Britain) between the ages of 20 and 45 liable for military service. The bill allowed many grounds for exemption, but the debate was acrimonious, bordering on ugly; one MP said that the only reason conscription was needed was because Quebec had failed to do its duty. Although the bill passed, it did not become law until late August, the first conscriptees were not called up until mid-October, and—because of Borden's pledge to wait for the results of the election—did not start training until January 1918. The term of Borden's government had run out in 1916, but was extended for a year by the agreement of parliament; a similar request for extension in July 1917 failed to pass, parliament was dissolved in October, and the election set for December. Between the end of August and mid-September, Borden forced two extraordinary bills through parliament, mostly by

invoking closure three times. One of these acts gave the vote—for the 1917 election only—to wives, widows, mothers, sisters, and daughters of any person, living or dead, male or female, who was serving or had served in the Canadian or British forces outside Canada (women were not considered to be "persons" under the BNA Act until October 1929 and thus did not have the right to vote in 1917). The other act took away the right to vote from all conscientious objectors and all Canadians of enemy extraction or birth who had been naturalized since 1902. Soldiers, however, were not allowed to vote for individual candidates, but simply for or against the government. Moreover, their votes could be applied to any electoral district in Canada. Despite this massive manipulation of the electoral process, less than two weeks before the election, Borden felt forced to promise that farmers' sons would not be conscripted, in reaction to fears that some rural Ontario ridings might vote Liberal. Not too surprisingly, his Unionist govern-ment took 153 seats to the Liberal's 82—but 62 of those were in Quebec. The civilian vote, however, gave a more accurate picture of where the country stood; only 53% were in favour of the government, while 92% of soldiers "voted" in favour of the government. Despite winning the election, Borden lost the conscription battle; by the end of the war, fewer than 84,000 men had been conscripted (out of some 400,000 who were eligible), less than 48,00 of those went overseas, and only 24,132 were actually sent to the Western Front. For those few soldiers, as Goodspeed points out in *The Road Past Vimy*, "the country had been deeply divided, French had been set again English, Catholic against Protestant, farmer against urbanite, soldier against civilian, and worker against employer." For the first time in Canadian history, there was serious talk of separation in Quebec and a bill to this effect was introduced in the National Assembly. The real irony was that 21,000 fully trained Canadian troops were sitting in England, twid-dling their collective thumbs, under the command of the ambitious but incompetent Garnet Hughes, son of Sir Sam Hughes (see Note 19). General Currie (see Note 54) refused to bring them over to France as a Fifth Division (which is what Sam Hughes wanted), as it would have meant overburdening the army with headquarters, corps, divisional, and brigade staffs, as well as supplying extra services such as artillery. In February 1918 the Fifth Division was broken up to reinforce the existing four divisions in the field. Sam Hughes never forgave Currie for this, and made him pay for it later, charging—from the floor of

Parliament, where he was safe from slander charges—that Currie had needlessly wasted Canadian lives in the closing days of the war. As a result of Hughes's efforts, Currie was denied the financial rewards that he so desperately needed—he was lauded widely but paid narrowly. The charges were resurrected in a newspaper report in 1927, long after Sam Hughes was dead. Currie sued for slander and won the case, but was awarded only a pittance because the jury assumed he was well off, which was not true. The strain of the trial destroyed Currie's health and he died a few years later.

53. **Henry John Hughes (1891–?)**—like many people who enlisted in the CEF in the first year of WWI, Hughes was a recent emigrant to Canada. He was born in Edmonton (now part of Greater London), England, in 1891, and had considerable military experience before he enlisted in Toronto on 12 April 1915. His attestation papers show that he had served for four years in the "R.G." (most likely a British regiment, although I have not been able to identify it) and three years in "12th York" (most likely the 12th York Rangers, a Toronto-area militia unit), and so was taken on strength as an officer. Like all other CEF battalions that went overseas after the Second Contingent, the 52nd (New Ontario Regiment) was absorbed into reserve battalions when it reached England, so it is quite likely Henry joined the ranks of The Unwanted. Exactly how he became an AO is not known, but he must have been good at it, as in August 1917 he was made an *Officier l'Ordre du mérite agricole* (see Note 67).

54. **Arthur William Currie (1875–1933)**—commander of the Canadian Army during WWI. Currie was born in Ontario, taught school there for a while, then moved to Victoria, BC, where he sold real estate. He joined the militia as a gunner in an artillery regiment in 1897, was commissioned three years later, and was the lieutenant-colonel of his regiment by 1909. In 1913 he raised and trained an infantry unit, the 50th Regiment, Gordon Highlanders of Canada. As soon as war broke out, Currie joined the regular army, along with his friend Garnet Hughes, son of Sam Hughes, and was sent to Europe with the First Contingent. He commanded the 2nd Canadian Infantry Brigade at the Second Battle of Ypres (1915), where his unit stood firm in the face of a poison-gas attack. Currie opposed the mass-attack tactics of Field Marshal Haig, and, along with General Julian Byng, was largely responsible for the Canadian victory at Vimy Ridge (April 1917). A critical feature of this battle was the use of a creeping barrage, in which the

troops advanced immediately behind the line of shell fire, and were on top of the German trenches before the troops could get out of their bunkers. Currie was also successful at Passchendaele—a battle which he considered to be totally unnecessary, but that was forced on him by Haig—later in 1917, but at the cost of 16,000 men (see Note 41). In 1917 he was promoted to general, the first Canadian to receive this honour during WWI, and took over command of the Canadian Corps, the first appointment to corps command of any officer in the British forces who was not a regular (career) soldier. Although history acknowledges him as a great general, he was not overly popular with his men; he was pear-shaped, pompous, and fussy, with a talent for ill-chosen remarks. He was, however, appreciated for his determination to be liberal with materiel and conservative with lives. Morton and Granatstein point out in *Canada and the Two World Wars* that Currie emerged as the best of the Canadian commanders, showing that "a big flabby real estate promoter could also be a great field commander."

55. **Herbert Stanley Monkman (1876–1915)**—a medical doctor from Vegreville, Monkman enlisted in the 3rd CMR in February 1915. He went overseas in the early summer of 1916 as second-in-command, under Major Frank Fane. He was killed on 1 December 1915, age 38. The Monkman and Hughes families knew each other before the war, as Dr. Monkman had practiced medicine in Vegreville since 1907 and had been the Medical Officer for the Saddle Lake Reserve since 1911. The front-page announcement of his death in the 8 December *Vegreville Observer* says Dr. Monkman was the first soldier from Vegreville to die in WWI. He is buried in the Berks Cemetery Extension, Comines-Warneton, Hainaut, Belgium.

56. **Major Grieve**—somewhat of a mystery; he is referred to seven times in the book, but only by rank and last name, no first name, not even an initial. Apart from this, all we know is that he was from Guelph. In the original manuscript, the name was spelled several ways; Grieve, Grieves, and Greive. As far as can be determined, no one by the name of Grieves or Greive enlisted in the CEF in WWI, so the spelling has been changed to Grieve, as some 90 men by that name did join up. The most likely candidate for the Major is James Broadfoot Grieve, a farmer from Rockwood, ON (just east of Guelph), who enlisted in the 153rd Battalion on 20 March 1916. He had served for five years in the 30th Wellington Rifles militia unit and held the rank of Captain at the

time, so it is quite likely he became one of The Unwanted when his unit arrived in England.

57. **Horatio Bottomley (1860–1933)**—one of the more bizarre figures to have trod the stage of WWI, he has been compared to Robert Maxwell and Jeffery Archer in modern times. Bottomley was raised in an orphanage, worked a court shorthand writer, became a journalist, and was elected MP for South Hackney in 1906. In the pre-war years he started several publications (none of which lasted very long), was forced into bankruptcy twice (the second time this happened, he was forced to resign his seat as an MP), and was hauled into court twice for fraud, although he was acquitted both times. He usually represented himself in court cases, and showed extraordinary skill as a lay lawyer; one judge advised him to go the Bar. At the start of the war he turned his weekly paper—*John Bull*, established in 1906, with a circulation of almost 2,000,000 at its peak—into a super-patriotic paper, giving his total support to Britain's decision to go to war, speaking at recruiting rallies, pushing for more aggressive prosecution of the war, and becoming more virulently anti-German as the war progressed. In 1919 he devised a scheme by which Britain's poorly paid workers (many of whom were ex-soldiers) could afford to purchase Victory Bonds. Bottomley promised to buy bonds on behalf of people who sent him as little as 20% of the cost of a bond, place them in the hands of trustees, and return anyone's investment any time they asked for it. Unfortunately, he had no head for business, forgot to factor in the cost of running the scheme (staff, advertising, office space, etc.), never bothered to appoint trustees, and soon found himself deep in debt and charged with fraud. In 1922 he was convicted of "fraudulently converting to his own use sums of money entrusted to him by members of the public" and sentenced to seven years in prison. He served five years, and went back to his journalistic ways after his release, though not with any great success, and was forced to apply for an old-age pension. His obituary in *The Times* (27 May 1933) stated that, "His career is full of interest, not only to the moralist, but to the student of national psychology." In a more modern assessment, an article by Matthew Engle in *The Guardian* (30 November 1999), says Bottomley "...was accepted 'as an acquaintance if not a friend' by the most powerful figures in the land. His flaws were obvious to anyone with half a mind. And the British public loved him." Engle adds that

Bottomley spent his money "wisely–ie on champagne, racehorses, and mistresses."

58. **German offensive of March 1918**—the last great German offensive of WWI. On 21 March 1918 64 German divisions attacked the Allied lines on a 54-mile front. The British 3rd Army held its ground, but the 5th retreated; by 26 March they were back to their defence line of 1916. On 12 April Haig issued his (oft-quoted) Order of the Day which stated that "There is no other course open to us but to fight it out. Every position must be held to the last man; there must be no retirement. With our backs to the wall and believing in the justice of our cause, each one of us must fight to the end." Haig, of course, was far behind the lines, where no fighting was taking place, and he was in no danger of having to defend any position "to the last man," The Germans captured Bailleul and the Messines Ridge in April, forcing the British to withdraw from Passchendaele, Gheluvelt, Poelcapelle, and Langemarke, all of which had been captured at great cost in 1917. By mid-April, however, the German effort was largely spent, and the tide slowly began to turn. The Germans attacked again in June and July, but these did not have the strength of the attacks of March and April, and soon ground to a standstill. It is estimated that between April and August, they suffered 800,000 casualties, and were left both depressed and exhausted, having gained little in real terms. Although the Allied casualties were almost as high, they had held onto the important points and stopped the offensive, so were in much better morale when the offensive ended. Also, the arrival of American forces was finally being felt, and with their help the Allies began to push the Germans eastward. On 23 August 1918 Canadian Prime Minster Borden noted in his diary, "The victories of the last four weeks would have been impossible but for the Americans."

59. **James Kennedy Cornwall (1869–1955)**—an early settler in Alberta and fierce promoter of the Peace River country, commonly known as "Peace River Jim." Cornwall was born in Brantford, ON, came to (what is now) Alberta in 1896, and spent two years building railways in the Crowsnest Pass area. He went to the Yukon briefly during the early days of the gold rush, returned to Alberta via the Peace River country, worked as a river pilot in Athabasca Landing in 1897-98, then settled in the Peace River area, where he worked as a trapper for some time, then opened a string of fur-trading posts. He sold the fur-trading posts to the Revillon Freres trading company in 1906 and formed the

Northern Transportation Company, which ran steamships on the Athabasca and Slave Rivers and Lesser Slave Lake. From 1908 to 1912 Cornwall was the Liberal member of the provincial legislature for Peace River, winning the riding by acclamation in 1909. By 1910 he was recognized as the greatest promoter of the Peace River country, but knew that efficient transportation was necessary if the area was to prosper. When the Edmonton Board of Trade turned down his request to promote the north, he invited and escorted a group of 18 prominent American and Canadian writers and agriculturalists through the as-yet-unsettled district. Partly because of his lobbying, the province opened up tracts of land for homesteaders and built a road called the Edson Trail through the barrier of muskeg and dense bush to the promised land. Cornwall was OC of the 8th Bn. and went overseas with the First Contingent in 1914. During the 1920s and 1930s he was president of the Athabasca Shipping Company, which ran steamships on the Mackenzie River and adjoining lakes.

60. **Ferdinand Foch (1851–1929)**—commander in chief of Allied forces on the western front during the closing months of WWI. Foch joined the French Army in 1871, served as a private in the Franco-Prussian War, became a Lieutenant of Artillery in 1874, entered the *École Supérieure de Guerre* (War College) in 1885, later taught military tactics there, and was appointed head of the school in 1908. He thought about war on a more abstract level than most officers of the day, and became a proponent of the idea that attack was the best form of defence. He was promoted to Brigadier General in 1907, Major General in 1911, and to the command of the 20th Army Corps in Nancy in 1913. By 1914 he was commander of the 9th Army. Foch was largely responsible for the French victory in the first battles of the Marne, despite the fact that the early part of the war disproved his ideas about the efficaciousness of always being on the offensive. He never abandoned the idea, however, but modified it to fit the circumstances. He became General Joffe's right-hand man and fell from favour when Joffe was forced out of command after the disasters of Verdun in 1916. He came back into favour in late 1917, however, and by May 1918 he was made Commander in Chief of the Allied forces. Foch is credited with holding the front together against the German offensive (see Note 58) until sufficient American troops had arrived to stem the enemy advance. He was made Marshal of France in July 1918, directed the final months of the war, and accepted the German surrender in

November. For his advice during the Polish-Bolshevik War of 1920 as well as for putting pressure on Germany during the Great Poland Uprising (a revolt by the people of Poznan and other towns against the Germans in 1919), Foch was awarded the title of Marshal of Poland. He was also made a British Field Marshal in 1919, and retired from active political and military life in 1920. Arthur Connan Doyle notes in *The British Campaign in France and Flanders January to July 1918*, that Foch achieved a "new unity of command" and was "famous for his writings in peace and for his deeds in war." In a speech in London after the war, Foch said, "I am conscious of having served England as I served my own country." But as Barrie Pitt points out in *1918—The Last Act*, "it was unfortunate that the price was so high."

61. **England's oldest ally**—the Anglo-Portuguese alliance is the oldest in the world. Britain and Portugal signed a Treaty of Alliance in 1373 when the English fought alongside the Portuguese against Spain. The two nations signed the Treaty of Windsor in May 1386 to formally confirm the alliance, and it has been a cornerstone of their bilateral foreign policy ever since. Portugal offered to help Britain in 1914 but did not actually declare war until March 1916, initially giving only naval assistance. It sent an Expeditionary Force of 50,000 men to Flanders in February 1917 and they saw action for the first time the following June. The war was not popular in Portugal, where many people could not see the connection between sending troops to France and the safety of shipping on the high seas. There was also wide social disparity between the troops and their officers; for example, officers took long leaves to go home, but the troops were not allowed to do the same. In short, the Portuguese Army was dispirited and close to a revolt by April 1918.

62. The British knew that the Portuguese position on either side of Neuve-Chapelle was vulnerable—on 5 April the 1st Division had been withdrawn, leaving the 2nd Division holding a front formerly held by two divisions—but Haig expected that even if they gave way, the flanking British units (40th and 55th Divisions) would hold firm until other British units could link up with them and maintain the line. At the insistence of Lieutenant-General DuCane of the neighbouring 15th Corps, the 50th and 51st Divisions were scheduled to relieve the Portuguese on the night of 9 April. But the Germans got there first. The preliminary shelling, which started at 0300 on the 9th, included some 40,000 mustard-gas shells and was so intense and widespread (it

extended far behind the lines, catching reinforcements and civilians)
that one battalion refused to go forward into the trenches. Just after
0800, the battered and demoralized 2nd Division was hit by seven full-
strength German divisions. Not too surprisingly, it was overwhelmed,
about 6,000 prisoners were taken, and a ten-kilometre-wide gap was
punched in the front line. Some Portuguese units held firm and
fought to the death, but by early afternoon, the commander of the
division reported, "Whole of Division lost or scattered." As expected by
Haig, the flanking British units held—until the 40th Division was
attacked from behind, then it too had to fall back. By noon of that day,
Ploegsteert, the greater part of Messines, and the crest of the
Wytschaete Ridge were in German hands. Over the next few days the
German advance far exceeded their expectations, and what had begun
as a diversion to relieve pressure on the Amiens front became a
primary operation. By 10 April the breach in the Allied line was 50
kilometres wide and the German commanders were being given all
the reserves they wanted (although probably not to the extent
suggested by John; decisions about wholesale rerouting of divisions
would have been taken by Ludendorff, and would have taken considerable time). As the Allies fought back, however, German casualties were
about twice that of the Allies, and, as Winston Churchill stated in *The
World Crisis 1916–1918 Part II*, "Here at last, though perilous, agonizing
and unrecognized, was the real battle of attrition." By 15 April the
advance had ground pretty much ground to a halt, the British had
managed an unhurried withdrawal from exposed positions, and the
Germans were exhausted. After one more costly, abortive assault on 29
April, the German offensive was abandoned. Captain B.H. Liddell Hart
states in *The Real War 1914–1918* that, "the Portuguese ruined
Ludendorff and saved their Allies by running away."

63. *estaminets*—a licenced establishment serving beer and wine.

64. **CCS**—Casualty Clearing Station, one of many points at which battle
casualties were taken care of. Advancing troops were not allowed to
stop and care for their wounded comrades; all soldiers carried a few
basic medical supplies and were expected to treat their own wounds if
possible. If they could not make their own way back to the lines, they
had to wait for the stretcher-bearers to arrive and carry them to the
Regimental Aid Post, which was typically in the reserve trenches. Here
Medical Officers cleaned wounds, applied dressings, and gave injec-
tions. Casualties might then be taken to an Advanced Dressing Station

where wounds were again treated and sometimes emergency amputations took place. If necessary, they were moved by Field Ambulance to the CCS (usually several kilometres behind the lines) where more complex surgery, if needed, might be carried out. Badly wounded soldiers were often kept at the CCS until they had recovered enough to be moved to field hospitals.

65. This conversation between John and Lord Radnor would have taken place before 8 August, as that was the date of the surprise attack by the Canadian—and the British, Australian, and French—troops at Amiens. It has been left where John put it in the original manuscript, however.

66. **Osborne de Vere Beauclerk, 12th Duke of St. Albans (1874–1964)**—educated at Eton, he served in the Boer War, was mentioned in dispatches, joined the 17th (Duke of Cambridge's Own) Lancers in 1901, and was a Major in the South Nottinghamshire Yeomanry from 1904 to 1910. In November 1914 he was made a temporary Captain in the 17th Lancers, two years later he was transferred to the General List, served for some time as ADC to Douglas Haig, and in October 1919 he relinquished his commission, while retaining the rank of Captain. His engagement to Lady Beatrix Frances, the Marchioness of Waterford, was announced in the 7 August 1918 issue of *The Times*, and his marriage to her (complete with detailed description of clothing and jewellery worn by the bride, and the names of the important guests, organist, singers, etc.) was announced in the 20 August issue. In January 1919 the Marchioness was appointed a Dame Grand Cross (Civil Division) of the Order of the British Empire for her services as head of the Irish War Hospitals Supply Depots, member of the Joint War Committee for Leinster, Munster and Connought, British Red Cross Society, and Order of St. John of Jerusalem in England.

67. *l'Ordre du mérite agricole*—established in 1883 by Jules Méline, the French Minister of Agriculture, to compensate for the insufficient number of rewards available within the Legion of Honour, which had been created by Napoléon Bonaparte to reward civil as well as military merits, both in times of peace and war. It is awarded by the French government, by way of a special order by the Minister of Agriculture, to its citizens and to foreigners for "continued, significant contribution to the quality, advancement, and success of the agricultural sector." There are three ranks; in ascending order, *Chevalier* (or, in English, Knight, created on 7 July 1883), *Officier* (created 18 June 1887),

and *Commandeur* (created 3 August 1890). One of the first recipients of this award was Louis Pasteur. Although the French suspended the award at the start of WWI, the French Military Mission asked that an exception be made when they saw what the British were attempting to accomplish along their portion of the western front with regard to agriculture. It was probably both an attempt to recognize what had been accomplished and to further spur it on. By the end of the war, four Canadians had been made *Officiers* and 52 *Cheveliers*. The *Officiers* are Lt. Colonel Gilbert Godson-Godson, DSO, 16th Infantry Bn. (civil servant, City of Vancouver); Lt. Colonel Robert Thomas Pritchard, 111th Bn., 10th Corps AO (farmer; see Note 34); Major Henry John Hughes, 52nd Bn., 1st Army AO (P.O. clerk, electrician; see Note 53); and Major John McKendrick Hughes, 151st Bn., 2nd Army AO (farmer). Known *Cheveliers* are Major John Fortescue Foulkes, Canadian Army Service Corps, 4th Canadian Division (professional soldier); Major Francis Bethel Ware, 1st Canadian Infantry Division (accountant); Captain James Davidson Doughty, 153rd Bn., 5th Army AO (grain merchant); and Lieutenant Percy Secombe Downe Harding, 130th Bn. (agricultural expert).

68. **Joseph Austen Chamberlain (1863–1937)**—Secretary of State for India and a member of the War Cabinet during WWI. The eldest son of statesman Joseph Chamberlain and the half-brother of Neville (the future Prime Minister of England), Chamberlain entered politics in 1892, was Postmaster General in 1902, and Chancellor of the Exchequer from 1903 to 1905. After WWI he was Chancellor of the Exchequer once again, as well as Lord Privy Seal and leader of the Conservative Party. Chamberlain was widely expected to succeed Arthur James Balfour (see Note 88) as PM in 1922, but he stepped aside in favour of Andrew Bonar Law, the only Canadian to ever become PM of England—and who, coincidentally, was born in the same small New Brunswick town as John McKendrick Hughes. As Foreign Secretary from 1924 through 1929, Chamberlain helped bring about the Locarno Pact, for which he shared the 1925 Nobel Peace Prize with USA Vice-President Charles Dawes.

69. **Edward Albert Christian George Andrew Patrick David Windsor, Prince of Wales (1894–1972)**—eldest child of King George V and later King Edward VIII. Although he trained for the Royal Navy, Edward received an Army commission at the start of WWI and served as a staff officer until the end of the war. After the war he travelled widely through the British

Commonwealth, where his informal behaviour won him good will. At home his popularity rivaled that of his grandfather. After succeeding to the throne in early 1936, however, Edward was indifferent to court ceremony and sympathetic to striking coal miners, neither of which endeared him to the Conservative government. He abdicated in December 1936 to marry Wallis Simpson, an American and a commoner.

70. **Captain Stubbs**—a Canadian officer working as an AO in mid-1918. Like many of the men referred to in this book, the identity of Captain Stubbs is—and will likely remain—a mystery. There are at least four possibilities;

- John Hamilton Stubbs, a civil engineer from Kaslo, BC, joined up on 27 September 1914 in Valcartier, Quebec, with the rank of Captain. He had seen service with the Royal Engineers in the Cape Colony, Orange Free State, and Transval between 1900 and 1902.
- Isaac Harald Stubbs, a member of the 3rd CMR, joined up in Medicine Hat, AB, on 29 December 1914, with the rank of Lieutenant.
- Clement Stubbs enlisted in the 192nd Bn. on 16 February 1916, in Blairmore, AB, as a Lieutenant. At the time he was a member of the 23rd Alberta Rangers.
- John Roger Stubbs joined the CEF in Shorncliffe, England, on 30 March 1916 with the rank of Lieutenant, having been in the 15th Light Horse in Calgary for a year.

It is quite likely some or all of these men joined the ranks of The Unwanted.

71. **Frederick Joseph Bloxham (1888–?)**—another of The Unwanted, working as an AO in 1918. A telephone engineer from Stratford, ON, Bloxham enlisted in the 110th Bn. on 16 Dec 1915.

72. **Hindenburg Line**—a vast system of defences in Northern France constructed by the Germans during the winter of 1916–17, with much of the work being done by some 50,000 Russian POWs. It stretched about 32 kilometres from the area around Arras to beyond St Quentin, and consisted of deep and wide trenches, thick belts of barbed wire, machine-gun positions, concrete bunkers, tunnels, and command posts. In March 1917 von Ludendorff moved his troops from an

exposed front back to the Hindenburg Line, freeing up 13 divisions which could be moved elsewhere. The Germans left a scorched earth behind them, which the British could not occupy for more than a month. One of the main connecting points between the Hindenburg Line and the main German lines north from Hill 70 to the Belgian coast was a place called Vimy Ridge and despite its importance to the Germans, it was taken by the Canadian Corps in April 1917. Despite this, the Germans considered the Hindenburg Line impregnable, and even General Currie (see Note 54) called it "one of the strongest defences on the Western Front." The successful Allied offensive of September 1918 proved it could be breached.

73. **Patrick Burns (1856–1937)**—farmer, rancher, meat-packer, and businessman. Born on an Ontario farm, he moved to Manitoba in 1878 to homestead, but soon found himself in the freight and cattle business. In 1885 he got his first contract to supply beef to the railway crews, and as his business grew he expanded into ranching, packing, and the retail meat business. By the early 1900s he was well established as one of Canada's most successful businessmen. Burns sold his meat-packing business for $15,000,000 in 1928, and was made a senator in 1931, but he retained possession of his vast cattle ranches until his death.

74. **Louis Stephen St. Laurent (1882–1973)**—corporate lawyer, law professor, Liberal politician, and PM of Canada for almost nine years. St. Laurent was asked by then-PM King to become Minister of Justice in late 1941, and despite his lack of political experience, he accepted. He was elected to parliament in February 1942. After the war St. Laurent was made Secretary of State for External Affairs, and promoted Canadian membership in NATO. He was selected by King to be his successor, and became PM in November 1948. His government was re-elected twice with strong majorities, but suffered defeat in June 1957. In early 1958 he retired from public life, resuming his career as a lawyer in Quebec.

75. **George Alexander Drew (1894–1973)**—lawyer, Conservative politician, and premier of Ontario from 1943 to 1948. Drew enlisted in the CEF in January 1915 and was severely wounded in France. After the war he studied law, was called to the bar in 1920, became the mayor of Guelph, ON, in 1925, and was elected leader of the Ontario Conservative party in 1938. In 1948 Drew became leader of the federal Conservatives, but could not defeat Louis St. Laurent, and resigned in 1956. He was appointed Canadian High Commissioner to London in 1957.

76. **German Army Farms**—The Germans seem to have developed their farms on at least as large a scale at the British, perhaps larger. An Associated Press news item that appeared in the *Montgomery Advertiser* (Alabama, USA) on 11 November 1918 describes how advancing French troops had already harvested 1.5 million bushels of wheat from German farms they had over-run in occupied France, and said they expected to retrieve at least another half-million bushels. Some of the wheat had already been harvested before the French troops got to the farms, and in most cases they had to supply their own harvesters, as virtually all the farm implements "had been taken away or destroyed." (See Note 86.)

77. **Aberystwyth**—market town, administrative centre, and seaport on the west cost of Wales, supposedly the ancestral home of the Hughes family.

78. **the flu**—the Spanish Flu epidemic, also known as the Great Influenza Pandemic, the 1918 Flu Epidemic, and La Gripe, an unusually severe and deadly strain of influenza that killed at least 25,000,000 and perhaps as many as 70,000,000 people world-wide in 1918–19. In most of western Europe the epidemic was know as the Spanish flu, because it received more press coverage there than.elsewhere in the world, primarily because Spain was neutral in WWI and there was no wartime censorship. In Spain the epidemic was known as the French flu. The virus first appeared in March 1918 (most likely at Fort Riley, Kansas), and was unusual in that it often killed many young and healthy victims, as opposed to most influenzas which normally kill the old and infirm. People without symptoms could be struck suddenly and be rendered too feeble to walk within hours, and many died within a day. Symptoms included a blue tint to the face and coughing up blood. Many cities, states, and countries enforced restrictions on public gatherings and travel to try to control the epidemic. Thousands of theaters, dance halls, and other public places around the world were shut down for over a year. Even in areas where there were few deaths, those laid low by the illness were often so numerous as to bring much of everyday life to a stop. In many places there were no healthy health-care workers to tend the sick and no able-bodied grave diggers to bury the dead. The virus ran rampant for 18 months, then disappeared; the actual strain has never been determined.

79. **Edith Cavell (1865–1915)**—an English nurse who was executed by the German Army for helping Allied soldiers escape from German-occu-

pied Belgium. Cavell was appointed the first matron of the Berkendeal Institute in Brussels in 1907, where she was responsible for major improvements in the standard of nursing. When the Germans invaded Belgium in 1914, the Institute became a stopping point for Allied soldiers escaping the Germans. Cavell became involved in an underground group which helped more than 200 soldiers return to their own lines, before being betrayed by a Belgian collaborator and arrested in August 1915. She and several others were court martialled and sentenced to death in October, and shot within a few days. Although the sentence was legally justified (she was charged with assisting English and Belgian soldiers to escape), it was considered outrageous and was widely publicized by the Allies. In May 1919 Cavell's remains were returned to England and buried in Norwich, where she was born.

80. **the Peeing Manikin, also known as Manikin Pis**—a famous statue in Brussels of a little boy peeing, considered by many to be a symbol of Belgium. Legend says that a man had lost his little boy, and when he spotted his son two days later, the child was peeing. As a token of gratitude, the father had a fountain with a statue of a peeing boy built. Today it is a famous tourist attraction, along with the Manikin Pis Museum, Manikin Pis Hotel, Manikin Pis Restaurant, and Manikin Pis Boulevard.

81. **John Samuel Jocelyn Percy (1871–1952)**—Chief of Staff to General Plumer in 1918. Percy joined the East Lancashire Regiment in 1891, served as Assistant Superintendent of Army Signalling during the Waziristan Campaign in the North West Frontier of India from 1894 to 1895, saw action in the Boer War, then returned to India where he was Deputy Assistant Adjutant General from 1908 to 1912. He was a General Staff Officer at the Royal Military College at Sandhurst in 1913–14 and with a number of Divisions in the British Armies in France from 1914 through 1916. From 1916 to 1917 he commanded a Brigade within the 9th Corps, was promoted to Major-General, and attached first to the General Staff of the 5th Army in 1917–18, then to the General Staff of the 2nd Army in 1918–19. After the Armistice was declared, he commanded the 3rd Brigade, London Division, of the British Army on the Rhine in 1919. From 1919 to 1920 he was a Brigadier General with the British Military Mission to Lt. General Anton Ivanovich Deniken in South Russia, then Commander of the British Military Mission to Forces of South Russia under General Baron Petr Nikolaivich Wrangel. He retired in 1920.

82. **Hudson Ewbanks Kearley, Lord Devonport (1856–1934)**—businessman, Liberal MP, first Food Controller for Britain, and for many years the Chairman of the Port of London Authority. Kearley started working at the age of 15 as an unpaid clerk in a firm of tea merchants. Within five years he had started his own business as a tea merchant, doing his own buying, blending, and travelling. He was elected to Parliament as a Liberal in 1892, where he made himself the spokesman for ordinary working man. In 1905 he was appointed Parliamentary Secretary of the Board of Trade; one of his achievements was the creation of the Port of London Authority. In 1908 he was made a Baron, and in 1909 he became the first chairman of the Port Authority. By late 1916 submarine warfare in the North Atlantic was severely affecting the supply of food in and to Britain, and in December Parliament created a new office, called Food Controller. The Controller's duties were to "regulate the supply and consumption of food in such manner as he thinks best for maintaining a proper supply of food, and to take such steps as he thinks best for encouraging the production of food." When PM Lloyd George appointed Devonport to this new post, *The Times* noted that he was responsible for "administering the recent Defence of the Realm Regulations for the purpose of regulating supplies and prices of food and for other action in connection with food control." Devonport felt that the idea of voluntary rationing should be given one last chance, but soon had to ask the government to impose rationing, and issued a host of regulations, many of them trivial in nature. Despite important successes, including developing means of controlling cereal crops and setting up a series of local Food Control Committees, he was not popular, and many aspects of the food-control system were in chaos by May 1917. Claiming ill-health, he resigned in June 1917, was replaced— with unconcealed reluctance—by David Alfred Thomas (Lord Rhondda, 1856–1918), was rewarded with the title of Viscount in June, and went back to being the Chairman of the Port of London Authority, a position he held until 1925.

83. **Ion Hamilton Benn (1863–1961)**—a businessman, MP, and very active member of local government for many years. He was educated at the Merchant Taylors' School, entered the business world as a young man, then got involved in local government. In the 1890s he became a member of the Greenwich Borough Council, was elected mayor of Greenwich in 1901–02, was an original member of the Metropolitan Water Board, served on London County Council from 1907 to 1910, was

elected to Parliament in 1910, holding his seat until 1922, and was a director of the Port of London Authority from its inception in 1909 until about six months before his death at age 98. During WWI he took a break from Parliament and commanded a flotilla of "little ships" which harassed German ships along the coast of Belgium. He was in charge of the motor launches during raids on the ports of Ostend and Zeebrugge in June 1917 (which were intended to block German access to those harbours and their associated canals), was mentioned in dispatched three times, and was awarded the DSO, CB, and *Croix de Guerre*. His first wife died in 1948, and two years later—at the age of 87—he married Katherine Winnifred Grier of Montreal.

84. **Arlington Augustus Chichester (1863–1948)**—a career British officer, he joined the Dorsetshire Regiment in 1884. Chichester served as a Captain in the Boer War from 1899 to 1901, was awarded a DSO in September 1901, promoted to Major in March 1902, and to Colonel some time before 1914. He served as DAQMG and Deputy Assistant Adjutant General in Hong Kong between 1903 and 1907. In August 1914 he was taken off the half-pay list and appointed an Assistant Adjutant QMG. He was promoted to Major-General in June 1917, appointed DQMG in November 1917, awarded a KCMG in January 1919, and relinquished his appointment in December 1919. His other awards and honours include CB, Legion of Honour (*Croix de Commandeur*), and *Croix de Guerre*. Chichester was the Colonel of the Dorset Regiment from 1922 to 1933.

85. **Arthur Frank Umfreville Green (1878–?)**—apparently more than a simple military man, he wrote at least four books on military matters: *Landscape Sketching for Military Purposes* (London: Hugh Rees, Ltd., 1908); *Evening Tattoo* (1940); *Home Guard Pocket Book* (1940); and *Questions Answered About Rifle Shooting* (1945). His first book was intended specifically for the use of junior officers in the field to help them understand the lay of battlefields and the military significance of landmarks.

86. **Armistice terms**—Article 231, Part VIII of the peace treaty between Germany and the Allies, which dealt with reparations, states, "The Allied and Associated Governments affirm and Germany accepts the responsibility of Germany and her allies for causing all the loss and damage to which the Allied and Associated Governments and their nationals have been subjected as a consequence of the war imposed upon them by the aggression of Germany and her allies." As well as

ATTESTATION - PAPER.

No. 911302

Folio.

CANADIAN OVER-SEAS EXPEDITIONARY FORCE.

QUESTIONS TO BE PUT BEFORE ATTESTATION.
(ANSWERS)

1. What is your surname? — Mc Kela
1a. What are your Christian names? — Nelson Felix
1b. What is your present address? — Fort Saskatchewan Alberta
2. In what Town, Township or Parish, and in what Country were you born? — Finland
3. What is the name of your next-of-kin? — Mrs Emma McKela
4. What is the address of your next-of-kin? — Bathgam Alberta Canada
4a. What is the relationship of your next-of-kin? — Mother
5. What is the date of your birth? — 21st April 1875
6. What is your Trade or Calling? — Salesman
7. Are you married? — No
8. Are you willing to be vaccinated or re-vaccinated and inoculated? — Yes
9. Do you now belong to the Active Militia? — No
10. Have you ever served in any Military Force? If so, state particulars of former Service. — No
11. Do you understand the nature and terms of your engagement? — Yes
12. Are you willing to be attested to serve in the CANADIAN OVER-SEAS EXPEDITIONARY FORCE? — Yes

DECLARATION TO BE MADE BY MAN ON ATTESTATION.

I, N. F. Mc Kela, do solemnly declare that the above are answers made by me to the above questions and that they are true, and that I am, willing to fulfil the engagements by me now made, and I hereby engage and agree to serve in the Canadian Over-Seas Expeditionary Force, and to be attached to any arm of the service therein, for the term of one year, or during the war now existing between Great Britain and Germany should that war last longer than one year, and for six months after the termination of that war provided His Majesty should so long require my services, or until legally discharged.

Date March 10 1916.

N. F. McKela (Signature of Recruit)
L. V. Miller (Signature of Witness)

OATH TO BE TAKEN BY MAN ON ATTESTATION.

I, Nelson F. McKela, do make Oath, that I will be faithful and bear true Allegiance to His Majesty King George the Fifth, His Heirs and Successors, and that I will as in duty bound honestly and faithfully defend His Majesty, His Heirs and Successors, in Person, Crown and Dignity, against all enemies, and will observe and obey all orders of His Majesty, His Heirs and Successors, and of all the Generals and Officers set over me. So help me God.

Date March 10 1916.

Nelson F. McKela (Signature of Recruit)
L. V. Miller (Signature of Witness)

CERTIFICATE OF MAGISTRATE.

The Recruit above-named was cautioned by me that if he made any false answer to any of the above questions he would be liable to be punished as provided in the Army Act.

The above questions were then read to the Recruit in my presence.

I have taken care that he understands each question, and that his answer to each question has been duly entered as replied to, and the said Recruit has made and signed the declaration and taken the oath before me, at Edmonton this day of March 1916.

(Signature of Justice)

The front page of the Attestation Paper filled out by Nels McKela when he enlisted in the CEF in March 1916. Although he had no military experience at the time, he was a Lieutenant when John ran into him in Bramshott, England, about a year later.

Source: Library and Archives Canada, RG150, Box 6954–5.

paying the sum of 20,000,000,000 gold marks by 1 May 1921 (and
another 40 billion within 30 years, plus an additional 40 billion "if the
reparations Committee shall decide that Germany can meet them"),
Germany was required to restore "cash, animals, securities, and
objects of every nature taken away, seized, or sequestered" by her
during the war. The Allied governments drew up lists of animals,
machinery, equipment, tools, and items of a commercial nature that
had been seized, destroyed, or used up by Germany, which were to be
replaced or restored by Germany. The list included 500,000 cows,
470,000 sheep and goats, and 370,000 horses and donkeys taken from
occupied France. The German Army had also destroyed buildings and
industrial machinery, flooded coal mines, ripped up railway lines, and
demolished bridges and tunnels. (It should be noted, however, that
not all atrocities were committed by the Germans; when Lord
Kitchener was informed of an incident involving British troops, he
said. "What is the good of discussing that incident? All war is an
atrocity.") Within three months of the signing of the treaty, Germany
was to deliver thousands of cows, horses, sheep, pigs, and goats to
France and Belgium. (Although the terms of the treaty were certainly
stiff, they were mild in comparison to the terms that Germany had
imposed upon Russia in 1917.) For many Germans, the end of the war
was met with relief, as the terms of surrender could be no worse than
what they had already endured. Since the start of the war, Germany's
food production had dropped dramatically, and by 1918 people were
rioting for food, normally law-abiding citizens took to stealing food to
avoid starvation, and crops previously considered fit only to be cattle-
feed were eagerly eaten by anyone who could get their hands on them.

87. **Nelson Felix McKela (1895–?)**—McKela was born in Finland but was
working as a salesman in Fort Saskatchewan, AB, when he joined the
army as an enlisted man—not an officer—in March 1916. His
Attestation Papers show that his mother was his next of kin, he was
single, had no militia or active military experience, and was assigned
to the 196th Bn. Notices in *The London Gazette* indicate he was seconded
for duty with the RFC on 11 September 1917 (by which time he was a
Lieutenant), and ceased to be seconded for service with the RAF on 24
February 1919.

88. **Arthur James Balfour (1848–1930)**—British statesman, educated at Eton
and Trinity College, Cambridge. In 1874 he was elected as a
Conservative MP for Hertford, which he represented until 1885. In

1878, his uncle, Lord Salisbury, became foreign minister and Balfour served as his private secretary until 1880. Under Lord Salisbury's administration Balfour was president of the Local Government Board, and later secretary for Scotland with a seat in the cabinet. When the chief secretary for Ireland was forced to resign due to illness, Lord Salisbury appointed Balfour to the post. His policy was that of coercion—such as his fearless administration of the Crimes Act—coupled with remedial legislation, and he enforced one while proceeding with the other, regardless of the risk of outrage outside the House and of insult within. In 1891, he became First Lord of the Treasury and leader of the House of Commons, and from 1892 to 1895 he was leader of the opposition. During Lord Salisbury's illnesses and absences, Balfour was in charge of the foreign office. He was responsible for the Transvaal negotiations in 1899, and when the Boer War began badly, was quick to realize the necessity of putting Britain's full military strength into the field. In 1900 he became First Lord of the Treasury, and when Lord Salisbury resigned in July 1902, succeeded him as prime minister. His principal concerns were education and defence, but his cabinet split on the issue of free trade. After several turbulent years in office, his Unionist government was defeated by the Liberals in 1905. The party did no better in the elections of 1910, and Balfour resigned as leader in 1911. He was succeeded by Andrew Bonar Law (see reference in Note 68). The Unionists joined Asquith's coalition government in May 1915, and Balfour succeeded Winston Churchill as First Lord of the Admiralty. When Asquith's government collapsed in December 1916, Balfour became Foreign Secretary, but was not included in the Cabinet, and was frequently left out of the loop. He resigned as foreign secretary after the Versailles Conference in 1919, but continued on in government as Lord President of the Council until 1922, when he resigned following the Conservative back-bencher revolt that put Bonar Law into office. In 1922 Balfour was created Earl of Balfour. He returned to the Cabinet in 1925, serving as Lord President of the Council in Stanley Baldwin's second government.

89. **Alexander Fedorovich Kerensky (1881–1970)**—Russian socialist and revolutionary. Kerensky studied law at the University of St. Petersburg, joined the Socialist Revolutionary Party in 1905, and became editor of the radical newspaper, *Burevestik*, for which he was arrested and briefly sent into exile. He returned to St. Petersburg in 1906 and soon developed a reputation for defending political radicals. Kerensky joined the

moderate Labour Party and in 1912 was elected to the State Duma. A socialist, he developed a strong following amongst industrial workers. He rejoined joined the Socialist Revolutionary Party in 1917 and called for the removal of Tsar Nicholas. When the Tsar resigned in March 1917, Kerensky helped form a Provisional Government, in which he was appointed Minister of Justice, and within a few months, Minister of War. He was soon the most powerful person in the government, and forced the Bolsheviks underground, arresting Trotsky and several others, and forcing Lenin to flee to Finland. The Russian Army was close to revolt, however, and, spurred on by defeats on the Eastern Front and encouragement from the Bolsheviks, demonstrated against Kerensky. A major offensive in July failed, due to a combination of low Russian morale and poor supply lines, and superior German troops and equipment. When Kerensky announced further summer offensives, the Russian soldiers first refused to move, then began to desert *en mass*. Despite the fact that Kerensky was Supreme Commander of the Russian Army, he was actively opposed by the Bolsheviks, and by October was unable to assert his authority. Upon learning that the Bolsheviks were about to seize power in early November, Kerensky left Petrograd for the Eastern Front, where he hoped to appeal to the army for support. He assembled an army of loyal troops from the Northern Front, but was defeated by the Bolsheviks at Pskov, and had to flee to Finland, where he remained in hiding until May 1918 when he escaped to London. Later he moved to France where he led a propaganda campaign against the Soviet Union. In 1939 he urged the Western democracies to attack the communists in Russia and the fascists in Germany. In 1940 Kerensky moved to the United States, and spent much of his time at the Hoover Institute in California, where he taught graduate courses and contributed to the Institute's archive on Russian history.

90. **William Albert Benn (1893–?)**—born in Richmond, ON, Benn was working as a clerk for the Canada Cement Co. in Dauntless, AB, at the time he enlisted in Medicine Hat on 3 February 1916.

91. **Kinmel Park, Rhyl**—a dispersal camp in northern Wales, about 40 kilometres west of Liverpool, where Canadian soldiers were held after the end of the war, while waiting for ships to take them home. It was the site of the first and most serious mutiny by Canadian soldiers in the aftermath of the war, and although the riot occurred while John was still in Germany, he certainly would have been aware of it. Conditions

at Kinmel Park in early 1919 were exceedingly poor; living standards were inferior to those in prison camps, men were sleeping on damp and drafty floors with very few blankets, there was insufficient coal for fires, and the food was described as little better than pigswill. Weeks passed, but few men left for home. The men were repeatedly told that their ships had been cancelled because dockworkers were on strike, but the authorities could not explain why thousands of American and Australian troops were able to sail for home each week. Another grievance was that recruits who had only just come over from Canada were being sent back first. It had long been understood that "first in, first out," modified by marital status, would be the rule for sending troops home. But this was opposed by Sir Robert Borden, General Currie, and other senior officers, who wanted to keep Canadian forces on an armed footing beyond the Armistice. It was also becoming clear to the troops that their economic prospects in Canada were grim, and that this was a factor in their delayed demobilization. Troops who had returned to Canada sent gloomy reports of discrimination in the job market in favour of officers, severe unemployment, and an aggressive anti-working-class policy. There were 12,000 unemployed in Montreal alone, and a similar number in Toronto; the Canadian war debt was hundreds of millions of dollars, and it looked like the working classes were expected to make the "necessary sacrifices" to ensure economic recovery. The grim conditions in Kinmel and the depressing news from home were a recipe for mutiny. The final straw was the arrival of Canadian newspapers showing pictures of a hero's welcome being given to soldiers who had not seen any fighting. On 4 March 1919 a meeting was held by the soldiers of Montreal Camp, a strike committee was elected, and William Tarasevich (a Canadian soldier of Russian extraction) was picked to give the signal to start the mutiny. Things quickly degenerated into looting and destruction of equipment. On 7 March under the headline "Riot in Canadian Camp: Twelve Killed and Many Injured. VC Trampled to Death" *The Times* reported that, "A serious disturbance by Canadian soldiers occurred at Kinmel Military Camp, near Rhyl, on Tuesday and Wednesday. As a result twelve lives were lost, including that of a Major of New Brunswick who had gained the VC. About twenty others were injured. In addition damage estimated at £50,000 was done to the camp." The disturbance was put down quickly and about 20 ringleaders, mostly of foreign extraction, were taken away. An enquiry determined that only five soldiers were killed, none of them were officers, and none of them had been awarded a VC, and just 21 soldiers, including two officers, were injured. The mutiny achieved certain immediate gains however; ships materialized as if by magic, and by the end of March, 30,000 men had been repatriated to Canada.

Notes to Appendix IV

1. **very nearly two hundred years ago**—On 27 October 1770 the barque Annabella arrived off the north shore of PEI and was promptly wrecked on a sandbar. It was carrying some 60–80 people, comprising about a dozen families. Among them were Lauchlan and Rachel MacKendrick and three of their children; Janet, Donald, and Duncan. John's mother is descended from Malcolm John MacKendrick, the first child born to Lauchlan and Rachel on PEI.

2. **on his seventy third birthday**—The 26 June 1890 issue of the St. Andrews (NB) *Beacon* reported that "William Hughes, Kingston (Kent Co.) was killed instantly by lightning during the storm on Wednesday. The unfortunate man was struck in the back of the head while lying in bed near the chimney." Another account of the storm in the same paper stated it occurred on June 18. The 19 June 1890 issue of the *Daily Telegraph* (Saint John, NB) stated that the storm passed over Albert County (next to Kent County) "between 1 and 4 a.m., and was one of the heaviest rain storms ever witnessed here." The 20 June 1890 issue of the Saint John (NB) *Daily Sun* reported "William Hughes, age 60, was killed by lightning which entered the house and struck Hughes, who was lying on the sofa close by the stove." It is assumed that his age as given is a typo, as other documents indicate William was born between 1815 and 1820, which would make him at least 70 in 1890.

3. **they had eight children**—This is not correct. According to the Richibucto Parish Register, William married Rebecca James on 9 September 1846 and they had nine children between 1847 and 1866.

4. **Catherine's niece Anna Campbell**—Anna Mattock Campbell was John's cousin, but she lived with Charles and Catherine for so long that John often referred to her as his sister. Anna acted as a housekeeper to John and Rob when they were homesteading north of Mannville.

5. **his uncle**—It is not clear which of Charles's brothers stayed in Minnesota with John that spring and summer of 1899. The oldest,

William John, settled in Chicago, while the other two, Abraham James and Jonathan Dickson, moved to Alberta. Abraham returned to Minnesota some time after 1901 but Jonathan stayed in Alberta.

6. **considered joining the force**—Many of John's stories dealt with Mounties. One of them, *Doctor Sweetapple*, concerns a NWMP veterinarian who gets pressed into service to deliver a baby in the midst of a blizzard. The name "Sweetapple" struck JRH as improbable, but a search on the web turned up this item from the Whitby (ON) *Chronicle* for 6 April 1888:

> Mr. C.H. Sweetapple, our popular young Vet. has left for the Northwest Territory. He has accepted a government position as veterinary for the mounted police, for which he gets a good salary. He will be succeeded here by Mr. Robt. Hickinbottom, V.S. who is a graduate of the Veterinary College, Toronto. We wish both success in their profession.
>
> Prior to leaving Brooklin the other day Chas. Sweetapple, V.S. was surrounded by a number of his friends and presented with a magnificent meerschaum pipe and case. The presentation was made in a short, witty and well-worded address by Mr. Jno. Spence on behalf of the contributors. The doctor was completely taken by surprise, but made a happy response. The company then sang "He's a jolly good fellow!" with becoming gusto.

His arrival in Fort Saskatchewan was noted in the 19 October 1893 issue of the *Edmonton Bulletin*. By 1923 Inspector Sweetapple was in charge of the detachment at the Fort. So the hero of John's story was a real person, but was the storm-bound birth a real event? We do not know.

7. **John appears to have worked on the homestead with him**—On Charles's sworn statement in support of his homestead application in 1909, he answered Question 6 (Of whom do [sic] your family consist: when did they first commence residence upon this homestead, and for what portion of each year since that date have they resided upon it?) with this; *"wife 2 sons in Fort Sask and on S.W. 4–52–8–W4"*, implying both John and Rob were homesteading the one quarter-section.

8. Within two months of receiving titles to their homesteads in 1909, both Rob and Charles sold the land to Nellie A. Berry, wife of Robert G. Berry, a farmer in Fort Saskatchewan, for $1600 per quarter-section. It appears that they homesteaded strictly as a money-making venture,

not because they particularly wanted to live on that specific piece of land. Charles kept the farm at Fort Saskatchewan for a few more years, then got a job as the Indian Agent at Saddle Lake Reserve in 1912. Rob may have worked his father's farm during WWI. After the war he moved to California for a few years, then returned to Canada in 1926 to work in the fruit-growing and -canning industries.

9. **British War Medal**—authorized on 29 July 1919, this medal was awarded to all ranks who rendered service to His Majesty's Forces between 5 August 1914 and 11 November 1918, or who had served in a theatre of war in 1919 and 1920.

10. **Inter-Allied Victory Medal**—agreed to by all allies in March 1919. All medals were to be almost identical to obviate the need to exchange allied medals and each was patterned after a French medal of 1870. The medal was authorized in Britain on 1 September 1919. It was awarded to all ranks of the fighting forces, to civilians under contract, and others employed with military hospitals who actually served on the establishment of a unit in a theatre of war between 5 August 1914 and 11 November 1918. It was also awarded to members of the British Naval mission to Russia 1919–1920 and for mine clearance in the North Sea between 11 November 1918 and 30 November 1919. This medal was never issued alone, but always with the British War Medal. A multiple-leaved emblem is worn on this medal when it was awarded to those "Mentioned-in-Despatches."

11. **Canadian Efficiency Decoration**—awarded for 20 years of meritorious service in a non-permanent active militia, RCAF Auxiliary, and Reserve until 17 August 1942. It was for commissioned officers who joined before 1 September 1939. A bar was awarded for 20 additional years of service. There have been approximately 3,700 issued. War service counted double for this medal. Half of the time spent in the ranks counted towards this medal.

12. **revolver**—Paul says that one day in about 1925, he and Ted found the revolver in John's desk drawer, along with a pouch of ammunition. Ted insisted on holding it, and, as guns are inclined to do under those circumstances, it went off, creating a very noticeable hole in the living room floor. Knowing that this would not be looked upon favourably by John or Sara, Ted and Paul filled the hole with putty, added a bit of shoe polish to make it look like a knot, and—miraculously—escaped detection. As far as Paul knows, that was probably the second and last time the revolver was ever fired.

13. **Frank Fane**—He was the son of Frank W.W. Fane, whom John met shortly after he arrived in Fort Saskatchewan in 1899. The elder Fane is referred to in the second paragraph of *The Saddle Lake Trail* (page 298).

14. **Walter Norman Smith**—Norm Smith was born in England, came to Canada in 1906, and worked in newspapers in Winnipeg, Calgary, Edmonton, and Regina. He served with the Machine Gun Corps during WWI, then worked for the Calgary *Albertan* from 1919 to 1921. He became education secretary for the United Farmers of Alberta in 1921, was appointed editor of the UFA newspaper when it was started in 1922, and held that position until it ceased publication in 1936. From 1921 to 1935, Smith prepared much of the UFA's political literature, and in the mid-1930s made an intense study of Social Credit philosophy. In 1936, he and his wife launched the *Western Farm Leader*, a bi-weekly farm newspaper, which they edited and published until their retirement in late 1954.

15. **1918**—This date is probably a typo on John's part, as he was in France in 1918. He may have meant 1919 or perhaps even a bit later, or he may have been referring to when the Co-op was originally formed, rather than when he got involved with it. Of course, there is always the (very remote) possibility that he got involved with it by correspondence while he was still in France.

16. **Red Fife**—Red Fife was grown in the Western Ukraine (where it was called Halychanka) as long ago as the 12th century. The first seeds were brought to Ontario in 1842, where it soon proved to be a great success, although it was not grown on the prairies until the 1870s. It was hardier, of better quality, and produced a higher yield than earlier varieties of wheat grown in Manitoba, but was still susceptible to the severe and unpredictable prairie weather conditions. Drought, frost, and hail damaged crops regularly throughout the 1880s and 1890s and into the 20th century. Despite this, over 100,000 acres of land in Alberta were seeded with Red Fife in the spring of 1905. By 1909, however, Charles Saunders had successfully crossed Red Fife with early-maturing Hard Red Calcutta wheat from India, resulting in the Marquis strain. It matured about eight days faster than Red Fife, and accounted for 90% of prairie wheat production by 1920. Virtually all wheat strains developed since then for use on the prairies are based on Red Fife.

17. **Johnny Borwick**—Johnny Borwick was a Métis who ran a stage coach out of Vegreville in the early 1900s. From 1914 until 31 October 1920 he

worked for Charles at Saddle Lake as an interpreter and driver. His salary started at $480 a year in 1914 and was up to $540 a year by 1920.

Selected Bibliography

Journals

Gibson, Craig, "The British Army, French Farmers and the War on the Western Front 1914–1918," *Past & Present 180, no. 1* (2003): 173–237. (This article won the Agricultural History Society's Wayne D. Rasmussen Award for the best article on agricultural history published by a journal other than *Agricultural History* in 2003.)

Wise, Sidney F. "The Gardeners of Vimy: Canadian Corps' Farming Operations During the German Offensives of 1918," *Canadian Military History 8, no. 3* (1999): 39–47.

Books

Aitken, Max. *Canada in Flanders, The Official Story of the Canadian Expeditionary Force.* Toronto: Hodder and Stoughton, 1916.

Anderson, P. I *That's Me, Escape from German Prison Camp and Other Adventures.* No publication data.

Berton, Pierre. *The Last Spike, The Great Railway 1881–1885.* Toronto: McClelland & Stewart, 1971.

———. *Vimy.* Toronto: McClelland and Stewart, 1986.

———. *Marching As to War, Canada's Turbulent Years 1899–1953.* Toronto: Random House of Canada., 2001.

Bird, Will R. *Thirteen Years After, The Story of the Old Front Revisited*. Toronto: Maclean Publishing, 1932.

Blake, Robert, ed. *The Private Papers of Douglas Haig 1914-1919*. London: Eyre & Spottiswoode, 1952.

Bliss, Michael. *Right Honourable Men, The Descent of Canadian Politics from Macdonald to Mulroney*. Toronto: Harper Collins Publishers, 1994.

Borsaton, J.H., ed. *Sir Douglas Haig's Despatches (December 1915- April 1916)*. London: J.M. Dent & Sons, 1919.

Bruce, Anthony. *An Illustrated Companion to the First World War*. London: Michael Joseph, 1989.

Burg, David F. and Purcell, L. Edward. *Almanac of World War I*. Lexington: University Press of Kentucky, 1988.

Canada. Department of Public Information. *Canada's Part in the Great War*. Ottawa: Government of Canada, 1919.

Chambers, Frank P. *The War Behind the War, 1914-1918, A History of the Political and Civilian Fronts*. New York: Harcourt, Brace and Co., 1939.

Churchill, Winston S. *The World Crises 1916-1918, Part II*. London: Thornton, Butterworth, 1927.

Dancocks, Daniel G. *Welcome to Flanders Fields, The First Canadian Battle of the Great War: Ypres, 1915*. Toronto: McClelland & Stewart, 1988.

Doyle, Arthur Conan. *The British Campaign in France and Flanders, January to July 1918*. London: Hodder and Stoughton, 1919.

Dyer, Gwynne. *War*. New York: Crown Publishers, 1985.

Fussell, Paul. *The Great War and Modern Memory*. Oxford: Oxford University Press, 1975.

Gilbert, Martin. *Atlas of World War I*. London: Dorset Press, 1970.

Goodspeed, D.J. *The Road Past Vimy, The Canadian Corps, 1914- 1918*. Toronto: Macmillan of Canada, 1969.

Granatstein, J.L. and Morton, Desmond. *Canada and the Two World Wars*. Toronto: Key Porter Books, 2003.

Gray, Edwyn A. *The Killing Time, The U-Boat War, 1914-1918*. New York: Charles Scribner's Sons, 1972.

Gray, Randal. *Chronicle of the First World War*. Oxford: Facts on File, 1991.

Hammerton, J.A., ed. *The War Illustrated, A Pictorial Record of the Conflict of the Nations*, Volumes 1 through 9. London: The Amalgamated Press, 1914 through 1919.

Johnson, J.H. *Stalemate! The Real Story of Trench Warfare*. London: Rigel
Publications, 1995.

Johnston, G. Chalmers. *The 2nd Canadian Mounted Rifles (British Columbia
Horse) in France and Flanders*. Vernon: The Vernon News Printing &
Publishing Co., (Undated; circa 1931).

Kelly, L.V. *North with Peace River Jim*. Calgary: Glenbow-Alberta Institute,
1972.

Kennedy, Joyce M. *Distant Thunder, Canada's Citizen Soldiers on the Western
Front*. Manhattan (KS): Sunflower University Press, 2000.

King, Jere Clemens, ed. *The First World War*. New York: Walker Publishing
Co., 1972.

Liddell Hart, B.H. *The Real War, 1914–1918*. London: Faber and Faber, 1930.

——. *Strategy*. London: Faber and Faber, 1954.

Livesay, J.F.B. *Canada's Hundred Days, With the Canadian Corps from Amiens to
Mons, Aug. 8– Nov. 11, 1918*. Toronto: Thomas Allen, 1919.

Mee, Charles L. *The End of Order, Versailles 1919*. New York: E.P. Dutton,
1980.

Meek, John F. *Over the Top! The Canadian Infantry in the First World War*.
Orangeville (ON): Privately published, 1971.

Montrose, Lynn. *War Through the Ages*. New York: Harper & Row, 1944.

Moore, William. *See How They Ran, The British Retreat of 1918*. London: Leo
Cooper, 1970.

Morton, Desmond. *A Military History of Canada, From Champlain to the Gulf
War*. Toronto: McClelland & Stewart, 1992.

Nasmith, George G. *On the Fringe of the Great Fight*. Toronto: McClelland,
Goodchild & Stewart, [1917].

——. *Canada's Sons and Great Britain in the World War*. Toronto: John C.
Winston Co., 1919.

Nicholson, G.W.L. *Canadian Expeditionary Force 1914 – 1919, Official History
of the Canadian Army in the First World War*. Ottawa: Queen's Printer,
1964.

Offner, Avner. *The First World War, An Agrarian Interpretation*. Oxford:
Clarendon Press, 1989.

Orcutt, Louis E. *Supplementary Volume to the Great War History, From the
Armistice November 11, 1918, to the Ratification of the Peace Treaty*. New
York: The Christian Herald, 1920.

Paschall, Rod. *The Defeat of Imperial Germany, 1917– 1918*. Chapel Hill: Algonquin Books, 1989.

Pendergast, Tom, and Pendergast, Sara. *World War I Almanac*. Detroit: Gale Group, 2002.

——. *World War I Biographies*. Detroit: Gale Group, 2002.

——. *World War I Primary Sources*. Detroit: Gale Group, 2002.

Pitt, Barrie. *1918, The Last Act*. London: Cassell, 1962.

Roy, Reginald H., ed. *The Journal of Private Fraser, 1914–1918, Canadian Expeditionary Force*. Victoria: Sono Nis Press, 1985.

Schaefer, Christina K. *The Great War, A Guide to the Service Records of All the World's Fighting Men and Volunteers*. Baltimore: Genealogical Publishing Co., 1998.

Seymore, William W. *The History of the Rifle Brigade in the War of 1914–1918*, Vol. II. London: n.p., 1936.

Shaw, Anthony, and Westwell, Ian. *World in Conflict 1914–45*. London: Fitzroy Dearborn Publishers, 2000.

Simons, Frank H. *History of the World War*, Vol. Five. Garden City: Doubleday, Page, & Co., 1920.

——. *They Won the War*. Freeport: Books for Libraries Press, 1968.

Smith, Gene. *Still Quiet on the Western Front, Fifty Years Later*. New York: William Morrow & Co., 1965.

Stevens, G.R. *A City Goes to War, History of the Loyal Edmonton Regiment (3 PPCLI)*. Brampton: Charters Publishing Co., 1964.

Stone, Norman. *The Eastern Front 1914–1917*. New York: Charles Scribner's Sons, 1975.

Terraine, John. *Mons, The Retreat to Victory*. London: B.T. Batsford, 1960.

Thompson, John Herd. *The Harvests of War, The Prairie West, 1914–1918*. Toronto: McClelland & Stewart, 1978.

Toland, John. *No Man's Land, 1918, The Last Year of the Great War*. Garden City: Doubleday & Co., 1980

Tuchman, Barbara. *The Guns of August*. New York: Macmillan, 1962.

Various Authorities. *Canada in the Great World War, An Authentic Account of the Military History of Canada from the Earliest Days to the Close of the War of the Nations*. Toronto: United Publishers of Canada, 1921.

Vermilion Old Timers. *Vermilion Memories*. Vermilion: n.p., 1967.

Vincent, C. Paul. *The Politics of Hunger, The Allied Blockade of Germany, 1915–1919*. Athens: Ohio University Press, 1985.

Watt, Richard M. *Dare Call It Treason, The True Story of the French Army Mutinies of 1917*. New York: Dorset Press, 1969.

Warner, Philip. *The Zeebrugge Raid*. London: William Kimber, 1978.

———. *Passchendaele, The Story Behind the Tragic Victory of 1917*. London: Sidgwick & Jackson, 1987.

Wilson, H.W. and Hammerton, J.A., ed. *The Great War, The Standard History of the All-Europe Conflict*, Vol. 5. London: Amalgamated Press, 1916.

Wolff, Leon. *In Flanders Fields, The 1917 Campaign*. New York: Viking Press, 1958.

Woodward, David R., ed. *The Military Correspondence of Field-Marshal Sir William Robertson, Chief of the Imperial General Staff, December 1915–February 1918*. London: Bodley Head, 1989.

Web Sites (current 2005)

Aftermath — http://www.aftermathww1.com/index.asp.

Battlefields of the Great War, 1914–1918 — http://battlefields1418.50megs.com/.

The Canadian Encyclopedia — http://www.thecanadianencyclopedia.com/.

The Canadian Letters and Images Project — http://www.mala.bc.ca/history/letters/.

Canadian Orders, Medals, and Decorations — http://www.vacacc.gc.ca/remembers/sub.cfm?source=collections/cmdp.

Commonwealth War Graves Commission — http://www.cwgc.org/cwgcinternet/search.aspx.

Encyclopedia of the First World War — http://www.spartacus.schoolnet.co.uk/fww.htm.

For King and Empire, Canada's Soldiers in the Great War — http://www.kingandempire.com/.

The Great War 1914–1918 — http://www.greatwar.co.uk/.

Hellfire Corner — http://www.fylde.demon.co.uk/welcome.htm.

Johnny Canuck's Wartime History of Canada — http://www.nt.net/~toby/.

K-G-Saur World Biographical Information System — accessed via Thompson Gale, http://www.gale.com.

The Laurier Centre for Military Strategic and Disarmament Studies —
    http://info.wlu.ca/~wwwmsds/.

Library and Archives Canada —
    http://www.collectionscanada.ca/history/index-e.html.

The London Gazette — http://www.gazettes-online.co.uk.

The (London) Times Digital Archives, 1785–1985 — accessed via
    http://www.gale.com.

The Long, Long Trail, The Story of the British Army in the Great War of
    1914–1918 — http://www.1914-1918.net/index.htm.

Orders of Battle — http://orbat.com/site/index.html.

Photos of the Great War — http://www.gwpda.org/photos/greatwar.htm.

Soldiers of the First World War (1914–1918) — http://www.collection-
    scanada.ca/archivianet/020106_e.html.

The War to End All Wars — http://www.firstworldwar.com.

The World War I Document Archive — http://www.lib.byu.edu/~rdh/wwi/.

Virtual Tour of Historic Vermilion —
    http://www.telusplanet.net/public/twnverm/virtualtour.htm.

Wikipedia — http://en.wikipedia.org.

World War One Photos — http://www.ww1photos.com/index.

Index

Note: Bold page numbers indicate photo captions.

Currie, General Arthur, 110,
161–62, 352–53n54

Devonport, Lord (Food
Controller), 216, 365n82
Drew, George (Canadian
politician), 192, 362n75

Earl of Folkestone, *see* Pleydell-
Bouverie, Jacob
English
countryside more lovely than
cities, 13, 36–38
farms contrasted with
Canadian farms, 13–15
longshoremen stronger than
Canadian soldiers, 13
reaction of locals to Canadian
officers, 38
trains/railways, 13

Falicon, Lieutenant, 106, 108,
344n39
Fane, Major Frank, 3rd CMR, 67,
280, 299–300, 374n13
Fat Fund, as source of money for
Army Farms, 5, 187, 226
Flanders, description of country
side and people, 58–63
flu epidemic of 1918–1919, 205–6,
363n78
Foch, Generalissimo Ferdinand
career, 356–57n60
informs Haig of dire situation
in France, 72

meets German delegates in
November 1918, 199
plans harvest of 1918, 148
refuses to commit all his
reserves in April 1918, 129,
136
Forrester, Captain, Chaplain, 38,
153
France/French
army camp at Versailles, 84
civilian areas damaged by
war, 49–50
civilian life, 61–63, 118
civilians' reaction to troops in
area, 50
effect of war on, 52–53, 58–59,
72, 342n36
farming practices, 59–60
requests help for farmers, 53,
252
running short of food in late
1917, 80
French interpreters assigned to
British Armies, **45**, 55–56,
255 56, 344n39
Frost, H.J. (Jack), 10th Canadian
Railway Corps, **25**, **55**

German Army Farms, 112, 115,
195, 197–98, 363n76
German offensive of March 1918
Allied anticipation of, 115–16
civilians flee from, 123–24,
134–36
farming conditions in the
midst of, 126

is halted, 140–42

over-runs Allied lines, 124–25, 130–39, 355n58

German retreat in late 1918, 177–80

Green, General Arthur, 222–24, 366n85

Griesbach, Major Billy, 23–24, 96, 337–38n22

Grieve, Major, 110th Bn.,

identity, 353–54n56

in charge of Army pig farms, 115–17

goes to Germany with John, 202, 207

member of John's mess, 196

replaces John on Armistice Commission, 223, 231

Guerney, Major, 116, 125

Haig, Field Marshal Douglas

career, 345–46n42

grants special leave to a friend, 165

supporter of Army agricultural activities, 90, 105, 148

tells Plumer he must take Passchendaele, 72–73

harvest of 1918, 159–60, 174–75

Harwood, Dr., 51st Bn., 24

Heyer, Captain, 2nd Army and Army of Occupation Chief Requisition Officer, 71, 210

introduces John to opera, 212–13

member of Mess Committee in Cologne, 215

replaced by John when on leave, 227

requisitions finest hotel in Cologne, 211

Hickey, Captain, 2nd Army Salvage Officer, 71

Hindenburg Line, 178, 361–62n72

Hindhead, England, **37**

Holman, General Herbert C., QMG, 4th Army

asks John to grow a garden for a million men, 3–6, 77

assigns Major Wheatley to John's staff, 78–79

career, 327–28n2

describes Canadians as "damned ignorant," 80

ensures John does not know the rules, 79, 83

enthusiastic about Army Farms, 80–81, 93, 105, 116

purchases supplies and equipment for Army Farms, 82

tours 4th Army farms with Lord Radnor, 91–94

Horne, General Henry, 73, 129, 346–47n43

horses

appearance of, 48 hours after being killed, 167

as a source of natural
fertilizer, 92–93, 264
pressed into service on Army
Farms, 105–6
Hughes, Major Henry John,
52nd Bn.,
1st Army AO, 103, 260
awarded *l'Ordre du mérite
agricole*, 360n67
enlistment details, 352n53
Hughes, John McKendrick
acquires land for Army Farms,
98, 263
affected by German offensive
of 1918, 123–39
arrives home in 1919, 244,
278, 306
arrives in England in 1916,
11–15
appointed 2nd Army AO,
69–71
appointed 4th Army AO, 5, 77
appointed 9th Corps AO,
51–52
appointed to the Armistice
Commission, 222–34, 291
as a storyteller, 287–90
as Acting Requisition Officer
for Army of Occupation,
227
as Area Commandant, 47–50
as censor, 46, 66
as horseman, 54–55
as hotel manager, 229–30
as OC, C Company, 151st Bn., 9

as traffic policeman in
snowstorm, 86–88
asked to go to Mesopotamia,
153
asked to grow a garden for a
million men, 3–6, 77
awarded *l'Ordre du mérite
agricole*, 167, **168**, 278,
360n67
brings 300 horses up to front
lines, 183–86
buys cows for General Plumer,
187–88
buys turkeys for Christmas
1918, 203, 215
called a "Fairy Godfather," 242
called an "ignorant colonial,"
173
can not live without his
porridge, 64
childhood and family history,
265–70, 289
comes and goes at will, 106–9
considered for a GHQ staff
position, 108
courtship with Sara, 275–78
declared to be "unwanted,"
18–19, 335–36n18
demoted to Lieutenant, 34–35,
339n26
describes his duties as 2nd
Army AO, 70
describes his duties as 4th
Army AO, 81, 98, 105–9, 111,
120–22